AGE IN AMERICA

MW00780240

Age in America

The Colonial Era to the Present

Edited by Corinne T. Field *and* Nicholas L. Syrett

NEW YORK UNIVERSITY PRESS
New York and London

NEW YORK UNIVERSITY PRESS
New York and London
www.nyupress.org

© 2015 by New York University
All rights reserved

References to Internet websites (URLs) were accurate at the time of writing.
Neither the author nor New York University Press is responsible for URLs that
may have expired or changed since the manuscript was prepared.

Library of Congress Cataloging-in-Publication Data
Age in America : the colonial era to the present / edited by
Corinne T. Field and Nicholas L. Syrett.
pages cm   Includes bibliographical references and index.
ISBN 978-1-4798-7001-1 (cloth : alkaline paper) — ISBN 978-1-4798-3191-3 (paperback :
alkaline paper)
1. Age—Social aspects—United States—History. 2. Age—Political aspects—United
States—History. 3. Age groups—United States—History. 4. Social classes—United
States—History. 5. Identity (Psychology)—United States—History. 6. Coming of
age—Social aspects—United States—History. 7. Aging—Social aspects—United
States—History. 8. Citizenship—United States—History. 9. United States—Social
conditions. 10. Political culture—United States—History. I. Field, Corinne T., 1965–
II. Syrett, Nicholas L.
HN90.S6A34   2015
305.260973—dc23   2014045475

New York University Press books are printed on acid-free paper,
and their binding materials are chosen for strength and durability.
We strive to use environmentally responsible suppliers and materials
to the greatest extent possible in publishing our books.
Manufactured in the United States of America
10 9 8 7 6 5 4 3 2 1

Also available as an ebook

CONTENTS

ACKNOWLEDGMENTS

First and foremost, we thank the contributors to *Age in America*, without whom the volume would not exist. They answered with enthusiasm when we first approached them about writing essays and responded to our revisions and suggestions with grace and good humor. At New York University Press, we thank Ilene Kalish, Alicia Nadkarni, Eric Zinner, Joseph Dahm, and Dorothea Halliday, as well as the two anonymous readers who gave helpful suggestions. Finally, we would like to acknowledge the Society for the History of Children and Youth, at whose biannual meeting we first met and began talking about this project, and whose vibrant and supportive community fosters such important work on age as a category of historical analysis.

Introduction

CORINNE T. FIELD AND NICHOLAS L. SYRETT

Sixteen. Eighteen. Sixty-five. In the United States today, we recognize these numbers as key transitions in the life course, precise moments when our rights, opportunities, and civic engagement change—when we become eligible to drive, cast a vote, or enroll in Medicare. Likely, we associate these chronological milestones with more subtle but no less pronounced changes in self-understanding—we recognize ourselves as more independent at eighteen, and worry that we are getting old at sixty-five. But these age markers themselves have a history; at a specific moment in the past Americans determined that eighteen, for instance, was the age at which citizens were capable of voting, imbuing that age with both symbolic and legal meaning. This book investigates how, when, and why age itself, as well as various specific ages, came to have significance in American culture.

Age is both a biological reality and a social construction. While human bodies change over time as they become older—they age—the numbers we assign to those bodies—their ages—are a human invention. It is clear that people of different ages—infants, for instance, or the elderly—are, by and large, unable to do things that those in the "prime of life" are capable of doing; human development is a biological process, in other words. At the same time, the meanings that we assign to precise ages—six, sixteen, twenty-one, thirty-five, sixty—are cultural constructions. Not all people reach puberty or intellectual maturity or incapacity at exactly the same ages, and yet cultural expectations, not to mention legal disabilities and responsibilities, are fixed to precise ages. Human beings have approximated; they have chosen specific ages to stand in for the beginnings and endings of life stages and the societal expectations that accompany them. The means by which Americans imposed chronological boundaries upon the ongoing and variable process of growing up and growing old offers a paradigmatic example of how people construct cultural meaning and social hierarchy from embodied experience. Furthermore, as the contributors to this volume argue, chronological age always intersects with other socially constructed categories such as gender, race, and sexuality. What makes age different from other categories such as whiteness and maleness is that, if we are lucky to live long enough, we will all pass through the chronological markers that define us as first young, then middle aged, and finally old.[1]

With these observations as a starting point, this book has three goals. The first is to document age in the American context, to demonstrate how and why specific chronological ages have come to have meaning over the course of American history, from the colonial period to the modern era. Some of these precise ages—like that for ending an indenture, for instance—are no longer applicable to the world in which we live. But many others—like the ages at which Americans may marry, vote, drink, drive, have sex, work, retire, immigrate, and enter legal, cultural, or religious adulthood—are so engrained into our consciousness that we scarcely question their origins. The ages of eighteen, twenty-one, and sixty-five, to take just three important examples, have come to seem natural precisely because we rely upon them so frequently to demarcate the beginnings of adulthood and of old age. But our reliance upon these ages has a past, and it is that history that imbues the ages with meaning. All eighteen-year-olds are not, in their very nature, any more or less mature than seventeen-and-a-half-year-olds or nineteen-year-olds. But our use of this specific number for the past century has made them seem so.

In demonstrating this, the contributors to *Age in America* also make clear that, as Corinne T. Field argues in her essay in this volume, these age markers are "arbitrary but necessary." They have been necessary, for lawmakers especially, as a means of apportioning legal incapacity and responsibility in a way that has seemed logical and all-encompassing, if not always equal and fair. But they have also been arbitrary in that the same lawmakers could have selected a different and perhaps proximate age for making their legal distinctions; recognizing this, opponents generally contested whatever ages were chosen. Many of these ages rely on precedents in the common law brought by English settlers; others hearken back to French or Spanish precedents in canon law or to religious traditions in Catholicism or Judaism. Legal commentators of the seventeenth century, for instance, attributed the ages of marriage under English common law, fourteen for boys and twelve for girls, to the ages at which both reached puberty. But contemporary historians have demonstrated that on average the onset of puberty was actually later than these ages during the early modern period.[2] The point is that those who first utilized the ages *believed* them to be accurate measures of the aging process, or as close to being accurate for at least some of the people they were designed to regulate as was possible. The ages, then, were arbitrary, but they were also necessary. There was no better way to describe the moment at which all children or all youth might arrive at a certain developmental stage that could also be effective as a matter of law; age could do so, but only if one accepted age qualifications as both arbitrary and necessary boundaries that always failed to account for individual variation but nonetheless offered an efficient means for apportioning rights and responsibilities to young and old.

The second goal of this volume is to demonstrate that age has, throughout American history, always mattered for at least some people. While a number of historians have argued that for much of early American history most settlers, and the Native Americans alongside whom they lived, were largely unaware of both their birthdays and their ages, there is plentiful evidence that many Americans were well aware of both. Literate New England colonists recorded birthdays in family Bibles. Catholic priests transcribed the ages of prospective brides and grooms in their matrimonial investigations in the territories of New Spain and New France. And many English colonists abided by the English common law, which stipulated the ages of majority, indenture, guardianship, and marriage, among others.

When individuals did not know their exact date of birth, colonial authorities were quite adept at choosing an age for them, likely based on a rough assessment of size and capacity. For example, illiterate European immigrants may not have recorded births in a family Bible, but town authorities nonetheless mustered their sons into the militia based on age. Enslaved Africans may not have known their exact date of birth, but masters often kept such records or otherwise recorded the ages of their slaves in case they wished to sell them. For many of these people, age did not matter in daily life, but it would be wrong to think that age was a meaningless category of identity for early Americans. While age consciousness—the belief that our ages are a fundamental part of our identity—was certainly not as widespread in colonial America as it would become in later eras, the legal function of age was clearly important to many, even if only at particular times in a person's life.

Contributors to this volume agree that reformers intensified the use of chronological age during the late nineteenth century. Indeed, research presented here deepens this narrative by explaining how exactly bureaucrats, lawyers, and politicians convinced ordinary Americans to conform to a proliferating number of age-based regulations. But other contributors reveal that this is not the whole story. They set Progressive Era innovations in a broader context, looking back to the colonial period to explain how Europeans, Indians, and Africans wrestled with the salience of age in defining civic obligations, interlocking dependencies, and relative status.

By the twentieth century, with age qualifications well established and accepted, debate intensified as to which ages, exactly, should matter. Spirited debates flared over when a person should be able to drink, vote, or claim Social Security benefits—all controversies detailed in this volume. The collection as a whole, then, documents the often overlooked significance of numerical age before the later nineteenth century, deepens our understandings of the significance of Progressive Era innovations in age stratification, and explores the debates surrounding modifications for various age-based privileges and responsibilities in the later twentieth century.

The third goal of *Age in America* is to encourage historians, and indeed all scholars of American culture, to incorporate age into their analyses as a key axis of identity for Americans. Imprecise and arbitrary as it may be, age has been a marker of identity fundamental to the way that citizenship has been constituted in American history, right alongside sex, race, class, and sexuality. Americans have used chronological age to construct race, gender, and sexuality, at the same time that they have used these other categories to shape the meaning of age. This has been true for the elderly and adults, just as it has been for children. While much of the work on age as a category of analysis has heretofore focused on young people, we hope this collection will serve as encouragement for all scholars of age-defined groups of people (children, youth, adults, and the elderly) to critically examine the ways that age markers themselves have been constructed historically, and refracted through the lenses of gender, race, class, and sexuality.[3]

***

Today it is a commonplace for historians to note a person's age as a means either to show something important about her or his identity or simply to allow the reader to place the person, to categorize her or him. Contemporary readers, historians assume, understand what it means *to be* five or thirty-five or seventy. But until relatively recently, few scholars have bothered to explore those ages themselves, what meanings people in the past ascribed to specific ages, and whether or not earlier Americans believed the same things about particular ages that we do. The scholarship on childhood and children on the one hand, and old age and the elderly on the other, has been plentiful. Some scholars have also explored the more ill-defined world of adulthood in between. But there has been far less scholarship on the history of age itself: which numbers are meaningful and why.

The few who have written on age can be roughly divided into two groups: those who have focused on the development of age consciousness, the belief that one's age is an important part of one's identity; and those who have studied age grading, that is, the organization of institutions such as schools, juvenile courts, and government welfare programs around age-based criteria. Those who have studied age consciousness have tended to employ the tools of cultural history—focusing as they have on a cultural phenomenon—whereas those who have studied bureaucratic uses of age have drawn on the tools of political, legal, and social history.

Of course the two have sometimes gone hand in hand. Howard Chudacoff's *How Old Are You? Age Consciousness in American Culture* (1989), until now the only book-length treatment on the subject of chronological age in U.S. history, combined both approaches to explore the intersections between age consciousness and age grading, both of which intensified after the Civil War. Chudacoff argues that many early Americans did not know their own birthdays or ages and that age consciousness did not begin to gain traction in the United States until the spread of pediatric medicine and age-graded schooling made age markers a meaningful part of people's identities. This occurred after the middle of the nineteenth century, first in the industrialized Northeast, spreading unevenly and gradually to other areas of the country. Chudacoff shows how birthdays, age scheduling (the idea that major life transitions should normally occur by a particular age), and thus age consciousness became meaningful for wider swaths of Americans over the course of the later nineteenth and twentieth centuries, so much so that age would eventually become a central "organizing principle" for how we interact with each other.[4]

While much of the work by historians since Chudacoff complements rather than contradicts his findings, particularly in its general conclusion that the use of age to regulate children and the elderly grew in the Progressive Era as it coincided with greater state bureaucratization, some more recent work also complicates his assertions. For instance, legal historians have long recognized that English common law, which formed the basis for the legal code in the Anglo colonies and later the United States, is riddled with precise ages: the age of majority, which governed the ability of adults to manage and convey property, or to make wills, or otherwise act independently of their parents; the ages of consent to marriage; and the ages when children might choose their own guardians. The French and Spanish carried their own particular age markers with them to the New World as well. These Europeans confronted Indians and Africans with their own distinct assumptions about age and life stage. Many colonies, and later states, passed statutory law that codified English, French, or Spanish age markers as meaningful transitions in the lives of young people.[5]

While the existence of legal age markers does not presuppose that most people either knew these markers or, for that matter, their own birthdays, more recent scholarship by Holly Brewer has demonstrated that the thinking of religious leaders, philosophers, and legal scholars both in England and its North American colonies underwent a profound shift in the early modern period that gradually coalesced around a consensus that children, who had previously been capable of marrying, contracting, bearing legal witness, and assuming criminal responsibility, were incapable of providing meaningful consent and thus should be denied those rights until age rendered them fit to do so. In the colonies this transition culminated in the revolutionary ideal that citizenship required informed consent, the kind that children were unable to give. But in order for that to work, various laws had to be passed stipulating the precise ages at which young people were eligible for the rights of adulthood; this occurred over the course of the colonial and early national periods. The overall point is that various ages did matter, at least legally, prior to the middle of the nineteenth century, indeed from the arrival of the first Europeans on North American soil. These ages may have mattered at the margins—that is, for only a minority of young people who were tried for a crime or attempted to marry or defy a guardian before reaching majority—but they mattered for those individuals and for people around them. And the laws' existence at all demonstrates that age mattered for legislators and practitioners of the law.[6]

As historians have shown, the military was one of the first institutions to rely upon chronological age as a means to demand obligations and provide benefits during fixed periods of life, though often only for white males. In both Europe and its colonies, governments employed age to define who had an obligation to muster for militia duty, who could qualify for service in government armies, and who was eligible for veterans' pension benefits. In the American colonies, the requirement that white males serve in the militia at a specified age, generally sixteen, created an intermediate stage of citizenship between boyhood and manhood. These youth were still legal minors who would not qualify to vote until they reached twenty-one and, what often took much longer, acquired property of their own. Nonetheless, these young and propertyless white men could stand proud on muster day knowing that they fulfilled obligations never demanded of their sisters and only rarely of their nonwhite peers. Recognizing that many of these youth lacked any written proof of age, militia laws empowered local officials to determine individuals' ages in the same way as they empowered tax assessors to fix the value of property. Numeric age thus came to define a clear path to citizenship for white males long before people could prove how old they were.[7]

As James Schmidt has argued, regulating the right to contract was more complicated. Some jurists in the new Republic sought to define age twenty-one as a universal qualification for both political and civil contracts, while others recognized that the shift from apprenticeship to wage labor, combined with widespread geographic mobility, necessitated that minor youth be empowered to contract their own labor. During the early years of the nineteenth century, judges in the Northeast generally worked to facilitate young people's participation in the labor market, whereas by the end of the century, a new generation of jurists helped build the consensus that young people belonged in school and not at work.[8]

Historians of slavery have demonstrated that chronological age functioned very differently for enslaved people, who could claim no rights on the basis of age, but nonetheless found that their vulnerability to sale and the demands upon their labor increased markedly as they grew from childhood to young adulthood. Masters, traders, and tax assessors relied upon chronological age to determine the monetary value of enslaved people, assigning the highest value to those in their mid- to late teens. To be sure, other traits such as sex, health, temperament, and skill entered into the equation, but the shorthand notation in account books was often name, age, and dollar value—age functioning as a rough gauge of capacity and hence of price. As a result, masters and mistresses were among the most careful recorders of births. Given the market incentives, however, slave owners likely quite often misrepresented ages to either save on taxes or boost a sale. Chronological age may have mattered less to enslaved people themselves, who generally lacked access to written records, but evidence suggests that enslaved parents used what power and influence they had to both shelter children from the worst aspects of exploitation and prolong childhood as long into the teenage years as possible.[9]

Fugitive slaves who joined the abolitionist movement in the North used chronological age to explain how enslaved people lacked the rights and protections routinely accorded their free peers. Frederick Douglass, for example, recalled his despair as an enslaved boy knowing his white peers would grow up to be "free at twenty-one." Harriet Jacobs contrasted the protections accorded white girls with the sexual exploitation she faced beginning in her "fifteenth year—a sad epoch in the life of a slave girl."[10] Indeed, narratives of fugitive slaves, coupled with the protests of disenfranchised adults in the North, suggest that age consciousness was particularly intense among those seeking equal rights for black men and all women, even as it may have been less salient to the enslaved in their day-to-day existence.[11]

To better understand the development of age consciousness over the course of the nineteenth century, historians have focused on the work of educators, doctors, and reformers, especially those in the urban Northeast, who first advocated the use of age-based criteria for determining social services, distributing rights, and organizing institutions. Chud-acoff credited age-graded schooling with doing much of the work of spreading age consciousness. Grouping together children in separate classes based on their birthdays resulted from the reformers' conviction that children should develop common characteristics, particularly the maturation of reason, as they aged. Once states and localities, begin-ning in the urban Northeast, started organizing their classrooms by age, the experience of age grading spread age consciousness to ever greater proportions of the population. This led to the belief that those children shared common characteristics, which increasingly they did, thanks to their shared schooling. This in turn inculcated the notion that age itself was a fundamental facet of one's identity.[12]

A number of scholars have demonstrated persuasively that rights and restrictions were also forged at the nexus of age, gender, and sexuality. Michael Grossberg shows that during the nineteenth century, age (along with race, medical fitness, and consanguinity and affinity) became a way for marriage and divorce reformers to "guard the altar" from those they believed might harm the institution of marriage. Marriage was for adults, not children, and age was the tool to make sure that this would henceforth be the case. Historian Mary E. Odem and political scientist Carolyn E. Cocca document the development of statutory rape laws in the nineteenth and twentieth centuries, respectively, demonstrating the ways that age was initially used to protect only girls, undergoing a revo-lution in the late twentieth century as the protections of statutory rape laws were extended to boys. Cocca also explores the ways that reformers developed age-gap exceptions to exempt the elder of two similarly aged teenagers from prosecution, even if one of them was actually younger than the legal age of consent. In particularly nuanced ways, historian Stephen Robertson has argued that by the twentieth century sexuality and sexual acts were always understood through the prism of age; in the courtroom and beyond, age structured how witnesses understood the sexual actions of a child, an adolescent, or an adult. Robertson also demonstrates, and in more recent work Nayan Shah further shows, that in legal cases of sexual abuse or same-sex sexual acts, both the ages and possible age differences, the sexes and possible sex differences, and the races and possible race differences of the two people involved all interacted in order to create plausible victims and assailants. Understandings of age structured whether a sexual act was legally a crime.[13]

Age has also been integral to the analyses of child labor laws and of the juvenile justice system as both developed at the turn of the twentieth century. In order for reformers to protect young people from what they perceived as the harm of the workplace and of culpability for criminal acts, age was necessary to define childhood in the first place. Indeed, arguments about these ages were key parts of the debate over just when childhood actually ended, and for what purposes. Perhaps inevitably policy makers did not always agree with lay people about these issues. James Schmidt has demonstrated in the realm of child labor, for instance, that working people in Appalachia long resisted the notion that just because a child had not reached a certain age he or she was ineligible for work; for these people a child worked when "big enough," not "old enough." And Joan Jacobs Brumberg has shown that supporters of leniency for juvenile criminals met with formidable resistance in the face of the horror of crimes committed by young people. Age clearly mattered in these circumstances, most especially in the legal framework designed to protect young people from work or criminal responsibility, but not all Americans necessarily agreed with lawmakers.[14]

Many scholars have also focused on the work of doctors, particularly the psychologist G. Stanley Hall's late nineteenth-century efforts to define adolescence as a distinct stage of life bounded by age.[15] Where Hall focused on young men, other doctors were more concerned with the health of young women, for whom menarche marked a clear transition to reproductive adulthood. Crista DeLuzio demonstrates that during the antebellum period, many doctors formulated age-based schedules for normative human growth and argued that young people—girls in particular—needed to postpone marriage and childbearing until their bodies and minds had fully developed, a slow process extending into the early twenties.[16] As doctors increasingly tracked female growth by age, they noticed something surprising: a marked decline in the age of menarche. By the late nineteenth century, many parents and medical experts were aware that American girls were maturing earlier than their mothers and grandmothers, a phenomenon that worried many and fueled efforts to protect the health and morals of young girls, particularly those who were white, native-born, and Protestant.[17]

At the same time, doctors concerned with the end of life worried that Americans used up their vital store of energy by late middle age and debated what to do with aging workers, whose capacity, they believed, declined with every passing year. Others optimistically argued that with proper habits, all individuals could enjoy health and productivity into their sixties and seventies, and, perhaps with the advance of science, for many decades more. Gerontology, which developed as a scientific and medical discipline in the twentieth century, took as its subject an elderly population defined by chronological age.[18] Medicine has thus also increased the significance attached to age, for men and women sometimes in different ways.

Historians interested in the history of retirement agree that individual capacity rather than chronological age generally determined individuals' decisions to withdraw from the labor force through the mid-nineteenth century. Many attribute the rise of age-based criteria for retirement to the expansion of the welfare state, first with the payment of military pensions for union veterans following the Civil War and then, even more important, with the passage of Social Security in 1935. Historians interested in the growth of state bureaucracies, and their reliance on chronological age to categorize population groups, agree that the expansion of government benefits led many Americans during the mid-twentieth century to regard retirement as a normative stage of life beginning at age sixty-five.[19]

Historians interested in old age have also debated the extent and impact of age discrimination in the labor market. From the late nineteenth through the mid-twentieth century, American corporations increasingly adopted age-based seniority and pension systems as a tool to manage their employees. Some social historians, however, have noted that the labor force participation rates of older workers remained fairly constant. All agree that because white men were most likely to qualify for private pension benefits, age discrimination affected men of color and white women in distinct ways, often rendering them less secure in old age.[20]

During the middle years of the twentieth century, chronological age also came to figure centrally in various efforts to market products. As sociologist Daniel Thomas Cook has demonstrated, retailers first began to market age-sized clothing to children and youth in the 1920s. Over the course of the twentieth century, marketers promoted ever more fine-grained age segmentation of the youth market, popularizing new age-defined terms such as "toddlers" in the 1930s, "teens" in the 1940s, and "tweens" in the 1980s. Of these markets, teenagers emerged as by far the largest. Increasingly concentrated in high schools, with free time and money to spend, teens developed an age-segregated youth culture in the years after World War II. Movie, record, and television producers profited by targeting their content to age-defined audiences. While many marketed to the young, some developed niche markets among older adults, often tapping into anxieties about old-age decline to market products that promised to prolong youth.[21]

Historians and sociologists have also traced the process by which medical experts, politicians, and lawyers have applied age-based measures of human development to the period before birth. In her history of the fetus in modern America, Sara Dubow shows how embryologists came to understand fetal life in terms of developmental stages measured by weeks since conception, and lawyers to pin new rights and obligations on fetal age, even as antiabortion activists confounded these stages by referring to fetuses as babies and seeking to classify embryos as persons. Sociologist Miranda Waggoner, meanwhile, explains how since the 1980s public health advocates have begun to target the months before conception as the crucial window during which potential mothers need to begin certain medical interventions—such as taking folic acid. The result is that the span of time relevant to human development has extended to encompass not only gestation but also a newly defined stage of prepregnancy.[22]

At the turn of the twenty-first century, sociologists, psychologists, and opinion leaders concerned with both youth and old age began to question whether chronological age was losing its relevance as a marker of distinct life stages. The psychologist Jeffrey Arnett coined the term "emerging adulthood" to refer to the period between ages eighteen and twenty-five as a prolonged phase of experimentation in which the markers of adulthood no longer come according to any fixed schedule or sequence. While sociologists and journalists debate the significance of this prolonged youth, all agree that variation and diversity in experience trump clear chronological norms.[23] Pursuing what is in some ways a parallel inquiry into the last stage of life, critical gerontologists noted that many baby boomers entering their sixties and seventies insisted that they felt much younger than their calendar age. Some see liberatory potential in the articulation of a postmodern life course, rooted in heterogeneity and indeterminacy rather than chronological milestones. Some worry that new models of aging are linked too closely to consumerist models of forestalling old age through the purchase of products, while others warn of a new and more virulent form of ageism lurking in advice that urges people to age well by concealing and denying how old they are.[24] By showing how age categories have changed over time for children, youth, adults, and the elderly, this book provides a richer historical context for understanding these contemporary debates.

As we hope to have demonstrated, chronological age has clearly not been absent from historical scholarship, though with the exception of Chudacoff's *How Old Are You?*, it has rarely taken center stage. Instead, scholars have grappled with how age has been one factor that structured the experiences of school, work, retirement, slavery, medicine, sex, and legal capability, and interacted with other identity categories like gender, race, and class in order to construct legible human subjects. Here we bring age to the fore, placing it at center stage, where we believe that, in conjunction with race, class, gender, and sexuality, it belongs.

The Contributors

Ann M. Little and Sharon Braslaw Sundue both demonstrate the salience of age categories in early America, and among a diverse cast of characters. Focusing on relations among French, English, and Wabanaki on the northern frontier in the seventeenth and eighteenth centuries, Little argues that the cross-cultural significance of ages four, seven, twelve, and fourteen shaped the experiences of children taken as captives and provided grounds for diplomatic agreements between warring peoples. Through a case study of gradual emancipation in Pennsylvania during the late eighteenth and early nineteenth centuries, Sundue shows how chronological age became central to debates over slavery and freedom in the early republic. In an era when historians have concluded that chronological age lacked meaning, Little and Sundue demonstrate that for some people, age was actually crucial to decisions about life, death, freedom, and citizenship.

Corinne T. Field, Jon Grinspan, Nicholas L. Syrett, and Yuki Oda all focus on how age categories intersected with gender, race, and class differences across the long nineteenth century. Field explores how politicians in antebellum America used the requirement that voters be twenty-one as proof that suffrage was not a natural right but a privilege that states could regulate at will, thus disqualifying white women and African Americans. Grinspan turns to diaries and letters to explore what voting at age twenty-one meant to young white men themselves and to party leaders eager to tap their support. Noting that most states enabled young girls to marry several years earlier than boys, Syrett argues that the differential age of marriage and of ages of majority in western and midwestern states constructed differently gendered prescriptions for adulthood, some of which paradoxically allowed girls opportunities not afforded to their brothers. Turning to immigration law, Oda shows that by the 1920s chronological age determined who could become a citizen, but in very different ways for European and Asian immigrants. All four show in distinct ways how lawmakers used age to construct the categories of race and gender, and in turn how some Americans internalized and battled against the identities forged at those crucial intersections.

Where other contributors trace the significance of age qualifications in law, Shane Landrum answers the important question of how exactly Americans proved their age by showing how the informal, personal records accepted by public officials in the nineteenth century were replaced by official, state-issued birth certificates common by the 1910s. James D. Schmidt covers a similar period and demonstrates another way that Americans came to know their ages: the twinned regulation of labor law and mandatory schooling. Schmidt argues that although they are often studied separately, they amounted to the same thing, both using chronological age to determine who belonged at work and who did not. Taken together, both essays help us further understand not just how lawmakers used age as a tool to regulate Americans, but how those same people came to see age as a fundamental category of their own identities.

By the early twentieth century, as more and more Americans could prove their age, the debate shifted to questions about which ages exactly should qualify the young and old for entitlements and responsibilities. No longer was age itself at issue, the fundamental question was which age. Taking a long view of attitudes toward old-age retirement, William

Graebner argues that chronological age became a dominant factor in retirement only in the 1930s with the creation of Social Security as an entitlement beginning at age sixty-five. Rebecca de Schweinitz, meanwhile, shows how the federal draft intersected with the expansion of public high schools to fuel support for the Vote 18 movement. However, even as Americans ratified the Twenty-Sixth Amendment and lowered the age of majority in many states, Timothy Cole demonstrates that a coalition of concerned parents and lawmakers organized to reassert their authority over adult teenagers, most notably by using federal highway funds to ensure that states would set the minimum drinking age at twenty-one. These three essays all show how the ages of sixty-five, eighteen, and twenty-one have come to have such salience in American culture today.

Stuart Schoenfeld and Norma E. Cantú both take a long view in their analyses of four enormously popular birthday-based rituals that have not just survived, but thrived, in the recent past: bar/bat mitzvah for Jewish Americans and quinceañeras/cincuentañeras for Chicanas and other Latinas. Schoenfeld shows the evolution of the significance (or lack thereof) of the age of thirteen for American Jews, as bar and bat mitzvah themselves have gained in importance over the course of the twentieth century as a performance of Jewish identity. Using the tools of a folklorist, Cantú argues for the importance of quinceañeras and cincuentañeras not just for marking status changes in a woman's life at ages fifteen and fifty, but also for reaffirming the importance of Chicana identity itself as a means of resistance in an Anglo-dominant culture.

Finally, W. Andrew Achenbaum suggests that in recent years chronological age has taken on a "paradoxical" meaning in the lives of older Americans as, on the one hand, ever more fine-grained age criteria confer a wide range of benefits from Medicare to discount movie tickets, while, on the other hand, gerontologists and many older people themselves insist that age predicts little about the physical, psychological, or spiritual experience of aging. As a fitting conclusion to a volume on the history of chronological age, Achenbaum wonders whether the revolution in longevity might lead Americans to turn away from age-based criteria toward more expansive, transgenerational definitions of social citizenship.

While it is true that age-based criteria proliferated with the expansion of government and corporate bureaucracies during the Progressive period, the contributors to this volume demonstrate that chronological age has been used to define the rights and obligations of citizens from the earliest days of European settlement to the present. Far from being a Progressive addition to more fundamental categories of citizenship such as nation, gender, and race, chronological age was one of the tools that early Americans used to define such differences. For example, governing officials relied on age to determine which children captured in war could choose their own allegiances, to enable young white men to cast their first vote, to require "free" black children to remain bound to service longer than their white peers, and to limit who could participate in the wage labor market or marry. Americans thus interwove age with other categories of citizenship from the very beginning, using age to shape the development of national boundaries, white manhood citizenship, and industrialization.

As contributors to this volume show, the study of chronological age throws into sharp relief the process by which Americans constructed categories of difference. Historians have long argued that gender, race, and national origins are not inborn traits but social constructions. Given that no one has ever claimed to be born a certain age, and that some Americans did not know or could not prove how old they were, the reliance on chronological age in law and public policy demonstrates the process of constructing categories of difference. Age not only intersected with other categories of difference but provided a fundamental means by which Americans learned to rely upon an artificial distinction—in this case calendar age—to distribute rights and obligations in a heterogeneous population riven by social contrasts but living in a nation dedicated to freedom and equality. That Americans continue to debate such issues as when young people should vote or older people claim Social Security benefits demonstrates that far from being resolved, age remains a paradigmatic example of how we learn to recognize, accept, and rely upon artificial categories of difference.

NOTES

1 Margaret Morganroth Gullette, *Aged by Culture* (Chicago: University of Chicago Press, 2004); Margaret Cruikshank, *Learning to Be Old: Gender, Culture, and Aging*, 2nd ed. (New York: Rowman & Littlefield, 2009); Stephen Katz, *Disciplining Old Age: The Formation of Gerontological Knowledge* (Charlottesville: University of Virginia Press, 1996).

2 Henry Swinburne, *A Treatise of Spousals or Matrimonial Contracts: Wherein All the Questions Relating to That Subject Are Ingeniously Debated and Resolved* (London: S. Roycroft, 1686), 47; Joan Jacobs Brumberg, *The Body Project: An Intimate History of American Girls* (New York: Random House, 1997), 27–56.

3 Other scholars have also called on historians, particularly, to note the centrality of age in constructing the past. See, among others, Stephen Robertson, *Crimes Against Children: Sexual Violence and Legal Culture in New York City, 1880–1960* (Chapel Hill: University of North Carolina Press, 2005), conclusion; James Schmidt, "The Ends of Innocence: Age as a Mode of Inquiry in Sociolegal Studies," *Law & Social Inquiry* 32, no. 4 (Fall 2007): 1029–57; Barbara Young Welke, *Law and the Borders of Belonging in the Long Nineteenth Century United States* (New York: Cambridge University Press, 2010), 12–13; and the following contributions to the Winter 2008 edition (vol. 1, no. 1) of the *Journal of the History of Childhood and Youth*: Steven Mintz, "Reflections on Age as a Category of Historical Analysis," 91–94; Stephen Lassonde, "Age and Authority: Adult-Child Relations during the Twentieth Century in the United States," 95–105; Leslie Paris, "Through the Looking Glass: Age, Stages, and Historical Analysis," 106–13; and Mary Jo Maynes, "Age as a Category of Historical Analysis: History, Agency, and Narratives of Childhood," 114–24.

4 Howard P. Chudacoff, *How Old Are You? Age Consciousness in American Culture* (Princeton, N.J.: Princeton University Press, 1989), 5 and chap. 2.

5 See, for instance, Michael Grossberg, *Governing the Hearth: Law and the Family in Nineteenth-Century America* (Chapel Hill: University of North Carolina Press, 1985).

6 Holly Brewer, *By Birth or Consent: Children, Law, and the Anglo-American Revolution in Authority* (Chapel Hill: University of North Carolina Press, 2005).

7 Corinne T. Field, *The Struggle for Equal Adulthood: Gender, Race, Age, and the Fight for Citizenship in Antebellum America* (Chapel Hill: University of North Carolina Press, 2014); Lisa Dillon, *The Shady Side of Fifty: Age and Old Age in Late Victorian Canada and the United States* (Montreal: McGill-Queen's University Press, 2008); Caroline Cox, "Boy Soldiers of the American Revolution: The Effects of War on Society," in *Children and Youth in a New Nation*, ed. James Marten (New York: New York University Press, 2009), 13–28; Joyce Lee Malcolm, *Peter's War: A New England Slave Boy and the American Revolution* (New Haven, Conn.: Yale University Press, 2009); Thomas F. Currran, "A 'Rebel to [His] Govt. and to His Parents': The Emancipation of Tommy Cave," in *Children and Youth during the Civil War Era*, ed. James Marten (New York: New York University Press, 2012), 65–76; Katz, *Disciplining Old Age*, 62; Carole Haber, *Beyond Sixty-Five: The Dilemma of Old Age in America's Past* (New York: Cambridge University Press, 1983), 111–12; Theda Skocpol, *Protecting Soldiers and Mothers: The Political Origins of Social Policy in the United States* (Cambridge, Mass.: Belknap, 1992), chap. 2.

8 James D. Schmidt, "'Restless Movements Characteristic of Childhood': The Legal Construction of Child Labor in Nineteenth-Century Massachusetts," *Law and*

History Review (Summer 2005): 315–50; James D. Schmidt, *Industrial Violence and the Legal Origins of Child Labor* (New York: Cambridge University Press, 2010).

9 Marie Jenkins Schwartz, *Born in Bondage: Growing up Enslaved in the Antebellum South* (Cambridge, Mass.: Harvard University Press, 2001), 15; Wilma King, *Stolen Childhood: Slave Youth in Nineteenth-Century America* (Bloomington: Indiana University Press, 1995), 102; Walter Johnson, *Soul by Soul: Life Inside the Antebellum Slave Market* (Cambridge, Mass.: Harvard University Press, 1999), 144, 2, 5–7, 19, 45.

10 Frederick Douglass, *Narrative of the Life of Frederick Douglass, an American Slave*, in *The Frederick Douglass Papers*, series 2, *Autobiographical Writings*, 2 vols., ed. John Blassingame, John McKivigan, and Peter Hicks (New Haven, Conn.: Yale University Press, 1999), 35; Harriet Jacobs, *Incidents in the Life of a Slave Girl: Written by Herself*, ed. Jean Fagan Yellin (Cambridge, Mass.: Harvard University Press, 1987), 27.

11 Field, *Struggle for Equal Adulthood*.

12 Chudacoff, *How Old Are You?*, 29–40; Joseph Kett, *Rites of Passage: Adolescence in America, 1790 to the Present* (New York: Basic Books, 1977); Stephen Lassonde, *Learning to Forget: Schooling and Family Life in New Haven's Working Class, 1870–1930* (New Haven, Conn.: Yale University Press, 2005), 26–32; James LeLoudis, *Schooling the New South: Pedagogy, Self, and Society in North Carolina, 1880–1920* (Chapel Hill: University of North Carolina Press, 1996), 21–25; Stephen Lassonde, "Age, Schooling, and Development," in *The Routledge History of Childhood in the Western World*, ed. Paula S. Fass (New York: Routledge, 2013), 211–28; Maris A. Vinovskis, David L. Angus, and Jeffery E. Mirel, "Historical Development of Age Stratification in Schooling," in *Education, Society, and Economic Opportunity: A Historical Perspective on Persistent Issues*, ed. Maris A. Vinovskis (New Haven, Conn.: Yale University Press, 1995), 170–93.

13 Michael Grossberg, "Guarding the Altar: Physiological Restrictions and the Rise of State Intervention in Matrimony," *American Journal of Legal History* 26, no. 3 (July 1982): 197–226; Mary E. Odem, *Delinquent Daughters: Protecting and Policing Adolescent Female Sexuality in the United States, 1885–1920* (Chapel Hill: University of North Carolina Press, 1995), chap. 1; Carolyn E. Cocca, *Jailbait: The Politics of Statutory Rape Laws in the United States* (Albany: State University of New York Press, 2004), esp. chaps. 2–3; Robertson, *Crimes Against Children*; Robertson, "Age of Consent Law and the Making of Modern Childhood in New York City, 1886–1921," *Journal of Social History* 35, no. 4 (Summer 2002): 781–98; Nayan Shah, *Stranger Intimacy: Contesting Race, Sexuality, and the Law in the North American West* (Berkeley: University of California Press, 2011), chap. 4. See also Estelle B. Freedman, *Redefining Rape: Sexual Violence in the Age of Suffrage and Segregation* (Cambridge, Mass.: Harvard University Press, 2013); Nicholas L. Syrett, "The Contested Meanings of Child Marriage in the Turn-of-the-Century United States," in *Children and Youth during the Gilded Age and Progressive Era*, ed. James Marten (New York: New York University Press, 2014), 145–65.

14 Schmidt, *Industrial Violence*, esp. chap. 1; Joan Jacobs Brumberg, *Kansas Charley: The Boy Murderer* (New York: Penguin, 2004); Anthony M. Platt, *The Child Savers: The Invention of Delinquency* (Chicago: University of Chicago Press, 1969); Steven Mintz, *Huck's Raft: A History of American Childhood* (Cambridge, Mass.: Belknap, 2004), 176–78.

15 G. Stanley Hall, *Adolescence: Its Psychology and Its Relations to Physiology, Anthropology, Sociology, Sex, Crime, Religion and Education*, 2 vols. (New York: Appleton, 1904); Kett, *Rites of Passage.*

16 Crista DeLuzio, *Female Adolescence in American Scientific Thought, 1830–1930* (Baltimore: Johns Hopkins University Press, 2007), 3, 9.

17 Brumberg, *Body Project*, 27–56.

18 W. Andrew Achenbaum, *Old Age in the New Land: The American Experience since 1790* (Baltimore: Johns Hopkins University Press, 1978); David Hackett Fischer, *Growing Old in America: The Bland-Lee Lectures Delivered at Clark University* (New York: Oxford University Press, 1977), chap. 4; Haber, *Beyond Sixty-Five,* chaps. 3–4; Thomas R. Cole, *The Journey of Life: A Cultural History of Aging in America* (New York: Cambridge University Press, 1991), pt. 3; Katz, *Disciplining Old Age.*

19 Haber, *Beyond Sixty-Five,* chap. 6; Martin Kohli, "The World We Forgot: A Historical Review of the Life Course," in *Later Life: The Social Psychology of Aging,* ed. Victor W. Marshall (Beverly Hills, Calif.: Sage, 1986), 271–303; Skocpol, *Protecting Soldiers and Mothers,* chap. 2; Dora Costa, *The Evolution of Retirement: An American Economic History, 1880–1990* (Chicago: University of Chicago Press, 1998), chap. 2; Katz, *Disciplining Old Age,* chap. 2.

20 For an overview of this debate, see chapter 9; William Graebner, *A History of Retirement: The Meaning and Function of an American Institution, 1885–1978* (New Haven, Conn.: Yale University Press, 1980); Brian Gratton, *Urban Elders: Family, Work, and Welfare among Boston's Aged, 1890–1950* (Philadelphia: Temple University Press, 1986); Carole Haber and Brian Gratton, *Old Age and the Search for Security: An American Social History* (Bloomington: Indiana University Press, 1994); Margaret Morganroth Gullette, "Inventing the 'Postmaternal' Woman, 1898–1927: Idle, Unwanted, and Out of a Job," *Feminist Studies* (Summer 1995): 221–53; Roger Ransom, Richard Sutch, and Samuel Williamson, "Inventing Pensions: The Origins of the Company-Provided Pension in the United States, 1900–1940," in *Societal Impact on Aging: Historical Perspectives,* ed. K. Warner Schaie (New York: Springer, 1993), 1–38.

21 Daniel Thomas Cook, *The Commodification of Childhood: The Children's Clothing Industry and the Rise of the Child Consumer* (Durham, N.C.: Duke University Press, 2004); Mintz, *Huck's Raft,* 348; Grace Palladino, *Teenagers: An American History* (New York: Basic Books, 1996); Thomas Doherty, *Teenagers and Teenpics: The Juvenilization of American Movies in the 1950s* (Philadelphia: Temple University Press, 2002); Stephen Lassonde, "Ten Is the New Fourteen: Age Compression and 'Real' Childhood," in *Reinventing Childhood after World War II,*

ed. Paula S. Fass and Michael Grossberg (Philadelphia: University of Pennsylvania Press, 2011), 51–67; Margaret Morganroth Gullette, *Declining to Decline: Cultural Combat and the Politics of the Midlife* (Charlottesville: University of Virginia Press, 1997).

22 Sara Dubow, *Ourselves Unborn: A History of the Fetus in Modern America* (New York: Oxford University Press, 2011); Miranda Waggoner, "Motherhood Preconceived: The Emergence of the Preconception Health and Health Care Initiative," *Journal of Health Politics, Policy and Law* 38 (April 2013): 345–71.

23 Jeffrey Jensen Arnett, "Emerging Adulthood: A Theory of Development from the Late Teens through the Twenties," *American Psychologist* 55 (May 2000): 469–80; Mary C. Waters, Patrick J. Carr, Maria J. Kefalas, and Jennifer Holdaway, eds., *Coming of Age in America: The Transition to Adulthood in the Twenty-First Century* (Berkeley: University of California Press, 2011); Michael Kimmel, *Guyland: The Perilous World Where Boys Become Men* (New York: Harper, 2008), chap. 2.

24 Stephen Katz, *Cultural Aging: Life Course, Lifestyle, and Senior Worlds* (Toronto: University of Toronto Press, 2009); Cruikshank, *Learning to Be Old*; Gullette, *Aged by Culture*; Toni M. Calasanti and Kathleen F. Slevin, eds., *Age Matters: Re-aligning Feminist Thinking* (New York: Routledge: 2006).

PART I

Age in Early America

1

"Keep Me with You, So That I Might Not Be Damned"

Age and Captivity in Colonial Borderlands Warfare

ANN M. LITTLE

Father Jacques Bigot was proud of his Acadian missionary work, but desperately worried during King William's War at the end of the seventeenth century that his youngest and most fervent English converts would be lost to him and their souls lost to perdition. In his annual letter to the Jesuit authorities in October 1699, he wrote about his and his converts' shared sorrow at the prospect of their being compelled to return to their parents in New England, and therefore to Protestant "heresy." He explained that according to an agreement between New France and New England, as well as Louis XIV, children "who are over fourteen years of age are free to remain with the enemy, but both sides have the right to take back those who are under that age, whether they like it or not. When they came to take away a poor boy of twelve or thirteen, you could not have restrained your tears had you seen how he begged the savages to keep him. 'I shall be lost,' he exclaimed, with sobs. 'Keep me with you, so that I might not be damned.'" He also wrote about "four English girls," who "positively refused to return to Boston, and preferred to live with our Savages rather than run the risk, they said, of being perverted by the ministers." Another child "thought nothing of enduring the hardships of the miserable and wretched life led by the Savages, provided she remained in the true religion." He even told a story about "seven little English boys" who attempted to take their fates into their own hands. When they "heard of the exchange that was to be effected, [they] hid themselves in the woods, through fear of being taken away." More ominously, he explained that "two others who were older, and who died some months ago after making their first communion here, had assured me positively that they would not return."[1]

Father Bigot was right that New England and New France had agreed to repatriate children who were under a certain age, but that age was twelve and not fourteen. Interestingly, this appears to have been a shared misunderstanding with Bigot's adult Wabanaki (the collective name for members of the Abenaki, Penobscot Pasmoquoddy, Maliseet, and Mi'qmac nations who once dominated Acadia) converts, whom he describes as the willing agents for the prisoner exchange. He writes, "Our Abnaquis have begun during the past few days to restore, by exchange, the English prisoners whom they had taken in war." Bigot makes it clear that it is not English soldiers or officers demanding the return of the young captives; rather, it was the Wabanaki who willingly cooperated with the return of captives under age fourteen. He writes about the boy who begged, "'Keep me with you, so that I might not be damned,'" and explains that it was "the captain of his nation, who came to effect the exchange." The reasons for the confusion about the treaty to return captive children under the age of twelve to their birth families are not entirely clear, but even this confusion suggests something important about the enduring cross-cultural significance of specific ages in childhood as legally and religiously meaningful.

Father Bigot's confusion also suggests something about the improvisational and fluid nature of authority in the northeastern borderlands. Perhaps Wabanaki diplomats thought that it was in their best interests to cooperate fully in the prisoner exchange, and to err on the conservative side of what Father Bigot told them; perhaps the twelve- and thirteen-year-olds whom Bigot describes as being readied for exchange were less valuable to them than the prisoners the Wabanaki hoped to reclaim. In the end, French and Anglo-American colonial officials, confused Jesuit priests, and the Wabanaki allies of the French all had a clear number in mind when it came to extending to some children the right of self-determination, and when the law would make that decision for them regardless of their own wishes.[2]

This is just one example of encounters in the colonial northeastern borderlands among French, English, and Wabanaki people that suggests that people in this era had not just a shared understanding of children as different from adults, but also ideas about how children of different specific ages might be treated as war captives, regarded as religious converts, and categorized as subjects of civil law. This essay examines children at three different approximate ages—toddlers (one- to four-year-olds), six- and seven-year-olds, and early adolescents (ages twelve and fourteen)—and argues that people in these contested lands held broadly similar views about these different stages of childhood. English colonists in New England, French colonists in New France, and the Wabanaki people in between the rival Euro-Americans had a great deal in common even as they waged brutal wars against each other for the control of North America.

Age Consciousness and Numeracy in Early North America

Even among historians of the family and of childhood, some have doubted that people in the early modern era were conscious of their specific ages. Innumeracy was widespread through the eighteenth century, and except for boys and young men being trained in book-keeping or navigation, "'rithmetic" was the last and least of the three Rs after "readin'" and "'ritin."[3] More recently, creative social, cultural, and economic historians have found evidence to suggest that even many middling and plebian seventeenth- and eighteenth-century Europeans were in fact aware of their ages and numerate to at least a basic degree.[4] Puritan minister Thomas Foxcroft wrote in 1722 that "[t]he anniversary celebration of birth-days is an *ancient custom*," so it is likely that most Anglo-Americans were well aware of their birthdays.[5] Perhaps more important, recent scholarship has demonstrated conclusively that English and Anglo-American people were acutely conscious of both the distinctive stages of childhood as well as legally significant specific ages within childhood. Both the civil and criminal law alike relied on parents, children, and others in their parishes and villages knowing children's specific ages, as so much of the common law hinged on the different and quite specific ages of majority for citizenship rights (voting, and jury and militia duty), culpability (for criminal acts), discretion (in terms of religious affiliation and national loyalty), and consent (to employment or marriage contracts).[6]

In reflecting on my own twenty years of experience in the archives, I have found that people's specific ages and birth dates were recorded in a striking number and variety of colonial-era European-language primary sources, including New England town, court, and church records,

English ship manifests, French Canadian sacramental records, the records kept by religious orders in Québec, and the sacramental records of French missionaries living in Algonquian villages. While I have seen some evidence of age heaping (the tendency of people to report ages ending in zero, five, or six, suggesting that people were giving approximate rather than specific ages) in the colonial records, colonial people appear to have been very careful about documenting the specific ages of children, probably because their young lives were marked by so many changes in rights and status up to the age of twenty-one.[7] By comparison, adults were more likely to round up, round down, or approximate their ages. In my estimation, colonial North American records concur with the recent European historiography on numeracy, demonstrating that specific ages were important and significant in the history of childhood.

Although there is no evidence that specific numerical ages were important to Native people, as we will see, they nevertheless also recognized a transition from babyhood and early childhood to a more serious period in which education and skills were acquired around age six or seven. They also recognized puberty and had formal rituals for acknowledging this developmental stage. Children's sizes and stages of mental and physical development were probably more important than chronological age in these significant transitions in Native children's lives. Because these life stages roughly correlated with the chronological ages regarded as significant in France and England, participants in the North American border wars shared a general understanding with regard to the timing of maturation in childhood and adolescence.

Survival and Captivity in North American Borderlands Warfare

The northeastern borderlands of North America suffered almost continual warfare from 1675 to 1763, nearly ninety years of conflict that were interrupted by a scant two decades of peace from the mid-1720s to the mid-1740s. The wars that dominated New England and New France were King Philip's War (1675–78), King William's War (1688–97), Queen Anne's War (1702–13), Dummer's War (also known as Ralé's War or Greylock's War, 1723–26), King George's War (1744–48), and the Seven Years' War (1756–63). While French, Native American, and Anglo-American warriors alike took live war captives, Indian people more frequently practiced captivity because taking live captives rather than leaving behind dead bodies was the traditional goal of Native warfare. English and French enemies and allies alike remarked upon the Native American preference for taking captives. Because most Algonquian-speaking Indians (like the Wabanaki) were allied with the French in these borderlands wars, there were more Anglo-American captives living in Indian country or New France than there were French or Native American captives living among the English. Although the taking of war captives predated the invasion by European colonial powers, the need to do so to replenish their ranks surely accelerated after the introduction of European infectious diseases, warfare with Europeans, and the episodes of devastating famine that followed both disease and warfare.[8] In a painstaking accounting over thirty years ago, Alden Vaughan and Daniel Richter estimated that there were a total of 1,579 Anglo-American captives taken in these wars, 392 females and 1,187 males. (These numbers include both soldiers taken in battle, which probably explains the preponderance of male captives, as well as women and children taken from their homes in guerrilla attacks on their villages.) No scholar has attempted, much less surpassed, their heroic efforts to document and analyze the scale and experience of borderlands warfare.[9]

Finally, the experience of Anglo-American captives is much better documented in English-language records and by former captives themselves, many of whom upon their repatriation to New England wrote about their experiences in a literary genre that came to be known as captivity narratives. These accounts, however ideologically driven, are especially valuable sources for understanding the experience of borderlands warfare on families and whole communities, as they, along with the letters preserved in *The Jesuit Relations* like the one from Jacques Bigot quoted in the introduction, are representative of the only sources we have for understanding the experiences of women, boys, and girls alike. Because the experience was more widespread and because the documentation is richer and more detailed, this essay is based on Anglo-American records. However, I attempt to read against the grain of these colonial sources to uncover the experiences of Native communities and French officials as well as that of the Anglo-American boys and girls in captivity.

The most brutal experience for the victims of an attack was at the beginning, when Native warriors either took captives on the battlefield, or turned Anglo-American homes into battlefields by attacking English settlements full of noncombatants as well as adult men. Most horrifying for families under attack is the fact that it wasn't just adult men wielding weaponry who were singled out for death. Indian warriors looking to take live captives saw toddlers as hindrances to their quick escape, so children too big to be babes in arms (twelve to eighteen months) and too small to walk dozens of miles a day without slowing down the group or crying out (under four years) often did not survive the initial attack on their families' homes. Appalling to English parents and even to modern readers, toddlers were frequently executed before their parents' eyes. Of course, the invaders were not asking detailed questions about the ages of the children they encountered—Native warriors probably relied on their own visual judgment of the children's relative health, strength, and physical development. Youngsters deemed unable to make the journey into captivity quickly and quietly on foot were unlikely to survive.

Elizabeth Hanson, whose New Hampshire household was attacked in 1725 during Dummer's War, describes the speed with which two of her children were executed on the first two pages of her narrative. Hanson had six children: two teenaged girls, a six-year-old, a four-year-old, a toddler, and a newborn just two weeks old. She writes that the Wabanaki warriors "killed one Child [the toddler] immediately, as soon as they entred the Door, thinking thereby to strike in us the greater Terror, and to make us more fearful of them." Hanson explained that she was home alone with a servant girl, the toddler, and the newborn, as "two of the little Ones [were] at Play about the Orchard." Presumably drawn by their mother's cries of distress,

> Two of my younger Children, One Six, and the other Four Years old came in Sight; and being under a great Surprize, cryed aloud, upon which one of the Indians running to them, takes one under each Arm, and brings them to us. My maid prevailed with the biggest to be quiet and still; but the other could by no Means be prevailed with, but continued screaking and crying very much, in the Fright, and the *Indians*, to ease themselves of the Noise, and prevent the Danger of a Discovery that might arise from it, immediately before my Face, knockt its Brains out.

Witnessing her toddler's and her four-year-old's violent deaths, Hanson's experience was sadly all too common among Anglo-American families under attack.[10] Although she never states the age of the first child who was summarily executed, it is likely that she was around two years of age, given the typical birth spacing of about two years among Anglo-American families in colonial America. The doomed child was probably playing in the corner or tied to a table with leading strings while her mother looked after her newborn sister and her elder siblings played outdoors.[11]

Susanna Johnson, who was taken from Fort Number Four with her entire family in August 1754, had considerably better luck with her toddlers than did Elizabeth Hanson. The Wabanaki invaders permitted not just her six-year-old son, Sylvanus, to live, but also her two- and four-year-old daughters, Polly and Susanna, perhaps because unlike most women, Johnson was taken with her husband and a teenaged sister, who might have been able to help comfort and carry the younger children. Johnson's experience of Indian captivity was far from easy, however— she was taken when due with a full-term baby, whom she gave birth to on the trail with the assistance of her sister, husband, and captors, who did their best to make her comfortable. Significantly, she named her youngest daughter "Captive," and her birth was celebrated by her Indian master, who cried "two monies for me, two monies for me," when he saw that a child had been safely delivered, as he planned to sell Johnson for French ransom money once he delivered her to Montreal.[12] The Wabanaki who captured Johnson and her family, like the Wabanaki who had taken Elizabeth Hanson a generation earlier, were keen to assist the women in their efforts to sustain their newborns' lives. In Hanson's narrative, she praises the Wabanaki for their "Humanity and Civility" in assisting her with the baby, and at one point they show her how to make a nutritious pap out of walnuts, cornmeal, and water for her baby after her milk dries up. Similarly, Johnson describes the pains the Wabanaki took with her infant as well, noting that the Indians "brought a needle and two pins, and some bark to tie the child's clothes, which they gave my sister, and a large wooden spoon to feed it with."[13] It was in everyone's best interests that as many captives as possible survive the overland journey, so long as most captives could walk long hours with little food or refreshment and not cry or complain.

Seven: The Age of Reason

Among the surviving captives, younger children of both sexes were the most fortunate, as they were the likeliest to be adopted into Indian families and would have found the transition to a Wabanaki home and family much easier than older children, adolescents, or certainly Anglo-American adults. Just as Native warriors had a shared understanding about the undesirability of toddlers as captives, so Native people, their French allies, and their Anglo-American enemies had a shared understanding about young childhood, and the transition from innocence to formal education around age seven.

The evidence we have for Native childhood is very scattered and almost completely dependent on European representations of Native families, but there appear to have been many broad similarities across colonial North America. Life stage structured Native households across North America and dictated a great deal of family etiquette. Elders enjoyed universal respect and deference, and children were lavished with affection and were never struck or disciplined harshly. Mothers and big sisters supervised babies and very young girls and boys alike. Father Joseph François Lafitau explained in 1724 that an Indian child's introduction to work happened early: "As soon as they have grown a little larger, they follow their mothers and work for the family. For this, they are trained to go fetch water from the river, to bring in little loads of wood as heavy as they can carry, and which they can regard as playthings rather than a burden." According to the Jesuit Lafitau, Native people saw early childhood as a time when children were morally unaccountable. "The mothers who are in charge of them, have not the strength to punish and correct them when they fail in their duties; they let them do everything that they like when they are very young, under the pretext that they are not yet at the age of reason and that, when they reach those years, they will follow the light and correct themselves." He remained dubious of this parenting strategy, calling it "a bad principle which favors vicious habits which they cannot shake off." However, he also conceded that the children were for the most part "docile enough" and respectful of their elders, "a thing which indicates that in methods of bringing up children, gentleness is often more efficacious than punishments, especially violent ones."[14]

By age seven, Native children were separated according to their sex and educated to work as women (farming, gathering, preparing food, and making or repairing household items) or men (hunting, fishing, fighting, and providing political and spiritual leadership). Algonquian-speaking people in New England and Acadia understood the life cycle as guided by spiritual forces. Everyday tasks were connected to the spirit world, so religious education was included in the sex-segregated work that boys and girls were expected to perform. Doing sex-appropriate work faithfully and skillfully was a means of channeling supernatural power and spiritual harmony for the benefit of the community, and children were expected to contribute by about the age of seven.[15] Nevertheless, a spirit of playfulness and gentleness accompanied these lessons. Lafitau observed of boys' education that

> [a]ll the instructions given the Indian children by their parents consist in things fitted to stimulate their courage by the examples of their ancestors, to inspire them to follow in the latter's footsteps, to instruct them in the early customs and usages, and to inculcate in them the glory to be gained by skill and courage. To this end, the bow and arrow are put in their hands; for a long time, they keep them as playthings; but, as their strength increases with age, they make a necessary exercise out of an amusement and a game, and, in a short time, make themselves very useful.[16]

Seven was also a highly significant number and age in the European Christian tradition: there are seven Catholic sacraments and seven deadly sins. Seven is also called "the age of reason" in the Catholic tradition, as children at that age are considered to have the power of moral reasoning. In addition, they are subject to church law, so they must observe ritual fasts and the sacraments of reconciliation and the Eucharist. The seven "ages of life" structured European thought about the life cycle from the middle ages through the eighteenth century, and the first stages lasted seven years (infancy to age seven, pueritia from seven to fourteen, adolescence from fourteen to twenty-one, and youth from twenty-one to twenty-eight or thirty-five). Seven as an age and as a number with spiritual meaning retained its power through the Reformation; Keith Thomas has argued that in early modern England, "[a]ges involving multiples of seven were deemed climacteric years, dangerous and critical."[17] Perhaps because of its religious significance, seven was widely understood in early modern Europe as the appropriate age at which to begin elite formal education for both girls and boys, with girls perhaps starting their educations a little later. Boys in Renaissance Florence entered boarding schools at age seven, as did both girls and boys in eighteenth-century France. The great mathematician and translator of Isaac Newton's *Principia*, the precocious Emilie du Châtelet, was enrolled at a Parisian convent school at age seven or eight in the twilight years of Louis XIV's reign.[18] In colonial Anglo-America, literacy education might have begun at age six or even younger, but seven was considered the absolute minimum age for instruction in writing, given the need for certain fine motor skills in using a quill pen and ink. It is interesting to note that although education was sex-segregated regarding what boys and girls were permitted to learn, if not also physically segregated in boarding schools, there was a broad and durable consensus through the early modern period that formal schooling should begin around age seven.[19] Being taken from one's family was certainly a "dangerous and critical" passage in the lives of young captives, but those who were taken around age seven were probably among the most fortunate of all war captives because both Native American and European families believed that children of this age were ready to learn and to perform some productive labor.

Even Euro-American children in the colonial period who never attended school were initiated into the sex-segregated work and clothing of adult life around the age of six or seven. From toddlerhood to this age, boy and girl children alike wore stays over their underclothing to shape their torso and support the development of proper posture, as well as identical gowns or smocks on top. Gowns for children this age were presumably easier and somewhat cleaner for the purposes of toilet training, as well as more practical for hand-me-downs in large families with rapidly growing children. Around age six or seven in both New England and New France, boys were "breeched," or permitted to wear breeches or trousers like adult men, and were expected to assist daily with the chores associated with men's work—fetching water, tending livestock, and helping in other ways on the farm. Significantly, this is also the age at which boys were liberated from their stays, whereas girls would continue to wear stays and gowns for the rest of their lives. While girls enjoyed no innovation in fashion, they too were expected by age six or seven to participate in women's work, helping out their families by assisting their mothers and older sisters with cooking, dairying, gardening, spinning, needlework, and other women's work. Because seven was such a transitional age for Euro-American children, captives taken at or around this age would have been prepared to learn from their new families, and would not have had much to unlearn from their lives before captivity.[20]

The tale of Susanna Johnson's six-year-old son Sylvanus furnishes more evidence that Native children around this age were also being introduced to the work and expectations of adult manhood, in addition to the tendency of children at this age to forget their native language, customs, and families. Sylvanus Johnson's experience as a Wabanaki captive called on him to learn the ways of Wabanaki manhood almost as soon as his journey into captivity was over. Upon her family's arrival in the Indian mission town of Odanak (St. Francis), Susanna was separated from the rest of her family and sold to another master. Johnson writes that her son "who was six years old, was in the mean time to be put to school at Springfield" (Massachusetts). She undoubtedly knew his birthday—the diaries of eighteenth-century Anglo-American women recorded their children's birth dates as a matter of course, and Puritans, like Catholics, kept baptismal records as well.[21] Sylvanus never made it to school, because he and his whole family were captured at Fort Number Four in the late summer of 1754, and he instead began his formal education as a Wabanaki boy. Johnson's former master retained her son Sylvanus, as she explained, "being a hunter, [he] wished for my son, to attend him on his excursions." Joining men on his first hunt would have been considered an exciting milestone in Native boyhood, but little Sylvanus didn't understand that he was being treated much like any other boy his age, and was terrified of leaving his birth family behind in Odanak. In mid-October of 1754, Johnson wrote, "[W]ho can imagine my distress, when my little son came running to me one morning, swollen with tears, exclaiming, that the Indians were going to carry him into the woods to hunt; he had scarcely told the piteous story, before his master came, to pull him away; he threw his little arms around me, begging in the agony of grief, that I would keep him." But of course, part of growing up is learning how to play the part, and Sylvanus's master insisted that he join the hunt. "The inexorable savage unclenched his hands, and forced him away; the last words I heard, intermingled with his cries, were, Ma'am I shall never see you again." We can imagine the fear he would have felt at having to walk many more miles that autumn, but from the perspective of his master, he was merely being expected to perform the role and do the work of other Wabanaki boys. Unlike younger children, who tended crops with their mothers and chased birds and rabbits away from growing corn and beans, joining the hunt was an honor, and a comparably exciting kind of work at that.[22]

Sylvanus Johnson's experience among the Wabanaki at Odanak also offers evidence of the efficacy of undertaking the education of six- or seven-year-olds. Susanna Johnson reports that she heard nothing of her son for four years. When in October 1758 she learned that her son was ill in Northampton, Massachusetts, she rushed to meet him, "and found him in a deplorable situation." Kindly, the residents of Northampton "had taken the charge of him," but she reports that "his situation was miserable; when I found him he had no recollection of me, but after some conversation, he had some confused ideas of me, but no remembrance of his father. It was four years since I had seen him, he was then eleven years old."[23] Even more significantly, Johnson reports that "during his absence he had entirely forgotten the English language, spoke a little broken French, but was perfect in Indian. He had been with the savages three years, and one year with the French." As one might expect, given the length of time and the significant childhood years he spent with the Wabanaki, "his habits were somewhat Indian: he had been with them in their hunting excursions, and suffered numerous hardships—he could brandish a tomahawk or bend the bow, but these habits wore off by degrees."[24]

The newer literature on the history of childhood suggests that trauma was a common, if not universal, experience of colonial childhood, and the lens of trauma certainly seems appropriate when we think about the experiences of child war captives.[25] Sylvanus Johnson appears to have been a very good Indian child, a boy adaptable enough to survive the challenges and hardships of three different border crossings in the northeastern borderlands during the Seven Years War. Did he view his return to Anglo-American society as a "redemption" from captivity, or was his removal from the French and Indian communities he lived in retraumatizing, an event that placed him once again among people who were strangers to him and whose language he no longer spoke?

The biographies of Esther Wheelwright and Eunice Williams, two Anglo-American girls taken from opposite ends of New England in the early raids of Queen Anne's War, furnish still more evidence about seven-year-olds taken into captivity. They both forgot how to speak English, and were very skilled adopted daughters of Catholic Indians and the French. Unlike Sylvanus Johnson, both of these women as adolescents took sacramental vows before their English families found them, so they remained with new families, new languages, and a new confession. They also illustrate an important fact about the captives who were of an age to decide, and who ultimately elected to remain with Native families or in New France: 70 percent of them were girls or women. Boys were much likelier to be offered incentives to return to New England—jobs as translators, for example—and in some families, their inheritances were held for them even if they wanted to return to their Native or French families. In contrast, girls were expected to respond to parental admonitions only without material compensation.[26]

Wheelwright, taken at age seven from Wells, Maine, in August 1703, was adopted by the Catholic Wabanaki for five years before being taken to Québec and enrolled in the Ursuline convent school there.[27] Not two years after her arrival in Québec, she indicated an interest in becoming a professed nun, and she took the vow at eighteen. In the only surviving evidence of correspondence with her natal family, Wheelwright wrote (through a translator) to her mother that the letter reporting her father's death was "faithfully interpreted unto me by a person of vertue," suggesting that she had long ago forgot how to read English (if she ever did), and probably had forgotten how to speak much English. Clearly, she became proficient at speaking Wabanaki as well as reading and writing French, languages that served her better in childhood as well as in her adult work as a lifelong teacher, officeholder, and mother superior of the convent. In her reply to her mother, the then fifty-one-year-old Esther suggested that she should instead consider moving to Québec: "Oh! what joy, what pleasure, what consolation, would it give me my dear Mother if you had the happiness of knowing this holy religion which a kind Providence hath made me embrace since I left you. An established religion which our Forefathers professed for a long time with much heed and fervour until the Schisme." Ever the evangelist, Mother Esther couldn't resist inviting her Puritan mother to join her church instead. Although we have only her voice in retrospect as a middle-aged adult, it is clear that Esther's captivity at age seven by Catholic Wabanaki set her on the path to a life devoted to Catholicism.[28]

Eunice Williams was also abducted at age seven in February 1704 in an unusual winter raid on Deerfield, Massachusetts.[29] She too apparently forgot how to speak English after spending nine years among the Catholic Mohawks at Kahnawake and marrying at sixteen a Mohawk husband. After a 1713 interview with Eunice (now called A'ongote, with the Catholic baptismal name of Margaret), John Schuyler, an agent of the governor of Massachusetts sent to try to lure her back to her Puritan family, paid tribute to her unshakable determination to remain with her Mohawk family from the moment he met her: "She looking very poor in body bashfull in the face but proved harder then steel in her breast, at her first Entrance into the Room." Schuyler wrote that after almost two hours of "long Solicitations" in which he begged her (with the assistance of a French priest) to return to her father's home, she refused to say more than two words: "(Jaghte oghte) which words being translated into the English Tongue their Signification (as may be not) but the meaning thereof amongst the Indians is a plaine denyall and these two words were all we could gett from her."[30] Although we have these glimpses of the women at very different stages in life—Mother Esther in middle age, A'ongote still an adolescent—both women, it seems, proved "harder than steel" when it came to solicitations for their return to New England, which would have meant giving up the church and the families they had found in Canada. Their experiences as fierce converts to a different religion, different languages, and different ways of life furnish evidence that colonial North Americans emphasized age seven in the education of children.[31]

How should we understand the experiences of children like Sylvanus Johnson, Eunice Williams, and Esther Wheelwright? On the one hand, Barry Levy has suggested that we must acknowledge the "traumatic reality" of early American childhood, "a sadder early America where children regularly face potentially traumatizing events and where parents and communities scurry to invent ways of handling their own and their children's desensitizing astonishment and crippling disassociations."[32] And these are the stories of boys and girls who survived their ordeals and were eventually restored to health if not also to their natal families—what of their Indian brothers and sisters, whose communities were ravaged by disease and starvation in addition to warfare? Something to consider when using the lens of trauma to understand children's experiences is that we are almost entirely reliant on adult narrators of children's experiences in this period. Susanna Johnson was the teller of her son's tales, so how can we know if the trauma she reported was her son's, or her own trauma at being reunited with a beloved child who no longer knew her as his mother and no longer even spoke her language? How would Esther Wheelwright's answer to her mother have differed if she were not already a middle-aged choir nun of more than thirty years? To what extent can we trust Schuyler's ultimately self-justifying account of his failure to induce A'ongote to return to New England with him as Eunice Williams once again? All of these questions must haunt those of us engaged in writing the history of children and childhood, as the mediation of adult narrators is almost inescapable.[33]

Alternatively, we can see these stories about seven-year-olds as clear evidence of children's resilience even amid the trauma and privations of warfare and captivity. Sylvanus, Esther, and Eunice/A'ongote alike all apparently lost their English and learned Wabanaki or Mohawk quickly, and Sylvanus and Esther both learned French as well. The two girls were enthusiastic converts to the Catholicism practiced in their Native families and in New France; Sylvanus was probably baptized and catechized, but because he returned to New England, he was undoubtedly forced to return to Protestantism. All of the children found loving and fiercely protective homes among Native peoples, as a son and daughters, and in A'ongote's case, as a wife. A'ongote's attachment to her Mohawk family and Esther's attachment to her Ursuline sisters and mothers was so strong that they remained among their new families for the rest of their lives. Not all children could make such an easy transition to life across these linguistic, religious, and national borders, but being age seven was undoubtedly a tremendous benefit to them. They were old enough to survive the initial assault on their families and strong enough to walk hundreds of miles into captivity, their minds ready to begin their formal educations and adult work roles; their stories demonstrate the tenacious resilience of children at this age.

Twelve and Fourteen: Discernment and Consent

European observers clearly recognized and were fascinated by the rituals Native American girls and boys observed at puberty. Lafitau devoted a large portion of his chapter on religion to "Initiation to the Mysteries," which offered a cross-cultural comparison of ancient Greek and Roman puberty rites to Native American puberty rituals from Brazil, Mexico, the Caribbean, Florida, Virginia, and the northeastern woodlands. Fasting and close attention to dreams were required of both male and female initiates across the Americas, as well as a rigid sex-segregation.[34] The Wabanaki were especially observant of the power associated with blood and bloodletting. Rituals surrounding menstrual seclusion for girls and women, and for boys and men preparing for the hunt or to go to war, were opportunities to acknowledge the divine as well as attempts to channel supernatural power by making the ritual observances.

Once again, it appears that chronological age was less vital to Native Americans than physical and emotional development. Girls' initiation rituals were almost entirely dependent on one sign of physical maturity, menarche. Lafitau writes that with the onset of menses both Iroquois- and Algonquian-speaking girls would be led away by a "matron" and kept in seclusion during their periods, a tradition they would be expected to observe through menopause. During their first periods, northeastern Native girls would "fast very strictly; and, as long as their fast lasts, they blacken their faces, the tops of their shoulders and their chests. In particular, they pay careful attention to their dreams and report them exactly to those in charge of them," and seek their mentors' advice on interpreting these dreams. "They also draw conclusions to determine for what these initiates ought to be fitted in the future, so that the test is a sort of vocational one." Boys too would spend time in seclusion in "vision quests," fasting and interpreting dreams with a mentor as they prepared to become men and warriors. Although the developmental markers Native men and women watched for in boys are unrecorded, presumably they were based on the physical changes wrought by adolescence. Like girls, they would be led into seclusion "into the woods, under an elder or a shaman's direction." There, their fasts would last "sometimes for a week and, at other times for ten days. Others have told me that they emerge from this cabin like skeletons and that sometimes they are carried out half dead." In addition to undergoing this puberty ritual, adolescent boys were encouraged to develop and display their physical prowess in swimming, running, and archery, among other activities, and to engage in competitive games with each other in the service of developing their skills as fishers, hunters, and warriors.[35]

Adolescence was recognized as a powerful passage by Europeans as well. Holly Brewer's important study argues that as birth and status became less important over time in the Anglophone Atlantic, the citizenship privileges once granted young aristocratic or wealthy children vanished. Although age was a more democratic means by which to distribute these rights, at the same time the minimum age for exercising these rights and responsibilities was adjusted upward over the course of the early modern era. Therefore the age at which children were considered morally culpable for their crimes moved haltingly from eight, to twelve, to fourteen by the early nineteenth century. So too did the right to vote or serve on a jury move from twelve to fourteen to twenty-one after the American Revolution.[36]

It is striking how often the ages of twelve and fourteen appear and reappear in English and Euro-American civil, criminal, and canon law, suggesting once again a broad consensus among Europeans and colonial Americans about the importance of early adolescence. The correspondence between the governor of New France and the king that explains the agreement with New England and New York for the repatriation of war captives in the fall of 1698 and the spring of 1699 states that "it was only children under twelve years who had no liberty to stay, notwithstanding the desire they had. We permitted this because [the Anglo-Americans] represented to us that they [children under twelve] don't have the power of discernment." Clearly the notion of discernment made sense to the officials both in New France and in the English colonies. Even Louis XIV and his councilors agreed, responding to the letter from New France by saying that children under twelve "must be returned following the rule that the English established themselves because they are not in a state to choose their own religion."[37]

For our purposes in puzzling out Father Bigot's confusion about the prisoner exchange policy being applied to those under fourteen instead of only to those captives under the age of twelve, research on the significance of particular ages in childhood offers us some important clues.

First of all, there may have been confusion about the policy in the mind of a Jesuit priest because according to canon law, the age of discretion was twelve for girls and fourteen for boys. The age of discretion was the age at which children could renounce their religion, which before the end of the eighteenth century usually was directly linked to one's citizenship. Up until that age, although children over seven had attained the "age of reason," they weren't held fully culpable for any errors or delusions they might have fallen into. As Brewer explains, "According to Catholic doctrine, active assent [to one's faith] at age fourteen was not necessary: only active dissent during that window of opportunity could break the connection." The connection between adolescence and active citizenship was also clear in Anglo-American law, as boys as young as twelve were required to swear oaths of loyalty in colonial America.[38] Therefore, considering the fact that Bigot's concern was mostly for the young boys in his charge, and given the long history of the importance of age fourteen in canon law in terms of religious assent or dissent, perhaps Bigot assumed that boys had to have achieved the age of fourteen in order to make their own decisions about faith and nation.

Interestingly, the consequence of ages twelve and fourteen with respect to the age of discernment maps directly onto the commonly understood age at which children could consent to marriage—once again, twelve for girls and fourteen for boys. This was the case not just in Europe according to English common law and Catholic canon law, but also in colonial New England and New France as well. As in the criminal law and other aspects of civil law, the age of marriage rose over time so that twelve and fourteen became the absolute minimum ages at which girls or boys (respectively) could lawfully marry. Over the course of the eighteenth and early nineteenth centuries, most English colonies or U.S. states also stipulated that brides under eighteen or grooms under twenty-one needed parental consent to marry. Because of the connection between marriage and independent adulthood in the minds of most early modern Europeans and colonial Euro-Americans, it might have been natural for them to link the age of consent for marriage to the age of discretion.[39] Of course, the legal minimum ages for marriage were directly related to the fact that children of twelve and fourteen were potentially becoming sexually mature and capable of having children themselves.[40]

Finally, just as in European and Euro-American communities, marriage marked the end of childhood for Native people as well. Wabanaki people appear to have had an especial reverence for the transition from the unmarried to the married state, suggesting that they too saw a great deal of the work of childhood and adolescence as complete or nearly complete once men and women made the decision to marry. Alice Nash argues that the Wabanaki were "brideservice societies," in which "men 'earn' wives by providing a woman's parents with meat and other gifts. It is a crucial requirement that men in brideservice societies must earn these gifts through their own effort so that they are beholden to no one, and their status as socially-recognized adult males is consequently dependent upon their ability to acquire and keep a wife."[41] Thus, the skills acquired in adolescence by Wabanaki boys especially were crucial to their achievement of adulthood, a status largely dependent on marriage.

Early adolescence, and specifically the ages of twelve and fourteen in European and Euro-American church and civil law, was a time in life recognized for its importance and power. Around the time they achieved sexual maturity, colonial Americans of all backgrounds and faith traditions recognized that adulthood was approaching, and they devised culturally and religiously appropriate customs in order to smooth the transition from childhood to maturity. It is perhaps no wonder that Father Bigot either mistook or confused the joint policy of New England and New France to repatriate children under twelve regardless of their personal preferences, because the age of fourteen for boys especially was so strongly a part of the church and civil laws observed in the colonial northeastern borderlands.

Conclusion

Early Americans of many different backgrounds and religious traditions had a shared understanding of the stages of childhood, and we have evidence that children's specific ages were very important to if not determinative of a child's experience of colonial borderlands warfare, captivity, and eligibility for repatriation. Toddlers, seven-year-olds, and children ages twelve and fourteen had some common experiences because of the shared understanding among French, English, and Native American people in the colonial Northeast. While some of these experiences may have been due to child development regardless of culture, it is important to remember that the common understandings of these ages were also culturally constructed. Children like Father Bigot's converts, Esther Wheelwright, Aòngote, and Sylvanus Johnson embodied religious and cultural change, but that change was successful only because of the deeper similarities that united all of the people in the colonial Northeast.

NOTES

1 Reuben Gold Thwaites, ed., *The Jesuit Relations and Allied Documents* (New York: Pageant, 1959), 65:90–93.

2 Ibid.

3 Patricia Cline Cohen, *A Calculating People: The Spread of Numeracy in Early America* (Chicago: University of Chicago Press, 1982), chaps. 1–3; Keith Thomas, "Numeracy in Early Modern England: The Prothero Lecture," *Transactions of the Royal Historical Society* 5th ser., 37 (1987): 103–32. In his foundational study of childhood and the family, Philippe Ariès describes the early modern era as the period when age consciousness began. See *Centuries of Childhood: A Social History of Family Life*, trans. Robert Baldick (New York: Vintage, 1962), 15–18.

4 Sean Takats, "Domestic Expertise: Literacy and Numeracy in the Eighteenth Century French Kitchen," *Proceedings of the Western Society* 32 (2004): 46–64; Jelle van Lottum and Bo Poulsen, "Estimating Levels of Numeracy and Literacy in the Maritime Sector of the North Atlantic in the Late Eighteenth Century," *Scandinavian Economic History Review* 59, no. 1 (2011): 67–82; Tom Wickman, "Arithmetic and Afro-Atlantic Pastoral Protest: The Place of (In)numeracy in Gronniosaw and Equiano," *Atlantic Studies* 8, no. 2 (2011): 189–212; Tine DeMoor and Jaco Zuiderduijn, "The Art of Counting: Reconstructing Numeracy of the Middle and Upper Classes on the Basis of Portraits in the Early Modern Low Countries," *Historical Methods: A Journal of Quantitative and Interdisciplinary History* 46, no. 1 (2013): 41–56.

5 Thomas Foxcroft, *The Day of a Godly Man's Death, Better Than the Day of His Birth* (Boston, 1722), 31.

6 Holly Brewer, *By Birth or Consent: Children, Law, and the Anglo-American Revolution in Authority* (Chapel Hill: University of North Carolina Press, 2005). Cohen's own evidence suggests that people were clearly aware of at least the approximate ages of afflicted community members in her discussion of the accounting of a diphtheria epidemic in Massachusetts in 1735. Cohen, *Calculating People*, 90–93.

7 DeMoor and Zuiderduijn, "Art of Counting," analyze age heaping with numbers that end in zero or five, while Thomas, "Numeracy in Early Modern England," found that in early modern England, duodecimo currency and weights meant that people engaged in age heaping with final digits of zero and six.

8 James Axtell, "The White Indians of Colonial America," *William and Mary Quarterly* 3rd ser., 32, no. 1 (1975): 55–88, reprinted in *The European and the Indian: Essays in the Ethnohistory of Colonial North America* (New York: Oxford University Press, 1981), 168–206; Axtell, *The Invasion Within: The Contest of Cultures in Colonial North America* (New York: Oxford University Press, 1985), 302–27; Daniel Richter, "War and Culture: The Iroquois Experience," *William and Mary Quarterly* 3rd ser., 40 (1983): 528–59; Richter, *The Ordeal of the Longhouse* (Chapel Hill: University of North Carolina Press, 1992), chaps. 2–3; Evan Haefeli and Kevin Sweeney, *Captors and Captives: The 1704 French and Indian Raid on Deerfield* (Amherst: University of Massachusetts Press, 2003), 1–7 and 95–163; Ann M. Little, *Abraham in Arms: War and Gender in Colonial New England* (Philadelphia: University of Pennsylvania Press, 2007), chap. 3, esp. 111–13.

9 Alden T. Vaughan and Daniel K. Richter, "Crossing the Cultural Divide: Indians and New Englanders, 1605–1763," *American Antiquarian Society Proceedings* 90 (April 16, 1980): 23–99.

10 Elizabeth Hanson, *God's Mercy Surmounting Man's Cruelty* (Philadelphia: Samuel Keimer, 1728), 5–6. For more on the attack on homes and the initial experience of Indian captivity, see, for example, Jill Lepore, *The Name of War: King Philip's War and the Origins of American Identity* (New York: Knopf, 1998), chap. 3; Haefeli and Sweeney, *Captors and Captives*, chaps. 5–6; Little, *Abraham in Arms*, 104–9.

For more on captivity narratives as a genre of literature and as useful historical sources, see James Axtell, "The White Indians of Colonial America," and *Invasion Within*; June Namias, *White Captives: Gender and Ethnicity on the American Frontier* (Chapel Hill: University of North Carolina Press, 1993); Pauline Turner Strong, *Captive Selves, Captivating Others: The Politics and Poetics of Colonial American Captivity Narratives* (Boulder, Colo.: Westview, 1999); Lorrayne Carroll, *Rhetorical Drag: Gender Impersonation, Captivity, and the Writing of History* (Kent, Ohio: Kent State University Press, 2007); and Teresa A. Toulouse, *The Captive's Position: Female Narrative, Male Identity, and Royal Authority in Colonial New England* (Philadelphia: University of Pennsylvania Press, 2007).

11 On the spacing of colonial Anglo-American women's families, see Susan Klepp, *Revolutionary Conceptions: Women, Fertility, & Family Limitation in America, 1760–1820* (Chapel Hill: University of North Carolina Press, 2009), 41–44. On leading strings and their uses on toddlers' gowns, see Linda Baumgarten, *What Clothes Reveal: The Language of Clothing in Colonial and Federal America: The Colonial Williamsburg Collection* (Williamsburg, Va.: Colonial Williamsburg Foundation, 2002), 166–67, 175.

12 Hanson, *God's Mercy*, 8–13, 25–26, quotation on 10; Susanna Johnson, *A Narrative of the Captivity of Mrs. Johnson, Together with a Narrative of James Johnson*, 3rd ed. (Windsor, Vt., 1814; repr., Bowie, Md.: Heritage Books, 1990), 26–36, quotation on 36.

13 Johnson, *Narrative*, 37.

14 Joseph François Lafitau, *Customs of the American Indians Compared with the Customs of Primitive Times*, ed. and trans. William N. Fenton and Elizabeth L. Moore (Toronto: Champlain Society, 1974), 1:355–61, quotations on 358 and 361.

15 For more on colonial Native American childhood, see Steven Mintz, *Huck's Raft: A History of American Childhood* (Cambridge, Mass.: Belknap, 2004), 34–37; R. Todd Romero, "'Ranging Foresters' and 'Women-Like Men': Physical Accomplishment, Spiritual Power, and Indian Masculinity in Early-Seventeenth-Century New England," *Ethnohistory* 53, no. 2 (2006): 281–329; Romero, "Colonizing Childhood: Religion, Gender, and Indian Children in Southern New England, 1620–1720," in *Children in Colonial America*, ed. James Marten (New York University Press, 2007), 33–47; and Romero, *Making War and Minting Christians: Masculinity, Religion, and Colonialism in Early New England* (Amherst: University of Massachusetts Press, 2011), 21–30. See also Dorothy Tanck de Estrada, "Indian Children in Colonial Mexico," in Marten, *Children in Colonial America*, 13–32.

16 Lafitau, *Customs of the American Indians*, 1:360.

17 Ariès, *Centuries of Childhood*, 18–22; Thomas, "Numeracy in Early Modern England," 125. See also Margaret L. King's excellent review essay of nearly fifty years of historiography, "Concepts of Childhood: What We Know, and Where We Might Go," *Renaissance Quarterly* 60, no. 2 (2007): 371–407.

18 Sharon T. Strocchia, "Learning the Virtues: Convent Schools and Female Culture in Renaissance Florence," in *Women's Education in Early Modern Europe: A History, 1500–1800*, ed. Barbara J. Whitehead (New York: Garland, 1999), 47–74; Carolyn C. Lougee, "'Its Frequent Visitor': Death at Boarding School in Early Modern Europe," in Whitehead, *Women's Education in Early Modern*, 207; Judith P. Zinsser, *La Dame D'Esprit: A Biography of the Marquise du Châtelet* (New York: Viking, 2006), 24; Dominique Picco, "Adults et Enfants en la Maison Royale de Saint-Cyr (fin XVIIe-XVIIIe siècles)," *Mélanges de l'École Francaise de Rome, Italie, et Méditerranée* 123, no. 2 (2011): 359–70; Pascale Mormiche, "Enfance, enfances de princes en France (XVIIe-XVIIIe Siècles)," *Mélanges de l'École Francaise de Rome, Italie, et Méditerranée* 123, no. 2 (2011): 395–407.

19 E. Jennifer Monaghan, *Learning to Read and Write in Colonial America* (Amherst: University of Massachusetts Press, 2005), 39–43, 363–65.

20 Mintz, *Huck's Raft*, 23. On Euro-American children's clothing and the breeching of boys, see Baumgarten, *What Clothes Reveal*, 156–76; Alice Morse Earle, *Two Centuries of Costume in America, 1620–1820* (New York: Macmillan, 1903), 1:271–320; Bernard Audet, *Le Costume Payson dans la Region de Québec au XVIIe Siècle Île d'Orléans* (Ottawa: Éditions Leméac, 1980); Pat Tomczyszyn, "*Le Costume Traditionnel*: A Study of Clothing and Textiles in the Town of Québec, 1635–1760" (master's thesis, University of Manitoba, 1999), 267–70; Tomczyszyn, "Sifting through the Papers of the Past: Using Archival Documents for Costume Research in Seventeenth- and Eighteenth-Century Québec," *Material History Review* 55 (Spring 2002): 4–15.

21 See, for example, Michelle Marchetti Coughlin, *One Colonial Woman's World: The Life and Writings of Mehetabel Chandler Coit* (Amherst: University of Massachusetts Press, 2002); Mehetabel Chandler Coit (1673–1758), *Mehetabel Chandler Coit, Her Book, 1714* (Norwich, Conn.: Bulletin Print, 1895) accessed via North American Women's Letters and Diaries, July 17, 2013, http://ezproxy2.library.colostate.edu:2952/cgi-bin/asp/philo/nwld/getvolume.pl?S3. See also diaries by Margaret Graves Cary (1719–62), Esther Edwards Burr (1732–58), Mary Vial Holyoke (1737–1802), and Christiana Young Leach, for example, all in North American Women's Letters and Diaries.

22 Johnson, *Narrative*, 25, 67, 69.

23 Ibid., 130–31. When reporting on his leaving for the hunt in 1754, Johnson had reported him as being merely six. Perhaps he turned seven that autumn.

24 Ibid., 131–32.

25 See, for example, Mintz, *Huck's Raft*. Significantly, Mintz's chapter on colonial childhood opens with a retelling of the 1704 attack on the Anglo-American village of Deerfield, Mass., by French and Indian warriors, 7–9. See also Marten, *Children in Colonial America*, esp. the foreword by Philip J. Greven (ix–xii) and the introduction by Marten (1–10); see also Barry Levy's review of Marten's collection in *William and Mary Quarterly*, 3rd ser. 64, no. 3 (2007): 668–72.

26 For more on the reasons why girls were likelier to remain in Canada and boys were likelier to return to New England, see Little, *Abraham in Arms*, chap. 4 (esp. 138–59).

27 Genealogical information about the Wheelwright family was published in the *Maine Historical Magazine* 9 (January 1894–January 1895): 77–80, and in Edmund M. Wheelwright, "A Frontier Family," in *Publications of the Colonial Society of Massachusetts, Transactions 1892–94* (Boston: Colonial Society of Massachusetts, 1895), 1:270–303.

I have never seen a surviving document from the seventeenth century recording Esther's birth as March 31, 1696, as the nineteenth-century family genealogies have it, but presumably the information was recorded at some point in Esther's brief life with her English family. All of her brothers and sisters listed in the *Maine Historical Magazine* genealogy have specific birthdates listed, so perhaps the information was recorded in seventeenth- and eighteenth-century family papers that have since been lost. Esther Wheelwright, like her three brothers and her elder sister, wasn't baptized until November 9, 1701, when her parents had them baptized all together (see the first page of baptismal records for the First Church of Christ, Congregational, Wells, Maine; Coll. 1249, Maine Historical Society, Portland, Maine).

28 Julie Wheelwright, *Esther: The Remarkable True Story of Esther Wheelwright—Puritan Child—Native Daughter—Mother Superior* (Toronto: HarperCollins, 2011); Coleman I: 429, Archives Personnelles Des Religieuses, Esther Wheelwright et famille, 1/G11, Sœur Esther Wheelwright Correspondence, Archives du Monastère des Ursulines de Québec, Québec, P.Q.

29 Steven West Williams, *The Genealogy and History of the Family of Williams in America* (Greenfield, Mass.: Merriam & Merrick, 1847), 92–94.

30 SC1 45X, Massachusetts Archives Collection v. 72: 13–15, Massachusetts State Archives, Boston; John Demos, *The Unredeemed Captive: A Family Story from Early America* (New York: Knopf, 1994), 101–8, 146–47.

31 Captive girls were likelier to remain in Canada than were boys. For more on this, see Little, *Abraham in Arms*, chap. 4.

32 Levy review, 669.

33 Ondina E. González discusses the inescapable voices of adults when attempting to uncover children's histories in her introductory essay in *Raising an Empire: Children in Early Modern Iberia and Colonial Latin America*, ed. Ondina E. González and Bianca Premo (Albuquerque: University of New Mexico Press, 2007), 5–7.

34 Lafitau, *Customs of the American Indians*, 1:180–219.

35 Ibid., 1:217. On both Native girls' and Native boys' adolescence, see Mintz, *Huck's Raft*, 34–47; on menstrual seclusion, see Alice Nash, "The Abiding Frontier: Family, Gender, and Religion in Wabanaki History, 1600–1763" (PhD diss., Columbia University, 1997), 236–39. Theda Perdue offers a similar analysis of menstrual segregation and taboos among the Cherokee in the eighteenth and nineteenth centuries in *Cherokee Women: Gender and Culture Change, 1700–1835* (Lincoln: University of Nebraska Press, 1998), 28–40. On boys' rituals, see Romero, "'Ranging Foresters'"; and *Making War and Minting Christians*, 25–27.

36 Brewer, *By Birth or Consent*, 40–44, 132, 140–41, 142–49, 211–29.

37 *Collection de Documents Relatifs a l'Histoire de la Nouvelle France* (Montreal: A. Coté et Cie, 1884), 2:309 and 327.

38 Brewer, *By Birth or Consent*, 48–70, 140–49, quotation on 65.

39 Ibid., 288–95; Carole Shammas, *A History of Household Government in America* (Charlottesville: University of Virginia Press, 2002); Stephanie Coontz, *Marriage, a History: From Obedience to Intimacy, or How Love Conquered Marriage* (New York: Viking, 2005).

40 We should probably regard age twelve as among the lowest ages at which a seventeenth- or eighteenth-century adolescent would begin to menstruate. In *The Body Project: An Intimate History of American Girls* (New York: Random House, 1997), 3–5, Joan Jacobs Brumberg has argued that the average age at menarche has dropped nearly four full years in the past two centuries, from fifteen or sixteen around the turn of the nineteenth century down to age twelve today.

41 Romero, "'Ranging Foresters'"; Nash, "Abiding Frontier," 148–99, quotation on 158–59.

2

"Beyond the Time of White Children"

African American Emancipation, Age, and Ascribed
Neoteny in Early National Pennsylvania

SHARON BRASLAW SUNDUE

In 1784, an unnamed free black woman approached the Pennsylvania Abolition Society seeking the organization's aid in protecting her two teenage daughters' fragile claim to freedom.[1] The woman and her girls, Charity and Deborah Pero, had been the slaves of Mary Burras in New Jersey until, at the end of the War for Independence, Burras brought them across state lines to Philadelphia. Once there, by virtue of Pennsylvania's 1780 emancipation law, the girls became entitled to their freedom after six months' residence. That law, the very first to abolish slavery in the United States, legally freed African Americans born in the state after its passage after serving a period of indenture to their mothers' master until twenty-eight, and likewise made provision for the emancipation of African American slaves brought into the state. Mary Burras never acknowledged the force of that law, and now planned to return to New Jersey with what she believed to be her human property. Deliberately circumventing the law, she applied to an unknowing municipal official at the Philadelphia workhouse, and without their mother's consent, Burras had the eleven- and sixteen-year-old girls contractually bound as her servants. Each was now bound to serve as her laborers until twenty-eight, a decade beyond the legal term of servitude for a white girl, and seven years beyond the chronological age of majority for free whites.[2] With papers in hand ostensibly certifying her right to the girls' labor, Burras trafficked the girls across the Delaware River back to New Jersey. Fifteen years later, the girls remained in Burras's New Jersey household, reduced to the status of slaves. After that point, they disappeared altogether beyond the historical record.

The Pero girls' sad story bears a resemblance to modern instances of child trafficking loudly protested by nongovernmental agencies in developing nations throughout the global South. And yet it was also a significant by-product of the process of emancipation of African Americans throughout the North in the aftermath of the American Revolution. By virtue of their move to Pennsylvania, Charity and Deborah Pero together with their mother became legally entitled to their freedom in Pennsylvania. Ironically, their mistress denied that freedom by taking advantage of the very same abolition law when she had them indentured to her, since that law provided that emancipated African Americans should be legally bound as "apprentices" to freedom to twenty-eight, an extended period of dependence, and thus essentially an extension of minority. The Pero girls' story highlights the ugliest implications of a redefined chronological length of servitude, and thus dependence, for nonwhites amid the first emancipation in the early national period. As historians including Gary Nash, Jean Soderlund, Graham Hodges, Joanne Melish, and John Sweet have detailed, this kind of "gradual emancipation," as it was enacted throughout most of the North, reflects the complicated relationship among northern whites' ideological opposition to slavery, their persistent demand for cheap, stable sources of labor, and the evolving construction of racial difference.[3] In Connecticut, for example, in 1785 the legislature passed an abolition statute freeing African American children born in the state after the law's passage, requiring service until age twenty-five. New York's 1799 abolition act likewise provided that females born after the law's passage would serve their mother's master to twenty-five, males to twenty-eight. Finally, New Jersey's 1804 abolition law freed children born after the law's passage after twenty-five years of service.[4] Robert Fogel and Stanley Engerman thus famously described northern emancipation acts offering "the opportunity to engage in philanthropy at bargain prices," given masters' ability to continue exploiting their former slaves as laborers.[5]

As this article argues, these terms of unfreedom also reflected widespread white presumptions concerning African Americans' mental and behavioral neoteny—delayed maturation and the persistence of childlike traits into physical adulthood—years longer than for whites. Strikingly, when lawmakers wrote an extended chronological age for black dependence in emancipation statutes, they also offered unscrupulous whites opportunities to circumvent the law. Over and over again, whites seeking to evade the emancipation law relied on the very same widespread presumption that *all* blacks must be liable for extended indenture because of inherently childlike traits, regardless of their actual legal status and the applicability of those extended legal indentures. The law extending servitude thus placed all young African Americans in danger of legal and economic exploitation regardless of whether they were born enslaved or free, given white assumptions regarding their status and the appropriate extended period of dependence.

Using Pennsylvania as a case study, this essay analyzes the social implications of the first emancipation law, which imposed legal servitude and thus dependence to the age of twenty-eight for emancipated African Americans. In order to reconstruct the consequences of this ascribed neoteny, this article analyzes evidence of exploitation documented by the Pennsylvania Abolition Society between 1784 and 1820. The Pennsylvania Abolition Society (hereafter the PAS) was the primary abolitionist organization in that state during this period and took as one of its chief responsibilities policing African Americans' fragile claims to freedom. As Nash and Soderlund have noted, a central strategy for the organization during its first decades was a moderate one, seeking ways to broaden the coverage of the 1780 law as much or perhaps more than seeking an outright abolition of slavery altogether via judicial precedent or legislation.[6] Given patterns of exploitation, therefore, one of the central issues in the PAS's efforts became the question of the appropriate terminus of legal dependence, which the organization fought to ensure, whenever possible, would not be "beyond the time of white children" for African American children not legally registered as slaves. In doing so, the PAS likewise relied on chronological age in order to make a powerful claim on equality for African Americans, and thus age would become vitally important for free African Americans.

Servitude for emancipated African Americans drew in part on much older legal precedents for the care of indigent minors; involuntary apprenticeship of impoverished minors was a central mechanism deployed for coping with the problem of impoverishment since the Elizabethan era. The intent of those pauper apprenticeships was explained in the 1576 English law that empowered local overseers of the poor to involuntarily remove boys and girls under twenty-one from their parents' homes and render them legal dependents to a more appropriate patriarchal authority either until the age of twenty-four or for seven years if the child was bound to learn a skilled trade. The intent of the law was clearly described in its preamble: "youth may be accustomed and brought up in labor and work, and then not like to grow to be idle rogues."[7] The law was modified in 1598 to enable parish overseers of the poor to bind out as servants "the children of all such whose parents shall not be thought able to keep and maintain their children," or, by the eighteenth century in the North American colonies, eighteen for girls and twenty-one for boys.[8] That terminus for servitude corresponded to the legal age of majority for boys, and the shorter term for girls corresponded to the legal age of marriage without parental consent in many states; presumably thereafter girls might marry and become appropriately dependent upon their husbands' patriarchal authority.[9]

When, during the era of the American Revolution, antislavery activists became increasingly vocal about the irreconcilability of slavery with the larger struggle for liberty, involuntary apprenticeship likewise took on a new meaning. By 1774, northerners were inundated with printed condemnations of slavery in the press and from the pulpit.[10] In the words of one editorial by Pennsylvania's Richard Wells, for example, how could Americans "reconcile the exercise of slavery with our profession of freedom"? "In vain shall we contend for liberty," he answered, "till this barbarous inhuman custom is driven from our borders."[11] Pennsylvania's Assembly took that lead and began to consider proposals for abolition during the war itself in 1778. In doing so, they acted on the instigation of Pennsylvania's Executive Council President George Bryan, who argued that if Pennsylvania abolished slavery, it would erase from within its borders the "opprobrium of America," regaining the respect of "all Europe, who are astonished to see a people eager for Liberty holding Negroes in bondage."[12] Those ambitions aside, this first American abolition bill offered freedom to no enslaved person already living. Why? Because, in Bryan's words, "the present slaves are scarcely competent of freedom."[13]

In short, widespread contemporary presumptions about differences between African Americans and whites and belief in blacks' inherent inferiority even among abolitionists worked against a universal approach to abolition. A key presumption working against a general or immediate abolition was the assumption that enslaved people were fundamentally more dependent than adult whites and less capable of exercising responsibility for themselves, and thus perpetually more juvenile in their tendencies than whites. In discussion surrounding a possible emancipation in the Pennsylvania newspapers in 1780, for example, even an advocate of emancipation conceded that "servants for life are without motive to industry, honesty and obedience."[14] The same author made reference to the widespread fear that "the emancipation of young blacks would be an injury to a race so indolent and helpless as the Africans, and place them in worse circumstances than their [enslaved] parents; a notion that can only arise from the experience we have of the vilifying effects of slavery, which, without doubt, destroy virtue, care and even industry."[15]

These anxieties about emancipated blacks' indolence were not confined to Pennsylvania; they were reiterated in other northern states contemplating emancipation in this period as well. The New York Abolition Society noted in 1790 that in advocating emancipation for African Americans they struggled against the presumption that "when liberated, and acting for themselves, they do not conduct so well as they did in a state of slavery, but in many instances contract vicious habits and lead disorderly lives."[16] Likewise, Connecticut's Levi Hart in his very early proposal for a general emancipation in 1774 conceded that "it is said that the Negros have not sufficient discretion to conduct their own affairs & provide for themselves, & that many of them are addicted to stealing, & other enormities now & would probably be much more so if they were not under the care & governance of masters who restrain them."[17] Further cementing African American neoteny in the nineteenth century was the increasingly common analogy made by southern slaveholders between slaves and children.[18] In short, concerns were widespread about the inability of emancipated African Americans to govern themselves with the necessary maturity and self-sufficiency demanded of an independent citizenry.

The language used to describe emancipated African Americans' incapacities was strikingly congruent with language used consistently to justify parents' and guardians' authority over minor children in the eighteenth and early nineteenth centuries. James Kent, for example, in his *Commentaries on American Law*, explained the principle of guardianship as deriving in large part from children's indiscretion: "The wants and weaknesses of children render it necessary that some person maintain them, and the voice of nature has pointed out the parent as the most fit and proper person."[19] In particular, he highlighted how "the necessity of guardians results from the inability of infants to take care of themselves; and this inability continues, in contemplation of law, until the infant has attained the age of twenty-one years."[20] That language echoed descriptions of African Americans' lack of "care" for themselves. Similar connections between minority and incapacity for self-governance were articulated in childrearing advice tracts. James Burgh, for example, in his very popular eighteenth century *Thoughts on Education*, had explained that "as persons arrived at years of discretion may be supposed (if they have had a proper education) in a great measure capable of conducting themselves; whereas the utter *incapacity* of Youth lays them almost wholly at the mercy of their Parents or Instructors for a set of habits to regulate their whole conduct through life."[21] These sentiments were elaborated in the next century by Baptist moral philosopher Francis Wayland, who worried about the dangers of disobedience by children to their parents, warning "what can be a surer indication of future profligacy and ruin, than that turbulent impatience of restraint, which leads a youth to follow the headlong impulses of passion, in preference to the counsel of age and experience."[22] Wayland's description of an absence of restraint in youth likewise bore uncanny resemblance to Levi Hart's acknowledgment about the absence of discretion among African Americans without masters to restrain their profligate behavior.

The consequence of these assumptions about the unfitness of blacks for freedom, and African Americans' retarded potential for mature self-responsibility was the adoption of a post-nati emancipation law by the Pennsylvania Assembly in 1780. Pennsylvania's law freed only children born after its passage, and left those already living in the state in slavery untouched, as long as they were registered with local officials within six months after the law's passage. And those African American children born to enslaved mothers after that point would be legally indentured to their mothers' masters in the capacity of involuntary apprentices until the age of twenty-eight, in some ways akin to involuntary pauper apprentices under existing poor laws. In the words of one editorializing advocate, "A negro child born of a slave in a man's family is to be considered as a white child abandoned by his parents and laid at his door.

Humanity will oblige him to preserve its life and give it all needful assistance but he is not bound to provide for it gratis; the child is bound to pay him by its labor as it grows up." This idea melded with the concern that "the public be in no danger to suffer much by their freedom." Thus, the law created a key difference for emancipated African American youth: an extended term of legal dependence in servitude beyond even what white pauper children owed their masters, as the greater demands of training them for personal responsibility "justly require that they serve their masters so much the longer time in consideration of the expenses and time spent in their schooling," which their own parents were assumed incapable of providing.[23] This model would subsequently be emulated by Connecticut, New York, and New Jersey as they enacted their own post-nati emancipation statues in 1784, 1790, and 1804, respectively, each of which prescribed some extended period of dependence beyond the legal age of majority and the terminus of involuntary apprenticeship for free white youth.[24]

An extended period of legal dependence in servitude for free blacks was not in itself new; it had been written into much older laws regulating the status of the children of free persons of African descent. In Pennsylvania in 1726, the General Assembly responded to anxiety about the growing presence of African Americans, both enslaved and free, in the colony by enacting a law "for the better regulating of Negroes," acknowledging that "'tis found by Experience, that free Negroes are an Idle, sloathful People; and often prove burthensome to the Neighborhood." The law thus decreed that "if any Negroe be set Free, under the Age of Twenty One Years, or where there shall be any Children of free Negroes, it shall and may be Lawful for the Overseers of the Poor to bind out to Service such Negro or Negroes, a Man child until he comes to the Age of Twenty four Years, and a Woman Child to the Age of Twenty One," three years beyond the equivalent term for a white pauper apprentice.[25] In that same law, following much older precedents set in southern colonies, children born to free mixed-race couples were required to be bound as servants for an even longer term of thirty-one years. In short, the legal ascription of psychological neoteny to free African Americans was based on a set of long-standing presumptions about blacks' delayed capacity for responsible behavior, and drew on older legal precedents. And via that older precedent, the remedy for concerns about African

American lack of self-control was an extended period of servitude during which white masters could rely on African Americans' labor, making their "dependence" on whites both self-serving and a self-fulfilling prophecy.

At the same time however, as a prohibition on future growth in the state's enslaved population, the 1780 abolition law required that any person arriving in the state with enslaved property register those African Americans within six months, entitling the slaveholder to legally bind them as servants for seven years if adults or to twenty-eight if they were minors. As a deterrent to ignoring the registration law, the act declared that "no Negro or Mulatto, now within this state, shall from and after the said first day of November, be deemed a slave or servant for life," unless he or she were registered.[26]

As the Pero girls' case suggests, however, widespread presumptions about an extended period of legal dependence for African American youth left even the unregistered (and thus legally free) young people in a very vulnerable position, ripe for exploitation by masters who attempted to manipulate the law in order to retain legal title to their youthful labor sources as long as possible. Bob's case in 1794 was typical. A decade before, the Abolition Society had identified the then eleven-year-old as having not been registered as a slave in accordance with the abolition law, and while the suit was pending Bob's master William Tharpe circumvented the law and brought Bob before Justice of the Peace William Rush, who unknowingly indentured him to Tharpe until twenty-eight.[27] Now twenty-one, Bob, apparently cognizant of his rights, left Tharpe's service, after which Tharpe had him arrested and jailed. Only at this point did Bob's predicament come to the attention of the PAS, whose members regularly visited the Philadelphia jail looking for African Americans unjustly deprived of their freedom.[28] Bob, they successfully argued, "having now reached to upwards of his 21st years of age we conceive ought to be Free—because he was not registered agreeable to the Act of 1780 ought to be considered as a white minor." Their advocacy is indicative of how, in the twenty years after the abolition law was passed, they would use the logic of chronological age to ensure that the law be followed to the letter in African Americans' favor. In short, given the emphasis in the 1780 law on date of birth and chronological age in defining access to freedom, the PAS and African Americans themselves

would do the same to make their claims, placing emphasis on chronological age in their advocacy on free blacks' behalf.

In advocating on behalf of emancipated African Americans like Bob,
after 1789 the PAS could turn to legal precedent that they had successfully helped to set in the Pennsylvania Supreme Court via *Respublica
v. Negro Betsey*.[29] That case was prompted by the questionable status
of twenty-year-old Betsey, born years prior to the Abolition Act's effective date, but whose master Samuel Moore had not registered her in
accordance with the law, thereby entitling her to freedom. Moore's attorney claimed that despite his failure to register her, he remained entitled
to her service until twenty-eight. Arguing on behalf of the notion that
Moore was entitled to that extended service, his attorney argued that
"the Legislature could not intend a greater favor to negroes and mulattos
born as slaves before the passage of that act, than to those born after."
Chief Justice McKean agreed with this logic, observing that the wording
of the law declaring nonregistered slaves "freemen and free-women" did
not however mean "that they shall be absolutely free from every species
of servitude."

In part, McKean's argument in support of that claim relied explicitly
on a presumption of continued dependence by emancipated African
Americans. Citing the portion of the law that demanded that masters
who did not register their human property would be answerable for
their maintenance should they become paupers, he argued that this gave
an "interest remaining to the owner." He concluded, "The negro Betsey
is in no worse situation, than if she had been born after the passing the
act, and I do not know a reason why she should be in a better. Were
she discharged from her master, she would be incapable to take care of
herself, and her parents are unable to educate her: She cannot suffer so
much by living with a good master, as being with poor and ignorant parents." Similar logic would apply to a white minor pauper; the significant
difference here is the presumption that Betsey remained "incapable to
take care of herself" at the age of twenty. By contrast, a white girl would
have been discharged from bound servitude at eighteen.

McKean's logic did not prevail; the other three justices sided with
Betsey, arguing that by neglecting to secure his right to her services by
registering her as his slave, her master should forfeit that right. Justice
Rush in his opinion directly responded to McKean's claim of continued

"interest" remaining with the master, arguing that the intent was to ensure that the master who retained legal title to slaves "shall always be liable for any necessary expenses the public may be put to, through his neglect to provide for him," unless he manumitted before twenty-eight years. But even Rush's logic on this point relied on an anxiety about African Americans' ability to care for themselves in adulthood. In his estimation, "Twenty-eight years was esteemed a proper age, in case of emancipation, under which, it might be reasonable supposed, that a Negro, by a course of industry for a number of years, might add to the public stock of wealth, as to be entitled to receive support from the public, if he should be unable to help himself." Once again, even in an opinion favoring a claim to liberty, Rush acknowledged the assumption that emancipated African Americans would take longer than white adults to earn entitlement to public support.

Legal precedent aside, just as in Bob's case, unscrupulous masters persisted in their efforts to circumvent the law by presenting unregistered African Americans before municipal officials even after 1789 in order to obtain indentures granting them access to African Americans' labor to twenty-eight. The implications of this extended period of legal dependence upon a master who stood to gain economically from a continuous denial of freedom was perilously serious; in the majority of the cases identified by the PAS in which a master attempted to circumvent the registration law, the young people's ultimate claim to freedom was immediately threatened by the master's plan to move them across state lines where their claims to freedom could not be readily policed. Thus illegal indenture to twenty-eight appears to have been a common strategy masters used to gain a title for the purposes of human trafficking.[30]

When Joseph Purcell attempted to take his former slave back to Trinidad in 1788, he readily adopted this strategy; his efforts highlight the methods masters could use to facilitate trafficking. Three years before, Purcell had come from the Caribbean to Pennsylvania, settling in Darby Township. He brought then ten-year-old Margaret with him, neglecting to comply with the law requiring that she be indentured to twenty-eight; as a consequence, by virtue of the law, Margaret became entitled to freedom after six months' residency in Pennsylvania.[31] Upon hearing of Purcell's likely return to Trinidad with the girl in tow, the committee acted to secure a writ of habeas corpus, and approached Purcell to get him to agree to an indenture for her labor to only her eighteenth year of age. Purcell, however, refused and "declared the girl was his slave and as such he intended to take her to the West Indies." The committee successfully petitioned the court in Philadelphia, which declared Margaret free. Purcell, still committed to retaining what he believed to be his property, then took Margaret before the unsuspecting Overseers of the Poor in Ridley, Pennsylvania, and obtained an indenture binding her to him to twenty-eight after unsuccessfully attempting the same ploy in adjacent Darby itself.[32] In doing so, Purcell was able to rely on both weak communication between municipal authorities in neighboring communities as well as the widespread presumption that an African American girl must be enslaved and liable for an extended indenture to twenty-eight.

Responding to Purcell's efforts to circumvent the law by obtaining an extended indenture after the fact, the Abolition Society's attorneys, Miers Fisher and John Coxe, secured a writ for Purcell to appear in court, ready to argue that "Margaret had been made free by the operation of the abolition act [and] is clearly entitled to the law and usage of white minor children consequently and cannot be held by indenture beyond the age of eighteen years, nor bound by any but legal representatives such as parents or next of kin."[33] After posting bond to appear, however, Purcell continued his plans for departure, "secreting" the girl. The Abolition Society lawyers approached Purcell, threatening to have him arrested; he promised to return her to Philadelphia after she reached twenty-eight. But the PAS was utterly unconvinced that this toothless promise would sufficiently protect Margaret, concluding "that she being taken to the Island of Trinidad where slavery much abounds her future liberty will be thereby endangered." Consequently, their intended strategy for arguing the case to protect her from trafficking relied on the question of the chronological age for the end of indentures, as they resolved that Margaret "is entitled to all the privileges of a free white minor child & ought only to be bound till she attains to the age of eighteen years."[34] Only if Purcell agreed to the shortened indenture and gave security that Margaret would not be removed from Philadelphia would the PAS agree to drop the proceedings against him. Purcell refused, and the case was remanded to the court docket.[35]

Like that of Margaret, many of these cases involved masters relocating across state lines with their indentured servants in tow. Yet these were not necessarily innocent instances of masters flouting the law to retain their own labor supply; the vast majority of the instances of trafficking outside of Pennsylvania investigated by the PAS involved overt cases of whites transferring indentured servants to new masters to sate labor demand, compromising their servants' legal rights in the process.[36] It appears that by 1800 some masters had found that even the sale of an additional few years could offer an opportunity for profiting from emancipated laborers in the short term. Kandene's situation illustrates the lengths to which masters might go. Kandene was born in slavery in Delaware. Years before, her master had sent her to live with his son-in-law John King in Penn's Valley, Pennsylvania, where she lived for more than a year, thus earning her freedom. At that point, King had her legally bound as his servant until she reached eighteen before two overseers of the poor and two justices of the peace. At some point in 1800, seeing an opportunity to profit from Kandene and take advantage of poor record-keeping by the local overseers of the poor, King "had her indentures destroyed and had her bound [again] to her 28th year of age before the Overseers of the Poor." King then returned with her to Delaware and sold her indenture, now no doubt worth considerably more, attempting to rob Kandene of the opportunity to profit from her own most productive years.[37]

Whites' assumptions about the appropriateness of African Americans' extended dependence were not limited to those born in slavery who had earned their freedom from their masters' failures to comply with the registration law or by virtue of a move to Pennsylvania. Those assumptions about extended dependence were also reflected in the treatment of African American children born to free parents to whom the 1780 law and its extended term of indenture simply did not apply. In more than 35 percent of the cases in which the PAS intervened prior to 1820 that involved questions about the appropriate chronological termination of an indenture, African American children born to free parents were erroneously indentured by municipal authorities beyond the legal age prescribed for white children.[38]

Many of these cases involved mixed-race children or their offspring who previously would have been subject to the 1727 law demanding that mulatto children be indentured to thirty-one as the price of their "base birth."[39] For example, in 1790 twenty-four-year-old Poll applied to

Ephraim Steele, justice of the peace in Carlisle, claiming that she was the daughter of a free white woman and was entitled to her freedom. Poll had been registered as a slave by her mother's master, James Caruthers of West Pennsbury, who claimed that the 1727 law warranted him holding her to thirty-one.[40] On Poll's behalf, the PAS argued that that provision was now superseded, as the "law does not warrant holding mulatto illegitimate children longer than white children." Ultimately, their case was persuasive; Caruthers acknowledged Poll's freedom. In order to protect her liberty, Caruthers was required to give her a certificate declaring that he would "forever discharge the said Polly from [his] service and request that she may be permitted to pass and repass where she may think proper to make a livelihood."[41] Strikingly, Caruthers needed to qualify her liberty in that document by declaring that "she behaving herself as becomes the subjects of this state." Even given her formal legal right to freedom, Poll needed Caruthers's reference to demonstrate that she behaved with sufficient self-control to warrant the privileges associated with full independence.

These situations involving free-born African Americans were not, however, on the whole the product of confusion about the relationship between the older "base birth" law and the 1780 emancipation act. The majority of the cases identified by the PAS in which children born to free mothers were indentured to twenty-eight instead reflected more generalized assumptions about black children's status and the complexities of policing their fragile claims to freedom. For example, in September 1789, the Abolition Society advocated on behalf of seven-year-old Jack and two-year-old Jenney, both of whom had been bound by their mother's master to twenty-eight. Their mother Nancy was not a slave, however; she had been manumitted in 1782, before either of the children was born.[42] By virtue of her legal freedom, both were unequivocally free from the moment of birth.

Not a month later, the PAS advocated in a similar case on behalf of Grace's son Caleb, a case that highlights the difficulties free black parents could face in protecting their own children's legal claims to freedom. Grace had been manumitted years before by her master in Philadelphia on the condition that she serve her former master until she reached thirty; over the subsequent years, Grace had been transferred among three masters living in three different towns, the last of whom, Daniel

Levan, Esq. of Berks County, had sold her to a resident of Adamstown, misrepresenting her in the bill of sale as a registered slave named Pegg and her son Caleb as a servant to twenty-eight. Caleb was subsequently transferred two more times before his mother approached the PAS on his behalf, seeking to reunite with him. Amid all of these transfers, Grace seems to have done her best to keep track of her son. Here, it is important to keep in mind the odds African American parents like Grace faced in trying to speak on behalf of their free-born children's rights. Like Grace, most free African American parents in Pennsylvania lacked any legal claim over their own children given their own status as servants or the impoverishment that had forced them to relinquish their children to white masters as pauper apprentices. Instead, that legal authority belonged to the child's master, who likely had other competing economic interests. And, in circumstances in which the parent remained a bondservant in the child's master's household, the ability to voice concerns about the child's lost claim to freedom via removal outside of Pennsylvania would be nearly impossible.

A striking common denominator across all of these cases involving masters' efforts to circumvent the law was the dangerous combination of weak premodern communication between the municipal officers who were charged with enforcing the emancipation law over time and space and their presumption that African Americans were not free and thus eligible to be bound to twenty-eight. Seventeen-year-old Harry's case illustrates how that dynamic threatened African Americans' nascent freedom in the era of the first emancipation. Harry's mother Susan had been manumitted by her Maryland master back in 1770 on the condition that she serve Maryland planter Isaac Gibbs for fourteen years; in the interim, she gave birth to Harry, who was, therefore, born free in the eyes of the law. When Isaac Gibbs died, his heir Benjamin Gibbs brought Harry, then about eleven, to Philadelphia. There he presented Harry to the managers of the Philadelphia House of Employment, the local workhouse, who, presuming that Harry must have been enslaved property, bound him to Gibbs for seventeen years in accordance with the law.[43] And no doubt Harry would have served Gibbs for that extended term, no questions asked, had Gibbs not decided six years later to return Harry to his plantation in Maryland. When Harry refused, Gibbs resorted to force, duplicitously sending Harry on an errand to deliver a message to a ship waiting in Philadelphia harbor. Once on board, Harry was "seized and fastened in the hold," and taken to Delaware. Harry was both tremendously resourceful and quite lucky; the teenager escaped and returned to Philadelphia, where he "maintained himself." Gibbs, however, was not willing to surrender his presumed entitlement to Harry's labor; he obtained from the city mayor an arrest warrant for Harry as a runaway servant.

Only Harry's presence in the city jail alerted agents of the PAS to his predicament, and led them to spring into action on his behalf. After investigating the case, they successfully argued that "because the boy was born of a Free woman and not bound by her to any person—and because he was not any expense to the Overseers of the Poor we conceive they had no right to place him with any person—and the binding him to the age of 28 years appears an additional Act of Oppression."[44] Here at once they advocated on behalf of her legal rights as a parent and invoked the extended term of servitude as an act of "oppression." Strikingly, however, despite their recognition that Harry had in fact been self-supporting, the PAS agents still could not conceive of Harry's ability to appropriately fend for himself; instead, they facilitated his hired service with Andrew Summers until he would reach twenty-one, finding it necessary to comment in their minutes that "he appears to behave himself well."[45]

By way of conclusion, it is essential to highlight a fundamental point about the evidence collected by the PAS documenting their intervention on behalf of emancipated African Americans who were indentured beyond the legal age of indenture for whites. This evidence represents only the handful of fortunate cases in which a threat to a young adult's legal entitlement to freedom was detected, through arduous private effort by the organization and ultimately a series of fateful circumstances that brought a situation to the PAS's attention. In well over a third of the cases in which the PAS intervened on behalf of a young person for whom the appropriate age of independence was questioned, agents identified the situation merely as a by-product of some other more obviously detectable issue that brought the case under scrutiny, whether it was the potential for trafficking beyond state lines or a report of cruelty or physical abuse by a master or the fact that the twentysomething-year-old African American was jailed as a runaway.[46] Outside of those circumstances, the next most likely mechanism for the PAS to identify these situations was for the illegally indentured African American himself or herself to appeal directly to an agent of the PAS for help.[47] In many ways, what is most significant about these stories, therefore, is what they suggest about circumstances in which trafficked African Americans were not able to find their way into the PAS records. The rare twentysomethings with enough knowledge about the law and their own biographies and the window of opportunity to abscond from their masters had significant advantages over minors, who depended upon their family or neighbors policing their vulnerable claims to freedom. And, to make a key point, African Americans lucky enough to know their own age likewise had an essential advantage, given the importance of date of birth for claiming freedom; chronological age was now vitally important for free African Americans. In short, the PAS did challenge the presumption that free-born African Americans were not capable of or entitled to legal independence equivalent to the "privileges of a free white minor child" after the same chronological terminus for indenture, making a powerful legal claim to equal treatment that was an essential piece of their efforts to dismantle slavery as an institution. But in their efforts they swam against a tide of attitudes presuming that African Americans were less mature and, as the price of their governance, whites were entitled to their labor for an extended period.

NOTES
1 Minutes of the Acting Committee, book I (1784–88), July 15, 1784, Papers of the Pennsylvania Abolition Society, Pennsylvania Historical Society (hereafter MAC).
2 Ibid., November 29, 1784.
3 Gary B. Nash and Jean R. Soderlund, *Freedom by Degrees: Emancipation in Pennsylvania and Its Aftermath* (New York: Oxford University Press, 1991); Graham Russell Hodges, *Slavery and Freedom in the Rural North: African Americans in Monmouth County, New Jersey 1665–1865* (Madison, Wis.: Madison House, 1997); Hodges, *Root and Branch: African Americans in New York and East Jersey 1613–1863* (Chapel Hill: University of North Carolina Press, 1999); Joanne Pope Melish, *Disowning Slavery: Gradual Emancipation and "Race" in New England, 1780–1860* (Ithaca, N.Y.: Cornell University Press, 1998); John Wood Sweet, *Bodies Politic: Negotiating Race in the American North, 1730–1830* (Philadelphia: University of Pennsylvania Press, 2003).
4 Artur Zilversmit, *The First Emancipation: The Abolition of Slavery in the North* (Chicago: University of Chicago Press, 1967), 181–82, 187–88, 192–93.

5 Robert Fogel and Stanley Engerman, "Philanthropy at Bargain Prices: Notes on the Economics of Gradual Emancipation," *Journal of Legal Studies* 3 (1974): 377–401.

6 Nash and Soderlund, *Freedom by Degrees*, 119–23.

7 Hugh Cunningham, *The Children of the Poor* (Oxford: Blackwell, 1991), 24; Holly Brewer, *By Birth or Consent: Children, Law, and the Anglo-American Revolution in Authority* (Chapel Hill: University of North Carolina Press, 2005), 243–44.

8 39 Eliz. I, c. 3 (1598). On the evolution of twenty-one as the standard termination for custodial relationships, see Brewer, *By Birth or Consent*, 240–63.

9 Brewer, *By Birth or Consent*, 314–37. Eighteen was first articulated as the age of marriage without parental consent in Pennsylvania in 1676; in 1730 that law was revised to demand parental consent for both males and females until twenty-one.

10 Zilversmit, *First Emancipation*, 109–37.

11 [Richard Wells], *Pennsylvania Packet*, January 8, 1774, cited in Zilversmit, *First Emancipation*, 97. See also Nash and Soderlund, *Freedom by Degrees*, 78–80.

12 *Pennsylvania Packet*, November 28, 1778, cited in Nash and Soderlund, *Freedom by Degrees*, 100–101.

13 Ibid.

14 *Pennsylvania Packet*, January 1, 1780.

15 Ibid.

16 *Daily Advertiser*, January 22, 1790.

17 Levi Hart, "Some Thoughts on the Subject of Freeing the Negro Slaves in the Colony of Connecticut, Humbly Offered to the Consideration of All friends to Liberty & Justice," ed. Samuel Hopkins and John Saillant, *New England Quarterly* 75 (March 2002): 120.

18 On presumptions of the inevitability of dependency for people of color and the role of these assumptions in the construction of emancipation laws in New England, see Melish, *Disowning Slavery*, 63–76. On the analogy between slaves and children that likewise emerged in this era in the South, see Brewer, *By Birth or Consent*, 355–59.

19 Chancellor James Kent, *Commentaries on American Law*, vol. 2 (New York: Halsted, 1728), 159.

20 Ibid., 191.

21 James Burgh, *Thoughts on Education* (London, 1749), 7.

22 Francis Wayland, *The Elements of Moral Science* (New York: Cooke and Co., 1835), 364.

23 *Pennsylvania Packet*, March 13, 1779.

24 In Connecticut, a 1780 bill to emancipate African Americans older than seven with a service requirement to twenty-eight was rejected; in 1785 the legislature passed a post-nati abolition statute requiring service until age twenty-five. New York's 1799 abolition act likewise provided that females born after the law's passage would serve their mother's master to twenty-five, males to twenty-eight. Finally, New Jersey's 1804 abolition law freed children born after the law's passage

after twenty-five years of service. Zilversmit, *First Emancipation*, 181–82, 187–88, 192–93.

25 *Acts Passed in the General Assembly of the Province of Pennsylvania* (Philadelphia: Andrew Bradford, 1726), 25.

26 Nash and Soderlund, *Freedom by Degrees*, 102.

27 MAC book I, July 8, 1784; book II, April 9, 1794. For a very similar case, see Dinah's case, MAC book II, March 4, 1795.

28 Of the forty-five cases in which the Pennsylvania Abolition Society's Acting Committee intervened between 1784 and 1800 that involved a question concerning the legality of an indenture beyond the legal age of majority for white youth, twelve involved cases of masters circumventing the law requiring registration within six months.

29 *Respublica v. Negro Betsey*, 1 U.S. 469 (1789).

30 Of fourteen cases identified by the PAS between 1784 and 1819 involving a master deliberately attempting to circumvent the registration law by indenturing young people to twenty-eight, in eight the master did so as part of an effort to remove them beyond Pennsylvania's borders.

31 MAC book I, October 8, 1788.

32 Ibid., November 12, 1788.

33 Ibid., October 22, 1788.

34 Ibid., November 29, 1788.

35 For similar cases, see ibid., July 1, 1784 (Adam had not been properly registered by C. Roquet and was about to be illegally removed to Virginia; Roquet manumitted him and bound him before Managers of the House of Employment to twenty-eight); October 22, 1788 (Joseph was about to be trafficked to the West Indies by his master William McFaden; he was found not registered and McFaden had him illegally bound to twenty-eight); book II, May 3, 1797 (Tom, slave to John Morgan, was not registered within six months; Morgan bound him to twenty-eight after the fact and sent him to New Jersey, still a slave state).

36 Of 279 cases of freed persons trafficked beyond Pennsylvania's lines identified by the PAS between 1784 and 1819, only ninety-four of the cases, or one-third, involved masters themselves relocating with their African American servants.

37 MAC book III, August 27, 1800.

38 Of the sixty-seven cases identified by the PAS involving inappropriately long indentures, twenty-four involved children born to free parents.

39 Of the twenty-four cases involving a child born to free parents, eleven were mixed-race children indentured to thirty-one according to the 1727 law.

40 MAC book II, October 6, 1790.

41 Ibid., December 15, 1790.

42 Ibid., September 2, 1789.

43 Ibid., July 17, 1793.

44 Ibid., May 26, 1794.

45 Ibid., May 7, 1794.

46 Of sixty-seven cases in which the PAS intervened regarding the appropriate terminus of service between 1784 and 1819, twenty-four had already been identified for other reasons, either because the African American in question was held in jail as a runaway, or a case was already under investigation for trafficking across state lines, or the person was a victim of physical abuse or cruelty.

47 An additional seventeen cases were initiated by African Americans approaching the PAS directly on their own behalf, 25 percent of the total cases in which the length of service was in question.

PART II

Age in the Long Nineteenth Century

3

"If You Have the Right to Vote at 21 Years, Then I Have"

Age and Equal Citizenship in the Nineteenth-Century United States

CORINNE T. FIELD

On the evening of June 27, 1867, delegates to the New York State constitutional convention gathered in the state assembly chamber with a large crowd of onlookers to hear women's rights activists Elizabeth Cady Stanton and Susan B. Anthony present their case for "universal suffrage," meaning the enfranchisement of black men and all women on the same terms as white men.[1] Horace Greeley, editor of the *New York Tribune*, liberal Republican, and chair of the convention's suffrage committee, presided as Stanton and Anthony offered several compelling arguments, most importantly that voting was an "inalienable right." Greeley challenged this natural rights argument by shifting attention from black men and women to the case of minors and immigrants denied the vote for fixed periods of time. "When does this inalienable right commence for young men and foreigners?" Greeley demanded. "Have we the right to say when it commences?" Anthony responded that the state certainly had a right to set age and residency requirements but that those should apply equally to all human beings. "If you have the right to vote at 21 years, then I have," Anthony contended. "All we ask is that you should let down the bars, and let us women and negroes in, and then we will sit down and talk the matter over."[2]

Thus a debate about the rights of black men and all women shifted to a debate about minors. Greeley mentioned the state's right to set age qualifications because he knew that he could count on Anthony to concede that even if age twenty-one was an arbitrary distinction between citizens, some age qualification was necessary or else New Yorkers would have to welcome young children at the polls, a contingency that even the most radical champions of "universal" suffrage did not support. Once Anthony conceded that New York had "the right to say" that a young white man must be twenty-one or older before he could vote, she had in effect disarmed all of her own arguments for she had acknowledged that voting was not a natural right but a privilege that states could regulate at will. Furthermore, she had conceded that paying taxes, serving in the military, and displaying clear political competence did not entitle a citizen to vote, since young men indisputably did all these things before they turned twenty-one.

Anthony's proposal that New York's revised constitution should apply age qualifications equally to all citizens fell flat as Greeley successfully used the disenfranchisement of young men to prove that American citizens did not have an inalienable right to vote but rather that delegates to the state constitutional convention had the right to limit suffrage as they saw fit. Over the next months, much to Greeley's frustration, Democrats beat him at his own game by arguing that if the state could prevent women and minors from voting then there was no reason to enfranchise adult black men either.[3]

This political strategy of defining chronological age as an arbitrary but necessary barrier to full citizenship, and then using age to justify other exclusions, was repeated by delegates to state constitutional conventions throughout the North from the Revolution through Reconstruction. Because no state allowed minors under twenty-one to vote at any point during this period, the age qualification for suffrage provided a clear and universal standard for full citizenship amid a welter of other variable requirements. Women, nonwhites, recent immigrants, and the poor all voted in at least one state after the Revolution, but minors nowhere. In contrast to vibrant movements for black manhood and woman suffrage, there were no sustained calls for the enfranchisement of minors. Rather, as I have argued elsewhere, the disenfranchised often couched claims to the ballot in terms of their right to be recognized as equal adults at age twenty-one.[4]

What turned age qualifications into such a powerful tool for politicians intent on limiting the franchise, however, was not simply that Americans agreed on the disenfranchisement of minors, but that they recognized age twenty-one as the most artificial of barriers, a distinction rooted in human rather than natural law, an abstract number that failed to measure the variable pace of human maturation. This was in sharp contrast to how both mainstream politicians and reformers talked about gender and race as differences rooted in natural or divine law. To be sure, some politicians who supported black manhood suffrage acknowledged the difficulties in determining who was "white," and a few worried about women who might pass as male, but most Americans, including even the boldest champions of human equality, tended to fall back on the assumption that at least some racial and sexual differences were inborn rather than arbitrary—an understandable conclusion at a time when being classified as white or not, male or not, profoundly shaped life chances. With even reformers believing in inherent racial and sexual differences, chronological age stood out as a particularly artificial distinction.[5]

In antebellum America, chronological age had force in law, but little relevance in daily life. Classrooms, workplaces, and leisure activities brought together people of various ages. Youth left school, began work, and married at different ages. Even within the realm of the law, statutes and judicial decisions set different age requirements for various purposes and, to further complicate matters, revised these ages over time. Finally, and perhaps most significant, many Americans did not know or could not prove exactly how old they were. As a result, when state lawmakers set age qualifications for particular rights and duties, they sometimes specified who would have the authority to determine a person's age in a dispute. Though counting birthdays might seem an obvious way to measure human growth, many Americans did not retain knowledge of their exact date of birth. Determining if a young man was old enough to vote often required a complex negotiation between an eager young voter and election officials, with the latter having the final say. Requiring voters to be twenty-one thus appeared to be a particularly arbitrary means of demarcating citizens in a democracy.[6]

Rather than denying the arbitrariness of chronological age, lawmakers from the 1770s through the 1870s emphasized the artificiality of imposing age-based distinctions while also adding the important caveat that age boundaries nonetheless had to be drawn in order to ensure the proper functioning of democratic government. Lawmakers stressed that a vast gulf separated infants from adults, harped on the idea that young children could not provide meaningful consent or care for themselves, and raised the prospect of babies at the polls as the reductio ad absurdum that proved not every citizen could be a voter. For all these reasons, setting some age qualification for suffrage seemed absolutely necessary.[7]

By defining age qualifications as arbitrary but necessary, lawmakers set age apart from other distinctions based on gender, race, ability, and nationality, which, while often defended as necessary, were not presented as completely arbitrary. To put this another way, legislators and judges did not see chronological age as analogous to other categories. Indeed, lawmakers often used age qualifications to separate minors from adults within distinct populations already defined by what they understood to be immutable differences based on race and sex. In some cases, state governments applied age qualifications exclusively to white males, for example requiring them to serve in militias at eighteen and enabling them to vote at twenty-one. In other cases, states set different age requirements, for example fixing the end of pauper apprenticeships at twenty-one for white males, earlier for white girls, and later for black youth. The result was that chronological age, a seemingly neutral measure, rarely applied to all citizens equally.[8]

When black civil rights activists and women's rights activists argued that this was profoundly unjust and urged state governments to apply age qualifications equally to all citizens, lawmakers turned to what they insisted was the arbitrary nature of chronological age itself to prove that states could set other boundaries as well, even if those might be equally arbitrary. Once politicians had established that states had the right to keep minors out of polling places, they could then use this to prove that states had no moral or constitutional obligation to, in Anthony's words, let "women and negroes in." Chronological age thus became central to debates over citizenship, not because Americans thought age accurately measured individual capacity, but because they recognized that it did not. Chronological age functioned at once as a tool to convey rights and responsibilities and as the final proof that those same privileges were not to be found in nature.

***

The centrality of chronological age to debates over citizenship can be seen clearly be focusing on two of the largest states in the Northeast, Massachusetts and New York, both of which held multiple constitutional conventions during the nineteenth century. The proceedings of these state constitutional conventions provide a rich and largely untapped source for exploring the political significance of chronological age. Whereas social and cultural historians have persuasively argued that birthdays had little relevance for school, work, romance, and leisure during this period, legal scholars have pointed out how legislators and judges relied upon chronological age to define legal standing. An analysis of political rhetoric reveals that lawmakers were quite aware that the main significance of chronological age was as an artificial tool by which states defined the rights and obligations of citizens.

In Massachusetts, the significance of chronological age as an arbitrary but necessary qualification for political rights emerged during the earliest phases of the Revolution. For example, in May 1776, Massachusetts patriots John Adams and James Sullivan debated whether or not the state's first constitution should enfranchise men without property.[9] In what historians have called the "Pandora's Box" argument, Adams warned Sullivan not "to alter the Qualifications of Voters. There will be no End of it. New Claims will arise. Women will demand a Vote. Lads from 12 to 21 will think their Rights not enough attended to, and every Man, who has not a Farthing, will demand an equal Voice."[10] Of all these limits, however, Adams understood age twenty-one to be the most artificial— and for that very reason, the most significant—criterion by which republican governments could deny political rights to worthy citizens. As Adams wrote Sullivan, "What Reason Should there be, for excluding a Man of Twenty years, Eleven Months and twenty-seven days old, from a Vote when you admit one, who is twenty one? The Reason is, you must fix upon Some Period in Life, when the Understanding and will of Men in general is fit to be trusted by the Public. Will not the Same Reason justify the State in fixing Some certain Quantity of Property[?]"[11] Adams did not find the same proof of state power in the disenfranchisement of women and young children, for he believed such people were naturally incapable of representing themselves. "Nature has made [women] fittest for domestic Cares," Adams wrote, and children "have not Judgment or Will of their own."[12] By defining age twenty-one, in contrast, as a distinction drawn by men rather than nature, and simultaneously insisting that establishing such a distinction was imperative, Adams justified setting a property requirement as well. His logic was persuasive. Though it would take voters in Massachusetts another four years to ratify a constitution, they eventually agreed to retain property and age requirements for suffrage, as did most states during this period.[13]

Adams's conviction that age twenty-one was both arbitrary and necessary was rooted in his experience of colonial age qualifications defining the rights and obligations of citizens. In English common law, twenty-one had long been recognized as the age of legal majority, the moment when an individual was freed from guardianship and granted the legal standing of an adult in all matters regarding person and property. Until that point, minors owed obedience to parents, guardians, or, if bound to service, masters. In terms of the obligations of citizenship, however, the Massachusetts Bay Colony made substantial claims on white males beginning at age sixteen, but carefully filtered these claims through teenage boys' legal dependence on adult heads of household. In 1646, Massachusetts set a pattern followed by other New England colonies when the General Court levied a poll tax on every male inhabitant, "servant or othr, of ye age of 16 yeares and upward," with exemptions only for those "uncapable of such rates" because of "sickness, lamenes, or other infirmity." The court specified that for servants and children "that take no wages, their mastrs or parents shall pay" the tax for them.[14] Militia service functioned in much the same way. All able-bodied males from sixteen to fifty years old, with some exceptions, were required to serve in local training bands, but whereas adult, propertied men had to provide their own equipment, the law specified that "parents, masters, and guardians shall furnish and equip those of the militia which are under their care and command."[15]

By filtering these age-based obligations through heads of household, Massachusetts legislators created an intermediary stage of citizenship in which young men were classed neither with young children nor with propertied, adult men. The same young men who relied on fathers or masters to pay their poll taxes and equip them for militia duty also relied on heads of household to represent them in town government. Selectmen in Massachusetts were notorious for allowing all householders a vote in local elections, even if they didn't meet the state-mandated property requirements, but these same selectmen almost always barred minors under twenty-one and adult sons living with fathers.[16] The result was that most young men continued to obey and be represented by fathers or masters until well into their midtwenties or even later when they were finally able to set up households of their own.[17]

The age-based obligation to pay a tax and muster for militia duty accorded well with broader cultural expectations that young men in their late teens and early twenties would begin to perform adult tasks while still obeying fathers or masters. The difference was that whereas cultural practices were not sharply defined by age or sexual difference—boys left home at widely varying ages, many girls left home as well—the obligation to pay a tax and muster for militia duty at age sixteen defined a precise moment when boys owed new obligations to the state not expected of their sisters.[18] At times, the General Court included black males in these age-based obligations, and at other times excluded them.[19] The result was that chronological age functioned to map out a path to full citizenship for white males, from which women were always and black men often blocked.

Revolutionary leaders retained existing age-based qualifications for poll taxes and militia duty when Massachusetts became a state. What changed was their significance. Because Americans redefined themselves as citizens consenting to government, rather than subjects born dependent on the king, the difference between childhood subjection and manhood freedom took on new weight as a matter of practical importance.[20] Militia duty in particular began to function as a path toward full citizenship from which young women were barred.

Revolutionary leaders faced scattered proposals to extend political rights to minors who served in state militias or the Continental Army. Yet Pennsylvania was the only state to grant teenage soldiers the right to vote in general elections, and only briefly in the spring of 1776 before reverting back to a minimum age of twenty-one in the state constitution drafted later that year. In Pennsylvania, as throughout the nation, constitutional delegates argued that young men made good soldiers but poor voters, precisely because they were accustomed to following orders rather than thinking for themselves. That colonial governments had always required military service of minors helped justify the belief that fighting for American liberty did not qualify an individual to govern himself. Amid a wide variety of other requirements for suffrage in the different states, age twenty-one stood out as the qualification upon which all could agree.[21]

This reliance on twenty-one is particularly striking given that the Revolutionary crisis raised pressing questions about how any individual's age could be known. With regard to militia service in particular, wartime commanders generally requested that soldiers be over sixteen, which was also the age used by most states for their draft. Continental Army recruiters and militia captains, however, often enlisted younger boys if they appeared strong and capable. Masters and fathers complained that servants and sons ran away by pretending to be older than they were. The presence of younger boys in the armed forces required leaders in the new nation to clarify how exactly a person's age could be proven.[22] Perhaps recognizing that too many teenagers had snuck into uniform during the Revolutionary War, Massachusetts's militia law of 1792 quite explicitly stated, "in all cases of doubt respecting the age of any person enrolled, or intended to be enrolled, the party questioned shall prove his age to the satisfaction of the Commanding Officer of the company within whose bounds he may reside."[23] With no specific form of proof defined in law, a young man's age was, for the purpose of military service, whatever his commanding officer declared.

During the colonial period, local officials were empowered to determine the age of young men and were quite accustomed to doing so. The Massachusetts poll tax law specified that an assessor elected by the freemen of each town was responsible, along with the town selectmen, for counting the "just numbr of their males" liable for the poll tax.[24] In small towns where residents knew each other from birth, assessors and militia captains could rely on personal knowledge to balance the testimony of young men and their fathers or masters. This system for assessing age was imprecise and open to fraud, but no more so than the very similar system for assessing the monetary value of taxable estates. Indeed, Massachusetts assessors must have considered themselves quite adept at estimating ages not only of human beings but of livestock, for the court set the tax on cows, horses, sheep, pigs, and asses based on age. Even material objects, such as tools, were assessed on the basis of age and wear. That people often lacked official written proof of their age may have struck town leaders as no more problematic than that their cows or saws did as well.[25]

Nonetheless, colonial officials in Massachusetts led the way in trying to provide for a system by which citizens could document how old they were. In 1639, the General Court required that towns keep records of births, deaths, and marriages as an aid to adjudicating probate. Individuals could then pay a fee to receive a certificate of their birth. Recognizing that this system was woefully inadequate—more than half of all births went unreported—leaders of the newly formed state tried to increase registration after the Revolution.[26] Massachusetts would continue to serve as a laboratory for the recording of vital statistics, providing models for other states and eventually for the federal government, but in the early national period the majority of citizens lacked any government record of their ages.

More widespread than official registration was the practice of recording births and deaths in a family Bible. Even illiterate parents asked others to make such records for them. In legal cases where age was in dispute, these family Bibles were the most common form of documentary evidence presented in courts of law throughout the nineteenth century.[27] While legislators in Massachusetts would have liked the registration of births to become universal, they were quite comfortable leaving the matter in the hands of local officials. So long as voting, jury service, and officeholding, not to speak of estate taxes, remained linked to property, estimating the value of things had higher stakes than judging the age of people. That a few stout boys of fourteen might assume obligations too young or a few slender youths avoid them too long did not particularly trouble the Revolutionary generation so long as age qualifications functioned overall to separate boys from men and both from women.

***

During the first decades of the nineteenth century, state governments throughout the nation abolished property requirements for suffrage while leaving the age requirement in place. This reform turned voting at twenty-one into both a political right and a rite of passage, but only for white men. As New Jersey stripped women of the right to vote and other states barred or limited the participation of black men, white manhood suffrage became the norm. Black civil rights and women's rights activists responded by insisting that state governments should apply age qualifications equally to all Americans regardless of race or sex.[28]

In 1820, Massachusetts held a constitutional convention at which champions of white manhood suffrage successfully abolished John Adams's cherished property qualification, enfranchising virtually all men, white and black, at age twenty-one. Questions remained, however, about the disjunction between the requirement to muster for militia duty, set at age eighteen for all white males in accordance with federal standards, and the assumption that young men could not represent themselves until twenty-one. The 1780 constitution, written under the leadership of John Adams, limited participation in militia elections to those twenty-one years and older. Militia commanders at the 1820 convention pointed out that this provision was never enforced until Adams's old colleague James Sullivan held the governorship from 1807 to 1808. Joseph Valentine, lieutenant colonel from Hopkinton, claimed that Sullivan's "prohibition had created great uneasiness and confusion in the militia, and had greatly diminished its spirit." The chair of the committee on the militia, U.S. Senator Joseph Varnum, defended the Revolutionary era view that allowing minors to vote in any election was a "violation of general principles" and that twenty-one should be a universal standard for electors. The majority of delegates, however, agreed with Valentine that allowing militiamen to vote for their own officers would boost morale. They revised the constitution so as to allow militia captains to be elected "by the members of their respective companies, without regard to age." But, delegates emphasized that the militia was "a case by itself" and that they had not "opened the door" for minors to vote in other elections. Delegates wanted to encourage teenage boys to perform their military obligation, but held fast to the long-established principle that minors should not be given the same political rights as adult men.[29]

Massachusetts was unusual in allowing black men to vote on the same terms as white, a result of the influence of Federalists who enjoyed large support among black voters. At the New York State Constitutional Convention of 1821, Republicans engineered a particularly arbitrary compromise: they eliminated property requirements for white voters, but required black voters to meet a $250 freehold requirement.[30] Delegates justified this racial distinction by pointing to the age qualification. As New York Chief Justice Ambrose Spencer explained,

> We have in our constitution determined that no man under twenty-one years shall exercise the right of suffrage, upon the presumption that they do not possess mature understandings, and therefore have not a right

to enjoy this privilege. Has the correctness of this principle ever been doubted? He [Spencer] believed not, although many arrive at maturity of understanding, and are ornaments of society, before they reach that age. It is necessary in establishing laws, to have general rules. He therefore had no hesitation to say, that with regard to the blacks if we think the exercise of this privilege by them will contravene the public good; we have a right to say they shall not enjoy it.[31]

Despite sustained appeals from black civil rights activists, New York State entered Reconstruction with the property requirement for black voters firmly in place.

In 1867, when Greeley's suffrage committee proposed enfranchising black men on equal terms with whites, delegates could no longer claim universal approval for the disenfranchisement of minors or women. Two of their colleagues, Republican newspaper editor Marcus Bickford and Democratic Superior Court judge Anthony L. Robertson, sponsored constitutional amendments to enfranchise young men between the ages of eighteen and twenty-one. No delegate even bothered to argue against this proposal, which was easily defeated by a margin of three to one.[32] Delegates paid more attention to woman suffrage because Anthony, Stanton, and other members of the Equal Rights Association had built a powerful lobby,[33] but delegates eventually defeated the woman suffrage resolution by an even larger margin of more than five to one.[34]

The only reform with a solid chance of passing was black manhood suffrage. Republicans controlled the convention and argued that black men deserved the right to vote because of their military service. Democrats, however, successfully countered this argument by pointing out, in the words of Judge Homer Nelson, that on "the rolls of that army which fought so bravely [were] long lines of honorable names of young men between the ages of eighteen and twenty-one" who could not vote.[35] Claiming that "we all know young men between the ages of eighteen and twenty-one, numbers of them, who would cast as intelligent a vote as perhaps any of us could cast, and yet they are excluded," Nelson argued that the age qualification, like the other "various exclusions," was "an arbitrary line" but "it must go somewhere."[36] Even Republicans who supported universal suffrage used the disenfranchisement of minors to prove that voting was not a natural right, as when Stephen Hand thundered, "Who gives you the right to say that the age of twenty-one years is the precise period of a man's life when he shall attain the privilege of the elective franchise? The fact shows that the right belongs to society coming together here in this Constitutional Convention."[37] The convention decided, after months of debate, to do nothing to reform suffrage. It was the Fifteenth Amendment that brought interracial democracy to New York State.[38]

Far from resolving these debates, however, the language of the Reconstruction era amendments to the U.S. Constitution ensured that chronological age would continue to figure as an arbitrary but necessary distinction between citizens. The Fourteenth Amendment, which introduced the word male and age twenty-one into the Constitution for the first time, reduced congressional representation for any state that denied the right to vote to "male citizens twenty-one years of age." The logic of the amendment deliberately and decisively rendered adult males the only population that counted for purposes of political representation. In 1875, the Supreme Court ruled in *Minor v. Happersett* that voting was not a right guaranteed to all citizens. Speaking for the court, Justice C. J. Waite reasoned that every state had always denied the vote to citizens under twenty-one, all but New Jersey had barred women as well, and the Fourteenth Amendment itself acknowledged these exclusions. Waite's ruling not only classed female citizens with minors, but, by ruling that voting was not a right guaranteed to citizens by the Fourteenth Amendment, also paved the way for state governments to disenfranchise many black men and poor white men.[39]

***

A hundred years later, Americans finally mobilized political support to enfranchise citizens between the ages of eighteen and twenty-one.[40] Despite this reform, it's worth pondering whether chronological age still serves a similar political function today as it did in the nineteenth century, reassuring us that even if limitations on political rights are arbitrary—as the disenfranchisement of those with criminal records and resident aliens may in fact be—some limits are necessary or else young children would be voters. Historians interested in the social construction of categories such as race and gender would do well to pay greater attention to chronological age, for at a time when many Americans still regarded other categories as natural they self-consciously discussed age twenty-one as a category of law while nonetheless insisting that this qualification was necessary for the functioning of democracy. Chronological age thus stands out as a particularly powerful example of how advocates of democratic government relied upon constructed categories to exclude those whom they regarded as incapable of full citizenship. By defending the moral and constitutional right of state governments to impose age qualifications for suffrage, champions of white manhood citizenship gained a powerful justification for imposing other distinctions that, even if arbitrary, could be construed as necessary.

NOTES

1 On the importance of this convention to New York state and the nation as a whole, see David Quigley, *Second Founding: New York City, Reconstruction, and the Making of American Democracy* (New York: Hill & Wang, 2004), chap. 4.

2 *New York Tribune*, June 28, 1867, 5. See also Ann D. Gordon, ed., *The Selected Papers of Elizabeth Cady Stanton and Susan B. Anthony*, vol. 2, *Against an Aristocracy of Sex, 1866–1873* (New Brunswick, N.J.: Rutgers University Press, 2000), 75–77. On the American Equal Rights Association's campaign for suffrage in New York State, see Faye E. Dudden, *Fighting Chance: The Struggle over Woman Suffrage and Black Suffrage in Reconstruction America* (New York: Oxford University Press, 2011), 100–103.

3 Greeley's committee report advocated enfranchising black men but not women or "boys above the age of eighteen years." *Documents of the Convention of the State of New York, 1867–68*, vol. 1 (Albany, N.Y.: Weed, Parsons, and Company, 1868), no. 15. Delegates repeatedly invoked the disenfranchisement of women and children to prove that voting was not a natural right, but a privilege that could be regulated by the state. Delegates noted that women and minors paid taxes and supported the military, but still could not vote. See, for example, *Proceedings and Debates of the Constitutional Convention of the State of New York, Held in 1867 and 1868, in the City of Albany*, vol. 1 (Albany, N.Y.: Weed, Parsons, and Company, 1868), 200, 213, 237, 243, 245, 260, 336–39, 347, 427, 432 (hereafter cited as *NYC 1867*). Alexander Keyssar noted that constitutional delegates throughout the nation often defeated arguments that voting was a natural right by pointing to the disenfranchisement of women and children; see *The Right to Vote: The Contested History of Democracy in the United States* (New York: Basic Books, 2000), 44. What I am arguing here is that delegates' acknowledgment of age twenty-one as an arbitrary distinction between young men made age qualifications a particularly potent proof of the state's power to limit suffrage.

4 Corinne T. Field, *The Struggle for Equal Adulthood: Gender, Race, Age, and the Fight for Citizenship in Antebellum America* (Chapel Hill: University of North

Carolina Press, 2014). Wendell W. Cultice argues that there was some real support for enfranchising teen militiamen in antebellum America, but his conclusions are marred by a tendency to misinterpret the broader context of debate in state constitutional conventions. For example, he characterizes delegates to the New York state constitutional convention of 1821 as arguing for the enfranchisement of young militiamen, when in fact they were demanding rights for propertyless militiamen over twenty-one. *Youth's Battle for the Ballot: A History of Voting Age in America* (New York: Greenwood, 1992), 7. Nathaniel H. Carter and William L. Stone, *Reports of the Proceedings and Debates of the Convention of 1821, Assembled for the Purpose of Amending the Constitution of the State of New York* (Albany, N.Y.: E. and F. Hosford, 1821), 202, 210–14, 252, 273–74, 359–60 (hereafter cited as *NYC 1821*); on voting at twenty-one, see chapter 4; on age qualifications, see Holly Brewer, *By Birth or Consent: Children, Law, and the Anglo-American Revolution in Authority* (Chapel Hill: University of North Carolina Press, 2005).

5 Richard Franklin Bensel, *The American Ballot Box in the Mid-Nineteenth Century* (New York: Cambridge University Press, 2004), 27, 123–37; Mia Bay, *The White Image in the Black Mind: African-American Ideas about White People, 1830–1925* (New York: Oxford University Press, 2000); William Leach, *True Love and Perfect Union: The Feminist Reform of Sex and Society* (New York: Basic Books, 1980); Nancy Isenberg, *Sex and Citizenship in Antebellum America* (Chapel Hill: University of North Carolina Press, 1998).

6 Joseph Kett, *Rites of Passage: Adolescence in America, 1790 to the Present* (New York: Basic Books, 1977), chaps. 1–4; E. Anthony Rotundo, *American Manhood: Transformations in Masculinity from the Revolution to the Modern Era* (New York: Basic Books, 1993); Howard P. Chudacoff, *How Old Are You? Age Consciousness in American Culture* (Princeton, N.J.: Princeton University Press, 1989); Bensel, *American Ballot Box*, 17–20, 42–43, 93–106.

7 See, for example, *Journal of Debates and Proceedings in the Convention of Delegates Chosen to Revise the Constitution of Massachusetts, Begun and Holden at Boston, November 15, 1820, and Continued by Adjournment to January 9, 1821* (Boston: Daily Advertiser, 1853), 377–80 (hereafter cited as *MA 1820*); *NYC 1821*, 189, 252; William G. Bishop and William H. Attree, *Report of the Debates and Proceedings of the Convention for the Revision of the Constitution of the State of New York, 1846* (Albany, 1846), 177, 191, 218, 233, 1018; J. V. Smith, Official Reporter, *Report of the Debates and Proceedings of the Convention for the Revision of the Constitution of the State of Ohio, 1850–51*, vol. 2 (Columbus, Ohio: S. Medary, 1851), 553.

8 Field, *Struggle for Equal Adulthood*, chaps. 1–2; Sharon Braslaw Sundue, *Industrious in Their Stations: Young People at Work in Urban America, 1720–1810* (Charlottesville: University of Virginia Press, 2009).

9 This idea of chronological age as arbitrary but necessary was fundamental to both John Locke and William Blackstone. Both influenced Adams. See Locke, *The Second Treatise of Government*, in *Political Writings of John Locke*, ed. David Wootton (New York: Mentor, 1993), 290–91; Blackstone, *Commentaries on the*

Laws of England, Reprint of the First Edition (1765; repr., London: Dawsons of Pall Mall, 1966), 1:441, 451; Holly Brewer, "The Transformation of Domestic Law," in *The Cambridge History of Law in America*, vol. 1, *Early America (1580–1815)*, ed. Michael Grossberg and Christopher Tomlins (New York: Cambridge University Press, 2008), 313–20.

10 John Adams to James Sullivan, May 26, 1776, in *The Adams Papers Digital Edition*, ed. C. James Taylor (Charlottesville: University of Virginia Press, 2008); on the "Pandora's Box" argument, see Keyssar, *Right to Vote*, 12–13.

11 Adams to Sullivan, May 26, 1776.

12 Ibid.

13 *A Constitution or Frame of Government, Agreed upon by the Delegates of the People of the State of Massachusetts Bay 1780* (Boston: Benjamin Edes and Sons, 1780), 19, 25.

14 Nathaniel Shurtleff, ed., *Records of the Governor and Company of the Massachusetts Bay in New England* (Boston: William White, 1853), 11:173, 213.

15 *The Acts and Resolves, Public and Private, of the Province of the Massachusetts Bay: To Which Are Prefixed the Charters of the Province, with Historical and Explanatory Notes, and an Appendix*, vol. 5, *1775–1776* (Boston: Wright and Potter, 1918), 445–48.

16 Selectmen in Sheffield did allow one eighteen-year-old to vote in 1751 because his father had died and he was functioning as head of the family; see Michael Zuckerman, "The Social Context of Democracy in Massachusetts," *William and Mary Quarterly* 25 (October 1968): 530–33.

17 W. J. Rorabaugh, *The Craft Apprentice: From Franklin to the Machine Age in America* (New York: Oxford University Press, 1986), chap. 1.

18 Kett insightfully argued that from age ten to twenty-one, youth entered a stage of "semidependence" that offered "a jarring mixture of complete freedom and total subordination," especially for boys who often left home to learn skills but retained obligations to fathers. *Rites of Passage*, 29. Poll taxes and militia duty followed this general pattern but, unlike work or school, were precisely scheduled to begin at age sixteen.

19 Joyce Lee Malcolm, *Peter's War: A New England Slave Boy and the American Revolution* (New Haven, Conn.: Yale University Press, 2009).

20 Joan Gundersen, "Independence, Citizenship, and the American Revolution," *Signs: Journal of Women in Culture and Society* 13 (Autumn 1987): 59–77.

21 Keyssar, *Right to Vote*, 16; Brewer, *By Birth or Consent*, 139–40.

22 The determination as to who was old enough to fight was decided through complex negotiations among boys, fathers, masters, military recruiters, and commanding officers. See Steven Mintz, *Huck's Raft: A History of American Childhood* (Cambridge, Mass.: Belknap, 2004), 62–63; Caroline Cox, "Boy Soldiers of the American Revolution: The Effects of War on Society," in *Children and Youth in a New Nation*, ed. James Marten (New York: New York University Press, 2009), 13–28; Rorabaugh, *Craft Apprentice*, chap. 1.

23 *Laws for Regulating and Governing the Militia of the Commonwealth of Massachusetts 1803* (Boston: Tomas and Andrews, 1803), 4.

24 Shurtleff, *Records of the Governor and Company of the Massachusetts Bay*, 174.

25 Ibid., 174. For discussions of how officials determined ages in later periods, see Bensel, *American Ballot Box*, chap. 2; and James D. Schmidt, who traces a shift from "big enough" to "old enough" in *Industrial Violence and the Legal Origins of Child Labor* (New York: Cambridge University Press, 2010).

26 Robert Gutman, "Birth and Death Registration in Massachusetts, I: The Colonial Background, 1639–1800," *Millbank Memorial Fund Quarterly* 36 (January 1958): 58–74; and "The Birth and Death Registration in Massachusetts, II: The Inauguration of a Modern System, 1800–1849," *Millbank Memorial Fund Quarterly* 36 (October 1958): 373–402; Sam Shapiro, "Development of Birth Registration and Birth Statistics in the United States," *Population Studies* 4 (June 1950): 86–111.

27 See chapter 6.

28 Field, *Struggle for Equal Adulthood*, chap. 3; Keyssar, *Right to Vote*; George P. Parkinson, Jr., "Antebellum State Constitution-Making: Retention, Circumvention, Revision" (PhD diss., University of Wisconsin, 1972); Chilton Williamson, *American Suffrage: From Property to Democracy, 1760–1860* (Princeton, N.J.: Princeton University Press, 1960).

29 *MA 1820*, 377–78; *Constitution or Frame of Government*, 32.

30 *NYC 1821*, 661; Phyllis Field, *The Politics of Race in New York: The Struggle for Black Suffrage in the Civil War Era* (Ithaca, N.Y.: Cornell University Press, 1982), 35–37.

31 *NYC 1821*, 195.

32 Bickford, a staunchly pro-Union newspaper editor commended for raising large numbers of volunteers during the war, argued that soldiers were full-grown men and deserved to be treated as such. Robertson, a prominent Democrat opposed to black manhood suffrage, was more intent on proving that "white 'boys' of eighteen" were more competent than black men over twenty-one. *NYC 1867*, 101, 102, 489–91, 541. On Bickford, see John A. Haddock, *The Growth of a Century: As Illustrated in the History of Jefferson County, New York, from 1793 to 1894* (Albany, N.Y.: Weed-Parsons, 1895), 314–15. On Robertson, see *Reports of Cases Argued and Determined in the Superior Court of the City of New York* (New York: Banks and Brothers Law Publishers, 1893), 61:xxvii–iii, and "A New Political Club," *New York Times*, November 13, 1865.

33 For the debate over woman suffrage, see *NYC 1867*, 207, 215, 364–76, 393, 427–69.

34 On July 25, the convention met for a roll call vote on both these measures. Twenty-six delegates supported substituting eighteen for twenty-one in the constitution; the majority of these (eighteen) were Democrats. Two of these Democrats were also the only members of their party to support woman suffrage. Of the eight Republicans who supported enfranchising minors, five also supported woman suffrage. For the partisan breakdown of these two votes, see *New*

York Tribune, July 26, 1867, 5. The committee of the whole voted on the proposal to enfranchise women on July 23 and eighteen-year-olds on July 24. The woman suffrage proposal lost by a vote of sixty-three to twenty-four, a margin of 62 percent. Bickford's resolution enfranchising eighteen-year-olds was defeated by a vote of eighty-two to thirty-three, a similar margin of 60 percent. More delegates were present the second day. There was no roll call. *NYC 1867*, 469, 490.

35 He also noted that many women had aided the war effort, but because he viewed women as naturally destined to occupy a more noble sphere than politics, he regarded sex as less arbitrary than age. *NYC 1867*, 261.

36 Ibid., 261.

37 Ibid., 214. On Hand, see Gordon, *Selected Papers of Stanton and Anthony*, 77n1. For other delegates of both parties invoking age twenty-one as arbitrary but necessary, see *NYC 1867*, 426, 428, 432.

38 Quigley, *Second Founding*.

39 *Minor v. Happersett*, 88 U.S. (21 Wall.) 162 (1875). Elizabeth Cady Stanton, Susan B. Anthony, and Matilda Joslyn Gage, *The History of Woman Suffrage*, vol. 2, *1861–1876* (1882; repr., New York: Arno, 1969), 234–42; Ellen Carol DuBois, "Outgrowing the Compact of the Fathers" and "Taking the Law into Our Own Hands: Bradwell, Minor, and Suffrage Militance in the 1870s," in *Woman Suffrage and Women's Rights* (New York: New York University Press, 1998), 98–108, 114–23; Eric Foner, *A Short History of Reconstruction, 1863–1877* (New York: Harper and Row, 1990), 222–25.

40 See chapter 10.

4

A Birthday Like None Other

Turning Twenty-One in the Age of Popular Politics

JON GRINSPAN

Nineteenth-century American youths lived with a frustrating lack of age boundaries. From the 1830s through the 1880s, men and women in their late teens and early twenties stumbled beyond the old structures of kin and region, into a confusing new world of economic and social uncertainty. Though pushed toward adulthood, few clear age boundaries signified real maturity. Millions of young men puzzled over where "childhood ends and youth begins and where youth ends and manhood begins."[1] The path was even more muddled for women. Each birthday heightened young Americans' concerns that they would never achieve adulthood.

One moment bucked this trend. When white men turned twenty-one and were finally able to vote, they celebrated a clear step into adulthood. This political rite of passage helped make chronological aging seem progressive and triumphant to otherwise drifting youths. Many young men looked forward to casting their first votes, and young women, denied the right themselves, nonetheless elevated its importance for the men in their lives. While Americans tended to greet their fifteenth or twentieth birthdays with chagrin, they honored an eligible man's twenty-first birthday as an unambiguous passage into adulthood.

The political culture welcomed them. During the age of popular politics—running from the 1840s through the 1880s—public democracy stood at the center of American life. Voter turnout peaked during this era, averaging 77 percent of eligible voters at presidential elections. Some heated races drew well over 90 percent of potential voters to the polls, and even the slowest presidential election, in 1852, had a higher turnout than any presidential race since 1900.[2] Nonvoters refused to stand on the sidelines: American women, children, and disenfranchised minorities played an active role at rallies, debates, and jollifications. Public political events served as the uniting centerpiece of American society; democracy enthralled many as the chief national pastime.[3]

This excited political environment offered young voters a crucial sense of importance. While scholars have studied the party dynamics, ideological conflicts, and campaign tactics of this political culture, few have examined the personal significance of young Americans' individual use of public politics. This study focuses on the private implications of Americans' linkage of democracy and maturity.

What many considered the most exasperating aspect of this political system—the arbitrary choice of twenty-one as the line between boyhood and manhood—may actually have been its greatest strength. Young men—floundering in new economic and social environments, struggling to find a job, to meet a spouse, to start a family—delighted in the idea that they won the right to vote without having to accomplish anything. In his 1888 book about turning twenty-one, civil rights activist Albion Tourgée wrote about the significance of this almost mystical transition, tied not to achievement but to simple chronology. Overnight, no matter how stunted the rest of his life appeared, an idle young man was "transformed into an effective agency."[4] The very arbitrariness of the voting age offered young men an unearned birthday present.

This cultural use of a political rite put young women in an unenviable position. Like their brothers and beaux, young women struggled with the titanic changes of nineteenth-century life. They expressed similar anxieties at each passing birthday, worrying about their failure to achieve success, stability, family, and respectability. And many followed party politics extremely closely; their diaries and letters often overflow with partisan rhetoric, favorite slogans, and campaign gossip. Unlike young men, however, American women were prevented from using their political interests against their personal anxieties. They were denied a satisfying transition at age twenty-one.

Instead, most women fumbled between three lesser options: vicariously appreciating the twenty-first birthdays of the men in their lives, celebrating their twenty-first birthdays as significant without explaining why, or pointing to the fundamental inequality of the system. None provided the sudden transition that young men found upon becoming voters, but each offered some semblance of a boundary in their otherwise hazy development.

Few African Americans, male or female, could use their birthdays in this manner. A very large proportion, born as slaves, could not mark a specific date of birth. Many knew only the season or an event, like a presidential election, that took place the year of their birth.[5] In addition, although millions of black men voted between 1840 and the 1880s, their right to vote was never a dependable moment to be anticipated. The chances were simply too high that a state legislature or election day terrorists would prevent a twenty-one-year-old black man from going to the polls. Young white men could look forward to their twenty-first birthdays as a moment of proud transition; few black men could be so certain about their age or their suffrage.

The extended period from the antebellum era through the Gilded Age witnessed two powerful social trends. On the one hand, a booming nation shook the transition from childhood to adulthood, challenging youths to make their own way in a world without the old boundaries. At the same time, the political system asserted its centrality in American culture, bringing citizens together in ways that—though unfair and corrupt—thrilled millions. It is no coincidence that this peak of young people's instability was also the most enthusiastic moment of popular politics, and many young men and women used one trend against the other. For millions of young people turning twenty-one each year, the age limits of politics offered a clear and welcome boundary in their otherwise muddled development.

***

Poor Benjamin Brown Foster. The awkward youth, growing up in an 1840s Maine lumber town, knew intimately the succession of stifled birthdays that failed to grant real maturity. Foster struggled toward adulthood at a time when the path seemed vague. The booming market economy pushed him to achieve, but the crumbling system of apprenticeship shuffled him from job to job, none promising real advancement. He yearned for a wife, but his financial problems disadvantaged him in courting. One wealthy young woman mocked him as "the dirtiest looking object she ever saw." Assessing his failures to achieve manhood in his frank, anxious diary, Foster sighed, "[M]y life is already probably a quarter or a fifth gone and with what result?"[6]

Concerns like Foster's are common in the diaries and letters of young Americans from the 1840s through the 1880s. A diverse cast expressed a shared belief that each year marked 365 wasted days. From the young Pennsylvanian who fretted that his big plans would probably "vanish for the lack of money" to the Tennessee girl who felt that she did "nothing but eat and wear and be in the way," a broad swath of American youths expressed the same mixture of self-improving ambition and self-pitying pessimism.[7] Most believed that they alone were failing to progress toward adulthood.

These worries were not limited to young Americans of a particularly morose type. Confident, arrogant, and smug youths shared this sense of obstructed progress. A Great Plains buffalo hunter who survived a stabbing at Deadwood, boxed for Calamity Jane's amusement, and kept track of all the animals he shot in his diary, frequently groaned about his future.[8] Charles Plummer, a nativist street preacher who could work massive Philadelphia crowds into frothing anti-Irish agitation filled his diary with lamentations that he was "qualified for nothing" and found it "humiliating indeed" that he still lived with his parents at age nineteen.[9] Something larger than personality held back all these uncertain young people.

What seemed like the individual failures of millions of youths was, in reality, the human impact of the massive structural forces unleashed in the nineteenth century. The unprecedented changes felt during the age of popular politics filled the lives of American youths with gnawing uncertainty. Pushed by a faith in progress and pulled by the disorderly modern world, young men and women hoped for success but saw no clear way forward.

In the mid-nineteenth century, young Americans' lives changed radically. Between 1840 and 1890, America's population quadrupled, splitting cities' seams and peopling the vast frontier. Patterns of work, family, courtship, and education changed dramatically. Such upheavals disturbed the earlier progression of youth, in which most young Americans planned to replicate their parents' lives. Beginning in the early decades of the nineteenth century, a growing market economy and an obsession with progress eclipsed that hope. By the Jacksonian era, few could plan to live as their ancestors had.[10] There was no sudden shift away from the milestones that marked adulthood—youths still worked to find a partner, a livelihood, and a home—but after 1840 young people seemed unsure that they were pursuing these goals at the proper pace. The world seemed to be speeding up just as young people worried that they were slowing down.

Massive social change altered young Americans' most intimate experiences. Romantic relationships grew more complex, as mobile men and women bounced around to new cities and territories. Americans courted more partners and married years later than their ancestors.[11] Finding work became another fraught decision; most young people had never before needed to find a job outside of their families' domestic economy or social network. As America refocused on unskilled industry, the tradition of apprenticeship that introduced so many young men to the middling classes crumbled. The market added formerly unimagined options, but most jobs were short-lived. Work that had once been collective, like farming, was replaced by individual labor and personal pressure. Though family and regional networks weakened, new institutions like schools and unions could not yet replace their beneficial structures.[12]

Just as their futures grew hazy, young people faced increasing social pressure to achieve. Each generation seemed more self-improving than the last, driven by what many came to call "the go-ahead principle."[13] Though committed to the idea of progress and individual achievement, most young people experienced a phase of "semidependence" in their late teens.[14] Many left home for six months of school or two years of work, but returned to rely on their family while planning their next move. A typical young man considered his teen years an alternating series of "buoyant hopes" and "baffling discouragements."[15]

Many young Americans lumped together concerns about financial success, proving their maturity, and asserting their masculinity or femininity. Adulthood and masculinity, for instance, were mutually reinforcing for young men, who considered manhood "a matter of age *and* gender," and used "manly" to distinguish men from boys as often as they used the term to separate the sexes. As the culture of self-made capitalism increasingly dominated American aspirations, many saw financial success as proof of adulthood and masculinity.[16]

For young ladies, usually barred from such capitalist strivings, a feeling of uselessness undermined their sense of womanhood. As the marriage age crept ever higher, many young women felt cut off from what was considered their primary mission: managing a household, husband, and children. Women frequently denounced themselves as foolish, frivolous, childish, and wasteful.[17] For these reasons, many educators, parents, and preachers considered "youth"—that hazy phase between childhood and adulthood—"the most dangerous period of human life."[18]

Birthdays brought these dangers to a point. For most of the year, youths experienced social and economic pressures as a miasmic weight, ever present but unarticulated. On their birthdays these burdens suddenly felt crushing. There was often a seasonal trend in such diaries: around New Year's young Americans filled pages with hopeful visions of the coming year, and on their birthdays they bemoaned every mistake and missed opportunity.[19] Many young Americans used the anniversary to express their darkest views of the past and their dimmest predictions for the future. Benjamin Brown Foster, the struggling Maine teen mentioned above, berated himself on his sixteenth birthday for being "ignorant, poor, fickle, wavering, without brilliancy, talents, wealth or influential friends."[20]

Both men and women expressed these feelings, usually following one of two models. Young women were more likely to simply castigate themselves as failures, to criticize their status without much consideration of other potential paths. Many marked their birthday with comments like "I am now eighteen and my feeling is regret—sincere regret" or "nineteen years of my unprofitable life are gone."[21] The African American activist Charlotte Forten Grimké felt her "own utter insignificance" on her birthday on August 17, 1854, marked August 17, 1856, as "saddest I have ever known," worried on August 17, 1857, that "the years are passing away, and I, Ah! how little am I improving them," and even on August 17, 1862, marveled that she had "lived a quarter of a century, and am so very, very ignorant."[22]

Such castigations did not resemble more modern concerns about growing old, but rather focused on a sense of personal stasis. Lacking much agency in nineteenth-century American culture, many young women found it difficult to point to specific mistakes that were holding them back. Some religious young women—particularly those immersed in the Calvinism that still dominated much of American spirituality—simply blamed their insufficient devotion, wishing, "Oh, that I had more faith in Jesus!"[23]

The other model, more common among young men, was to list specific setbacks on one's birthday, measured against an idealized vision of where one should be at that point in life. Benjamin Brown Foster's birthday diary entries did this, enumerating the jobs he failed to win, the friends he lacked, and the trappings of manhood that eluded him.[24] Oliver Wilcox Norton wrote, during his service in the Civil War, that on his birthday, "It is time I was a man if ever I am to be one," but though "[m]y years would indicate that I ought to be a man, but I must confess to much of the boy in my nature yet."[25]

Many youths worried about this disconnect between their chronological age and place in life. For this reason, it is wrong to suggest that age consciousness had little importance in nineteenth-century America. Many youths felt like the aspiring preacher Lyman Abbott, who wrote on his birthday, "I am 20 years of age. To say that I do not realize it, would not begin to express my want of conception of who I now am and who I used to be. Even now as I walk the room I cannot conceive who I am that am twenty years old."[26] An awareness of one's chronological age was not absent; it merely failed to sync with lived experience. Many craved a decisive moment when chronological age matched self-image.

A stunted romantic life added to the list of woes. Over the course of the nineteenth century the average age of marriage crept up, until by 1890 men married at 26.5 and women at 23.5, a peak not returned to until the late 1980s and 1990s.[27] Individual young women and men experienced this demographic shift as a personal delay. Many poured out their deepest worries on their birthdays. When turning twenty, Emily Hawley Gillespie's mother nagged her, saying, "Here you are twenty years old and not married yet," while Oliver Wilcox Norton wrote in a birthday letter, "Do you think I will be married before I am thirty? I don't see much prospect of it."[28] Very few of these young people pointed out that they were part of a larger trend; most saw their "single wretchedness" as an individual failing.[29]

This was the usual model, expressed with particular self-recrimination between ages fifteen and twenty-one. Some Americans kept criticizing themselves on their birthdays for the rest of their lives, but this tone peaked as anxious young men and women struggled to find a path toward manhood or womanhood. Most expressed some version of Norton's worry that, though "a man" in years he remained "the boy" in life experience. This disconnect between chronological age and expected maturity dogged millions. Many cast about for a clear, decisive boundary, a chronological marker that would really change their status.

**

In the face of all these melancholy anniversaries, one date stands out. Though young Americans bemoaned their failings on their seventeenth or twentieth birthdays, they reveled in their twenty-firsts. Young white men in particular used proud, triumphant, and nationalistic language to mark that anniversary. While they looked backward on other birthdays, considering mistakes they had made or paths they might have taken, on their twenty-first they looked forward to adulthood and citizenship.

The Union Army veteran, radical Republican, and civil rights activist Albion Winegar Tourgée best articulated the political weight of turning twenty-one. In his book *Letters to a King*, he implored young men not to lose interest in politics—as enthusiasm began to wane in the late 1880s—but to locate their manhood in democratic participation. Writing to an archetypal young adult, Tourgée announced, "This is your twenty-first birthday. Yesterday you were an infant; to-day you are a man." Turning twenty-one meant more than manhood, Tourgée went on: "Yesterday you were a subject; to-day you are a sovereign." The political system coronated young men; the nation, Tourgée wrote, "enjoins you to *be a king!*"[30]

It was not just pushy reformers who felt this way; triumphant twenty-first birthdays jump out from young Americans' otherwise anxious diaries. Charles Plummer, the anti-immigrant street preacher mentioned above, provides a clear example of this in his prolific diary spanning the 1840s. In his late teens he lived in Philadelphia, worked in a shoe factory, and spent his free time preaching evangelical Christianity. Though his associates described him as a brilliant speaker, he saw himself as a failure. Plummer ignored his success as a lecturer and focused on his struggle to establish financial independence. It was really the aftershocks of the 1837 depression that kept him from achieving, but Plummer berated himself for living in his parents' cramped house and working in his brother's unventilated shoe factory.[31]

As his twenty-first birthday neared, his tone changed. Plummer focused less on his personal status and more on the political conflicts roiling 1840s Philadelphia. In long entries he discussed which political party represented the "real democracy of the country," vacillating from the Whigs to rising anti-immigrant organizations. He bemoaned his failures less, and began to write with more self-assurance, even aggression. While his politics leave nothing to admire, his confidence clearly grew as he saw himself as a mature political arbiter. Finally, on March 29, 1842, Plummer declared—with characteristic soapbox bombast—"All Hail, I am 21 Years of Age to day. Thanks be to God! . . . the Laws of the Land declare me to be a man and a Citizen."[32] Gone was his humiliation at living at home and his concerns that he was "qualified for nothing." Instead, by simply turning twenty-one, Plummer earned manhood and citizenship.

Similar entries sprout from young men's diaries across the country for the next several decades. Even young immigrants, like those Charles Plummer ranted against, saw turning twenty-one as an introduction to citizenship and manhood. Michael F. Campbell, an Irish-born youth struggling in a Gilded Age New Haven factory, expressed this clearly. Campbell kept one of the most anxious diaries of the era, in which he continually worried about work, romance, identity, health, masculinity, and even his weight. For all his carping and moaning, Campbell greeted his twenty-first birthday with stammering pride, proclaiming, "Today is an important day in my life no doubt for on to-day I am to commence my career as a man and not as a boy . . . for on this beautiful day in may I have completed my twenty one years in this world."[33]

Pride at turning twenty-one could drown out regional, social, economic, and ideological differences. Cowboys and clerks, Union and Confederate soldiers, Democrats, Republicans, Whigs, Free Soilers, and Socialists often met their twenty-first birthdays with similar language. They were not united by background or even strong feelings about politics. Most of these excited twenty-one-year-olds shared a self-reflective tone in the months before their big birthdays. It was not external politics, but internal anxieties, that made attaining the voting age so significant for millions of anxious young men.[34]

Achieving the voting age was not simply a happy rite of passage upon which young men stumbled. Many struggling youths spent their late teens anticipating the proud day. In preparation for their twenty-first birthday, or for the first election following it, young white men grew mature facial hair or "sleeked up" in other ways. In the 1876 election—the presidential vote with the highest turnout in U.S. history—the *Milwaukee Daily Sentinel* mocked twenty-one-year-olds' affectations of maturity. A typical young man, the paper joked, awoke hours before dawn, fussed with his appearance, blustered at the breakfast table, argued politics with his father, dismissed his sister's views, and spent the day preening around the polls, his pockets stuffed with extra ballots.[35] Up in Maine, Benjamin Brown Foster felt overwhelmed by these aspirations while observing an election well before his twenty-first birthday. Watching grown men cast ballots, Foster wished "that I was for one year, and on this one topic, a man, a voter."[36]

Many twenty-one-year-old men felt that they earned this new sense of agency twice, first by turning twenty-one and then by casting a vote in an election following that momentous birthday. Crossing the chronological boundary marked an abstract transition in "the Laws of the Land," in the "eyes of God," and in their own self-identity.[37] After that personal milestone, casting one's first ballot at a widely attended election, surrounded by most of the men in their community, publicly declared that self-knowledge. A young man's first ballot offered concrete proof of his birthday's abstract transition. As one Union Army captain wrote, when he first voted, "This has been a red letter day, for with many others, I have cast my first vote for President." This young captain saw two simultaneous victories: he "cast my first vote," and he did so "with many others."[38]

While most young white men could hop over the boundary between youth and adulthood twice, other populations could never fully embrace their twenty-first birthdays. White women, by far the largest disenfranchised population, usually faced their twenty-firsts with an odd mixture of vague pride and inarticulate yearning. Living in the same culture as their beaux and brothers, they felt that turning twenty-one had greater meaning than other birthdays, but could not point to any concrete change.

Many looked forward to their twenty-firsts, but when the celebrated date arrived, they fumbled in explaining its significance.[39] In April 1859 midwestern farm girl Emily Hawley Gillespie wrote that it was her "twenty-first birthday; am now of age, some say 'can do as you please,'" while seven years later New York Quaker Phebe Hallock Irish announced, "My twenty-first birth-day. I have tried to be dignified, as becomes my age."[40] Twenty-one-year-old women felt that they now held greater freedoms and responsibilities, but they lacked the clear pronouncement of adulthood and citizenship that their brothers relished. Even those who were deeply interested in party politics celebrated their twenty-firsts, but knew that they could not expect their big day to usher in a new political identity.[41]

Most women who saw a connection between chronological age and political maturity focused on the birthdays of men in their lives. Isabella Maud Rittenhouse Mayne took this approach in the early 1880s. Though she "must always cry on my birthday," Mayne took a different tone when marking her suitor's, bragging, "His birthday is Saturday. He'll be 21 and able to vote."[42] Other women pushed men to celebrate their twenty-first birthdays and to be sure to cast their first vote when able. In 1868, the Indiana Sunday school teacher Mattie Thomas reminded her long-distance beau that his first vote was approaching, nudging, "I would feel real vexed if you would not vote this fall," while Georgia belle Ella Gertrude Clanton noted with palpable disappointment that her fiancé was too sick to cast his first ballot.[43] Though few women said so explicitly, these diaries give the sense that many saw their husband or beau's transition into political manhood as a personal victory as well.

The most poignant discussions of twenty-first birthdays came from mid-nineteenth-century women who railed against a system that declared men "kings" at twenty-one, but offered women no similar coronation. Women's Christian Temperance Union president Frances Willard provided the strongest denunciation of this inequality. In her autobiography and in speeches to the National Council of Women, Willard reflected on her relationship with her brother Oliver, whom she had always viewed as a peer. "Then my brother came to be twenty-one," Willard declared, and "dressed up in his best Sunday clothes" and went off to vote with the men, leaving his sister behind. "Lo and behold!" Willard told a crowd in 1888, "there came a day when there was a separation. I saw that voting made it, and it seemed to me the line was artificial."[44] Oliver enjoyed one of the era's few transitions based on chronological age, crossing an "artificial" line, with his sister left on the other side. The fact that the division was arbitrary made it more accessible to Oliver and more galling to Frances.

While her brother's twenty-first birthday provided a clear initiation, Willard's birthdays seemed to only limit her freedom. On one her mother insisted that she was too old to wear her hair down and had it "done up in woman-fashion," complete with eighteen painful pins. She bemoaned that birthday as "the date of my martyrdom." When Willard used her eighteenth birthday to assert her independence by reading *Ivanhoe*, a novel forbidden by her strict father, the Willard family laughed at her attempt to link a birthday with growing independence.[45] Oliver Willard's birthday offered a clear rite of passage, while Frances's meant decreasing freedom.

Frances Willard's attacks on the inequalities in nineteenth-century American society are familiar to many scholars working today, both because they are incredibly compelling and because such writing was not very common. Though a core of activists railed against the disenfranchisement of women, most young Americans did not. Far more celebrated their twenty-first birthdays as vaguely meaningful or honored the rite of passage for the men in their lives. Most women (like men) accepted the culture in which they lived, and never expected to vote at twenty-one. They tended to see men's birthday initiations as part of a fundamentally different path through life. Young men and women lived in an environment with few distinct boundaries, so they were apt to uphold and even celebrate the few clear lines they encountered.

***

In 1888—as Frances Willard denounced the artificial boundary her brother's twenty-first birthday created—Albion Tourgée published the last great paean to turning twenty-one. Tourgée's *Letters to a King* overflowed with bold pronouncements about the meaning of that crucial birthday. Tourgée stressed that though many youths might think that he was "inclined to magnify the importance of the legal transition from

youth to manhood which marks the opening of your 21st year," its significance could not be exaggerated.[46]

Tourgée protested too much. *Letters to a King* represented both the
apogee and the rapid plunge of the importance given to turning twenty-
one. He wrote against a growing trend—fewer young men were voting at
each election, especially among the respectable classes—acknowledging
that his views might make him seem like an "old fogy." He challenged
those young men who saw the voting age as "an effete and worthless
system, which holds its place only in the brains of narrow-minded stick-
lers for legal form and antiquated custom." Instead, Tourgée argued that
turning twenty-one meant an inescapable destiny, commanding, "The
citizen-king cannot abdicate. I mean that you are required to 'go into
politics' whether you desire to do so or not."[47]

Tourgée read the cultural winds; turning twenty-one seemed to mean
less for new generations of youth. Fewer men mentioned their twenty-
first birthdays or first votes in their diaries. Many of the larger trends
that had made twenty-one a valuable chronological marker began to
weaken. New institutions like schools, workplaces, and youth associations helped offer much-needed structure to young people's education,
employment, and entertainment. Parents, teachers, and reformers established doctrines for incorporating, or at least distracting, young men
and women trapped in that nether region between childhood and adulthood.[48] At the same time, the vibrant public political culture became
more private, more secretive, and less focused on entertainment than
it had been from the 1840s through the 1880s. The path to adulthood
stabilized, and the world of public politics withered.[49]

Suffrage helped aging, and aging helped suffrage. Young Americans
wove these two concerns together, living at a time when voting seemed
crucial and maturity seemed problematic. Albion Tourgée hailed this
link as wonderfully arbitrary, while Frances Willard saw it as mad-
deningly "artificial," but both acknowledged the tremendous power of
the capricious dividing line. In a world of foggy boundaries and vague
transitions, a blunt, unthinking separation based on simple chronology
served as a useful tool. For those allowed to cross the line—mostly white
men—it offered an unearned victory. They delighted in the transition it
promised, turning a simple legal boundary into a powerful cultural celebration. For those who could never cross, however, turning twenty-one

marked just another stifled birthday in a youth made up of ambiguous moments.

Those awarded full citizenship at age twenty-one, and those forced to watch from the sidelines, shared something larger. They all craved a line in the sand, a sense that by surviving to a designated age they were entitled to maturity. A "go-ahead" zeal for progress disrupted the old traditions, leaving floundering youth to yearn for a moment when their official age and their felt maturity finally connected. Struggling through the age of popular politics, and counting birthdays in "the most dangerous" phase of life, mid-nineteenth-century youths found meaning in the arbitrary.[50]

NOTES

1 William Fletcher King, *Reminiscences* (New York: Abingdon Press, 1915), 64.

2 John P. McIver, *Historical Statistics of the United States, Millennial Edition*, ed. Susan B. Carter and Scott Sigmund Gartner (New York: Cambridge University Press, 2006), series Eb62–113.

3 See Joel Silbey, *The American Political Nation, 1838–1893* (Stanford, Calif.: Stanford University Press, 1994); Richard Franklin Bensel, *The American Ballot Box in the Mid-Nineteenth Century* (New York: Cambridge University Press, 2004); Michael E. McGerr, *The Decline of Popular Politics: The American North 1865–1928* (New York: Oxford University Press, 1986).

4 Albion Winegar Tourgée, *Letters to a King* (Cincinnati: Cranston and Stowe, 1888), 37.

5 Henry Clay Bruce, *The New Man: Twenty-Nine Years a Slave, Twenty-Nine Years a Free Man* (York, Pa.: P. Anstadt & Sons, 1895), 11; Ned Cobb, *All God's Dangers— The Life of Nate Shaw*, ed. Theodore Rosengarten (New York: Knopf, 1974), 11; William S. McFeely, *Frederick Douglass* (New York: Norton, 1991), 8.

6 Benjamin Brown Foster, *Down East Diary*, ed. Charles H. Foster (Orono: University of Maine at Orono Press, 1975), 107, 76.

7 Lester Ward, *Young Ward's Diary*, ed. Bernhard J. Stern (New York: G.P. Putnam's Sons, 1935), 8, 25; Amanda McDowell Burns, July 5, 1861, in *Fiddles in the Cumberland*, ed. Amanda McDowell and Lela McDowell Blankenship (New York: Richard R. Smith, 1943).

8 Rolf Johnson, *Happy as a Big Sunflower: Adventures in the West, 1876–1880*, ed. Richard E. Jensen (Lincoln: University of Nebraska Press, 2000), 160–96.

9 Charles W. Plummer, September 27, 1840, Charles Henry Plummer Diaries, Pennsylvania Historical Society, Philadelphia.

10 Charles G. Sellers, *The Market Revolution: Jacksonian America, 1815–1846* (New York: Oxford University Press, 1991), 12; Daniel Walker Howe, *What Hath God Wrought: The Transformation of America, 1815–1848* (New York: Oxford University

Press, 2007); Mary Ryan, *Cradle of the Middle Class: The Family in Oneida County, New York, 1790–1865* (New York: Cambridge University Press, 1981); Paul E. Johnson, *A Shopkeeper's Millennium: Society and Revivals in Rochester, New York, 1815–1837* (New York: Hill & Wang, 2004).

11 Ellen K. Rothman, *Hands and Hearts: A History of Courtship in America* (New York: Basic Books, 1984); Howard Chudacoff, *The Age of the Bachelor: Creating an American Subculture* (Princeton, N.J.: Princeton University Press, 1999).

12 Walter Licht, *Getting Work: Philadelphia, 1840–1950* (Cambridge, Mass.: Harvard University Press, 1992); Walter Licht, *Industrializing America: The Nineteenth Century* (Baltimore: Johns Hopkins University Press, 1995).

13 "The Go-Ahead Principle," *American Review: A Whig Journal* 4 (1849): 287. Also see the infamous minstrel routine "Zip Coon on the Go-Ahead Principle" (Boston: L Deming, 1832); Timothy Templeton, *The Adventures of My Cousin Smooth* (New York: Miller, Orton, & Mulligan, 1855), 2.

14 Joseph Kett, *Rites of Passage: Adolescence in America, 1790 to the Present* (New York: Basic Books, 1977), 11–13.

15 King, *Reminiscences*, 64.

16 E. Anthony Rotundo, *American Manhood: Transformations in Masculinity from the Revolution to the Modern Era* (New York: Basic Books, 1993), 20; Kett, *Rites of Passage*, 173.

17 For examples, see Amanda McDowell Burns, May 1861, in *Fiddles in the Cumberland*; Alice Bradley Haven, February 1852, in *Cousin Alice: A Memoir of Alice B. Haven*, ed. Cornelia Richards (New York: Appleton, 1868), 135–37; Ellen Tucker Emerson to Addie Manning, September 8, 1856, in *The Letters of Ellen Tucker Emerson*, ed. Edith W. Gregg (Kent, Ohio: Kent State University Press, 1982), 1:118–20.

18 "A Lecture to Young Men, L. K. Washburn," *Boston Investigator*, October 3, 1888; also see *Before He Is Twenty: Five Perplexing Phases of Boyhood Considered* (New York: F.H. Revell, 1894).

19 David Schenck Papers, December 31, 1849 and December 31, 1850, Southern Historical Collection, University of North Carolina at Chapel Hill; Isabella Maud Rittenhouse Mayne, *Maud*, ed. Richard Lee Strout (New York: Macmillan, 1939), 48–52; David Beardsley, "Birthday Commentaries on His Life," in *Visions of the Western Reserve*, ed. Robert A. Wheeler (Columbus: Ohio State University Press, 2000).

20 Foster, *Down East Diary*, 124.

21 Ella Gertrude Clanton Thomas, April 1852, in *Secret Eye: The Journal of Ella Gertrude Clanton Thomas, 1848–1889*, ed. Virginia Ingraham Burr (Chapel Hill: University of North Carolina Press, 1990), 103; Chloe Bridgman Conant Bierce, *Journal and Biological Notice of Chloe B. Conant Bierce* (Cincinnati: Elm Street Printing, 1869), 98.

22 Charlotte L. Forten Grimké, August 17, 1854, August 17, 1856, August 17, 1857, August 17, 1862, in *The Journal of Charlotte Forten Grimké: A Free Negro in the Slave Era*, ed. Ray Allen Billington (New York: Dryden Press, 1953), 47, 72, 94, 120.

23 Susan Allibone, Diary, July 1833, in *A Life Hid with Christ in God*, ed. Lee Alfred (Philadelphia: J.B. Lippincott & Co., 1856), 46–49.

24 Foster, *Down East Diary*, 124.

25 Oliver Wilcox Norton, December 18, 1864, in *Army Letters, 1861–1865* (Chicago: O.L. Deming, 1903).

26 Lyman Abbott, *Reminiscences* (Boston: Houghton Mifflin, 1914), 113.

27 Diana B. Elliot, Kristy Krivickas, Matthew W. Brault, and Rose M. Kreider, "Historical Marriage Trends from 1890–2010: A Focus on Race Differences" (paper, Population Association of America annual meeting, May 3–5, 2012); Chudacoff, *Age of the Bachelor*, 48.

28 Emily Hawley Gillespie, April 1858, in *My Only Confidant: The Life and Diary of Emily Hawley Gillespie*, ed. Judy N. Lensink, Christine M. Kirkman, and Karen P. Witzke (Iowa City: State Historical Society of Iowa, 1979), 291–92; Oliver Wilcox Norton, December 18, 1864, in *Army Letters*.

29 Uriah W. Oblinger to Mattie V. Thomas, September 14, 1866, Uriah Oblinger Family Collection, Nebraska State Historical Society, digitally collected at the Library of Congress, http://memory.loc.gov/ammem/award98/nbhihtml/pshome.html.

30 Tourgée, *Letters to a King*, 13, 36, 34.

31 Charles W. Plummer Diary, September 27, 1840, Historical Society of Pennsylvania, Philadelphia; Charles W. Plummer is described by his contemporary William Brock Wellons in *The Life and Labors of Rev. William Brock Wellons, D.D.*, ed. and comp. Rev. J. W. Wellons (Raleigh, N.C.: Edwards, Broughton & Co. Steam, Printers and Binders, 1881), 124.

32 Plummer Diary, March 29, 1842.

33 Michael F. Campbell Diary, May 7, 1881, Sterling Library, Yale Special Collections, New Haven, Conn. For other immigrants on the power of turning twenty-one and casting one's first ballot as an American, see Edward W. Bok, *The Americanization of Edward Bok* (New York: Scribner, 1920), 441–46; Joseph J. Mersman, *The Whiskey Merchant's Diary*, ed. Linda A Fisher (Athens: Ohio University Press, 2007), 142.

34 John J. McCarthy, "When I First Voted the Democratic Ticket," collected by Bessie Jollensten, October 19, 1938, American Life Histories: Manuscripts from the Federal Writers' Project, Library of Congress; William Saunders Brown Diary, November 4, 1844, University of Virginia Special Collections, Charlottesville; Leander Stillwell, *The Story of a Common Soldier of Army Life in the Civil War, 1861–1865* (Kansas City: Franklin Hudson Publishing Co., 1920), 96; Campbell Diary, May 7, 1881; Abbott, *Reminiscences*, 105–13; Lew Wallace, *An Autobiography*, vol. 1 (New York: Harper & Brothers, 1906), 205; John C. Chase, "How I Became a Socialist," *Comrade* 2 (November 1902): 109.

35 "The Young Man Who Deposited His Maiden Vote on Nov. 7," *Milwaukee Daily Sentinel*, December 11, 1876.

36 Foster, *Down East Diary*, 69, 141.

37 Plummer Diary, March 29, 1842.
38 Charles G. Hampton, "Twelve Months in Rebel Prisons," in *War Papers Read before the Michigan Commandery of the Loyal Legion of the United States, Volume Two* (Detroit: James H. Stone, 1898), 242.
39 Mary Elizabeth Hawes Van Lennep, April 1842, in *Memoir of Mrs. Mary E. Van Lennep*, ed. Louisa F. Hawes (Hartford, Conn.: Belknap and Hammesley, 1847), 150–57.
40 Emily Hawley Gillespie, April 1859, in *A Secret to Be Buried: The Diary and Life of Emily Hawley Gillespie* (Iowa City: University of Iowa Press, 1989), 19–20; *Phebe M. Hallock Irish Diary*, March 25, 1866 (Philadelphia: Thomas William Stuckey, 1876), 66–67.
41 Annie L. Youmans Van Ness, July 1869, in *Diary of Annie L. Youmans Van Ness, 1864–1881* (Alexandria, Va.: Alexander Street Press, 2004).
42 Mayne, November 4, 1885, November 1, 1882, *Maud*, 361, 136–42.
43 Mattie V. Thomas to Uriah W. Oblinger, September 3, 1868, Oblinger Collection; Thomas, November 1852, in *Secret Eye*, 115–17.
44 Frances E. Willard, *Glimpses of Fifty Years: The Autobiography of an American Woman* (Chicago: Women's Temperance Publication Association, H.J. Smith & Co., 1889), 69–70; Willard, "Address at Washington Meeting of National Council of Women, 1888," extract in *Glimpses of Fifty Years*, 593.
45 Willard, *Glimpses of Fifty Years*, 69, 72.
46 Tourgée, *Letters to a King*, 35.
47 Ibid., 41–42.
48 Kett, *Rites of Passage*, 111–211; David Macleod, *Building Character in the American Boy: The YMCA, the Boy Scouts, and Their Forerunners, 1870–1920* (Madison: University of Wisconsin Press, 1983); Licht, *Getting Work*; Chudacoff, *Age of the Bachelor*; *Before He Is Twenty*.
49 McGerr, *Decline of Popular Politics*; Mark Lawrence Kornbluh, *Why America Stopped Voting: The Decline of Participatory Democracy and the Emergence of Modern American Politics* (New York: New York University Press, 2000); Silbey, *American Political Nation*.
50 "A Lecture to Young Men, L. K. Washburn," *Boston Investigator*, October 3, 1888; also see *Before He Is Twenty*.

5

Statutory Marriage Ages and the Gendered Construction of Adulthood in the Nineteenth Century

NICHOLAS L. SYRETT

When legislators in California first met in 1850, they passed a statute mandating that a man could marry at twenty-one and a woman at eighteen; below those ages they needed parental consent. California, a relative latecomer to the United States, was following a well-established tradition. From the first moment that colonies, and later states, passed laws regulating when young people could marry, or when they might need their parents' permission to do so, almost all kept some age gap intact. The gap in ages, even when raised significantly, stemmed from the English common-law ages for marriage: fourteen for boys and twelve for girls, which themselves had been justified on the basis of when girls and boys were presumed to arrive at puberty. From the seventeenth century till the 1970s, only about one-fifth of the colonies/ states at any point had an equal age of marriage for girls and boys. In all others, and even most of those during certain periods, girls were able to marry before boys, or they could do so earlier without their parents' permission, or both. The age disparity echoed the biological basis in common law and yet, when regulating those in their late teens and early twenties, was no longer about biological capacity to marry, have sex, or reproduce. Legislators were using age to construct gendered adulthood rather than simply to measure the maturation of the human body.[1]

This gap clearly indicated that legislators expected girls to marry before boys, in large part because, unlike boys, girls were not expected to be of an age when they might support a new spouse at the time of their marriage; they were meant to be dependents. A lower age of marriage for girls also reflected beliefs about fertility and pregnancy; allowing girls to marry earlier enabled them to produce more children and, crucially, may have been a way to cut down on pregnancy out of wedlock as well (girls' indentures ended sooner for the same reason). But using lower age standards for girls, while in keeping with these goals, also had contradictory effects. Different marriage laws, and the differential ages of majority that I argue stemmed from them, allowed girls to make adult-like decisions and gain some privileges before boys. This was clearly not in keeping with a regime that emphasized the greater legal capacities of men, not women. Until the twentieth century, women did not vote or serve in the military, so the ages of twenty-one and eighteen were largely meaningless for them. But in the realm of marriage, women reached the crucial age markers before men did, allowing them legal capacities that their brothers did not possess until they became older.[2]

I argue that lower statutory ages of marriage allowed—or forced, depending on your perspective—girls to become adults earlier than boys. This essay is concerned with the contradictions that inhered in these marriage laws, what those differences meant in practice, and what all of this can tell us about how age and sex worked in tandem to construct differently gendered versions of adulthood in the nineteenth and early twentieth centuries. In legislators' eyes age was a descriptive characteristic, a way of dividing those girls and women who were ready for marriage from those who were not. However, because the marriage contract is meant to be voluntary, indeed can be nullified if entered through force or coercion, picking specific ages above which girls could make their own choices about marriage also empowered those same girls. For state legislators, age functioned to describe a class of people, but it also imbued those people with legal capabilities; this is what produced the contradictory outcomes.[3]

The disadvantages of lower ages of marriage were much discussed by nineteenth-century women's rights advocates. But that the laws' unintended consequences sometimes benefited women has received far less attention. Persuasive arguments can be made in support of both the disadvantages and the advantages of these lower ages. One useful way of thinking about the issue is that lower ages of marriage (and their relationship with a lower female age of majority, which I discuss below) were detrimental to women in the aggregate, but beneficial to some girls and women individually. The dual nature of the outcomes is more comprehensible if we remember that the legislators who passed the statutes were in the position of thinking of themselves as both (potential) husbands and fathers, and that these two roles might have different interests. A lower age of marriage could benefit men in search of wives, and a state or colony in need of more legitimate children, even as it worked to erode paternal control. A lower female age of majority allowed women to control property in a way that might benefit potential husbands or the men with whom they might do business, even though it also undermined fathers' and guardians' control of women and their property. Beside the fact that almost all state legislators demonstrated their belief that age of marriage was significant by regulating it (for women and men), it is clear that age, especially when combined with sex, was not neutral. It was also contradictory: it circumscribed women's lives even as it might also give them unexpected opportunities.

***

State legislatures could approach the marriage age question in one of five ways. They could pass no law on the subject, in which case the minimum ages were understood to be the common-law ages of fourteen and twelve (for boys and girls) and no parental permission was required. This strategy was most common in the South where early marriage was frequent. One modification of this was to avoid setting overall minimums in a state's marriage law, but to criminalize the act of marrying a girl below a certain age without her father's or parents' permission. This was usually done to protect inherited property and was also more common in southern states. It amounted to having a minimum age for girls but not for boys. The third option was that states could set minimum marriageable ages for both sexes; until the 1970s almost all colonies and states that chose this route instituted different ages for men and women. This strategy was most common in the states of the Midwest, which tended to pass marriage legislation upon organizing as territories and often used each other's statutes as models. Fourth, states could choose no minimums, and stipulate only that those below certain ages (usually twenty-one for boys, eighteen for girls) required parental permission. In those states, the common-law ages of fourteen and twelve were retained as the minimum marriage ages. Reflecting a concern for familial order and filial deference, this strategy was common in New England and usually dated from the colonial period. Finally, states could combine the last two practices and set both minimums and ages below which children required consent. Eventually all states adopted this position, some more recently than others. State legislatures that chose any option that necessitated parental consent were walking a middle ground, preserving the rights of fathers to oversee their children's marriage choices, at the same time setting maximum ages above which they believed that young people should have the right to marry. Potential husbands could benefit in this situation, but only if fathers approved of them.

We have little comprehensive data about the rates of early marriage nationwide until 1880, when the U.S. Census Bureau began to publish reports that linked age with marital status. That said, individual states sometimes kept vital records (Massachusetts was the first, beginning in 1842), and there is plentiful evidence of individual cases from across the growing nation to indicate that marriage in the middle teen years, and sometimes earlier, while by no means the norm, was relatively common. In New York State in 1847, for instance, of the 11,347 marriages reported that year, 3,013 brides were younger than twenty, compared to only 325 grooms. Twenty years later, Massachusetts found that of 14,300 marriages that year, 2,877 brides were younger than twenty (including 13 widows) and only 237 grooms, meaning that about one-fifth of the women who married in 1867 did so before they reached legal adulthood in that state. Of these, 587 were under eighteen; the youngest recorded bride in Massachusetts in 1867 was twelve. The numbers, documenting just a handful of states, tell us only so much. But combined with the fact that most state legislatures regulated the age of marriage and most state high courts heard some cases where age of marriage was at the heart of a dispute, it is clear that young people married throughout the nineteenth-century United States.[4]

***

It is also clear that parents, judges, social reformers, and legislators debated their ability to do so. The question of the advantages and disadvantages of early marriage for girls depended largely on perspective: To whom was it advantageous and why? Who benefited and for what reasons? Mid-nineteenth-century women's rights activists believed that society encouraged early marriage for girls, that it was detrimental to them, and that parents should not permit their daughters to marry before they had been educated or trained in particular skills. These activists were often blind to the class implications of such arguments, in that working-class girls might have little to gain through the postponement of marriage; the activists clearly saw young marriage as detrimental both to individual wives and to women as a whole. While they rarely framed their arguments in terms of specific states' statutes, they did invoke common-law ages of majority and of marriage and noted that girls were legally able to marry at younger ages than boys. Activists like Abby Kelly Foster, Matilda Joslyn Gage, Lydia Pierson, and members of the influential Blackwell family all railed against early marriage in women's rights conventions during the 1850s. They wanted to protect girlhood as a period of life, which they believed was too quickly foreshortened by early marriage. Some also argued that young brides made for bad mothers and that early marriage was indicative of a decline in civilization and the degeneration of Americans. Others pointed specifically at the inequalities of marriage law, and their critique is the most germane to this essay.[5]

Elizabeth Oakes Smith, who herself married at sixteen, wrote extensively about early marriage in a series of columns in the *New York Tribune* beginning in 1850, later assembled in a single volume called *Woman and Her Needs*, published the next year. Writing of the marriage contract itself, Smith contrasted the two who were entering it: "One party is mature in life—experienced not only in the world, but in the nature of his own soul, its needs, its capacities, infirmities, and powers. The other party is a child, an infant in law, whose pen to a commercial contract would be worthless. . . . Yet this girl, this child, is party to a contract involving the well-being of her whole future life; a contract by which she is consigned to sickness, care, suffering, coercion, and her individuality completely suppressed." Using the actual legal language of the common law and some state statutes—"infant" and "idiot"—to talk about those who were incapable of contracting, she highlighted the problem with allowing children to contract marriage: "Can she, who is an infant, an idiot in a worthless account of dollars and cents, be capable of entering into a contract involving such tremendous interest? Can this child, whose nature has been so outraged even before she can even understand its laws, be held responsible for after results?" Smith went on to indict any man (which would presumably have included her own husband) who would enter such a contract with a legal infant, precisely because he was availing himself of her inexperience in gaining her assent to the marriage in the first place. The problem for Smith was not just that early marriage abbreviated the joys of girlhood (which was really a problem for girls privileged enough to enjoy such a period in their lives) but also that they were too young to understand the import of their decision.[6]

Elizabeth Cady Stanton agreed, framing her concerns in terms of the youthfulness of some brides, and also emphasizing just how much a young girl did not understand of the legal implications of any marriage she might enter. Women's rights advocates targeted coverture—the legal inequality of marriage derived from the common law—in its own right, so for Smith, Stanton, and others like them, the reason that early marriage was particularly problematic was that the contract itself was so detrimental to women's autonomy. It was one thing for grown women to submit to its terms, quite another for a girl who did not understand what she was getting herself into to agree to be bound by its strictures. In an 1860 letter to the editor of the *New York Tribune*, Stanton explained, "The contract of marriage is by no means equal. The law permits the girl to marry at twelve years of age, while it requires several years more of experience on the part of the boy. In entering this compact, the man gives up nothing that he before possessed—he is a man still; while the legal existence of the woman is suspended during marriage, and henceforth she is known but in and through the husband. She is nameless, purseless, childless—though a woman, an heiress, and a mother." While by 1860 activists like Stanton had been successful in modifying some of the regulations of coverture as they related to women's right to retain property or earnings, much of the institution remained hopelessly skewed against women. The fact that these activists recognized the cruel unfairness of the marriage contract—for all women—only intensified their belief that girls should not be encouraged or permitted to enter it.[7]

For this reason, and because a lower age of marriage for girls presumed wifely submission and dependence, equalization of the marriage age remained on the legislative agenda for women's rights groups well into the twentieth century, to which I return below. On the whole, however, mid-nineteenth-century women's rights activists tended to focus on cultural reasons for early marriage, not the law that allowed for it. And in an era when common-law or informal marriage was quite frequent, the law was not as effective at regulating the institution of marriage as it is now. That said, the law of marriage is still significant both as a symbol of legislators' own prescriptions for marriage and because it had real consequences. Even at a time when age consciousness may have had less traction in the United States, many young girls married because legally their states allowed them to. That the law allowed for this encouraged parents to believe that it was acceptable, and so they consented to the unions of their youthful daughters. Returning to the effects of the law thus remains worthwhile. It is also where we see the contradictions that allow us to appreciate that while early marriage might be detrimental for women in the aggregate, some girls took advantage of the ability to make marital decisions at early ages in ways that did benefit them individually.

The first set of contradictions is broad in scope: Girls got to make decisions (and not just about marriage, as I will demonstrate presently) at an earlier age than boys did, even though most Americans were agreed that greater age allowed human beings the capacity to fully understand their decisions, the ability to practice informed consent. This was the revolution in the understanding of consent that Holly Brewer writes about in *By Birth or Consent*. Even in a society that generally did not put much stock in girls' or women's intellectual development, girls were presumed capable of making the decision to marry sooner than boys were. Of course, as we have seen, women's rights advocates did not believe that young girls were really capable of making the choice to marry, that they were coerced into this decision. Nevertheless, as parental influence over marriage partners waned by the nineteenth century, allowing girls to make this decision before boys was not insignificant. Second, girls could legally have sex earlier than boys could. When these laws were first passed, fornication statutes were still on the books, and still very much enforced in some places: legally sex was supposed to take place in marriage alone. And while historians have demonstrated that understandings about female passion underwent profound shifts during the late eighteenth and early nineteenth centuries—with women increasingly understood to be passionless—almost all states gave legal sanction to *earlier* legal sexual activity for girls than boys. Both of these contradictions can be explained away if we discount the degree to which legislators actually thought about what girls themselves wanted, a not unreasonable supposition: letting girls marry earlier was what men wanted, in other words. Precisely because women did not benefit from aging and its attendant rights and responsibilities the way men did, it did not much matter when girls married because their femaleness trumped their age. So these laws were passed because they suited male legislators' needs and desires, even if they also gave girls a certain amount of decision-making power and the right of having sex legally earlier than boys.[8]

But even if it is clear that the laws were not passed to benefit women, what strikes me about the laws are the ways they could inadvertently upend a legal order that clearly favored men. It is in those moments that we most see men's rights as potential husbands trumping their rights as fathers. For instance, a girl who wanted to escape a volatile home life was legally empowered to do so at an earlier age than her brother, because marriage to whomever she herself chose legally emancipated her from the control of her father. In an 1844 Pennsylvania case Juliann Bertron married without her father's permission, but still above the common-law age of twelve for girls. She testified that when her father was in "the habit of intoxication" he frequently forced her and her mother outside to sleep in the stable. While she admitted that he did this only when he drank and when sober was "kind enough," the drinking was habitual and she married her husband after an acquaintance of only three or four days. Juliann Bertron thus married to escape an intolerable home life; she could do so at a younger age and in defiance of her father's wishes because the laws of Pennsylvania allowed her to do so.[9]

Marriage law also affected labor. During the period of minority—which under the common law was twenty-one—girls and boys owed service to their parents. After they reached the age of majority, or they married, the fruits of their labor were legally their own if they were boys, or their husband's if they were girls. So an earlier age of marriage allowed a girl, especially after the passage of some of the married women's property acts of the mid-nineteenth century, to work for her chosen family instead of for her father, and to do so at an earlier age than her brother, for instance. In an 1881 case from Mississippi, Richard Holland's daughter married without his permission and below the age of eighteen. Holland sued the official who had improperly issued her the marriage license, arguing that the clerk's actions had deprived him of his daughter's services. The Mississippi Supreme Court held, as most state supreme courts did, that while the clerk should not have issued the license, the marriage was nevertheless valid and Holland's daughter could not be required to serve her father any longer. In this case Holland's unnamed daughter had broken the law to marry, but in all states where the minimum marriage age was lower for girls than boys, or those like Mississippi that used the common-law ages as their minimums, any girl who married above those minimum ages, illegally or not, was no longer obligated to serve her father, either by working for him in his home or by turning over her wages to him. Marriage could emancipate her from parental control, and it could almost always do so earlier for a girl than for her brother. While this might well mean that she simply transferred the obligation of service to her husband, from the perspective of the young wife herself, working on behalf of the family she had chosen, rather than the one into which she was born, may well have been a meaningful distinction.[10]

Marriage also terminated guardianship. Anyone who had inherited and had that inheritance held by a guardian was entitled to the control of the inheritance at the age of twenty-one or at marriage. So while the fate of a married girl's inheritance probably depended a good deal upon the behavior of her husband, the fact remained that the inheritance did pass to her upon her marriage, which could always happen earlier for her than for her brother. In another Mississippi case, this from 1838, Frances Nixon Wood used her marriage as a minor to gain control of the estate that was being held for her by her guardian. Marriage, the Mississippi Supreme Court held, terminated a minor's wardship; her guardian was thus obligated to deliver to Robert N. Wood, Frances's husband, "all the goods, effects, and property, belonging to said ward [Frances], according to law." The doctrine of coverture meant the property was now controlled by Robert, not Frances, and we cannot know if he did a better job in its management than her guardian might have done. From Frances's perspective, however, marriage may have provided access to what she saw as her rightful inheritance. And marriage was legally possible for Frances at a younger age than it would have been for any brother she might have had.[11]

Perhaps the most important age-related difference between boys and girls was the age of majority, which I have already alluded to several times. Under the common law, in use in all the English colonies before the United States became a country, and in continued use afterward (often codified through statute), the age of majority was twenty-one; below that age, one was legally an infant. At the age of twenty-one a man or woman could inherit in his or her own name and control that property, convey real estate, keep his or her own wages, and make a will; it was also the age of voting for men (subject to property and racial and residence qualifications so long as those lasted). There were limits, of course, to the meanings of being of full legal age, especially because there were always other ages that made young men and women adult-like before the age of majority: not just marriage, but the ability to support oneself through waged labor, for instance, or to serve in the military. And of course the period of minority was meant to protect minors, who were perceived as being too young to make many important decisions; certain contracts (though not marriage) were voidable because of infancy. In its most basic formulation, the age of majority was the age at which one became an adult and was thus legally significant. It was, if nothing else, the age at which a father was no longer able to legally control his children. Legally they weren't "children" anymore.[12]

All of this may seem unrelated to the age of marriage. But the vast majority of western and midwestern states as well as two in the East, Arkansas and Vermont, actually modified the common-law age of majority through statute. They lowered the age of majority for women by three years, meaning that in those states women were legal adults earlier than men were. The statutory age of majority for women aligned with one of their marriage ages in almost all of these states; the new age of majority for women, eighteen, was the age below which they were required to have parental consent to marry. States that lowered their ages of majority did so, in most cases, after they had set their ages of marriage. California, for instance, revised its ages of majority in 1854, four years after passing its marriage statute; the ages were identical. I argue that states made women legal adults at eighteen because they had already allowed them to marry at that age. They saw marriage as the purpose of adulthood for women and they wanted women to have the rights to their property as they entered marriage, rights that would, of course, be circumscribed through marriage. While this lowered age of majority was not meant to benefit women, it inadvertently gave some women the ability to exercise the perquisites of adult citizens three years earlier than their brothers.[13]

In trying to evaluate whether or not this is significant, bear in mind that even in those states that did not have a lower age of majority, girls already achieved their majority through marriage. And if they were wards their guardianship ceased and they got their property if they had any. Marriage below the age of majority made for a seamless transition from the status of female infant to that of wife. If the only thing that legislators were concerned about was the safe passage of property from a woman—who was temporarily holding it because her father or another relative had died—to a husband, marriage *already* did this, no matter what the age of majority was, eighteen or twenty-one.[14] So aside from the fact that the legislatures actually did pass the laws in the first place, that they wrote them this way has to be significant, has to mean that they believed there was some consequence to them. Making women adults before men was legally meaningful, and yet also somewhat contradictory: these states were declaring girls to have greater legal capacities than their same-aged male peers.

While some of the bills that fixed this lower age of majority reveal very little of the legislators' intent, others tell us much more. In Ohio's 1834 Act for Fixing the Age of Majority, for instance, the legislators declared that men of at least twenty-one years and women of at least eighteen "shall be capable of contracting respecting goods, chattels, lands, tenements and any other matter or thing which may be the legitimate subject of a contract." The second part of the act repealed any laws in the state that "restrain any unmarried female person, of the age of eighteen years and upward, from making any contract, or from conveying any lands, tenements or hereditaments." When California updated its minority statute to clarify what the common law already said, that marriage ended a girl's minority, the senator proposing the amendment explained "that the object of the bill was to allow married females under the legal age of majority (eighteen) to sign contracts, deeds of conveyance, in conjunction with their husbands, etc."[15]

A similar focus on property animates the laws where differential minority is spelled out through guardianship statutes. Guardians had a number of duties on behalf of their wards, but property management was one of them. In the statutes of four states the stipulation about girls' minority ending at eighteen is tacked on at the end of a section where financial arrangements are addressed. After explaining that guardians shall manage the money and property of their wards and have the ability to lease their real estate, the statutes end by explaining that "such leasing shall never be for a longer time than during the minority of the ward; and the minority of females shall cease at the age of 18 years." Given the subject matter of the clause itself, this reads as something of an afterthought, but its placement is crucial in revealing the intent of lawmakers: the management of girls' property by their guardians ceased at eighteen, when they were legally adults. This was the true meaning of girls' different age of majority in these states: girls could manage any property they had earlier than boys could. As one Iowa legislator explained, "[T]he female is to reach her majority at the age of eighteen years, and is a legal 'infant' under that age, as in Iowa (being unable to contract marriage except by consent of parent or guardian, and by marriage she as all minors attains majority). . . . The evident intent of the law is to protect her property interests during that period." That period ended three years earlier for Iowa girls than it did for their brothers because they were expected to marry earlier.[16]

There are a couple reasons that newer and more western states were the ones that modified the common law to declare eighteen the age of majority for girls. The vast majority of them had been settled as territories after the colonial period; their ties to English legal culture had not been established prior to statehood and they felt less need to abide by it. It also seems logical that in midwestern and western states, especially as they were coming into being (and many of these statutes date from the territorial period), legislators were concerned about the ability of people to marry and to sell and convey property when their parents might not be present, either because they had not accompanied them on the journeys to these western territories or because they had died en route or after arrival. Statutes like these allowed for the easier transfer of property in places where death was not uncommon and where it was essential that property could pass from person to person in order to encourage settlement.

But these are the reasons that the laws were passed. What about their consequences? While a good argument can be made that making girls adults at eighteen actually deprived them of the protection that being a minor was meant to ensure, it was also the case that individual girls might find they could control their own destinies in ways that boys could not, or at least they could do so three years earlier than boys could. A number of examples attest to this. In 1859, a twenty-year-old woman named Emily McDonough had her lawyer file a writ of habeas corpus on her behalf, claiming that she was being held against her will by her father. Because she was twenty and thus "above the age of majority for females" in California, the judge granted the writ and ordered her released. Age of majority also factored in inheritance where it was customary to dictate in a will that one's minor children would receive their inheritance when they reached their majority. When Joanna Raymond died in 1872, she left the bulk of her estate to her husband but also various amounts to her children from a previous marriage, two sons to inherit at age twenty-one and a daughter at age eighteen. All three were also to receive "board, lodging, and protection until they arrive at the age of majority." The daughter, Mary McCarthy, received less money and three years' fewer board and lodging, but she also got her money earlier. In this case parents like Joanna Raymond and state legislators seem to have been in agreement in their expectation that girls would never really be independent; they collectively expected Mary McCarthy to marry earlier than her brothers, thus obviating her need for support through the age of twenty-one. It is debatable whether Mary McCarthy was better off than her brothers in this scenario, but given that Mary was not really going to be in better shape until the entire legal regime was restructured to eliminate gender-based discrimination sometime in the late twentieth century, this might be better than nothing. It was a gendered expectation, filtered through the legal device of age, which had given Mary McCarthy something that her brothers lacked.[17]

Ambivalence about the different ages in the laws is also apparent in the early twentieth century as the National Woman's Party, concurrent with their plans for a federal Equal Rights Amendment, set about trying to dismantle all the state laws that made women and men unequal. The author of a 1922 report called "Michigan Laws Discriminating Against Women," noted that "under the Common Law, women were 'protected' from themselves in being placed *under the guardianship of father* or husband." When "protected" is in quotations marks, the cynical point here is that women don't need this protection, and that indeed it is not protection at all: it is control. They say this explicitly: "Modern women do not wish 'protection' as inferior beings." Note, however, that one of the protections that the NWP was eschewing was the guardianship of a father to his daughter, not just of a husband to his wife. Just six pages later when describing the differential marriage ages in Michigan, the author notes that "since minority is meant as a protection to young people, the law should extend this protection to girls as long as boys." While the National Woman's Party was seeking to equalize all laws, even the ones that would in some ways end up disadvantaging women, they also seem not to be able to make up their minds about whether "protection" is a good thing or not. Clearly they believed that protecting grown women amounted to consigning them to inferiority, but they also advocated for more protection for girls. The difference, of course, was one of age. That the NWP's attitude toward minority and parental consent was sometimes contradictory (even within the same document) is not surprising, however, given what we have already learned. Eschewing protection could be detrimental for women, but sometimes it was beneficial; it depended upon whether the woman in question was being "protected" by her father or her husband and what her relationship with each might have been. The very thing that disadvantaged one girl was the best hope of another.[18]

Almost thirty years later, in 1950, when much had changed for American women, Frieda S. Miller, director of the U.S. Women's Bureau, under the auspices of Maurice J. Tobin, secretary of the U.S. Department of Labor, compiled a listing of what she called "State Laws of Special Interest to Women." They described this as "a simple digest . . . of significant State laws which have particular value for women." They divided each state's laws into those that benefited wives and mothers, widows, or working women. Varying state by state, the section for wives and mothers tended to describe some combination of a husband's support obligations, a wife's right in regard to her own earnings, and occasionally her right to live free from "dangerously violent conduct." For many states, among the advantages for women was that "legal age of consent to marriage [is] lower for females" and, in states where it remained true, "earlier age of majority for females." Chronicling the forty-eight states of the day, the memos listed thirty states with a lower age of consent to marriage for girls and seven with a lower age of majority. The memos, perhaps because they were based on inaccurate or incomplete sets of revised statutes, were actually undercounting, but the point is that the compilers saw both lower ages as advantages for women and girls. This was as debatable in 1950 as it was exactly one hundred years earlier when Elizabeth Oakes Smith identified the lower age of marriage as one of women's primary obstacles to full equality. By 1950, with the age of first marriage plummeting to an all-century low, the ability to marry at a younger age was cast as an advantage, not just by some individual girls who wanted that right, but by the United States Women's Bureau, an organization founded to advance the rights of working women.[19]

American women in 1950 were living in a society that would have been unrecognizable to their predecessors of a century earlier. And indeed that women were still marrying earlier and forsaking their educations to do so would have horrified the likes of Elizabeth Oakes Smith. The midcentury glorification of early marriage was to prove short-lived; the advantages that Miller and her colleagues at the Women's Bureau saw in the ability to marry early in 1950 were precisely those decried by organized feminists just over a decade later, when Betty Friedan pointed to early marriage as one of the factors leading to "the problem that has no name."[20] It also bears noting that the advantages that some married girls had made of youthful marriage in earlier eras—the way that it allowed them to claim legal adulthood and all that could mean for them— were not what Cold War teenage brides tended to see in the institution. These few brief examples highlighting key differences and disagreements, however, lead us back to the central point: the legal possibility for girls' early marriage was never always positive or always negative. Its benefits and disadvantages depended on one's individual circumstances and whether one evaluated the effects of early marriage in the aggregate or at the individual level.

***

In 1975 the U.S. Supreme Court, in *Stanton v. Stanton*, a Utah case adjudicating the obligation of a man to support his minor son longer than his minor daughter, ruled that different ages of majority for men and women were unconstitutional; that ruling only further affirmed that different marital ages might also be so.[21] While some states had already eliminated the gendered age differences in their marriage laws, by the late 1970s and 1980s almost all other states followed suit, equalizing both minimum ages and those below which children needed their parents' consent.[22] These changes were guided by the belief that marriage was not supposed to be a different experience for men and women. Though that ideal is far from a reality—and one symptom of this is that girls continue to marry earlier than boys nationwide, with much larger numbers of them doing so as legal minors—the legal distinction between boys and girls in terms of age and marriage law has largely been eliminated. When it did exist, however, it was clearly a gendered prescription: an expression of legislators' beliefs about how marriage should function and the roles they believed that wives and husbands were meant to fulfill. But precisely because this was a prescription that was legally determined on the terrain of age, the laws produced unintended consequences. Encouraging girls to pursue one path at earlier ages necessitated allowing them to choose that path, but once they were permitted to do that, some of them might make choices contrary to those envisioned by legislators. Age was a marker that allowed legislators to write gendered expectations into the law, but also a legal tool that girls could manipulate to their own ends. That it functioned as both simultaneously is what produced the divergent and contradictory outcomes.

NOTES

1 *The Statutes of California, Passed at the First Session of the Legislature* (San Jose: J. Winchester, State Printer, 1850), 424–25; William Blackstone, *Commentaries on the Laws of England*, 4 vols. (Oxford: Clarendon, 1765–69), 1:424–25. While it is difficult to ascertain when exactly boys and girls actually reached puberty in early modern England—and most evidence for the colonies suggests that twelve and fourteen would be earlier than what was common—legal commentators relied on puberty as the explanation for the ages. See Henry Swinburne, *A Treatise of Spousals or Matrimonial Contracts: Wherein All the Questions Relating to That Subject Are Ingeniously Debated and Resolved* (London: S. Roycroft, 1686), 47; Joan Jacobs Brumberg, *The Body Project: An Intimate History of American Girls* (New York: Random House, 1997), 3–4, 23, chap. 2. Most states with an equal age had no minimum marriageable age and simply mandated that those below twenty-one (or under their parents' control, which meant age twenty-one) required parental consent. These states' minimum ages, by default, would have been the differently gendered twelve and fourteen, meaning that even those that appeared to be equal were not really so; Connecticut, Massachusetts, Pennsylvania, and Rhode Island fall into this category. See *The Code of 1650, Being a Compilation of the Earliest*

Laws and Orders of the General Court of Connecticut (1821; repr., Storrs, Conn.: Bibliopola Press, 1999), 68; *The Acts and Resolves, Public and Private, of the Province of the Massachusetts Bay* (Boston: Wright and Potter, 1869), 1:61; *Purdon's Digest: A Digest of the Laws of Pennsylvania, from the Year One Thousand Seven Hundred, to the Twenty-Second Day of April, One Thousand Eight-Hundred and Forty-Six*, 7th ed. (Philadelphia: James Kay Jr., and Brother, 1852), 794–95. Rhode Island, in the colonial period, made it necessary for a girl (but not a boy) to obtain her parents' consent to marry but by the late nineteenth century amended the law to read like the ones cited above, i.e., permission for minors of both sexes. See *General Laws of the State of Rhode Island and Providence Plantations* (Providence: E. L. Freeman and Son, 1896), 623. Tennessee, for most of its time, maintained the common law ages of marriage by default because it had no law on age of marriage, and later passed statutory law setting sixteen as the marriageable age for both boys and girls. See *Public Acts of the State of Tennessee Passed by the Seventieth General Assembly* (Nashville: Printing Department, Tennessee Industrial School, 1937), 262–65. And Florida, despite a nominally equal age for boys and girls, also made it a crime to marry a girl, and only a girl, below the age of eighteen without her parents' consent. See *Compilation of the Public Acts of the Legislative Council of the Territory of Florida, Passed Prior to 1840* (Tallahassee: Samuel P. Sisley, 1839), 88 and *Compiled General Laws of Florida, 1927* (Atlanta: Harrison Company, 1929), 2327. Idaho began as a territory with unequal ages but switched to eighteen for both sexes in 1887. See *Compiled and Revised Laws of the Territory of Idaho* (Boise City: Milton Kelly, 1875), 643–44. Colorado and North Carolina both had differential ages for most of their history, but switched to equal ages in 1945 and 1947, respectively. See *Colorado Revised Statutes, 1953* (Chicago: Callaghan, 1953), 4:618; *State of North Carolina, 1947 Session Laws and Resolutions* (Raleigh: Published by Authority, 1947), 455.

2 On the meaninglessness of age markers for women, see Corinne T. Field, "'Are Women . . . All Minors?': Woman's Rights and the Politics of Aging in the Antebellum United States," *Journal of Women's History* 12, no. 4 (Winter 2001): 113–37.

3 For more on this final point, see Steven Mintz, "Reflections on Age as a Category of Historical Analysis," *Journal of the History of Childhood and Youth* 1, no. 1 (Winter 2008): 91–92.

4 Norma Basch, *In the Eyes of the Law: Women, Marriage, and Property in Nineteenth-Century New York* (Ithaca, N.Y.: Cornell University Press, 1982), 178; *Twenty-Sixth Report to the Legislature of Massachusetts, Relating to the Registry and Return of Births, Marriages, and Deaths in the Commonwealth, for the Year Ending December 31, 1867* (Boston: Wright & Potter, State Printers, 1869), 18–21. While Massachusetts collected vital statistics beginning in 1842, the published reports do not record anything beyond the average age of marriage until 1845; from that year onward the reports make clear that the number of girls who married as legal minors was always higher than the corresponding number for

boys and that there were always a handful of girls who married as young as twelve, thirteen, and fourteen. See *Fourth Annual Report to the Legislature, Relating to the Registry and Returns of Births, Marriages, and Deaths in Massachusetts, for the Year Ending April 30th, 1845* (Boston: Dutton and Wentworth, Printers to the State, 1845), 38–40, 75–78.

5 *The Proceedings of the Woman's Rights Convention, Held at Syracuse, September 8th, 9th, 10th, 1852* (Syracuse, N.Y.: J. E. Masters, 1852), 40; *Proceedings of the Ohio Women's Convention, Held at Salem, April 19th and 20th, 1850* (Cleveland: Smead and Cowles, 1850), 20–21; Nancy F. Cott, *Public Vows: A History of Marriage and the Nation* (Cambridge, Mass.: Harvard University Press, 2002), 11–12; Basch, *In the Eyes of the Law*, 17; Marylynn Salmon, *Women and the Law of Property in Early America* (Chapel Hill: University of North Carolina Press, 1986), xv.

6 E. Oakes Smith, "Woman and Her Needs, No. V," *New York Tribune*, March 4, 1851, 3; Elizabeth Oakes Smith, *Woman and Her Needs* (New York: Fowler and Wells, 1851).

7 Elizabeth Cady Stanton to the editor of the *New York Tribune*, May 30, 1860, quoted in Elizabeth Cady Stanton, Susan B. Anthony, and Matilda Joslyn Gage, eds., *History of Woman Suffrage*, 6 vols. (Rochester, N.Y.: Charles Mann, 1889), 1:738.

8 Holly Brewer, *By Birth or Consent: Children, Law, and the Anglo-American Revolution in Authority* (Chapel Hill: University of North Carolina Press, 2005), esp. introduction; Nancy Cott, "Passionlessness: An Interpretation of Victorian Sexual Ideology, 1790–1850," *Signs* 4 (1978): 219–36. For the argument about women's aging being trumped by their femaleness, see Corinne T. Field, *The Struggle for Equal Adulthood: Gender, Race, Age, and the Fight for Citizenship in Antebellum America* (Chapel Hill: University of North Carolina Press, 2014).

9 *Stansbury v. Bertron*, 7 Watts & Serg. 362 (Pennsylvania, 1844). Pennsylvania's marriage statute stipulated that children below the age of twenty-one required their parents' consent to marriage, but judges routinely ruled that those who married without that permission were still legally wed if over the common law ages of twelve or fourteen, even if they (or the official who issued them a license) had broken the law in order to marry.

10 *Holland v. Beard*, 59 Miss. 161 (1881). While Mississippi passed the earliest married women's property act (in 1839), it pertained only to real property that a woman brought into a marriage, not to her wages (if she earned any), and it would not have nullified her duty to serve her husband by laboring in his home, another facet of coverture, which itself was predicated on the understanding that a husband would owe support to his wife in return. On women and property, see Salmon, *Women and the Law of Property*.

11 *Wood and Wife v. Henderson*, 3 Miss. 893 (1838); Ransom H. Tyler, *Commentaries on the Law of Infancy* (Albany, N.Y.: William Gould and Son, 1882), 135–36; Frank Keezer, *The Law of Marriage and Divorce* (Boston: William J. Nagel, 1906), 21; Michael Grossberg, *Governing the Hearth: Law and Family in Nineteenth-Century*

America (Chapel Hill: University of North Carolina Press, 1985), 95–96, 106–7; Nicholas L. Syrett, "'I Did and I Don't Regret It': Child Marriage and the Contestation of Childhood in the United States, 1880–1925," *Journal of the History of Childhood and Youth* 6, no. 2 (Spring 2013): 314–31.

12 James Kent, *Commentaries on American Law*, 2nd ed. (New York: O. Halsted, 1832), 2:233; Blackstone, *Commentaries*, 1:451; T. E. James, "The Age of Majority," *American Journal of Legal History* 4 (1960): 22–33. See also Barbara Young Welke, *Law and the Borders of Belonging in the Long Nineteenth Century United States* (New York: Cambridge University Press, 2010), 12–13.

13 The age when girls' indentures ended, in the common law and in many state statutes, was also lower for girls than for boys, but it did not necessarily match their age of majority. My contention would be that these lower indenture ages were themselves a result of the expectation that girls marry at earlier ages, meaning that both ages (indenture and majority) actually tie back to marriage. The states that modified the age of majority were Arkansas (in 1873: *A Digest of the Statutes of Arkansas* [Columbia, Mo.: E. W. Stephens, 1894], 874); California (in 1854: *The Statutes of California Passed at the Fifth Session of the Legislature, January 4, 1854 to May 15, 1854* [Sacramento: B. B. Redding, State Printer, 1854], 44); Colorado (at least by 1867: *Revised Statutes of Colorado, Passed at the Seventh Session of the Legislative Assembly* [Central City: David C. Collier, 1868], 348); Hawaii (by 1884, when still the Kingdom of Hawaii, to eighteen and twenty: *Compiled Laws of the Hawaiian Kingdom* [Honolulu: Hawaiian Gazette, 1884], 483); Idaho (in 1864: *Laws of the Territory of Idaho, First Session* [Lewiston: James A. Glascock, 1864], 515); Illinois (probably in 1809: *The Statutes of Illinois: An Analytical Digest of all the General Laws of the State, in Force at the Present Time, 1818–1868* [Chicago: E. B. Myers and Company, 1868], 332); Iowa (in 1839: *Revised Statutes of the Territory of Iowa* [Iowa City: Hughes and Williams, 1843], 432); Kansas (in 1868: *General Statutes of the State of Kansas* [Lawrence: John Speer, 1868], 580); Minnesota (at least by 1866: *The General Statutes of the State of Minnesota* [St. Paul: Davidson & Hall, 1866], 399); Missouri (at least by 1879: *The Revised Statutes of the State of Missouri, 1889* [Jefferson City: Tribune Printing Company, 1889], 1274); Montana (at least by 1879: *The Revised Statutes of Montana* [Springfield, Ill.: H. W. Rokker, 1881], 554); Nebraska (at least by 1866 as a territory: *The Revised Statutes of the Territory of Nebraska* [Omaha: E. B. Taylor, 1866], 178); Nevada (in 1861: *The Compiled Laws of the State of Nevada, Statutes of 1861 to 1873, Inclusive* [Carson City: Charles A. V. Putnam, 1873], 105); North Dakota and South Dakota (at least by 1877 as Dakota Territory: *The Revised Codes of the Territory of Dakota, A.D. 1877* [Canton, D.T.: Sioux Valley News, 1883], 208; on the retention at statehood, see *The Revised Codes of the State of North Dakota, 1895* [Bismarck: Tribune Company, 1895], 606, and *The Revised Codes 1903, State of South Dakota* [Pierre: Ripple Printing Co., 1904], 593); Ohio (in 1834: *The Public Statutes at Large of the State of Ohio: From the Close of Chase's Statutes, February 1833, to the Present Time* [Cincinnati: n.p., 1853], 116); Oklahoma (in 1890: *The*

Statutes of Oklahoma, 1890 [Guthrie: State Capital Printing Co., 1891], 752); Oregon (in 1864: *The Organic and Other General Laws of Oregon* [n.p.: Eugene Semple, 1874], 564); Utah (in 1852: *The Compiled Laws of the Territory of Utah, Containing All the General Statutes Now in Force* [Salt Lake City: Deseret News Steam, 1876], 345); Vermont (at least by 1839: *The Revised Statutes of the State of Vermont, Passed November 10, 1839* [Burlington: Chauncey Goodrich, 1840], 319, 331); and Washington (in 1866: *Code of Washington Containing All Acts of a General Nature* [Olympia: C. B. Bagley, 1881], 409). Maryland did not have a separate age of majority for girls but did pass a law that allowed a girl to convey real estate before boys, at age eighteen. See James Kent, *Commentaries on American Law*, rev. ed., ed. William M. Lacy (Philadelphia: Blackstone, 1889), 2:36.

14 The common law was pretty clear about this, but so too were individual state statutes, which tended to spell out the fact that a girl's minority ceased at her marriage. California updated its 1854 law in 1858, declaring the differential ages of majority in order to make it perfectly clear that a married woman below the age of eighteen was also no longer a minor. See *The Statutes of California Passed at the Ninth Session of the Legislature* (Sacramento: John O'Meara, State Printer, 1858), 108; "California Legislature," *Sacramento Daily Union*, February 24, 1858, 1.

15 *Public Statutes at Large of the State of Ohio*, 116; *Laws of the Territory of Idaho*, 515; *Revised Statutes of* Montana, 554; *Compiled Laws of the State of Nevada*, 105; *Statutes of Oklahoma*, 752; *Compiled Laws of the Territory of Utah*, 345; *Organic and Other General Laws of Oregon*, 564; *General Statutes of the State of Kansas*, 580–81; "California Legislature," *Sacramento Daily Union*, March 2, 1858, 1, and "Laws of California," *Sacramento Daily Union*, April 3, 1858, 4.

16 *Public Statutes of the State of Minnesota*, 399; *Digest of the Statutes of Arkansas*, 874; *Revised Statutes of the State of Missouri*, 1274; *Revised Statues of the Territory of Nebraska*, 178; *Statutes of Illinois*, 332; *Revised Statutes of Colorado*, 348; *Revised Statutes of the Territory of Iowa*, 432; Z. H. Gurley, "Raise the Age of Consent," *Arena* 13 (1895): 218–19.

17 "Mooney on Habeas Corpus," *Sacramento Daily Union*, April 15, 1859, 2; "Wills," *Daily Alta California*, December 18, 1872, 4. See also "The Jennings Estate," *Daily Alta California*, June 28, 1890, 8.

18 "Michigan Laws Discriminating Against Women," 1922, 2, 8, folder 20, box 203, group II, Records of the National Woman's Party, Library of Congress, emphasis added.

19 Frieda S. Miller and Maurice J. Tobin, "State Laws of Special Interest to Women," January 1, 1950, folder 4, box 210, Group II, Records of the National Woman's Party.

20 Betty Friedan, *The Feminine Mystique* (New York: Norton, 1963), 16, 276–77, 302.

21 *Stanton v. Stanton*, 421 U.S. 7 (1975); Warren Weaver, Jr., "Justices Void Law on Majority Ages," *New York Times*, April 16, 1975, 21; "Court Decision Might Control Marriage Age," *Farmington Daily Times*, April 16, 1975, 4A. The case before the

court concerned child support and the differential ages until which a Utah father was obligated to support a son versus a daughter. While the court limited its opinion to the issue of support, Justice Blackmun was also clear that different societal expectations for girls and boys could not be a rational reason for treating them differently (by age) under the law.

22 Arkansas, Mississippi, New Hampshire, Ohio, and Rhode Island continue to maintain different marriageable ages for boys and girls. In many other states girls below the statutory minimum age may marry if they are pregnant and gain the permission of a judge. That said, some states also grant this exception to a boy below the same age if he is the father of a child (either in utero or already born).

6

From Family Bibles to Birth Certificates

Young People, Proof of Age, and American
Political Cultures, 1820–1915

SHANE LANDRUM

In late March 1839, Mississippi resident Samuel Robb had just turned twenty, or so he claimed later in court. Although he was not yet old enough to make a legal contract, he cosigned a note with two other men, attaching his name to a $450 commercial debt. At the time, the young man believed his signature was a formality, a favor to two reputable associates. However, nearly a decade later, long after his cosigners had gone bankrupt, Robb was still trying to escape the debt by pleading his age at signing—what was known, in law, as his infancy. His only written proof was "the bible belonging to his family, in which the register of his birth was and yet remain[ed]." After a lengthy search, he had not been able to locate the book, and his only corroborating witnesses had failed to appear in court. Without any way of proving his age to the court's satisfaction, Robb lost his case.[1]

Samuel Robb was one of countless Americans in the nineteenth century who relied on privately kept records to prove their own age and the facts of their identity. For generations, American Protestants had used the flyleaves and blank pages of their Bibles to record their family histories, following essentially similar formats over time.[2] Anglo-American common-law traditions held that a record in a family Bible was valid evidence of the information it contained about "pedigree," simply because the family who owned it had common access to its records and represented it as true.[3] As Robb's case shows, Bible records were vulnerable to the vagaries of weather and circumstance. Even so, the vast majority of Americans relied on privately maintained records to prove their own age and the other facts of their identity. During the 1840s, every American state had laws that allowed parents to record their children's births and deaths, but they did not compel adherence. As a result, American birth certificates did not become useful identity documentation at a mass level until sometime in the early twentieth century. How and why did Americans begin to believe that all citizens should have access to government-issued proof of their own age?

The answers to this question lie primarily in the late nineteenth- and early twentieth-century movements for better public health and improved attention to children's welfare. Beginning with the idea that babies and children had a right to good health, reformers created bureaucratic systems that simultaneously compelled the registration of births and collected data on infant mortality. The data collected enabled a wide range of public health reforms. The most important of these, including sanitation systems, pure-milk regulations, and compulsory vaccination, have been addressed ably by historians.[4] An additional wave of Progressive Era reforms targeted children's well-being more generally; these included mothers' pensions, statutes on compulsory education and child labor, and age-based restrictions on sexual consent and marriage.[5] However, existing works have overlooked the bureaucratic infrastructures that enabled these reforms and made it possible for most Americans to routinely prove their own identities using a piece of paper.

Newly compulsory systems for birth and death recording, also called civil registration, were a fundamental government tool for both demographic statistics and individual identity documentation. Administered by municipal and state health departments, these laws standardized family recording across faiths, nations of origin, and cultural practices. By the 1910s, compulsory birth registration systems in some cities and states began routinely to provide the youngest Americans with documentary proof of their ages—that is, birth certificates. In these places, birth certificates became the documentary cornerstones of young people's social and political rights.

At the same time, birth registration systems were an offshoot of public health agencies, which varied widely from state to state and presided over deeply racialized policies.[6] As a result, the ability to prove one's own age was a marker of access to legal rights and protections, and it varied widely by geography, race, and class. The ability of Americans to prove their age with reference to a written document varied over time and reflected distinctive political cultures in different regions of the country.

For most literate Americans during the early nineteenth century, family Bibles were the standard way of keeping a family record. By the middle of the nineteenth century, Bibles were common gifts to young women, like twenty-two-year-old Carrie Belle Nichols of Wells, Vermont, who received a "small bible" from her mother in 1882. Within the next five years, she kept a very typical family record in the book. It included her marriage to John W. Hurlburt of Castleton, the births of two children, and each child's death. Charles Horace, "aged 5 mo. 24 days," and Etta Mary, "aged 4 mo. 24 days," died during the late summer in 1885 and 1886. Thanks to newly affordable printing technologies, American consumers could choose from a range of Bible editions with ornamented family record pages.[7]

By contrast, before the Civil War, African American family records were less likely to appear in Bibles than in account books. In slaveholding states, records of slaves' ages were important legal evidence for the market value of human property.[8] In Dinwiddie County, Virginia, one slaveholder's family maintained a family record that also contained a "Register of Negroes" on a separate page:

> Phillis was born April ye 13th in 1777
> Batt was born, July 1785
> Siliom was born August ye 26th 1790
> Lucinda was born, 29th January 1797
> Holly was born, August 1799
> And departed this life 1800[9]

The family of Coleman Tucker, who wrote these words, maintained the record until sometime in the 1850s, but the enslaved Tuckers probably lacked access to it. Frederick Douglass, perhaps the most famous ex-slave of the antebellum period, stated that "I have no accurate knowledge of my age, never having seen any authentic record containing it. I do not remember to have ever met a slave who could tell of his birthday." When Douglass was a child, his white playmates (and potential future owners) knew their own ages, but Douglass's master scolded him sharply for trying to determine his own. He held on for years to a small morsel of knowledge: that sometime during 1835 his master had said that he was about seventeen years old.[10] After the Civil War, African Americans acquired both literacy and Bibles in increasing numbers, but, except for the relatively small number who had been free before the war, they generally lacked written records of their own lives.

Privately kept family records had a range of evidentiary uses in nineteenth-century courts. They were probably most frequently used in probate cases, since they provided a presumably complete list of a man's legitimate heirs. In cases concerning wrongful-death claims and life insurance benefits, working men's survivors used them to prove the number and ages of the deceased man's children. Family Bibles also appeared as evidence in statutory rape cases, usually presented by a parent to validate oral testimony of the age of a young woman.[11]

Proof of age held particularly serious consequences for youthful defendants in criminal cases. In North Carolina, the state Supreme Court ruled that youthful felony defendants could not escape conviction without written proof of their ages. In 1851, defendant Elijah Arnold "appeared to be a small boy" at his trial; when he did not provide any form of evidence for his own age, he was convicted. Chief Justice Ruffin declared that "the reputed age of every one is peculiarly within his own knowledge, and also the persons by whom it can be directly proved."[12] Three decades later, a murder defendant argued that he had been under the age of fourteen when the alleged crime was committed. His own mother's testimony "[rendered] it somewhat uncertain whether he was of that age," but other witnesses seemed to agree that he was about seventeen years old. Without written proof of his age, he could not escape conviction.[13] In states that did not reliably record births, access to a family Bible record could be a matter of life and death for juvenile defendants. North Carolina, like many heavily rural states in the South and Southwest, did not officially register 90 percent of each year's births until the 1920s. This had profound effects on North Carolinians' ability to prove their own ages, especially compared to Americans born in cities or in the Northeast.

Beginning in the 1840s, states in New England and cities around the country began to modernize their laws for birth recording in response to a range of new pressures. Nationally, Massachusetts was at the forefront of these reforms. Its modernized civil registration laws compelled parents and attending physicians to report births, although it is unclear how often violators were actually fined. Furthermore, in a time when home births were the norm, the Bay State required all householders to report births under their roofs. These laws did more than enable the routine recording of births and deaths. They also provided for the comprehensive collection of statistical data based on these records. By specifying particular items of data that were to be collected about each birth, Massachusetts regularized the legal categories of personal identity. Over time, these records became useful for Massachusetts-born people both as individual records and in aggregate, as government officials generated data on birth rates, infant mortality, and common causes of death.[14]

Comprehensive civil registration transferred the responsibility of family recording to government, asserting the growing importance of the state to a country with deeply religious roots. It defined individuals not by their relationships to God, to a faith community, or to the market, but by their existence on a government-issued piece of paper. The expansion of civil registration systems in the nineteenth century was sporadic, and the laws were incompletely enforced, but they provided an alternate means for Americans to prove their ages and the facts of their existence. Although jurisdictions collected very different kinds of data at birth, they universally recorded at least the child's sex and the father's full name.[15]

By the first decade of the twentieth century, reforms in civil registration were most successful in jurisdictions that shared certain aspects of political culture. In New England, relatively high population density and strong traditions of local democracy built wide support for birth registration. In cities throughout the country, strong traditions of police power allowed municipal governments to compel birth registration. In the Upper Midwest, Minnesota and Michigan also built well-organized, well-publicized systems between 1890 and about 1915.[16] Minnesota's success probably owed much to the state's large population of immigrants from Scandinavia, which had practiced civil registration for over a hundred years. Although many other states in the Midwest and West had revised their birth registration laws during the nineteenth century, they generally did not enforce these laws effectively until the twentieth century.[17]

In the states and cities that built effective birth registration systems, birth records served as a key infrastructure for improving babies' and children's health. Because infant mortality rates were calculated as the number of babies who died within their first year of life, registering *all* births was an important part of getting an accurate measurement. Once a city knew its annual infant mortality rate, it could measure the success of infant-saving measures such as pure-milk laws and midwifery restriction.[18] For older children, the chief use of birth records was as proof of identity and especially as proof of age. In an increasingly mobile and urban society, government-kept birth records became a significant form of identity documentation for the youngest Americans.

Such population-based government strategies were a key part of modern government administration in Europe; there, nation-states used identity documents to exercise fairly precise regulation over individual citizens' lives.[19] Across the Atlantic, Americans avoided such forms of centralized national power, but some cities and states built powerful infrastructures of identification based on the ideology of "protecting children." Over time, this complex of ideas came to justify almost every practical usage of birth certificates as identity documents until the New Deal expanded federal entitlements and labor regulations in the mid-1930s.[20]

Especially in New England and in urban areas, birth registration laws evolved hand in hand with other policies that were built on age distinctions, so that birth certificates became proofs of "childhood." The most important of these statutes forbade child labor, compelled school attendance, and prohibited underage marriage and statutory rape. Each of these classes of legislation created a legal definition of childhood based on age. Although reformers may have debated about whether childhood ended at fourteen or fifteen or sixteen, states with well-developed birth registration had the government machinery to allow for such fine-grained distinctions. They could understand a state's children as a particular population, with particular demographic characteristics, and they could generate public policies designed to benefit them.

The enforcement of age-based public policies in progressive-minded states relied on bureaucratic institutional forms. Bureaucratic approaches to proof of age required systems that could be administered quickly, easily, in rule-based ways, according to procedures and files rather than according to personal relationships.[21] A family Bible was, almost by definition, not useful for bureaucrats. Because there was only one original, it was liable to loss, damage, or fragmentation, and all individuals who moved away from the family Bible that authenticated their age would be left without reliable proof of the information it contained. However, with access to a government-authenticated birth certificate, geographic mobility and proof of age were no longer mutually exclusive.

A simple example of the transition from family Bibles to birth certificates concerns the age of marital consent. In the nineteenth century, clergy and civil officials who solemnized marriages in which the bride or groom was underage could face civil prosecution. In one such case, a Missouri judge ruled that "if [a clergyman] saw fit to determine for himself [a bride's] age, by her looks, he did so at his peril."[22] By the early 1900s, newspapers reported that young women were bringing copies of birth certificates to marriage license clerks, using documentary proof of their ages to speed the process. In Washington, D.C., in 1901, the legal age of marital consent was eighteen, but it was twenty-one in Charlottesville, Virginia, where Mary Jane Gardner lived. To evade Virginia law, Gardner and her intended, Price Blackwell, took a morning train to the capital city, where they acquired a license despite her father's protest by rush telegram. When he arrived later that afternoon by train, he found the newlyweds exiting a church, much to his dismay.[23] Newspapers reported these stories as novelties, both revealing the unusual nature of the brides' acts and spreading the word to other readers who might contemplate similar behavior.

By 1915, the cities and states that had become most effective at registering births were increasingly deploying age-based bureaucracies for governing young people. Perhaps the most complex and wide-reaching use for birth certificates concerned regulations that kept young people in school and out of the paid labor market. In 1905, New York State law declared that employers must verify the ages of all young workers, not employing any "child" under sixteen. When this system proved unenforceable in New York City, municipal officials implemented a work permit system administered by the city's Board of Health. By 1908, hundreds of teenagers lined up at the board's offices every week, waiting to show proof of their age so that they could get officially issued work permits. However, unlike courts, the Board of Health would not trust a parent's word. When an applicant lacked official documentation of age, he or she could receive a work permit only after filing a parental affidavit and waiting forty-five days. Although civil courts of the same period tended to trust a parent's word about a child's age, states with effective protections against child labor assumed that all parents and young people had concrete reasons to falsify their ages.[24]

Building upon the successful implementation of New York City's work permit system, the city's National Child Labor Committee argued forcefully against weaker child labor laws elsewhere in the country that allowed judges to use personal discretion, rather than proof of age, to issue a work permit. One minister, investigating Georgia's child labor permit system, noted that a particular judge "appears to think he is doing a kindness every time he gives permission for a child to work in the mills."[25] At least in theory, birth certificates were a fair, objective tool for keeping young people in school and out of paid work. However, support for compulsory birth registration relied on political assumptions that much of the United States did not yet support.

Although some cities in the Reconstruction era South built moderately effective systems for birth registration, the states of the former Confederacy generally ignored the subject altogether. With their state budgets crippled by the burden of Confederate war debt, they had little money to spare for policy innovations.[26] Moreover, compared to those of New England, southeastern states had larger land areas and more rural populations, making enforcement of registration laws more difficult. Georgia's situation was typical. Its two major port cities, Savannah and Augusta, kept substantial birth records beginning in the mid-nineteenth century. One of the state's last Reconstruction era legislatures passed a modernized registration law in February 1875, but it was mostly ineffective. The original birth certificates collected under this law for the next two years amounted to a stack of paper less than six inches thick. By 1877, doctors seem to have ignored the law altogether.[27] Virginia and North Carolina both attempted to register births by enlisting tax collectors, so that each taxpayer would report all births and deaths that occurred during the past year in his family or the families of his nonpaying "servants or employés." However, this system resulted in birth data so incomplete that the state considered it useless to tabulate and print them.[28]

Compared to New England states, southern states were less locally democratic, and their governments relied much more on the political wills of well-off landowners.[29] Particularly in the regions within each state where tenant farming, sharecropping, and textile milling were common occupations, their civil registration systems would have under-reported the births of children in working-class white and black families, just as poll tax systems discouraged their fathers from voting.[30] By 1896, Virginia's legislature had cut funding for the state board of health so sharply that the state kept no birth records at all.[31] As a result, the implementation of effective modern birth registration systems in the South generally lagged until the twentieth century.

Despite the increasing importance of birth certificates in some jurisdictions, the majority of Americans did not register their children's births with government until sometime in the 1920s. Many babies were still born at home, with the assistance of a doctor in richer families or of a midwife in poorer ones. Parents continued their own cultural traditions for welcoming a child into the community, whether by baptism, circumcision, or a formal naming ceremony, and they recorded their children's names as their own parents had done for them. Civil birth registration was, for many parents, an afterthought if it entered their minds at all.

Although southern states were slow to build birth registration, they increasingly recognized that their states could not improve infant mortality rates without adequate birth recording. In 1909, Virginia's State Board of Health described the state's lack of a functional birth registration statute as a "very serious handicap." Within three years, the state legislature had enacted a new vital statistics law, strengthening the state's previously toothless and underfunded Board of Health.[32] In the heart of Appalachia, government officials described their newly improved registration system as "Kentucky's Big Family Bible," which enabled "the privilege of establishing and maintaining family history under the care of the State." Not to be outdone, North Carolina's Board of Health urged readers of its bulletin to lobby legislators for a registration law of their own. "Don't you wish that North Carolina had a great big family Bible like Kentucky's," the editors wrote, "where as one big family, a great commonwealth of brethren, our births and deaths would all be recorded together? Then ask your representative in the General Assembly of 1913 to go get us one." The North Carolina legislature did pass a registration law, but one of the nation's leading experts still declared that "the most urgent public health need of the South is accurate vital statistics."[33] Moderniz-ing the region's economy meant, partially, modernizing its government.

Even though better birth registration supported the goal of child labor regulation, southern states themselves often placed a low priority on both reforms.[34] Virginia was a notable exception. Although its child labor laws were not particularly well enforced, the project of birth reg-istration found considerable support because it aligned with the state's goal of documenting racial genealogies and legally restricting racial in-termarriage. States generally failed at effective birth registration when their political cultures resisted expanding government budgets, priori-tized local communities' decisions over the will of the state legislature, or fought against the imposition of federal power. As a result, expansion of effective age documentation was a slow and gradual process, requir-ing a modification of states' political cultures and government priorities.

Consistent measuring of infant mortality and consistent enforcement of child labor laws required effective compulsory birth registration sys-tems. The Census Bureau had been working to promote birth regis-tration since its establishment as a permanent federal agency in 1903. However, it lacked the constitutional power to compel states to register births.[35] Most states simply did not have the government infrastruc-ture to register births effectively. With the establishment of the federal Children's Bureau in 1912, this began to change. Although the Children's Bureau is usually known more for pioneering the policies of the federal welfare state, its congressional mandate to "investigate the questions of infant mortality [and] the birth rate" required good state-level birth reg-istration systems.[36]

Using a combination of medical and social science expertise, the Chil-dren's Bureau supported state-level boards of health and women's orga-nizations that were lobbying for better birth registration in their own states. It mobilized the expertise of Census Bureau statisticians, public health experts, and actuarial mathematicians and spread information about the importance of birth registration through every possible chan-nel. Although the federal government had no constitutional power over birth registration, the Children's Bureau and Census Bureau worked to-gether to generate grassroots support at the state level for standardized birth registration systems.[37] When, during the 1920s, numerous rural states expanded programs for maternal and child health using federal dollars, the Children's Bureau ensured that birth registration was on these states' agendas. Because African Americans and Spanish-speaking Americans still lived largely in rural areas, federal funding played a key role in reducing racial and language-based disparities in birth registration rates.

Any state that wanted its citizens to use an officially issued document to prove their own age made significant efforts to educate parents about birth certificates. Early twentieth-century birth certificates themselves explained why they were important. New York State's official form announced that it was an "IMPORTANT NOTICE TO PARENTS." All four margins reminded them to "carefully preserve this certificate by having it framed." Below, it instructed the reader very specifically:

> The official record of birth of which this is a certificate is very valuable as a proof of age and citizenship; it is necessary to have such proof in the future life of this child for the purpose of entering or leaving school, obtaining working papers or marriage license, inheriting property, holding public office, entering civil or military service, and for many other important objects.
>
> If the child's given name does not appear on this certificate, the parents must report it as soon as possible to the local registrar. They should also report to him any mistakes in dates or spelling on this certificate.[38]

The text continued with "extracts from the vital statistics law," explaining the state requirements for birth registration within five days, supplemental filing of a child's name, and that all parents receive a copy of their child's birth certificate within ten days of its filing.

In Virginia, parents received a similar notification of birth registration in postcard format, which informed them that "[t]he Commonwealth of Virginia has an interest in the welfare of this individual, from birth through life, and issues this certificate as a protection." Like the New York City birth certificates, it listed the many important uses that a birth record might have, and it encouraged parents to safeguard the notice for its "historic value to future generations."[39] These messages on the reverse of birth certificates served to educate parents about the new

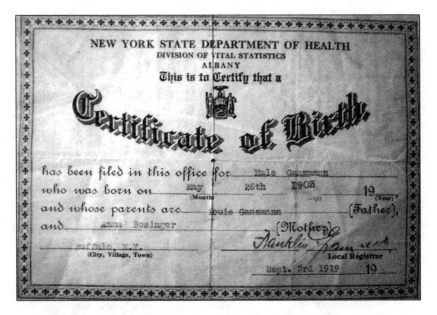

Figure 6.1. Like many extant birth certificates from personal papers, this birth certificate was issued just after its owner's sixteenth birthday. Measuring about five by seven inches, it was folded into a wallet-size shape, suggesting that its bearer used it to navigate child labor laws. New York State birth certificate for Male Ganzmann, born Buffalo, N.Y., May 26, 1903, issued September 3, 1919, in collection of author.

bureaucracies that required birth certificates in an increasing number of situations. By speaking in the terms of individual rights, they promoted the idea that government birth registration was not an arbitrary expansion of state power but served a positive social good.

Many state boards of health spread the news about birth certificates using graphical means. Illinois appealed to livestock farmers, depicting pedigreed pigs who were registered and babies who were not. Other cartoons rendered the lack of a birth certificate as a moat or wall that separated a young man from his goals. Still others were more abstract, depicting the questions that might surround a young man who had no birth record.[40]

The editors of the *Virginia Health Bulletin* put the matter more succinctly, arguing that a birth certificate was "necessary to prove one's kinship, one's title to property, one's right to one's name. The birth certificate, in a word, is man's proof that he is himself."[41]

Even the nascent silent film industry spread the message. Chicago's Essanay Film Manufacturing Company produced at least one title, *The Error of Omission* (1912), illustrating the lifelong tribulations of "Tommy," who lacked a birth certificate. On the day he was born, his father had registered a purebred bulldog puppy, but not his son's birth. As a result, Tommy faced difficulty entering school, could not get a work permit at the age of fourteen when his father died, could not vote, could not obtain a marriage license, and could not claim an inheritance. In despair, he looked for family records, where he discovered, on the back of the bulldog's registration paper, his father's words, "Became father of

Figure 6.2. Promoters of better birth registration systems appealed to parents' interest in their sons' future careers. "Your Boy May Be Up Against This," *Bulletin of the State Board of Health of Texas* 8, nos. 11–12 (1914): 5.

TEXAS YOUNG MEN SHOULD BE EQUIPPED TO ANSWER THESE QUESTIONS.

Figure 6.3. Publicity about birth certificates and birth registration also appealed to young people's interests as members of an increasingly mobile population. "Texas Young Men Should Be Equipped to Answer These Questions," *Bulletin of the State Board of Health of Texas* 8, nos. 9–10 (1914): 99.

a fine, bouncing boy on this date, also." With this proof, the young man was able to claim his inheritance and marry. When his first son arrived, he immediately registered the child's birth to save the boy a lifetime of trouble. Films with similar plots seem to have circulated throughout the 1910s, judging from illustrated synopses that appeared elsewhere.[42]

The situation depicted in the film was not a literal reality anywhere in the country, but it was on the horizon. Cities' requirements for birth certificates sometimes lasted well past a child's first schooling. In New York City, which had one of the nation's best-enforced birth registration systems, compulsory education and child labor laws kept young people from paid labor outside their homes until they had completed an eighth grade education and passed their fourteenth or sixteenth birthday. An examination-based civil service system had replaced patronage placement. To get a work permit or to join the civil service, a birth certificate was required. At least theoretically, these systems ensured equitable administration of government and equal protection of all young workers. However, their reliance on documentary evidence exposed another challenge to the state-building project of birth registration: what to do with Americans who had no birth certificates.

By 1916, citizens in at least ten states, covering almost a third of the nation's adult population, had begun to register their children's births consistently. Their doctors filed birth reports to avoid civil penalties, but parents probably responded more to the increasingly pervasive message that, by registering a child's birth, they were securing his or her individual rights. Newspaper readers hardly could have

THE PROBATION OFFICER: "TOO BAD, SONNY, BUT WE CAN'T LET YOU GO TO WORK UNTIL YOU ARE FOURTEEN, AND YOU'RE SUCH A LITTLE CHAP THAT YOU CAN'T BE MORE THAN TWELVE." THE BOY: "HONEST I AM FOURTEEN!" THE PROBATION OFFICE: "LETS SEE YOUR BIRTH CERTIFICATE THEN"

Figure 6.4. This cartoon drawn from a silent film's plot illustrated the importance of a birth certificate for young people seeking work permits. Detail from Katherine Field White, "Without Proof," *Illinois Health News* 2, no. 6 (June 1916).

Figure 6.5. Amid increasing enforcement of age restrictions on marital consent, access to a birth certificate (or lack thereof) could enable or constrain young people's plans. Detail from Katherine Field White, "Without Proof," *Illinois Health News* 2, no. 6 (June 1916).

avoided the numerous fictional and nonfiction accounts in which an inheritance, wedding, or border crossing depended on access to a birth certificate.[43]

Early twentieth-century state and municipal governments that relied on birth certificates as identity documents frequently had to accommodate the possibility that their native-born citizens might not be able to produce one. In New York City, European-born immigrants could write back to civil or religious authorities in the old country to obtain birth records, but many American-born children had difficulty doing the same. The case of fourteen-year-old Ida Kolonsky was typical. The daughter of Russian Jewish parents, she lived with her older siblings in a densely packed immigrant neighborhood in Brooklyn. In 1902, at her birth, the city had not yet perfected its birth registration systems; by 1916, the city's child labor enforcement was strict enough that she needed to prove her age using a birth certificate. Unfortunately for Ida, the midwife who had attended her mother was dead, and she had never filed a record of Ida's birth with the city. Neither the Board of Health nor the Board of Education could prove that Ida was old enough to leave school and obtain a work permit. Her only recourse was to contact the state registrar of vital statistics personally and hope that he could offer a solution.[44]

The institutional problems with requiring birth certificates as proof of age existed in any jurisdiction where birth registration had not been well established for decades. In 1914, the city of Oakland, California, considered requiring birth certificates for admission to the public schools. The policy may have been intended to restrict the public schools to native-born white pupils. However, Japanese American midwives registered births more consistently than white physicians because Japanese law and custom had long required that each child be entered into a government registry of families. As a result, Oakland's proposed policies likely would have excluded more white children than children of Japanese descent.[45] After a review of the proposed policy, the state board of health's attorney advised against it, declaring that "it would only result in endless controversy and trouble."[46]

Beginning in the fall of 1916, the nation's first federal child labor statute exposed the large-scale problems with expecting individuals to have written proof of their own ages. Although the Keating-Owen Act was ruled unconstitutional within twenty-four months, during that time the problems of age proof that it posed became clear. Because Virginia had not recorded births at all between 1896 and 1912, only about 6 percent of the state's work permits were issued to teens who presented a birth certificate as proof of age. Most of the state's children who had written proofs of their age relied on life insurance policies held by their parents. For young people in Georgia, a family Bible record was more common, since the state's last effective birth registration law had ended with Reconstruction almost forty years before. Many young people who received work permits under the Keating-Owen Act had no written record of their age at all. To get a work permit, they had to be examined by a physician who would declare their approximate age based on physical markers of development.[47] Without a more reliable system for age proof, child labor regulation in southern states was bound to be an inexact process. The political cultures that had enacted compulsory birth registration effectively in New England and had slowed it in the South had far-reaching effects on young people's ability to document their own ages.

If the child labor law didn't get American adults' attention about the importance of being able to prove one's age, the Selective Service

Figure 6.6. In Illinois and many other states, lack of reliable proof of age posed challenges for running an effective military conscription system. "How Can We Prove It?," *Illinois Health News* 3, no. 7 (July 1917): rear cover.

Act of 1917 did. It required all men between the ages of twenty-one and thirty-one to register for the military draft and to carry their draft cards at all times. It was easy enough to prove that one had registered for the draft, but more difficult to prove that one was not required to register. As with the child labor laws, some proof of age was important to have: if not a birth certificate, then an insurance policy, family Bible record, or church or synagogue registry. These documents became particularly important during the fall of 1917, when the volunteer-run American Protective League conducted so-called slacker raids, which detained thousands of men for suspected draft dodging. One California senator complained that both "beardless boys" and older men were being forced to "demonstrate [their ages] by a birth certificate a thousand miles away."[48] His constituents, living in a frontier state, may have faced this problem frequently. Any Californian born before 1887 was old enough to be exempt from the draft, but relatively few American cities—and almost no states—registered births with near universal accuracy until the twentieth century. In Illinois, the State Board of Health declared that the problem of age-related draft evasion could have been solved "if the [state] birth registration law had been enacted years ago."[49]

By 1920, the transition from the family Bible to the birth certificate was far from complete, but it was well under way. In many places, new forms of government birth recording began to render this time-honored and legally binding practice increasingly obsolete. For some of the newest Americans—the children of native-born and immigrants alike—a birth certificate confirmed one's entitlement to the protections offered by a growing, if minimal, federal state.[50] Between 1915 and 1937, this generation would come to use birth certificates in increasing numbers. At the same time, some of them would face new constraints created by age-based regulatory systems that demanded a document they could not produce. Young people born in the South, the Southwest, and the rural West were much less likely to have their births registered by government, especially if they were nonwhite or Spanish-speaking.[51] For these Americans, the decline of the family Bible would have dramatic effects on their abilities to interact with the government bureaucracies their birth-certificate-holding peers increasingly took for granted.

NOTES

The research for this article was conducted with the support of a dissertation fellowship from the Gilder Lehrman Institute of American History, a research fellowship from the New England Research Fellowship Consortium, the Hugh Davis Graham Award from the Policy History Conference, a Beveridge Travel Grant from the American Historical Association, and a Provost's Dissertation Research Grant from Brandeis University. I am grateful to these organizations and institutions, without which my research would be much more limited.

1 *Robb v. Halsey*, 19 Miss. 140 (1848).

2 For a family Bible record that was begun in 1854 and contained dates ranging from 1774 to 1954, see Jeter Family Bible Record, Amelia County, Virginia, 1774–1954, accession 24435, Library of Virginia, Richmond (repository hereafter cited as LVA). For examples of the quantity and varying forms of family Bible records over time, see Virginia Daughters of the American Revolution Genealogical Records Committee, *Miscellaneous Bible Records Collection No. 45, 1747–1977* (1982), accession 36280, LVA; *1509 Family Bible Records, 17 Volumes, Collected by Mrs. Eli Thomas, State Chairman D.A.R.*, bound typescript, 1938, Georgia Archives, Morrow.

3 *Carskadden v. Poorman*, 10 Watts 82 (1840); G. Pitt-Lewis, *A Treatise on the Law of Evidence as Administered in England and Ireland; With Illustrations from Scotch, Indian, American and Other Legal Systems*, 9th ed. (London: Sweet and Maxwell, 1895), 422–23; *People v. Ratz*, 115 Cal. 132 (1896).

4 Richard A. Meckel, *"Save the Babies": American Public Health Reform and the Prevention of Infant Mortality, 1850–1929* (Baltimore: Johns Hopkins University Press, 1990); John Duffy, *The Sanitarians: A History of American Public Health* (Urbana: University of Illinois Press, 1990); Michael Willrich, *Pox: An American History* (New York: Penguin, 2011).

5 Theda Skocpol, *Protecting Soldiers and Mothers: The Political Origins of Social Policy in the United States* (Cambridge, Mass.: Belknap, 1992); Kriste Lindenmeyer, *"A Right to Childhood": The U.S. Children's Bureau and Child Welfare, 1912–46* (Urbana: University of Illinois Press, 1997); Molly Ladd-Taylor, *Mother-Work: Women, Child Welfare, and the State, 1890–1930* (Urbana: University of Illinois Press, 1994).

6 On the deeply racialized nature of public health in the United States, see Tera W. Hunter, "Tuberculosis as the 'Negro Servants' Disease,'" in *To 'Joy My Freedom: Southern Black Women's Lives and Labors after the Civil War* (Cambridge, Mass.: Harvard University Press, 1997), 187–218; Nayan Shah, *Contagious Divides: Epidemics and Race in San Francisco's Chinatown* (Berkeley: University of California Press, 2001); Natalia Molina, *Fit to Be Citizens? Public Health and Race in Los Angeles, 1879–1939* (Berkeley: University of California Press, 2006); James C. Mohr, *Plague and Fire: Battling Black Death and the 1900 Burning of Honolulu's Chinatown* (New York: Oxford University Press, 2005).

7   Family Record of John W. Hurlburt transcribed by Elmer I. Shepard, Williamstown, Mass., November 10, 1945, New England Historic Genealogical Society, Boston; Colleen McDannell, "The Bible in the Victorian Home," in *Material Christianity: Religion and Popular Culture in America* (New Haven, Conn.: Yale University Press, 1995), 67–102.

8   In Virginia, slave owners could not uphold claims of a slave's market value without a record of his or her age; *Dabney v. Green*, 1809 Va. LEXIS 31 (1809), 13. On other aspects of age in slave sales, see Walter Johnson, *Soul by Soul: Life Inside the Antebellum Slave Market* (Cambridge, Mass.: Harvard University Press, 1999).

9   Tucker Family Bible Record, Dinwiddie County, Virginia, 1765–1852, accession 33235, LVA.

10 Frederick Douglass, *Narrative of the Life of Frederick Douglass, an American Slave, Written by Himself* (Boston: Anti-Slavery Office, 1845), 2. My thanks to John Huffman and Walter Johnson for bringing this to my attention.

11 *Louisville, Cincinnati and Lexington Railroad Co. v. Mahony's Administratrix*, 70 Ky. 235 (1870); *People v. Ratz*, 115 Cal. 132 (1896); *Buzzard v. Commonwealth*, 134 Va. 641 (1922).

12 *State v. Elijah Arnold*, 35 N.C. 184 (1851) at 192.

13 *State v. George McNair*, 93 N.C. 628 (1885).

14 Robert Gutman, "Birth and Death Registration in Massachusetts, II: The Inauguration of a Modern System, 1800–1849," *Milbank Memorial Fund Quarterly* 36, no. 4 (1958): 373–402; Robert Gutman, "Birth and Death Registration in Massachusetts, III: The System Achieves a Form, 1849–1869," *Milbank Memorial Fund Quarterly* 37, no. 3 (1959): 297–326; Robert Gutman, "Birth and Death Registration in Massachusetts, IV: The System Attains Its Basic Goals, 1870–1900," *Milbank Memorial Fund Quarterly* 37, no. 4 (1959): 386–417.

15 "Proceedings of Conference on Vital Statistics," *National Board of Health Bulletin* 5 (1880): 16. All jurisdictions surveyed except Galveston, Texas, also recorded the date of birth.

16 "The Vital Statistics—How to Overcome the Chief Obstacles to Their Collection," *Public Health in Minnesota* 3, no. 1 (1887): 5–7; "An Act to Provide for the Collection of Vital Statistics," *Public Health in Minnesota* 3, no. 1 (1887): 12; "Vital Statistics–Births and Deaths," *Public Health in Minnesota* 7, no. 46 (1891): 38–39; "Important to Health Officers and Town Clerks," *Public Health in Minnesota* 9, no. 10 (1893): 103–4; William H. Guilfoy, "The Past and Future Development of Vital Statistics in the United States: III, Cressy L. Wilbur," *Journal of the American Statistical Association* 21, no. 155 (1926): 272–74; James H. Cassedy, "The Registration Area and American Vital Statistics: Development of a Health Research Resource, 1885–1915," *Bulletin of the History of Medicine* 39 (1965): 221–31, 224–25.

17 For California's 1905 establishment of a Bureau of Vital Statistics to oversee all registration, and the state's prior failures, see *Seventeenth Biennial Report of the State Board of Health of California, for the Fiscal Years from June 30, 1900, to June*

30, 1902 (Sacramento: W. W. Shannon, 1903), 22–23; *Nineteenth Biennial Report of the State Board of Health of California, for the Fiscal Years from July 1, 1904, to June 30, 1906* (Sacramento: W. W. Shannon, 1906), 11–12, 39–43.

18 Meckel, *"Save the Babies"*; Julia C. Lathrop, "The Safeguarding of the Child," *Woman's Home Companion*, May 1914, 3, 46.

19 Michel Foucault, *The History of Sexuality*, vol. 1 (New York: Vintage, 1990), particularly the third section. On the role of identification documents, see Jane Caplan and John C. Torpey, eds., *Documenting Individual Identity: The Development of State Practices in the Modern World* (Princeton, N.J.: Princeton University Press, 2001); John C. Torpey, *The Invention of the Passport: Surveillance, Citizenship, and the State* (Cambridge: Cambridge University Press, 2000).

20 Southern states used birth certificates' racial designators as a tool for enforcing racial marriage restrictions. Virginia's system has been especially well documented. Peggy Pascoe, *What Comes Naturally: Miscegenation Law and the Making of Race in America* (New York: Oxford University Press, 2009), 131–62; Peter Hardin, "'Documentary Genocide': Families' Surnames on Racial Hit List," *Richmond Times-Dispatch*, March 5, 2000, 1; Richard B. Sherman, "'The Last Stand:' The Fight for Racial Integrity in Virginia in the 1920s," *Journal of Southern History* 54, no. 1 (February 1988): 69–92.

21 Max Weber, "Bureaucracy," in *From Max Weber: Essays in Sociology*, ed. H. H. Gerth and C. Wright Mills (New York: Oxford University Press, 1958), 196–244.

22 *State v. Griffith*, 67 Mo. 287 (1878) at 288.

23 "Papa's Protest of No Avail," *Washington Post*, July 14, 1901, 5. For a similar story from Chattanooga, Tennessee, see "True Lovers Prove Romance Not Dead," *Chicago Daily Tribune*, December 11, 1904, 7.

24 "The Labor Laws," *New York Times*, May 22, 1905, 6; "Watch on Working Children," *New York Sun*, July 26, 1908, 2nd sec., 2. For pictures of young people waiting in line at New York City's work permit office, see S. Josephine Baker, *The Bureau of Child Hygiene of the Department*, 3rd ed. (New York: Department of Health of the City of New York Monograph Series No. 4, January 1915), 151–52.

25 A. J. McElway, *Child Labor in Georgia* (New York: National Child Labor Committee, [1910]), 12–15.

26 Richard Harrison Shryock, *The Development of Modern Medicine: An Interpretation of the Social and Scientific Factors Involved* (New York: Knopf, 1947), 227.

27 Georgia Historical Records Survey, *Guide to Public Vital Statistics in Georgia* (Atlanta: Georgia Historical Records Survey, 1941); *Acts and Resolutions of the State of Georgia*, January Session 1875, 32–36, box 1 (DOC-2612), Vital Statistics Records 1875–1876, Georgia Department of Public Health Vital Records, Georgia Archives, Morrow.

28 Lecture Notes [undated, ca. 1870–99], "Statistics, Vital—Death Rates" folder, box 43, reel 38, John S. Billings Papers, New York Public Library.

29 This was largely a continuation of antebellum political cultures in each region; Robin L. Einhorn, *American Taxation, American Slavery* (Chicago: University of Chicago Press, 2006).

30 Edward Ayers, *The Promise of the New South: Life after Reconstruction* (New York: Oxford University Press, 1992), 50–54, 148–49. For a twentieth-century southern registrar who recorded only the deaths of white persons in a district that was three-quarters African American, see "The Humor of Vital Statistics," *Illinois Health News* 4, no. 7 (1918): 138–39, 139.

31 Virginia Acts 1895–1896, chap. 612, 674–75, and chap. 575, 611–12, 616.

32 "Vital Statistics," *Virginia Health Bulletin* 1, no. 7 (January 1909): 225; Virginia Acts 1912, chap. 181.

33 *Bulletin of the State Board of Health of Kentucky* 2, no. 2 (March 1912): 11–12; "The Value of Vital Statistics," *Bulletin of the North Carolina State Board of Health* 27, no. 6 (1912): 202–6, 202; Cressy L. Wilbur, quoted in "Wherein the South Has Been Negligent," *Bulletin of the State Board of Health of Texas* 7, no. 11 (1913): 32–33.

34 Child labor legislation was unpopular in southern states for a variety of reasons, which included resistance to federal power and the region's dependence on young people's labor, particularly in agricultural and textile industries. Jacquelyn Dowd Hall et al., *Like a Family: The Making of a Southern Cotton Mill World* (Chapel Hill: University of North Carolina Press, 1987). On the culture of age reckoning in the Appalachian South, see James D. Schmidt, *Industrial Violence and the Legal Origins of Child Labor* (New York: Cambridge University Press, 2010), 166–75.

35 U.S. Census Bureau, *Extension of the Registration Area for Births and Deaths: A Practical Example of Census Methods as Applied to the State of Pennsylvania* (Washington, D.C.: Government Printing Office, 1907).

36 Children's Bureau, U.S. Department of Labor, *Establishment of the Children's Bureau* [1912], http://mchlibrary.info/history/chbu/20364.pdf.

37 Children's Bureau, U.S. Department of Labor, *Birth Registration: An Aid in Protecting the Lives and Rights of Children*, 3rd ed. (Washington, D.C.: Government Printing Office, 1914).

38 Birth certificate of Male Ganzmann, born May 25, 1903, Buffalo, N.Y., in possession of author.

39 Birth certificate postcard of unnamed white male child born to Mrs. J. Wine, Flat Rock, Va., June 27, 1914, in possession of author.

40 "Your Boy May Be Up Against This," *Bulletin of the State Board of Health of Texas* 8, nos. 11–12 (1914): 5; "Texas Young Men Should Be Equipped to Answer These Questions," *Bulletin of the State Board of Health of Texas* 8, nos. 9–10 (1914): 99.

41 "Virginia's Roll of Life and Death," *Virginia Health Bulletin* 5, no. 11 (1913): 178–91, 178–80.

42 "The Value of Vital Statistics; Details from Katherine Field White, 'Without Proof,'" *Illinois Health News* 2, no. 6 (June 1916).

43 Molly Ladd-Taylor, "'Grannies' and 'Spinsters': Midwife Education under the Sheppard-Towner Act," *Journal of Social History* 22, no. 2 (1988): 255; "The Registration Area for Births," *American Journal of Public Health and the Nation's Health* 7, no. 8 (1917): 714–16. For selected examples of newspaper publicity from different cities, see W. A. Evans, "How to Keep Well: Recording Future Heirs," *Chicago Daily Tribune*, March 20, 1920, 6; "News of Women's Patriotic Societies: Registration System for State Should Be Uniform," *Atlanta Constitution*, March 31, 1912, D12; "Real Man without a Country," *Boston Daily Globe*, January 16, 1910, 35; "Quiltmaker an Heir to Wealth of Beggar," *New York Times*, February 20, 1905, 1; "How Old Is Sammy Katz?," *New York Times*, April 24, 1904, 7.

44 Ida Kolonsky, Brooklyn, N.Y., to Children's Bureau, June 16, 1916; Julia Lathrop to Kolonsky, June 23, 1916; both in File 4-0-1, box 23, Central File 1914–1920, Records of the United States Children's Bureau, RG 102, National Archives and Records Administration, College Park, Md.

45 State Board of Health of California, *Biennial Report, for the Fiscal Years from July 1, 1914 to June 30, 1916* (Sacramento: California State Printing Office, 1916), 226–27; Susan L. Smith, *Japanese American Midwives: Culture, Community, and Health Politics, 1880–1950* (Urbana: University of Illinois Press, 2005), 99–100; David Chapman, "Geographies of Self and Other: Mapping Japan through the Koseki," *Asia-Pacific Journal: Japan Focus*, http://japanfocus.org/-David-Chapman/3565.

46 Louis S. Roseberry, "Opinion No. 186: In re Power of Board of Education of Oakland to Require Birth Certificates upon School Registration," November 25, 1914, Series 14 (Attorney Opinions 1911–1923), Records of the Legal Division, California Department of Public Health, California State Archives.

47 On the Keating-Owen Act, see Lindenmeyer, "*Right to Childhood*," 120–26; Hall et al., *Like a Family*, 57–60; *Hammer v. Dagenhart*, 247 U.S. 251 (1918). On southern birth registration systems, see "Virginia's Roll of Life and Death," 1913; on Georgia specifically, see *Smith v. State*, 160 Ga. 857 (1925), which ruled Georgia's 1914 birth registration law unconstitutional.

48 Quoted in "Draft Raids Here Anger Senators," *New York Times*, September 6, 1918, 1–24, 24. Christopher Capozzola, *Uncle Sam Wants You: World War I and the Making of the Modern American Citizen* (New York: Oxford University Press, 2008), 46–49; "Seize 20,000 Here in Slacker Search," *New York Times*, September 4, 1918, 1–17; "Second Day Nets Few Slackers Here," *New York Times*, September 5, 1918, 3; "Harlem Slacker Raid Nets Forty," *Philadelphia Inquirer*, May 26, 1918, 5.

49 "How Can We Prove It?," *Illinois Health News* 3, no. 7 (July 1917): rear cover.

50 Children's Bureau, *Birth Registration*; Lathrop, "Annual Report of the Chief of the Children's Bureau," in *Reports of the Secretary of Labor and Reports of Bureaus* (Washington, D.C.: Government Printing Office, 1915), 114–15.

51 Robert D. Grove, "Studies in the Completeness of Birth Registration; Part I, Completeness of Birth Registration in the United States, December 1, 1939, to March 31, 1940," *Vital Statistics Special Reports* 17, no. 18 (April 20, 1943): 224–96.

7

"Rendered More Useful"

Child Labor and Age Consciousness in the Long Nineteenth Century

JAMES D. SCHMIDT

Manufacturing, Alexander Hamilton famously wrote in 1791, could save children from the throes of idleness. Indeed, he declared, by working outside the home, "women and Children are rendered more useful and the latter more early useful by manufacturing establishments, than they would otherwise be." A century later, Hamilton's cheerful predictions with regard to young people were both true and increasingly becoming anathema in polite society. The nineteenth century had witnessed rapid growth of remunerative labor for young workers outside the household, but at the same time middle-class reformers had mounted a long campaign to regulate and, in more extreme cases, abolish this particular form of wage work. During the Progressive Era, those efforts expanded into a national campaign that secured restrictions across the country.[1]

In the process, child labor reform contributed centrally to the creation of chronological age consciousness. In this essay, I explore the role of law, labor, and education in this vital epistemological shift. Beginning in New England in the 1820s and 1830s, middle-class reformers created a legal regime in which child labor, compulsory attendance, and truancy laws became a mutually reinforcing apparatus that focused the attention of people, young and old, on increasingly fine demarcations of age. While humanitarian concerns would eventually dominate discussions of child labor by the Progressive Era, the original impetus lay in political concerns about educating citizens for participation in a republic where inherited means of social and political cohesion had been swept away by the Revolution. These social and political assertions ran squarely into a considerably different outlook on youthful labor held by working people across the United States. Working people often measured the capacity to labor in physical terms, by size and ability, not calendar years. Moreover, young workers and their families, especially in rural areas, often did not reckon calendar age in the ways becoming common among the urban-industrial middle class. Birth dates, if remembered at all, might be counted by season or against some significant community event. The coming of child labor, compulsory school attendance, and truancy laws changed that, for working people now had to know, for certain, exact calendar ages in order to acquire the certificates needed to get a job. This fact often led to outright lying as well as convenient forgetfulness about age and birth dates, but as the legal web drew tighter, working people slowly adapted to the assumptions encoded in statute. By the middle twentieth century, accommodation was becoming more common, but resistance never died out completely.[2]

As a system of knowledge, child labor law in the United States constituted a particular sort of age consciousness. While some reformers sought outright abolition of wage work for young people, the legal process almost always produced statutes that created gradations of age. This outcome both reflected ideas of working people themselves and altered them by cementing fluid notions of capacity with the power of the calendar. As a prime example of James Scott's model of "state simplification," child labor and compulsory education law made age matter as it had never before. Young people would no longer be "rendered more useful" at an early age depending on their physical and mental development. Instead, they would look to the number of candles on the cake to tell them whether they were ready for the adult world of work or whether they should remain in the realm of the schoolhouse.[3]

Age consciousness about work constitutes a peculiar sort of ideological standpoint. It might be seen as a subset of class consciousness. It is certainly tied directly to questions of political economy, those that ask who should work and how. In the history of the United States, considerations of work for young people have been intertwined with conflict over slavery, women's work, immigrant labor, and the degradation of labor for white adult men. The ongoing resolution of tensions about work and youth forms part of the larger adjustment of home and work during the transition to capitalism, especially to the general nineteenth-century obsession with "idleness." But what about young people themselves? How does one come to know "I work. I labor," or alternatively "I do not work. I do not labor"? These are questions of the good, both of morality and political economy. Because of the dependences of youth—physical, moral, legal—this kind of consciousness includes an element of being imposed from without, by parents, community elders, or more distant entities such as factory inspectors or truant officers.[4]

At least with regard to labor, these ideas were born and raised in the modern West, especially in the nineteenth and early twentieth centuries. To understand the epistemological shift involved in "child labor," we must think about a period before that notion took hold, one before the rise of child labor law, a category that should include compulsory attendance, truancy, and reform school legislation. Indeed, law must be central to our inquiries, for child labor is a prime example of what legal scholars call the "constitutive power of law." From time immemorial, at least some young people have worked inside or outside the home, for wages or other compensation, in bound or free arrangements, but the modern notion of age-demarcated boundaries of legitimation for these kinds of labor was, and remains, a function of legal precepts erected and maintained by the modern state, the administrative apparatus that came slowly into place in the West and beyond over the course of the nineteenth and twentieth centuries. In the areas that touched on the work of young people, the state-building process began in the early decades of the nineteenth century in the United States, Britain, and other parts of Europe, but it was not complete until the middle decades of the twentieth century. To think about child labor and age consciousness, we first need to consider what came before that legal regime and analyze carefully its earliest phases.[5]

When Hamilton penned his famous exhortation about useful labor, his sentiments about the necessity of work for young people were not out of line with majority views in the Atlantic world. Certainly not all young people worked, and even by the middle eighteenth century, elite and middling folk in port cities had begun to outline a vision of youth spent in school, not at work, but most young people in the Atlantic system toiled in some fashion or other from a relatively early age. At the time of the American Revolution, apprenticeships, either craft arrangements or bound situations established by local poor authorities, controlled the labor of many young people. Another large swath of youth toiled in chattel slavery. For free children, work in the predominantly agricultural economy of British North America seemed perfectly natural. Culturally, a prevailing fear of idleness enjoined people to work. In reality, of course, children of the elite spent their youthful hours learning how to rule (as in all hierarchical societies), but most young people expected to be doing something other than learning from books and playing with toys. Such expectations persisted across the nineteenth century, especially in rural America, but also among its burgeoning immigrant working population.[6]

Under this work regime, age consciousness mattered in ways different from those that would obtain a century or so later. On the one hand, majority and minority meant a great deal. Twenty-one was an important age that signaled the acquisition of legal personhood, especially in matters of property. As the voting age in many states coalesced around twenty-one for white males, entrance to the most significant badge of citizenship beckoned. As for labor itself, twenty-one usually ended most apprenticeships for young men. The much smaller portion of young women in apprenticeships usually escaped at eighteen. Slavery, of course, cut across these lines in two ways. Until emancipation, eighteen and twenty-one might have social and cultural meaning for bondspeople, but they were not legal divisions, except for the few slaves who toiled in craft apprenticeships. In the older free states, the process of gradual emancipation heightened the significance of other age demarcations. In short, one birthday mattered a great deal, and it occurred at the end of childhood.[7]

Unlike the child labor and compulsory education era that followed, young people in the early parts of the nineteenth century had little reason to ask "*exactly* how old am I?" If that question were to be asked at all, it would much more likely be connected with such matters as the common-law ages for consent to marry. This legal situation combined with a more general lack of knowledge about age that persisted into the twentieth century. Howard Chudacoff's famous observation that people before the middle nineteenth century often did not know their own ages is certainly true, and such inattention to age persisted into the later part of the century as well, especially in rural America. People often reckoned age more by ability and less by the calendar. All of this is not to say that alternate markers for life stages meant a complete ignorance of age. People did record birthdays: in family Bibles, in memo books, on scraps of paper, on quilts. What mattered is that only rarely did they need to compute their *exact* age *to the day* in a way that counted in their economic and social lives. In other words, at least for labor, nothing in the social and legal world of work compelled people to bring age consciousness to the forefront of the meanings they gave to their daily activities. While we might speculate that young people calculated age as the end of bound relationships approached, their working lives were not dissected into discrete parts as they would be under the modern statutory regime. Moreover, while poor authorities might police the terms of pauper apprenticeships or craft workers might bring suit, these actions did not equate with the widespread attention to age promoted by the later regime of child labor, compulsory attendance, and truancy laws.[8]

Across the course of the nineteenth century, a new epistemology of age arose. While present in many areas of society and culture, the legal regime that came to control work and education presented one of the strongest compulsions for calculation of exact calendar age. Indeed, Chudacoff argues that age-graded schooling was the opening wedge for age consciousness, becoming "entrenched" by the 1870s. While his assertions about the early ubiquity of age-graded schooling are open to question, there is no doubt that the spread of schools and the legal regime that accompanied it altered age consciousness in ways nothing else could. In fact, though historians only occasionally notice the fact, child labor laws and compulsory education laws began as essentially the same thing, a development that should force us to focus on the when and where of why this shift started.[9]

The classic story of child labor reform places it in the social justice humanitarianism of the Progressive Era, but in fact its conception and gestation can be found in the antebellum era, in a different set of concerns. In the late eighteenth and early nineteenth centuries, the Atlantic economy for young people was in flux. For one thing, the rapid demographic expansion of slavery in early nineteenth-century America meant that its slave population was overwhelmingly young. At the same time, rapid industrialization in Britain and the northeastern United States created wage work for children and youth in ways that surpassed Hamilton's Federalist fantasies. Simultaneously, craft apprenticeship declined along with the craft economy in general. A broad shift in political economy meant that hireling labor, once seen as akin to slavery, increasingly became the norm for both young and old, especially in New England and the older states of the Middle Atlantic.[10]

Given this tale of transformation, it would be tempting to explain the earliest child labor laws as a functional response to economic change. In a manner of speaking, such an explanation fits the story of the British Factory Acts better, for there humanitarian agitation did drive the regulation of work for young people. Moreover, events across the Atlantic pricked the conscience and consciousness of many an American reformer. But the initial regulation of child labor in the United States had more to do with the heritage of its political revolution than with the disruptions of its market revolution. As states democratized their constitutions in the late eighteenth and early nineteenth centuries, political elites increasingly came to fear the power of uncontrolled masses of voters in a free polity. From at least the 1780s onward, calls for training republican citizens became an almost annual ritual. Industrialization heightened the level of anxiety behind these exhortations, but the impetus was already there.[11]

When combined, the fear of political and economic upheaval led to the first child labor laws in American history. Some bits of legislative action occurred earlier in the Northeast, but what is usually recognized as the first child labor act became law in Massachusetts in 1836. Both its provisions and its title evinced what would become the core of child labor regulation into the early twenty-first century: getting young people out of the labor market and into the school house. A short, simple text, this portentous statute was titled An Act to Provide for the Better Instruction of Youth Employed in Manufacturing Establishments. More a hopeful assertion than an actual regulation, the law established a new and meaningful calendar age. Young people under fifteen who wanted industrial employment had to have attended school for at least three months during the previous year. Manufacturers hiring young workers without such credentials faced a fifty-dollar fine, which, appropriately, would be passed on to the common schools in the area. The original statute remained silent about how this process would be verified, but two years later, the Bay State invented the work certificate, requiring youthful job seekers to acquire a testament to their legality from local school officials. By 1842, the state moved in two new, significant directions, involving local school officials in enforcement by giving local school committees the power to bring suits and, more important, introducing actual age-based regulation by enacting the ten-hour day for workers under twelve. Workers younger than twelve could not labor more than ten hours a day, a change that represented a victory for the ten-hour movement but which also signified a departure in child labor law by beginning to restrict the actual terms of employment in an abstract way tied to age and the clock.[12]

Across New England, other states followed suit, often simply copying the text of the Massachusetts statutes. What makes these statutory assertions important is that they started to establish new markers of age where none had been before and that they backed up those assertions with the power of the state. In 1840, for instance, Rhode Island required proof of three months of school before allowing labor for anyone under twelve. New Hampshire's 1846 statute copied that education requirement but upped the age to fifteen. It has often been noted, at the time and since, that these laws were rarely "enforced." While true, this hardly matters for our current purposes. What matters is the epistemological virgin birth that these laws represented. Unlike apprenticeship regulations, which generally placed an age on the end of a particular work relation for young people, these laws specified a beginning point, and that point was much earlier in life. The earliest child labor and compulsory attendance statutes aligned with not much in the common law. They were lower than common-law consent to marry ages in most places, but they were higher than ages being established under child vagrancy and truancy statutes. One gets the impression that the varying ages established in states' child labor statutes were more or less guesses, given that they arose before, or at most with, the scientific language of developmental psychology. In any case, these statutes contributed a new way of looking at the daily lives of younger people. Once fully formed, they declared that below a certain age, you cannot work for wages, so you will be in school; between certain ages, you can work for wages under certain conditions and restrictions, so you might be in school; above a certain age, you may work, so you need not be in school. Most important, these are not general ages; they will be calculated to the day based on the date certain of your emergence from the womb. The calendar now mattered in ways it never had before.[13]

This regime did not descend fully formed. Rather, it was more like a picture coming into view, and that picture took more than a century to clear up. We can see this process of increasing clarity by looking at a single state; hence, here and below I frequently focus on Illinois. The first true child labor law passed the Illinois legislature only in 1891, but the legal history of youthful work and education in the state extended much further back. Tracing out that story reveals how the dawning consciousness of child labor always connected to a broader concern about education and to worries among elites about crime and social order generally. The state's initial vagrancy code, passed by the first legislature in 1819, provided the usual sort of compulsory education that existed under older legal understandings of children and youth. If it turned out that loiterers and wanderers were minors, sheriffs could bind them out "to some person of useful trade or occupation" until age twenty-one, with no statutory distinction for boys and girls. If such compulsory apprentices deserted these salutary arrangements, they would be "dealt with as other apprentices who leave their masters before expiration of their apprenticeship." In 1826, the state went much further, establishing a full-fledged apprenticeship code that authorized local poor officials to bind out any poor child whose parents were deemed unfit. Fathers who had lost their legal capacity, who had abandoned their families, or who were habitual drunkards could lose their children to binding out. Mothers who allowed begging for alms, who were of "bad character," or who allowed their children to grow up in "habits of idleness" faced a similar fate. Such laws, similar to those in the older states, regulated youthful work habits, but they did so in ways that reached back for centuries, emphasizing the power of local poor law authorities and using age limits from indenturing as the significant markers of time.[14]

The power of the state to determine the experiences of young people in Illinois grew dramatically in the 1850s and 1860s with the establishment of reform schools, first in Chicago and then for the entire state. The Chicago Reform School, which opened its doors in 1856, was primarily the project of one man, Methodist minister and missionary Danforth B. Nichols. Reports about juvenile crime had appeared in the Chicago papers as early as 1853. A letter writer who signed as "Illinois" (perhaps Nichols himself) called for a House of Refuge to educate wayward waifs. "The mind of every child in the Nation is the *Nation's property*," the missive asserted. "It must not be permitted to run to waste." Nichols won approval from the common council to experiment with a reform school on the south edge of town. In its first year, the institution took in more than 150 youngsters for everything from petit larceny to general uncontrollability. School officials dutifully recorded the "moral condition" of the inmates, finding boys who had destitute or drunken parents, who had avoided Sunday school, or who had been generally "profane" or "untruthful." Unintentionally recording slices of boy life at midcentury, they also noted those who had "slept out in barns, merchandise boxes, sugar hogsheads, and in stables" as well as those who had attended theaters and circuses or who had "set up ten pins in bowling saloons." A few months after the school opened, the state legislature granted an ex post facto stamp of approval, and ten years later the state established a school on the CRS model for the whole state.[15]

The enabling acts for CRS and for the state reform school in Pontiac are important, for they created new age and gender demarcations and authorized the state to make them real. The statute for CRS allowed Nichols and associates to nab boys between the ages of six and seventeen, a gender division that prompted almost immediate calls for a similar institution for girls. The state reform school law set the ages at eight and eighteen and envisioned children of both sexes, allowing girls in Chicago to be sent to the separate division founded there in 1863. Establishing another line of age, the state statute allowed binding out after the age of fourteen. In a manner that evinced the omnibus purpose of such statutes, the bill envisioned the "discipline, education, employment, and reformation of juvenile offenders and vagrants."[16]

Similar to laws in other states, the state reform school laws in Illinois should be seen as part of the history of child labor and compulsory education, not as part of a separate narrative concerning juvenile crime. This relationship is demonstrated most clearly by the fact that the state reform school bill passed at the same time that agitation for compulsory education heated up in the state and across the country. Prior to the Civil War, only a few states had experimented with direct compulsory attendance laws, that is, ones not tied directly to child labor regulation. As per usual, Massachusetts was one of the earliest, passing a truancy statute in 1850 for children aged six to fifteen and a compulsory attendance law two years later that dealt with young people aged eight to fourteen. During Reconstruction, efforts to enact compulsory attendance expanded rapidly in the North. Occurring simultaneous with and informed by debate over the British Elementary Education Act of 1870, which set Britain on the road to compulsory education, the postbellum era saw the beginning of a debate about school attendance and authority that would last for decades. The press around the country took sides, mostly favoring coercive learning. "It is eminently proper," opined the *New York Sun* in 1867, that children's "natural and legal protectors should be obliged by law to afford them every facility for obtaining a substantial and practical English education." Other commentators were not so sanguine. As one New Hampshire paper put it, the state could and should provide education, but to enforce penalties for not using it was "anti-Democratic—call it anti-Republican if you please."[17]

In Illinois, debate over compulsory attendance began in earnest during the 1860s, with the Republican *Chicago Tribune* leading the charge from 1867 onward. Careful to acknowledge fears about state intervention in the home, the *Tribune* nonetheless flatly asserted that "parents are the natural guardians of their children, but they are not their owners." Young people must be afforded all the advantages of "a fair start in life." Holding up the Prussian system of compulsory schooling as a model, the paper noted that it "cuts off vagrancy, encourages industry, excites ambition, and makes children emulous of good names and honorable deeds." By 1871, bills for compulsory attendance bubbled up in the Illinois statehouse, prompting further resistance from some quarters, often falling along party lines. The Democratic *Chicago Times* responded to one such bill in 1874 by declaring that it created "the crime of liberty in education." The proposed legislation, the paper maintained, would criminalize parents who chose something other than what the "papa-government prescribes by statute." By then the pro-compulsory-attendance argument had begun to shift even more strongly toward education as a means of social and political control. Reflecting on the governmental failures of the 1870s and following the rightward shift in the Republican Party, the *Tribune* outlined the matter bluntly in 1874: "If the conviction forces itself upon us that the people suffer when the people rule, then it behooves us to enlarge our educational system and make it compulsory."[18]

More years of agitation produced a compulsory attendance bill for the state of Illinois in 1883, but this initial assertion was only the beginning of a web of law that would recalibrate understandings of work and education around remembering birthdays. The 1883 statute set the school age as between eight and fourteen and required twelve weeks of yearly attendance. Reformers found this woefully lacking, and pushed for a wider age span and a longer school term. These efforts culminated in the late 1880s when a committee of Chicago elites began pushing for new legislation simultaneously on three fronts: child labor, compulsory attendance, and truancy. In turn, this push had grown out of a local movement spearheaded by the Chicago Women's Club and others that had compelled the Board of Education to begin enforcement of local truancy ordinances. Now the group hoped to expand the reach of the state, both lengthening the period of compulsory attendance and prohibiting as much as possible employment under age thirteen. Radicals on the committee wanted much more. Corrine Brown of the Chicago Women's Alliance objected to a provision that would limit compulsory attendance to twenty-four weeks, asserting that "forty weeks were none too much to require."[19]

Radicals such as Brown did not get anything close to what they desired out of the Illinois statehouse, but over the next several decades reformers slowly fashioned a system of law that accomplished most of their aims. The 1889 attendance statute included seven-year-olds in the regime of compulsion, increased the required term to sixteen weeks, eight of which had to be consecutive, and authorized the creation of local truancy forces. Two years later, the first full-fledged child labor law in the state prohibited employment under age thirteen without a special certificate granted by school authorities. Such certificates required the eight-weeks consecutive attendance of the school law. The 1893 legislature increased the period of consecutive attendance to twelve weeks, and in 1897 the child labor age rose a year to fourteen. New child labor and compulsory education laws in 1903 pulled together many of these threads. With an additional compulsory attendance law four years later, these pieces of statute created what would remain the common understanding of child labor and education for the foreseeable future. Employment under fourteen was generally prohibited during school hours, employment between fourteen and sixteen was regulated, and (after 1907) the school-leaving age was set at sixteen.[20]

By the early twentieth century a mutually reinforcing system of child labor, compulsory attendance, and truancy statutes defined the boundaries of youthful activity. But statutory assertions do not consciousness make. Ideally, consciousness of this sort is not simply a matter of "I must" or "I will," but rather "I am." Here we run back into the thorny theoretical problem of age "consciousness." As that notion has been deployed in Western academic and political discourse, it has usually meant a dawning sense of oppression and a politics of action to alter that political, social, economic, or cultural position. In short, it is about claiming capacity, legal and beyond. Read in the lexicon of child labor, age consciousness for young people is the opposite: it is about incapacity, in both theory and practice. Young people must learn that they are incapacitated legally, and ideally naturally, from performing labor for wages (or at all) before a certain calendar age. So how did people learn this consciousness of age? As with any major cultural shift, the growth of a new system of meaning about work and education for young people was multifaceted. A national ideology that increasingly stressed education over exertion as the ticket out of deprivation helped. A cottage industry in child labor denunciation in the popular press, in high gear by the late nineteenth century, contributed. As I have argued elsewhere, the encounter with the inherent dangers of industrial technology taught working people that their producerist vision for young people could not be carried out in an era of heartless machines and the heartless men who owned them. Here I focus on two elements of the new regime: work certificates and compulsory attendance. Both of these legal elements of the new regime concentrated attention on calculating and remembering calendar age, a critical prerequisite to full-blown age consciousness about work and education. How this process occurred can best be seen in the ways people resisted its operation.

The violation or evasion of child labor regulation was rife well into the twentieth century. What this indicates about consciousness of age is complicated. On the one hand, some young workers and their parents "broke the law" simply because they did not know it existed or because they thought it meant something other than it did. This clash of values appeared particularly clearly in the South, where industrialization proceeded rapidly in the years after the Civil War. Frequently, young people and their families who migrated from the countryside to southern industrial towns remained ignorant of child labor laws, or broke them knowingly, or simply followed old customs and violated statutes involuntarily. For instance, a young worker in Virginia, Johnson C. Monroe, professed ignorance of the state's child labor laws. "Did you know it was necessary to be over sixteen to get a job?" he was asked in a 1918 personal injury trial. "No, sir," he responded. His father, James, faced a similar line of questioning and produced a similar response. "Did you ever have any knowledge of the fact that if they were over fourteen and under sixteen they would have to have a certificate?" the attorney inquired. "No, sir, I thought anybody could work if they could get a job." In other instances, evasion was a conscious act, sometimes at the prompting of employers, sometimes carried out by workers on their own accord. When eleven-year-old Charley Burke applied for job at a West Virginia coal mine, he was allegedly told by the manager that he would "have to make himself twelve." The need for evasion could thus be implied by employers or practiced outright by would-be employees. An example from Tennessee is particularly clear. Paul Spitzer hoped to work for the *Knoxville News* in its printing plant, a position explicitly prohibited for boys such as himself who were under sixteen. To get any employment at his age, he should have had the proper certificate. Paul, however, knew that he looked the proper age: he was "about one hundred and forty-five pounds, was about six feet tall, wore a number eight or nine shoe, and had been shaving." So he applied. Asked later about what transpired, he gave this account of his conversation with the hiring agent: "How old did you tell him you were? I told him I was sixteen. Why did you tell him you were sixteen? I was afraid I would not get the job."[21]

While such conflicts were particularly keen for agrarian families in the South, working with, against, and around the new legal regime occurred across the United States. Finding ways around the law in this fashion could become a complicated game of inferences. Historians have often understood the operation of child labor and compulsory attendance statutes as two different things, but since school officials issued work permits, the two types of law went hand in hand, in both enforcement and evasion. When Ora Rookstool wanted to work at an Omaha meatpacking plant in early 1910 some days short of his fourteenth birthday, his mother and the local truancy officer, a Mr. McAuley, solved his deficiency of age. Ora's mother produced a birth certificate showing Ora to be underage, but McAuley "wanted him to be a little bit older on account of helping me out," Ora's mother recalled. In fact, Ora was thirteen going on fourteen, and McAuley "knew it positively. [Ora] went to school in South Omaha ever since he was five years old," she maintained. An instance from New Jersey suggests that working families learned how to leverage school officials even without such obvious collusion. John Feir got work at a Boonton, New Jersey, silk factory before reaching his thirteenth birthday, a relatively gross violation of New Jersey's child labor laws. John's hiring was no case of ignorance. At a later trial, a baptismal certificate established his calendar age quite clearly, but when he applied for work at Boonton, John had a more effective piece of paper. Previously, John and his mother had applied to school authorities in Shamokin for a work certificate, claiming John was the quite exact age of "fourteen years nine months and sixteen days." Subsequently, John went to live with an uncle in Boonton. The uncle worked for the silk mill and applied for a position for John. Both he and John then lied about John's age and for proof offered the falsified work certificate obtained in Shamokin.[22]

These rather stark examples raise questions about the relationship between resistance to law and consciousness of age. On the one hand, families such as the Feirs and Rookstools had not fully accepted the meanings for youthful labor and education proffered by the reformers who pushed through calendar-based legislation. While it is quite likely that they expected and even demanded education for younger children (Ora, after all, attended school from age five), they clung to different understandings about when a young person might be rendered useful. Viewed in that light, James Monroe's notions about when one could work were literally true: "working" and the ability to procure a position were the same thing. But if such working families resisted, their very means of resistance required they mind the calendar in ways undreamed of a century earlier. An apprenticeship that ended at majority was not the same thing as a work certificate that required both an exact record of birth and a healthy knowledge of what was allowed at which age (for instance, that working in a print shop was prohibited). John Feir's case, in particular, evinces a keen notion of age consciousness for the purpose of avoiding the very laws that required it.

How long this kind of resistance and accommodation lasted can be seen in a remarkable set of compulsory attendance enforcement records from the Office of the Superintendent of Public Instruction in Illinois. From the late nineteenth century into the middle twentieth, local school officials, concerned community members, parents, and even some students wrote to the office seeking clarification of, and relief from, the state's laws concerning compulsory education. These personal, often poignant, communications reveal an ongoing effort to reconcile the realities of daily life with the demands of the law. Part of the story arrived in the complaints of the enforcers. From Marshall in 1935, a man signing himself only as "Rube" decried the state of local truancy enforcement, particularly with regard to the progeny of one Ed Reese. Rube, it seems, had marshaled the resources to hire an honest truant office, but Mr. Reese still refused to send his daughter because she was "too nervous" and because he could not furnish her with the necessary clothes and books. Rube was incensed. "I WANT TO KNOW WHAT IS WHAT ABOUT THIS," he yelled in the general direction of Springfield. "This thing of having confounded brats loafing around on the streets smoking cigarettes and loafing in the pool rooms and doing nothing but let their minds rot or soak up a lot of devilment doesn't suit me." Less dramatic but equally problematic, William Tucker of Cambridge noted the case of schools being too far for children to walk, while Lewis Morgan from DuPage County inquired about whether a licensed teacher could avoid compulsory attendance by teaching her children at home.[23]

Compulsory education was on the minds of more than local school officials. In 1935, Mrs. Owen Greenfield of Forreston wrote to complain about the unfair nature of enforcement. "Can our boy be forced to go to school when two other children in the same district under sixteen do not have to go," she indignantly inquired. "Must we pay fine[s] and sheriff calls when they don't even send these others a notice?" It was not like she did not know the law. "The State Law says all children under sixteen, here in our district they are taking some of the children." We should not conclude, however, that all such complaints were made on behalf of students or parents wanting to leave school for work. Miss Marie Forck wrote on behalf of Geno Christiani, a twelve-year-old eighth grade graduate. Geno wanted desperately to attend high school, but "his folks radically declare[d] that he is going to stay home and work." Many of the requests to the state office, however, were for exemptions in order to work, none more touching than that of Edna Mae Shanks who wrote to receive a special permit for her son. A divorced mother whose husband refused to pay support, Shanks strove to maintain the family farm while troubles approached. Short on food, fuel, and money, she needed the wood he could cut and the cash he could collect at a job, noting proudly that her son was "a big boy, larger than most 16 year old boys and so he can do the work very well." She promised to send the boy to school every day he was not actually working, but her straits were dire. "If I receive no permit to keep him out of school when I need him, then we will loose [sic] our home." By 1942, Illinois Superintendent of Education John Wieland had no choice but to see like a state. "I regret our ability to assist you in this matter," he replied, "but I trust you will be able to adjust your affairs in some way so that the boy will be able to return to school and receive the education to which he is entitled."[24]

Shanks's plea and Wieland's response expose the calendar in control. Had Wieland wanted to alleviate Shank's suffering, which he likely did, he could not. Both parent and state official lived in an era when the peculiar age consciousness that reformers had developed over the previous century came to shape the lives of all it took within its ken. The legal instruments of compulsory attendance and child labor had carved growing up into discrete packets of time that did not exist before the nineteenth century. Starting with hopes and fears about a republican citizenry, the apparatus of age regulated work and labor and had become a machine that ran itself by the middle twentieth century.

NOTES

1 Alexander Hamilton, *Report on Manufactures* (Washington, D.C.: Government Printing Office, 1913), 13.

2 I have considered these matters at much greater depth in *Industrial Violence and the Legal Origins of Child Labor* (New York: Cambridge University Press, 2010). See also Hugh D. Hindman, *Child Labor: An American History* (Armonk, N.Y.: M.E. Sharpe, 2002).

3 James C. Scott, *Seeing Like a State: How Certain Schemes to Improve the Human Condition Have Failed* (New Haven, Conn.: Yale University Press, 1999). My use of Scott's conceptions has been influenced especially by Karl Jacoby, *Crimes Against Nature: Squatters, Poachers, Thieves, and the Hidden History of American Conservation* (Berkeley: University of California Press, 2001).

4 Howard P. Chudacoff, *How Old Are You? Age Consciousness in American Culture* (Princeton, N.J.: Princeton University Press, 1989), 3–8, 87–91.

5 A particularly good survey of youthful labor and education in colonial British North America is Sharon Braslaw Sundue, *Industrious in Their Stations: Young People at Work in Urban America, 1720–1810* (Charlottesville: University of Virginia Press, 2009).

6 Ibid.; Marie Jenkins Schwartz, *Born in Bondage: Growing Up Enslaved in the Antebellum South* (Cambridge, Mass.: Harvard University Press, 2001).

7 Holly Brewer, *By Birth or Consent: Children, Law, and the Anglo-American Revolution in Authority* (Chapel Hill: University of North Carolina Press, 2005); Karen Sánchez-Eppler, *Dependent States: The Child's Part in Nineteenth-Century American Culture* (Chicago: University of Chicago Press, 2005); Joanne Pope Melish, *Disowning Slavery: Gradual Emancipation and "Race" in New England, 1780–1860* (Ithaca, N.Y.: Cornell University Press, 1998).

8 Chudacoff, *How Old Are You?*, 34–38; Schmidt, *Industrial Violence*, chaps. 1 and 5.

9 Ibid.

10 Schwartz, *Born in Bondage*; W. J. Rorabaugh, *The Craft Apprentice: From Franklin to the Machine Age in America* (New York: Oxford University Press, 1986).

11 Carl F. Kaestle, *Pillars of the Republic: Common Schools and American Society, 1780–1860* (New York: Hill & Wang, 1983).

12 *Laws of Massachusetts, 1836*, 950–51; *Laws of Massachusetts, 1838*, 398–99; *Laws of Massachusetts, 1842*, 517–18. In the interest of shortening notes, I have cited all state statutes simply as "Laws of" plus the year. Readers should understand this as shorthand for the much lengthier titles of individual volumes of session laws.

13 For example, see *Laws of Rhode Island, 1840*, 92; *Laws of Connecticut, 1842*, 40–42; *Laws of New Hampshire, 1846*, 298. On child development, see Crista DeLuzio, *Female Adolescence in American Scientific Thought, 1830–1930* (Baltimore: Johns Hopkins University Press, 2007).

14 *Laws of Illinois, 1819*, 88; *Laws of Illinois, 1826*, 54–59.

15 *Chicago Tribune*, May 9, 1853, October 3, 1853, August 20, 1856; *Second Annual Report of the Officers of the Chicago Reform School* (Chicago: Chicago Daily Press, 1857); *Laws of Illinois, 1857*, 650–55; *Laws of Illinois, 1867*, 38–44.

16 *Laws of Illinois, 1857*, 651; *Laws of Illinois, 1867*, 38; *Chicago Tribune*, August 6, 1859, March 7, 1862.

17 *Laws of Massachusetts, 1850*, 468–69; *Laws of Massachusetts, 1852*, 170–71. The modern history of compulsory education is scant. See Michael S. Katz, *A History of Compulsory Education Laws* (Bloomington, Ind.: Phi Delta Kappa, 1976). For a solid compendium of legislative efforts, see a classic progressive era study: Forest Chester Ensign, *Compulsory Education and Child Labor* (Iowa City: Athens Press, 1921); *New York Sun*, repr. *Milwaukee Sentinel*, April 20, 1867; *Concord (N.H.) Daily Patriot*, September 5, 1871.

18 *Chicago Tribune*, July 30, 1867; *Chicago Times*, quoted in *Chicago Tribune*, January 26, 1874.

19 *Laws of Illinois, 1883,* 167–68; *Chicago Tribune,* November 11, 1888, December 2, 1888, December 30, 1888; *Chicago Daily Inter-Ocean,* February 17, 1889.

20 *Laws of Illinois, 1889,* 237–38; *Laws of Illinois, 1891,* 87–88; *Laws of Illinois, 1893,* 128; *Laws of Illinois, 1897,* 164; *Laws of Illinois, 1903,* 187–93, 308; *Laws of Illinois, 1907,* 180–83.

21 *Standard Red Cedar Chest Company, Inc., v. Monroe,* 125 Va. 442 (1919), case no. 6180, Virginia Supreme Court Records, Library of Virginia, n.p.; *Burke v. Big Sandy Coal and Coke Co.,* 68 W. Va. 421 (1910), case no. 76-6, West Virginia Supreme Court Records, West Virginia Library and Archives, 21; *Knoxville News Co. v. Spitzer,* 152 Tenn. 614 (1925), 619.

22 *Rookstool v. Cudahy Packing Co.,* 100 Neb. 851 (1917), 860; *Feir v. Weil and Whitehead,* 92 N.J.L. 610 (1918), 610.

23 "Rube" to Otis Keeler, September 25, 1935, Communications Received, Attendance—Compulsory, Illinois Office of Public Instruction; William Tucker to Mr. Reynolds, September 6, 1935; Lewis Morgan to John Wieland, December 7, 1935; all in Illinois State Archives, Springfield.

24 Mrs. Owen Greenfield to John Wieland, December 6, 1935; Marie Forck to John Wieland, October 20, 1935; Edna Mae Shanks to John Wieland, December 1, 1942; Wieland to Shanks, December 1, 1942; all in Illinois State Archives, Springfield.

8

"A Day Too Late"

Age, Immigration Quotas, and Racial Exclusion

YUKI ODA

In 1921, immigration authorities in New York excluded Freda Berman, a ten-year-old from Poland. Her father had lived in the United States since 1914 and sent for her after World War I, but the Polish quotas were full upon her arrival, and she was excluded for oversubscription and for not being a child of a U.S. citizen.[1] In 1924, immigration authorities in Seattle excluded a ten-year-old boy named Chin Bow from China. His father was a U.S. citizen, but Chin Bow was excluded because he was an "alien ineligible to citizenship."[2] Exclusion of these two young people reflected how the age of children, intertwined with race and citizenship, would become a critical factor in family immigration during the 1920s. This essay examines how age mattered in relation to two pillars of immigration restriction that emerged in the 1920s: the numerical restriction of Southern and Eastern European immigrants and the racial exclusion of Asian immigrants.

Age and Quotas Restriction: Age in the Era of Open Migration

Reference to age in immigration law was a companion to the tightening of immigration control and the increasing grounds for exclusion in the late nineteenth century, which resulted in a higher possibility of families being separated due to the exclusion of one member. At the core of family provisions in immigration laws was the idea that men had the right to have their immediate families together. At the same time, this "right" was conditional upon citizenship status or alienage. The key characteristic of the immigration restriction regime that emerged in the 1920s was an emphasis on the acquisition of formal citizenship as a prerequisite for family admission. This framework necessitated that fathers prove their children were below a certain age and thus still dependents within the definition of the law.

In 1903, in response to increasing immigration from Southern and Eastern Europe, Congress significantly expanded the grounds for exclusion. The 1903 act was the first immigration law with age-based exemptions from qualitative restriction, providing that the "wife and minor [under age twenty-one] children" of a permanent resident who had filed the "preliminary declaration to become a citizen" would not be excluded for contagious disease.[3] Naturalization was a two-step process until 1952, and the 1903 act placed emphasis on the filing of a "declaration of intention" to naturalize, which had to be filed at least three years before applying for naturalization. This emphasis on declaration had dual meanings. On the one hand, Congress expressed the idea of endowing immigrants on the road to citizenship with rights closer to citizens, with less emphasis on final naturalization.[4] On the other hand, it also reflected how physical admission to the United States in itself was not of high value during this period when the country had no numerical restrictions on immigration.[5]

A few years later, Congress lowered the significant age from twenty-one to sixteen to conform with age-based restrictions on child labor. The age of sixteen made a child independent in the context of immigration law. In the Immigration Act of 1907, Congress barred entry of immigrants under sixteen unaccompanied by either parent.[6] While this was initially intended more as a protection of children from child labor, acquisition of independent status also meant subjection to restrictions.

World War I reduced European immigration from one million to an average of 235,000 between 1915 and 1919, but the wartime antiforeigner sentiment empowered those seeking further restrictions. In 1917, Congress finally introduced a literacy test, championed by nativists since the 1890s. Following the 1907 act, Congress allowed immigrants above sixteen to travel without their parent(s), but also coupled this independent status with increased restrictions by requiring immigrants above sixteen to take the literacy test.[7]

After much contestation, Congress agreed to exempt dependent family members of "any admissible alien" and "any citizen."[8] Age and marital status were the two criteria defining dependence. Congress subjected men, considered as labor competition, to a more rigid standard. The literacy test was mandatory for all men between the ages of sixteen and fifty-five. Once over the age of fifty-five, the 1917 act exempted fathers and grandfathers, treating them as dependent on their children and grandchildren. For women, the law expressed the idea that females were dependent on their husband/father, and therefore placed more emphasis on marital status than on age. Regardless of age, the law exempted from the literacy test all wives, mothers, and grandmothers. Furthermore, a father could send for his daughter of any age without the literacy test provided she was unmarried or widowed. Thus, the test was obligatory only for men between the ages of sixteen and fifty-five, but for all others applicability depended on familial relationship, not just to citizens, but to any "admissible alien."[9]

As a result of both this family exemption and an improved literacy rate, the 1917 act did not reduce immigration from Southern and Eastern Europe, and postwar immigration rose from 430,000 in 1920 to 805,000 in 1921. Restrictionists began to push for a strict ceiling on the number of immigrants.[10] In the era of numerical restriction, familial relationships would be defined more narrowly, and age became even more critical as a sharp division.

Age in the Era of Numerical Immigration Restriction

The Emergency Quota Act of 1921 closed the era of open immigration to the United States. Between 1921 and 1965, Congress restricted immigration from Europe by annual quotas varying widely in size depending on country of birth. The 1921 act marked the beginning of modern immigration control where enforcing a ceiling became the norm.[11]

During the 1920s, the most pressing issue was whether prequota immigrants living in the United States could bring over family members still in Europe. In 1920, approximately 13.9 million U.S. residents were foreign-born (13.1 percent of the total population) and 6.6 million were noncitizens (47.6 percent of the foreign-born population).[12] Immigrants who had planned to send for their families were shocked by the new law that narrowed or closed that possibility. The significance of the family-based exemptions changed fundamentally. For instance, the earlier 1917 act did not exempt sons above sixteen from the literacy test, nor did the law exclude such sons as long as they passed the test. In contrast, under numerical restriction, there was no "passing" other than by unauthorized immigration. Numerical restriction meant lengthy if not indefinite waits for admission, and the whole point of quota restriction was to make otherwise qualifying immigrants wait for a spot to become available, if that ever became possible. The question of who counted as a dependent based on age thus became much more pressing.

The quotas system included two types of consideration for European immigrant families: admission outside the ceiling (nonquota) and priority (preference) over others within the quota. These privileges were a result of intense struggle from immigrant groups and their advocates. Restrictionists created the quotas system specifically for the purpose of discounting family ties as admission criteria. After the war, however, the House Immigration Committee chair Albert Johnson (R-Wash.) suggested an alternative idea of restriction: to suspend immigration save for certain families of citizens and those who had declared their intention to become U.S. citizens.[13] Congress rejected this scheme for two reasons. First, it lacked a firm numerical ceiling. Second, due to prerestriction migration patterns, congressmen believed that an emphasis on unifying families would favor immigration from Southern and Eastern Europe over immigration from Northern and Western Europe.[14] Congress originally designed quotas not only to rank nationalities according to ethnoracial hierarchy but also as an absolute numerical ceiling that could not be pierced. The original quotas thus included few if any family provisions. For example, the bill passed in 1920, pocket vetoed by President Wilson, included no family exemption.[15] The following Congress rejected proposals to exempt parents, siblings, children, and grandchildren of citizens; parents, siblings, and children of citizens; and parents and children of citizens. (Wives were beside the point, since the U.S. government recognized any woman who married as having the citizenship of her husband.) The only exception finally agreed on was children under eighteen, expected to be some thirty to forty thousand.[16] Age thus became central to immigration debates.

This was a significant limitation on various modes of family migration that were previously possible. Permanent residency or declaration of the intent to naturalize would no longer enable immigrants to reunify their families; only full citizens would have that privilege. With a very small chance of immigration within the quotas (in 1924 Congress would assign a quota of no more than a hundred to some twenty countries), naturalization became crucial for immigrants' family members to be placed ahead of the waiting list.[17] This required people to naturalize even before their families had ever lived in the country. Contributors to the *Interpreter*, published by the Foreign Language Information Service, protested this change, arguing that the period before naturalization was a time for preparation, for families to experience U.S. society to decide whether to become citizens, not the period for families to be separated and one member to apply for naturalization so that the others could come to the country for the first time.[18]

Under the new quota system, families of noncitizens faced harsh treatment. The exclusion of ten-year-old Freda Berman in 1921 in New York was one such instance. Her father Jacob had been in the United States for seven years and, like many other immigrants, sent for his family after the end of World War I. But she was excluded for oversubscription, since a child of an immigrant who had not yet naturalized did not qualify for any exemption.[19]

In addition to the neglect of relations such as parents and siblings, the second limitation was that only children below a certain age (initially eighteen, and raised to twenty-one in 1928) were exempted from the quotas. A one-year difference of age came to divide the possibility of immigration, separating elder siblings over age eighteen or twenty-one from younger ones below those ages. Contemporary systems of identification, or travel documents such as passports and visas, became the norm in the early twentieth century. Congress first adapted the visa system in 1917 as a temporary wartime measure (formalized by the Passport Act of 1918), requiring all foreigners to obtain a visa before departing for U.S. soil.[20] Age identification in the countries of origin became crucial for obtaining a visa and for admission to the United States.[21]

Coupled together, the citizenship requirement and age limitation were dual restrictions on the common mode of immigration where certain members preceded others in order to find employment, secure housing, and lay the groundwork for following family members and relatives. Immigration in this manner thereafter required that one person attain citizenship before reuniting the immediate family. That citizenship took at least five years to obtain complicated the age requirement for children. Calculating which children would still be young enough to qualify for nonquota status by the time of the parent's naturalization became a crucial factor to consider in deciding whether, when, and which family members should immigrate to the United States.[22] Prior to 1921, neither formal citizenship nor age of the child was decisive, and nonlegal factors such as financial conditions of the family decided the timing of immigration. As long as one met all requirements there was no reason for admitting a child under eighteen but not the older sibling of nineteen, or for compelling families ready to immigrate to wait for an extensive period.

Family separation became even more acute after 1924. The 1921 act claimed to be an "emergency" measure, but what followed was a permanent and much more severe restriction. Congress halved the total quotas to 155,000, allocating only 20 percent for Southern and Eastern Europe. Under the 1921 act, immigration officials had admitted certain families through a liberal reading of the law, but this was no longer possible as the Supreme Court ruled in 1924 that "however harsh the consequences" might be, quotas applied to everyone unless the law specifically stated otherwise.[23] Unmarried children under eighteen and wives of U.S. citizens were the only family allowed to enter the country outside the quotas without a lengthy wait for a visa.[24]

Appeals to stop the separation of Southern and Eastern European immigrant families were voiced from various circles. Especially strong were calls that relief be granted to earlier immigrants because they could not have expected the consequences of the new laws. Organizations of Southern and Eastern European immigrants, who were most affected by the quota acts, protested vehemently.[25] In addition to immigrant organizations, social service organizations showed particular concerns about the matter. In February 1926, thirty-five immigrant aid agencies from Europe and the United States met in Geneva for the second International Conference of Private Organizations for the Protection of Migrants. They addressed the separation of migrant families as an urgent problem. Classifying family separation into several types, such as seasonal migration, illness, war, and political persecution, conference participants reported that "it is the American Law of 1924 which, by its characteristics, has most struck the Associations and public opinion in this matter."[26] Immigrant aid agencies and social work organizations carried out studies on how the new law affected families.[27]

These studies showed how immigrant families were forced to make hard choices. The family of "T" came from Poland in 1922 during the first quota act. Just before sailing, one child contracted measles, and the father traveled to the United States with the two older children, while the mother stayed behind with the sick child. Before the child recovered, the 1924 act went into effect, and much smaller quotas closed the possibility of the wife and the child receiving a visa. The only chance was to wait until the naturalization of T, but the child was going to be over eighteen by then. T and the two children could continue to live in the United States, and T's naturalization would allow his wife to immigrate outside the quotas. However, the child over eighteen would have to be left behind in Poland. To avoid separation from the child, the only option was to give up residence in the United States and return to Poland. Thus, the age of one child affected the entire family.[28]

Contributors to the *Interpreter* argued that requiring citizenship as a prerequisite for family unification was tantamount to "direct coercion" to naturalization. While this argument was based on the recognition that immigrants did not all come to the United States determined to remain, other immigrant advocates assumed that most immigrants were likely to become U.S. citizens but that requiring separation during the prenaturalization years was unjust. If citizenship had to be the requirement for family unification, some argued, the deadline for children's age should be removed or raised (to twenty-one) to reduce the chance of children being separated from their parents or younger siblings.[29]

Family-oriented immigration reform faced intense opposition from nativists including the two authors of the 1924 act, Representative Albert Johnson and Senator David Reed (R-Pa.). These politicians understood that the admission of families outside the quotas would undercut the new law. While immigrant advocates called for admission outside the quotas as the only means to shorten the period of separation, nativists viewed it as a matter of increasing the volume of immigration. Those in favor of quotas saw not families trying to reunify, but "a struggle between the Anglo-Saxon stock and the new immigration for control of our country."[30] The most ardent nativists believed that immigration restriction consisted not only of limiting new admission but also of in-

ducing emigration from the United States and saw limiting family unification rights as a way to achieve both ends.[31]

Yet drastic reduction of immigration had the effect of relaxing the
anti-immigration sentiment to a certain extent. As historian Matthew
Frye Jacobson argues, the year 1924 was not the "closing gate" but "the
high-water mark" of the discourse of Anglo-Saxon supremacy.[32] A
large part of the support for expanding family-based admission derived
from the assumption that a limited revision of the 1924 act would not
invite large immigration. In addition to immigrant families struggling
to send for their relatives, and organizations working with immigrants
from Southern and Eastern Europe, many who had supported the quota
acts but were relieved by the drastic reduction of new immigration supported the limited admission of families as a way to incorporate pre-
1924 immigrants into American society.[33]

The resulting act of May 29, 1928, was a mixed product. First, Congress raised the age of dependent children from eighteen to twenty-one.
Second, whereas only men could send for their spouses outside the quotas restriction, the 1928 act extended this privilege to women, so long as
they were married before May 31, 1928. Next, within the quotas, the law
reserved half for husbands of citizens married after May 31, 1928, and
for parents of citizens. The remainder of the quota could be filled by
the children and wives of permanent residents who were not citizens.
These reforms enabled some new categories of adult relatives to enter
the United States. At the same time, the adjustments retained the fundamental idea that chronological age would determine who counted as a
dependent child and who did not. So long as the quota system remained
in place, Southern and Eastern Europeans would need to carefully consider the ages of their children when making decisions about migration
to the United States in order to avoid indefinite family separation.[34]

As the next section makes clear, however, the notion that a male citizen had a right to have his wife and children in the same household
applied only to white European immigrants. The 1924 act and following
court rulings stripped U.S. citizens of any family unification rights if the
arriving family member was of Asian descent, and the issue for Chinese
American families was whether citizenship mattered at all. The age of
children would become critical for Chinese Americans in the 1930s, but
in a very different way than for European immigrants.

Age in Racial Exclusion and Citizenship Jus Sanguinis

As immigrants from Southern and Eastern Europe were struggling to bring their families to the United States, Chinese Americans were fighting for the admission of their families on entirely different grounds. The second pillar of the 1924 act was racial exclusion of "aliens ineligible to citizenship," a euphemism for Asian immigrants.[35] The Nationality Act of 1870 had limited naturalization to "white" persons and persons of "African nativity and descent," and in the early 1920s the Supreme Court ruled in a series of cases that Asian immigrants were not "white" and were therefore ineligible for naturalization. In 1924, instead of referring to specific countries in Asia, Congress barred immigration of any "alien ineligible to citizenship."[36]

By the time the act of May 29, 1928 accorded nonquota status to children from Europe under twenty-one, the only immigrants from Asia who could enter the United States were children of Chinese Americans. However, whereas children of European immigrants attained nonquota immigrant status after naturalization of their parents, it was not merely by virtue of being children of U.S. citizens that children of Chinese Americans were admitted to the country but because they had acquired U.S. citizenship at birth and therefore were not "aliens" subjected to immigration restriction. Although ineligible for naturalization, persons of Chinese descent could acquire citizenship either by birth in the United States under the Fourteenth Amendment or, if born abroad, by deriving citizenship at birth from a U.S. citizen father under the jus sanguinis rule, as provided by nationality law.[37] For Chinese American families, it was in relation to this jus sanguinis rule of nationality law that the age of children came to matter in the 1930s.

The overall purpose of the 1924 act was the complete exclusion of immigrants from Asia, which began with Chinese exclusion in the late nineteenth century. Under the Immigration Act of 1917, Congress barred immigration of natives of "the Asiatic Barred Zone" that covered most of continental Asia and the Pacific.[38] What remained by 1924 was immigration from Japan, based on the Gentlemen's Agreement between the United States and the Japanese government. As a result, the primary target of the new exclusion clause, which spoke of race instead of nationality, was Japanese families, especially wives.[39] Despite the unmistakable intention of Congress to completely exclude immigration from Asia, enforcement of the 1924 act left one question to be contested during the late 1920s: whether racial exclusion applied to family members of U.S. citizens or whether the claims of U.S. citizens trumped racial exclusion.

Although the 1924 act barred families from both Japan and China, the two involved different claims, which had to do with factors such as generational differences between Chinese immigrants and Japanese immigrants and how immigration laws and intergovernmental treaties and agreements had determined excludability. Pre-1924 immigration from Japan concerned families of first-generation Japanese immigrants, as more recent immigrants to the United States who were ineligible for naturalization and therefore without U.S. citizenship. The second generation was yet to come of age to marry and to send for their families.[40] On the other hand, pre-1924 immigration from China consisted largely of the families of U.S. citizens, the dependents of U.S.-born Chinese Americans. Immigration officials inferred the admissibility of citizens' families from the treaty rights of merchant class noncitizen Chinese to bring their families.[41]

When immigration authorities excluded families of Chinese Americans after the 1924 act, families brought their cases to court, pointing to how the 1924 act exempted children under eighteen and wives of citizens from quotas restriction. They argued that as a right granted to male U.S. citizens the same should apply to them regardless of the racial exclusion. However, in 1925 the Supreme Court denied this claim and ruled that the foremost test was the race of the immigrant, not the rights of U.S. citizens to send for one's family members (*Chang Chan et al. v. Nagle*). Family ties could not supersede the racial exclusion.[42]

With the court denying relief, Chinese American organizations such as the Chinese American Citizens Alliance lobbied for legislative reform.[43] In 1930 Congress passed a limited amendment to the 1924 act, exempting Chinese wives from pre-1924 marriages.[44] Notably, the 1930 act did not exempt Chinese children of any age from racial exclusion, marking a contrast with how Congress in 1928 had extended nonquota status to the minor children of European immigrants.[45]

In 1927 the Supreme Court (*Weedin v. Chin Bow*) excluded the thirteen-year-old son of a Chinese American U.S. citizen father as an "alien ineligible to citizenship."[46] The Chins' transnational family formation was typical of many Chinese American families by the 1920s, with a U.S. citizen husband/father living in the United States, the wife/mother in China, and the Chinese-born children—mostly sons—hoping to immigrate to America at a certain age.[47] Between 1908 and 1924, some 16,400 Chinese-born children who acquired citizenship under the jus sanguinis rule immigrated to the United States, the largest group of persons of Chinese descent admitted during this period.[48] Chin Bow's grandfather was born in the country in 1878, among the first generation of Chinese Americans born under the Fourteenth Amendment. Chin Bow's father, Chin Dun, was born in China in 1894, deriving U.S. citizenship from his U.S.-born father. In 1922, Chin Dun moved to the United States at the age of twenty-eight, while his wife and son remained in China. However, when Chin Dun sent for his son, ten years old, in 1924, immigration officials in Seattle excluded him as an "alien ineligible to citizenship."[49]

The case was important on two levels. First, it indicated that the grandsons of first-generation U.S.-born Chinese Americans had reached an age to come to the United States. And the immediate issue was the rule surrounding third-generation citizenship derivation on jus sanguinis grounds, which would determine whether Chin Bow was a U.S. citizen or not. The Court did not recognize Chin Bow as a U.S. citizen because his father had never lived in the United States before Chin Bow's birth. The Court ruled that a foreign-born U.S. citizen did not have the power to transfer his citizenship to his child until he took residence in the country, which was a formally race-neutral rule.[50] Second, the court confirmed that children of Chinese Americans were admissible only if they were U.S. citizens themselves, not simply by virtue of being a child of a U.S. citizen. Unlike children from Europe, noncitizen children of Chinese descent were racially inadmissible to the U.S.[51]

With both wives (*Chang Chan et al. v. Nagle*) and noncitizen children (*Weedin v. Chin Bow*) excluded by the 1924 act and the Supreme Court rulings, and with Congress's refusal to exempt noncitizen Chinese children of any age (1930 act), what remained were children—but not grandchildren—of Chinese American citizens who had lived in the United States. These children were still citizens under the jus sanguinis rule. As long as they were citizens, foreign-born children were not subjected to immigration law, which applied only to aliens. Exclusionists such as the American Federation of Labor directed their attack against nationality law that endowed children of Chinese Americans with U.S. citizenship. Restrictions on the acquisition or retention of citizenship on jus sanguinis rule could make children of Chinese Americans into "aliens ineligible to citizenship," which in turn would bar their entry to the United States. It was in this context that age became a crucial factor in determining citizenship jus sanguinis.

Chinese Americans found the citizenship of their children under attack amid the movement to "equalize" nationality law. Citizenship on jus sanguinis rule descended only from the father but not from the mother, and organizations such as the National Woman's Party had been engaging in a campaign to equalize nationality rights between men and women. Until 1922, the nationality of a nuclear family was based solely on the husband/father. A foreign woman automatically became a U.S. citizen upon her marriage to a U.S. citizen (marital naturalization) or upon the naturalization of her husband. This was coupled with marital expatriation, which deprived a woman of her U.S. citizenship upon her marriage to a foreigner. Abolition of both practices by the Cable Act of 1922 created households where the spouses held different nationalities, but citizenship of children continued to be determined by the father. Equal nationality rights between fathers and mothers became the demand of women's organizations.[52] Exclusionists sought to take advantage of this movement to amend nationality law in such a way as to deny jus sanguinis citizenship to children of Chinese Americans altogether or to raise the hurdle for their acquiring and retaining citizenship. The American Federation of Labor, for instance, insisted that the organization would not agree to extending the right to women, unless the new law restricted the citizenship of children of Asian Americans.[53]

Congress included these exclusionist motions in the 1934 bill and the eventual law. Most explicitly, the House Committee on Immigration reported out an "equalization bill" that allowed both fathers and mothers to pass on their citizenship but only if the noncitizen parent was racially eligible for citizenship.[54] The committee argued that the children of a parent racially excluded from attaining U.S. citizenship through naturalization should not be able to acquire it through derivation either.[55] Drawing on rulings affirming the constitutionality of antimiscegenation laws, the Immigration Committee argued that it was an "equal" bill that applied to any citizen including "a white man who may marry a Chinese girl in China," but the obvious targets were children born to Chinese American fathers and Chinese mothers.[56]

Chinese American organizations filed a strong protest, arguing that the bill "originated to establish equality between male and female" was bringing "injustice to American citizens of Chinese race."[57] The House eventually defeated the explicit racial bar, but the opposition was grounded in the no less racist idea that when deprived of jus sanguinis citizenship, Chinese American men might try to marry white American women, which congressmen found unacceptable.[58]

Congress included restrictionists' proposals in the Nationality Act of 1934, in clauses that were formally race-neutral but legislated with Chinese Americans in mind. One amendment concerned citizenship derivation by the third generation. The new law reaffirmed the Chin Bow ruling that the parents' residence in the United States before the birth of their children was mandatory to pass on their U.S. citizenship. Another was age, which had never before been a factor in jus sanguinis citizenship derivation. The law provided that citizenship would be lost unless the foreign-born U.S. citizen resided in the United States for five years between his or her thirteenth and eighteenth birthdays. In other words, failure to take residence in the country before reaching age thirteen resulted in an automatic loss of citizenship.[59]

To consider these changes in relation to Chin Bow, the issue contested in the case was whether Chin Dun had the power to transfer his U.S. citizenship to his son Chin Bow, who was born before Chin Dun first came to the United States. The admissibility of Chin Bow, who had to be a U.S. citizen to enter the country, depended on his father. To solidify the ruling, the 1934 act expressed in clear language that a foreign-born citizen must establish residence prior to having children in order to pass on his citizenship.[60] Moreover, now at stake under the new age requirement was not only the power of foreign-born U.S. citizens to transfer their citizenship to others but the issue of their own citizenship. Congress questioned the citizenship of foreign-born citizens as well by pointing to the age that they first moved to the country, which was twenty-eight in the case of Chin Dun. Under the new act, foreign-born citizens of any race who continued to live abroad after reaching thirteen (later raised to sixteen by the 1940 Nationality Act) ceased to be U.S. citizens. Although the 1934 act was not retroactive, the retention deadline applied to any foreign-born citizen born after May 24, 1934.[61] In 1950, as the first generation of post-1934 foreign-born children approached the deadline, a rush to retain citizenship would occur.

Conclusion

By 1934, the age of the child living abroad had become critical for families, since being unable to send for the child before hard deadlines closed the possibility of immigration to the United States, but in different ways. For immigrants from Southern and Eastern Europe, of utmost importance was the age of twenty-one. Although the 1928 act gave certain preferences to children of permanent residents, it had little practical meaning when the visa backlog exceeded the quotas by years, if not decades. To apply for naturalization and to send for a child before reaching twenty-one was critical for families. On the other hand, such limitations were of little importance for immigrants from countries with large quotas, since visas were readily available even without any exemptions. Thus, age was not a stand-alone criterion, but its significance was intertwined with a hierarchy among immigrants from Europe.

For Chinese American families, the age of thirteen was the deadline to retain U.S. citizenship of their Chinese-born children (later raised to sixteen by the 1940 Nationality Act). To be sure, this was a formally race-neutral rule that applied to any foreign-born children of U.S. citizens, but the consequence of loss of citizenship was particularly grave for children of Chinese Americans, since it immediately made them into "aliens ineligible to citizenship" permanently barred from the United States.[62] Age intertwined with race and citizenship to draw a hard boundary between "white" children and Asian children of U.S. citizens.

In 1965, Congress would eventually abolish the immigration system based on explicit quotas, but along with the principle of numerical immigration restriction, citizenship and age continue to be crucial factors in the lives of immigrant families. For instance, until this day immediate admission of family members (immigration outside the annual numerical ceiling) is reserved for U.S. citizens. Children of U.S. citizens can receive visas outside the annual ceiling only before reaching twenty-one, which is a legacy of the 1928 act that defined nonquota children as those under that age (raised from eighteen). Today, in countries with a large demand for immigration visas, such as Mexico and the Philippines, the visa waiting period for older children of citizens extends as long as ten (the Philippines) or even twenty years (Mexico). Intertwined with other criteria, such as citizenship status of the visa sponsor, age continues to determine who is eligible to immigrate to the United States and how soon they are eligible.

NOTES

1 "Harding Takes Up Aliens' Exclusion," *New York Times*, September 13, 1921.
2 *Weedin v. Chin Bow* 274 U.S. 657 (1927).
3 Section 37, Immigration Act of March 3, 1903 (32 Stat. 1213); Edward P. Hutchinson, *Legislative History of American Immigration Policy, 1798–1965* (Philadelphia: University of Pennsylvania Press, 1981), 506–7.
4 Hiroshi Motomura, *Americans in Waiting: The Lost Story of Immigration and Citizenship in the United States* (New York: Oxford University Press, 2006), 115–23.
5 Adena Miller Rich, "Naturalization and Family Welfare: Doors Closed to the Noncitizen," *Social Service Review* 14, no. 2 (1940): 260.
6 Section 2, Immigration Act of February 20, 1907 (34 Stat. 1228); "New Immigration Law," *American Journal of International Law* 1, no. 2 (1907): 452–58.
7 Section 3, Immigration Act of 1917 (39 Stat. 874); John Higham, *Strangers in the Land: Patterns of American Nativism, 1860–1925* (New Brunswick, N.J.: Rutgers University Press, 1986), 191–93, 202–3; Bill Ong Hing, "'Translate This': The 1917 Literacy Law," in *Defining America through Immigration Policy* (Philadelphia: University of Pennsylvania Press, 2004), 51.
8 "Admissible alien" meant that along with other qualifications such as health, the new immigrant himself or herself had to pass the literacy test. Literacy was not required of citizens.
9 Section 3, Immigration Act of 1917 (34 Stat. 874): When the literacy test was proposed in 1896, one version required all immigrants above fourteen to pass the test, while the other version required only males between sixteen and sixty to pass. As a compromise, all immigrants over sixteen were required to pass the test, but a male immigrant's wife, children, and aged parents were exempted. Nancy F. Cott, *Public Vows: A History of Marriage and the Nation* (Cambridge, Mass.: Harvard University Press, 2002), 141, 155.
10 Higham, *Strangers in the Land*, 312–24; Aristide R. Zolberg, *A Nation by Design: Immigration Policy in the Fashioning of America* (Cambridge, Mass.: Harvard University Press, 2006), 223–42.
11 Immigration Act of May 19, 1921 (41 Stat. 5); Immigration Act of 1924 (43 Stat. 153). For discussion of the shift from open to closed migration, see Mae Ngai, *Impossible Subjects: Illegal Aliens and the Making of Modern America* (Princeton, N.J.: Princeton University Press, 2004), 18–25.

12 U.S. Census Bureau, *Fifteenth Census of the United States–1930—Population, Volume II: General Report, Statistics by Subject* (Washington, D.C.: Government Printing Office, 1933), 406–7.

13 This was the idea of Representative Albert Johnson (R-Wash.), future author of the Immigration Act of 1924, H.R. 66-14461 (1920); Higham, *Strangers in the Land*, 307.

14 Senator William P. Dillingham (D-Vt.), former chair of the U.S. Immigration Commission (1907–11), had proposed the quotas restriction as early as 1913. 60 Cong. Rec. 3447 (1921) (Senator William Dillingham); Desmond King, *Making Americans: Immigration, Race, and the Origins of the Diverse Democracy* (Cambridge, Mass.: Harvard University Press, 2000), 58; Roger Daniels, *Guarding the Golden Door: American Immigration Policy and Immigrants since 1882* (New York: Hill & Wang, 2004), 46–47; U.S. Immigration Commission, *Reports of the Immigration Commission: Vol. 1. Abstracts of Reports of the Immigration Commission* (Washington, D.C.: Government Printing Office, 1911), 24, 42. For return migration, see Mark Wyman, *Round-Trip to America: The Immigrants Return to Europe, 1880–1930* (Ithaca, N.Y.: Cornell University Press, 1993), 9–12. For male predominance in prerestriction migration, see Donna Gabaccia, *From the Other Side: Women, Gender, and Immigrant Life in the U.S., 1820–1990* (Bloomington: Indiana University Press, 1994), chap. 3.

15 *Restriction of Immigration*, H.R. Rep. No. 67-4 (1920); *Emergency Immigration Legislation*, S. Rep. No. 67-17 (1920).

16 61 Cong. Rec. 562, 563, 570, 579 (1921), sec. 2(a), 2(d). Preference within the quotas was accorded to other family members of citizens: wives, parents, siblings, and fiancées. Family members of declarants and World War I veterans were also given preferences: children under eighteen, wives, parents, siblings, and fiancées.

17 Florence C. Cassidy, "The Increasing Importance of Naturalization: Its Legal and Education Significance" (paper, International Institutes annual conference, 1925), 11–12, YWCA of the U.S.A. Records, reel 100, microdex 6, Sophia Smith Collection, Smith College; H. F. Gosnell, "Non-naturalization: A Study in Political Assimilation," *American Journal of Sociology* 33, no. 6 (1928): 935–36.

18 "Americans in a Hurry," *Interpreter* 3, no. 1 (January 1924): 3–4.

19 "Harding Takes Up Aliens' Exclusion."

20 John Torpey, *The Invention of the Passport: Surveillance, Citizenship, and the State* (Cambridge: Cambridge University Press, 2000), 117–21.

21 Until 1924, immigration officials at the ports of entry charged the quotas by the number of immigrants who actually arrived in the United States, and consuls issued more visas than the annual quotas. Thus, many immigrants with visas were turned away at the ports due to quota oversubscription. After 1924, consuls took on the primary responsibility of numerical immigration restriction and charged the quotas by the number of visas issued.

22 Cecilia Razovsky, "America's Present Immigration Policy: The Visa and Quota Laws as They Affect the Clients of Social Agencies," in National Conference of Social Work, *Proceedings 1927* (Chicago: University of Chicago Press, 1927), 600.

23 *Commissioner of Immigration v. Gottlieb*, 265 U.S. 310 (1924); Martha Gardner, *The Qualities of a Citizen: Women, Immigration, and Citizenship, 1870–1965* (Princeton, N.J.: Princeton University Press, 2005), 125–27.

24 Section 4 (a), Immigration Act of 1924 (43 Stat. 153).

25 Sheldon Morris Neuringer, *American Jewry and United States Immigration Policy, 1881–1953* (New York: Arno Press, 1971), 190–91.

26 "International Conference of Private Associations," *Monthly Record of Migration* 1 no. 40 (1926): 17–20; International Conference of Private Organisations for the Protection of Migrants, *Separation of Families of Migrants: Reports and Resolutions* (Geneva, 1926), 6–7, box 32, National Catholic Welfare Conference Department of Immigration General Correspondence, Collection 23, Center for Migration Studies, Staten Island, N.Y.

27 For example, in 1926, the YWCA gathered some 520 cases from fourteen states. The National Conference of Social Work's Division of Immigrants conducted a survey in 140 cities, sending questionnaires to community councils, immigrant aid societies, family welfare agencies, travelers aid societies, and Red Cross chapters. The conference cooperated with the International Association of Organizations for the Protection of Migrants to report cases from both sides of the Atlantic. Cecilia Razovsky, "Humanitarian Effects of the Immigration Law," in National Conference of Social Work, *Proceedings 1925* (Chicago: University of Chicago Press, 1925), 520; Aghavinie Yeghenian, "Separated Families: A New Foreign-Born Problem Growing out of Restricted Immigration," *Woman's Press* (November 1927): 157.

28 Ethel Bird, *Separated Families and the Immigration Law* (New York: YWCA, 1927), 5–6, YWCA of the U.S.A. Records, reel 100, microdex 1, Sophia Smith Collection, Smith College.

29 "Broken Homes," *Interpreter* 5, no. 9 (November 1926): 12.

30 "Oppose Any Change in Immigration Law," *New York Times*, April 8, 1926; Allied Patriotic Societies, *Third Annual Report of the Committee on Immigration of the Allied Patriotic Societies* (New York, 1926), 8, folder 2, box 3, National Catholic Welfare Conference Department of Immigration, General Correspondence, Center for Migration Studies.

31 Roy L. Garis, "Is Our Immigration Policy Satisfactory?," *Annals of the American Academy of Political and Social Science* 156 (1931): 39–40; Candice Lewis Bredbenner, *Nationality of Her Own: Women, Marriage, and the Law of Citizenship* (Berkeley: University of California Press, 1998), 129; Rich, "Naturalization and Family Welfare."

32 Higham, *Strangers in the Land*, 324–30; Matthew Frye Jacobson, *Whiteness of a Different Color: European Immigrants and the Alchemy of Race* (Cambridge, Mass.: Harvard University Press, 1998), 93.

33 Julius Drachsler, "The Immigrant and the Realities of Assimilation," *Interpreter* 3, no. 9 (September 1924): 3–4.

34 Act of May 28, 1928 (45 Stat. 654); Hazel G. Omsbee, "Jenkins Say Reunite," *Women's Press* 23, no. 7 (July 1929): 473–74. Congress did not fully equalize the right of men and women to send for their spouses until 1952.

35 Section 13 (c) Immigration Act of 1924 (43 Stat. 153).

36 Nationality Act of July 14, 1870 (16 Stat. 254); *Ozawa v. United States*, 260 U.S. 178 (1922) on naturalization of Japanese immigrants, and *United States v. Bhagat Singh Thind* (1923) on naturalization of Indian immigrants. Ian Haney López, *White by Law: The Legal Construction of Race* (New York: New York University Press, 2006), chap. 4.

37 For birthright citizenship regardless of race, see *United States v. Wong Kim Ark*, 169 U.S. 649 (1898); Erika Lee, *At America's Gates: Chinese Immigration during the Exclusion Era* (Chapel Hill: University of North Carolina Press, 2005), 103–6.

38 *Ozawa v. United States*, 260 U.S. 178 (1922) on naturalization of Japanese immigrants, and *United States v. Bhagat Singh Thind* (1923) on naturalization of Indian immigrants. López, *White by Law*, chap. 4.

39 For Japanese exclusion, Roger Daniels, *The Politics of Prejudice: The Anti-Japanese Movement in California and the Struggle for Japanese Exclusion* (Berkeley: University of California Press, 1962).

40 In 1930, the average age of the second-generation Japanese Americans with birthright citizenship was ten. Ronald Takaki, *Strangers from a Different Shore: A History of Asian Americans* (New York: Back Bay Books, 1998), 115.

41 On admission of families of merchant-class Chinese, *United States v. Gue Lim*, 176 U.S. 459 (1900). While there was no Supreme Court ruling on excludability of Chinese wives of U.S. citizens, after *Gue Lim*, the immigration authorities inferred that if a noncitizen merchant was entitled to send for his or her family, so was a U.S. citizen; Sucheng Chan, "The Exclusion of Chinese Women," in *Entry Denied: Exclusion and the Chinese Community in America, 1882–1943*, ed. Sucheng Chan (Philadelphia: Temple University Press, 1990), 116–17.

42 *Chang Chan et al. v. Nagle*, 268 U.S. 346 (1925). By contrast the court ruled that families of merchant class Chinese were admissible. Chan, "Exclusion of Chinese Women," 124–26; Bredbenner, *Nationality of Her Own*, 128.

43 For the Chinese American Citizens Alliance, see Sau Fawn Chung, "Fighting for Their American Rights: A History of the Chinese American Citizens Alliance," in *Claiming America: Constructing Chinese American Identities during the Exclusion Era*, ed. Kevin Scott Wong and Sucheng Chan (Philadelphia: Temple University Press, 1998), 95–116.

44 Act of June 13, 1930 (46 Stat. 581).

45 *Wives of American Citizens of Oriental Race, Hearing before House Committee on Immigration and Naturalization*, 70th Cong. 551 (1930) (Edward Shaughnessy, Bureau of Immigration).

46 *Weedin v. Chin Bow*, 274 U.S. 657 (1927).

47 Lee, *At America's Gates*, 103–6.

48 During the same period, 2,800 wives of U.S. citizens immigrated to the United States. Upon return from China, Chinese American men with wives in China often reported birth of children while abroad. Reports of births of sons outnumbered those of daughters more than tenfold, which involved a strategy to secure a

spot for other men (relatives or otherwise) to immigrate to the United States as so-called paper sons. Lee, *At America's Gates*, 115–16, 126–31.

49 *Weedin v. Chin Bow* 274 U.S. 657 (1927).

50 Nationality law stated that U.S. citizenship "shall not descend to [foreign-born] children whose fathers never resided in the United States," and the issue was whether the father had to have resided in the United States before the child was born, or whether a child born before the father first took residence in the country acquired U.S. citizenship.

51 Warner A. Parker, "Ineligible to Citizenship Provisions of the Immigration Act of 1924," *American Journal of International Law* 19 (1925): 42.

52 For equal nationality rights movement, Bredbenner, *Nationality of Her Own*, esp. chap. 6; Linda K. Kerber, *No Constitutional Right to Be Ladies: Women and the Obligations of Citizenship* (New York: Hill & Wang, 1998); 41–43; Nancy F. Cott, "Marriage and Women's Citizenship in the United States, 1830–1934," *American Historical Review* 103, no. 5 (1998): 1440–74; Gardner, *Qualities of a Citizen*, 172.

53 William C. Hushing, Legislative Representative, American Federation of Labor, to House Committee on Immigration and Naturalization, April 3, 1933, "H.R. 3673, 5 of 6" folder, box 72, 73A-D11, RG 233, National Archives and Records Administration, Washington, D.C.; Gardner, *Qualities of a Citizen*, 172.

54 Beatrice Loftus McKenzie, "American at Birth: United States Birthright Citizenship in Nation and Empire, 1866–1934" (PhD diss., University of Oregon, 2006), 195–96.

55 Memorandum for H.R. 7673, "H.R. 7673, 2 of 3" folder, box 71, 73A-D11, RG 233, National Archives and Records Administration.

56 78 Cong. Rec. 7330 (1934) (Samuel Dickstein, D-N.Y., House Immigration and Naturalization Committee chair); Peggy Pascoe, *What Comes Naturally: Miscegenation Law and the Making of Race in America* (New York: Oxford University Press, 2009), 108.

57 Oakland Lodge of Chinese American Citizens Alliance to Samuel Dickstein, April 14, 1934; "H.R. 7673, 2 of 3" folder, box 71, 73A-D11, RG 233, National Archives and Records Administration.

58 78 Cong. Rec. 7349 (1934).

59 Section 1, Nationality Act of May 24, 1934 (48 Stat. 797).

60 Whereas previous nationality law stated that U.S. citizenship "shall not descend to [foreign-born] children whose fathers never resided in the United States," the 1934 Nationality Act required that "the citizen father or citizen mother" must have "resided in the United States *previous to* the birth of such child." Section 1, Nationality Act of May 24, 1934 (48 Stat. 797), emphasis added.

61 The deadline was raised to sixteen by the Nationality Act of 1940 (54 Stat. 1137) and to twenty-three by the Immigration and Nationality Act of 1952 (66 Stat. 13), and remained part of nationality law until 1973.

62 Section 1, Nationality Act of May 24, 1934 (48 Stat. 797).

PART III

Age in Modern America

9

Age and Retirement

Major Issues in the American Experience

WILLIAM GRAEBNER

Age and retirement. Two peas in a pod? Jack and Jill? "Love and Marriage" ("you can't have one without the other")? In a sense, yes. Even in affluent America, and with the exception of the wealthy, the injured, and the bored few, most people retire from work late in life. Moreover, in the second half of the twentieth century, retirements spiked at two ages: at sixty-two, when Social Security benefits became available for men under 1961 amendments to the original Social Security Act; and at sixty-five, when full retirement benefits were available under the original legislation and corporate mandatory retirement programs—still legal well into the 1970s—compelled retirement, most commonly at age sixty-five.[1] Besides these legal incentives and restrictions, age conspired to produce involuntary retirements among older workers who were deemed by employers to be relatively inefficient and hence not worth keeping on, or who, because of age discrimination, could not find a job once unemployed.

Yet there are reasons to be skeptical even of the arguments made above. The retirement bumps at sixty-two and sixty-five, while triggered by chronological age, are in fact about money and politics: the results of political decisions that in the decades after 1950 made benefit payments sufficient to allow large numbers of people to leave the workplace. As for mandatory retirement plans, which were especially common between 1945 and 1978, mandatory retirement was less about getting older, inefficient workers out of the workplace than it was the necessary capstone of a mutually beneficial long-term contract between employer and employee, through which employees were encouraged to work harder by being paid less in early years and more in later ones. Although there is substantial anecdotal evidence for late nineteenth- and early twentieth-century age discrimination—and therefore for the causal relationship between age discrimination and retirement—constant labor force participation rates between 1890 and 1930 suggest that age discrimination may not have been determinative in compelling retirement.[2]

Although it would be wrong to suggest that chronological age and retirement are not causally linked, many other factors aside from chronological age, or in conjunction with it, have influenced the timing of retirement and the retirement experience. Among these are the American Civil War (and the veterans' benefits it induced), industrialization and urbanization, rising life expectancy, *ideas* about aging and older workers, health (and health-related benefits), disability (and disability benefits), the declining cost of leisure, the marketing of the retirement lifestyle, gender and class, deindustrialization and globalization, and intergenerational conflicts. While retirement is undeniably grounded in chronological age, it was, and is, a highly variable experience.

Despite this variability, the relationship between chronological age and retirement can be charted and understood over four time periods. In the colonial and into the early national era, *functional* age—what people could do and how they felt in old age—determined when one would stop working. *Chronological* age emerged as a determinant of retirement only late in the period, and for very few people. In the late nineteenth and early twentieth centuries, under the impact of rapid industrialization, small numbers of workers were affected by the chronological age provisions of the new corporate pension plans, which pushed some workers into retirement, and many older workers were subject to *life-stage* ideas of age—in this case, age discrimination—which pushed some older workers, perhaps a substantial number, into an unwanted, early retirement. While chronological age was not generally a significant cause of retirement in this period, it was a very important factor in the retirement of Civil War veterans, especially after 1890.

Chronological age emerged as a dominant factor in retirement only in the 1930s, when the federal government used chronological age in the Railroad Retirement Act (1934) and the Social Security Act (1935). Social Security was especially important, for it linked money (benefit payments) with an age—really, the *idea* of an age, sixty-five—that quickly became *the* age of retirement. The impact of chronological age was deepened by the pension boom of the 1940s and 1950s, when corporations and unions used mandatory retirement to shed older workers and to allocate work and wages between age groups.

The "age of chronological age" lasted for about fifty years, into the 1970s and even the 1980s, but one could see a new paradigm emerging in the 1960s, when federal law made age discrimination illegal, the first in several steps that would, in 1986, make mandatory retirement (and its mechanism, chronological age) illegal in most public and private employment. Social security remained a stimulus to retirement at sixty-two and sixty-five, but even in the 1970s, large numbers of workers retired *before* benefits became available. In addition, the emerging global economy, with its demands for worker flexibility, helped sever the link between chronological age and retirement.

Beyond identifying the key historical periods, a deeper understanding of the history of retirement and its relationship to age can be gleaned from applying "push" and "pull" models. Were older workers *pushed* into retirement, or onto the scrap heap, by ageism, age discrimination, the infirmities of old age, or systems of mandatory retirement? Or were they *pulled* into retirement by Social Security payments, mounting personal savings, and the security offered by private and public pension plans, including the Civil War pension system? Very broadly (there are exceptions), the first model foregrounds age and ideas about it, tends to conceptualize the elderly as victims, and focuses attention, though not exclusively, on the decades *before* 1930. The second model foregrounds money and affluence, tends to conceptualize the elderly as agents making thoughtful choices about how to spend later life, focuses attention on the decades *after* 1930, and features public and private retirement systems that utilized chronological age.

***

The colonial era was "no golden age of senescence" (in historian Carole Haber's phrase), in which the old were invariably venerated, but the elderly were certainly more admired than they are today, perhaps because their control over the main source of power—landed wealth—was protective.[3] In this economic environment, and in a society where the great majority of men were farmers, chronological age was not a factor, and retirement as we understand it today did not exist; older men and women worked as long as they could, then stopped working, whether gradually or abruptly. New England ministers might be asked to retire, but as "a duty," or for "cause," rather than at a fixed age determined by church policy. The first signs of mandatory retirement appeared between 1790 and 1820, when laws in some states required the retirement of public officials, beginning with judges, usually at age sixty or seventy. Changing *ideas* about age were one cause, particularly a new enthusiasm for youth (including the abolition of primogeniture) brought on by the American Revolution.[4]

The forced retirement of judges notwithstanding, mandatory retirement remained a minor part of the American retirement experience until well into the twentieth century. Of more significance in the intervening years, and especially in the last decades of the nineteenth century and first several of the twentieth, was a deep current of age discrimination, forcing some older workers into premature "retirement." Age (the *fact* of being old) may not have mattered, but ageism (the *idea* of being old) did. Ageist assumptions advanced across a wide variety of late nineteenth-century and early twentieth-century institutions, including the military, large corporations, state and federal civil service bureaucracies, and charity and relief organizations. Encouraged by scientists, physicians, efficiency experts, and other professionals, these institutions and others developed rigid, age-based criteria—unproved and, indeed, false—that classified older people as "unproductive and useless."[5]

The U.S. Pension Bureau, charged with writing checks to Civil War veterans, claimed that it was "overstaffed with the elderly." In the printing industry, the spread of the Mergenthaler line-casting machine after its invention in 1884 threatened older men, who responded by dyeing their hair. By 1900, the anxiety caused by the prospect of moving into old age had led to "age rounding" in the census—the practice of reporting one's age as younger than it really was. Turn-of-the-century newspaper advertisements regularly discriminated on the basis of age—sometimes chronological age, sometimes life stage—requesting applications from workers who were "young" or in a particular age category, such as twenty-five to forty (and hence *rejecting* inquiries from those over forty). Private pension plans, which usually contained provisions for mandatory retirement at a specified age, had by the late 1920s become a factor in the matrix of age discrimination, covering more than

15 percent of employees in mining, office work, manufacturing, and transportation. The bellwether event in the history of age discrimination occurred in 1905, when William Osler, the esteemed Johns Hopkins physician, insisted that the creative work of the world was accomplished between the ages of twenty-five and forty, and—taking the concept from novelist Anthony Trollope—broached the idea of retirement at sixty, a year of contemplation, then a "peaceful departure by chloroform."[6]

The issue, then, is not whether age discrimination existed—it seems clear that it did—but whether it produced forced retirements among older workers, whether workers subject to discrimination ended up on the "scrap heap," as it was called.[7] Not all did. Many superannuated workers in public and private employment were spared the scrap heap because their employers felt awkward dismissing workers who had no pension plan to cushion their later years or, as was generally the case, little or no savings. By 1900, the Department of the Treasury—and it was not unique—had become a caretaking agency, a kind of informal retirement home for superannuated employees, mostly low-income clerical workers, protected from layoff by supervisors who would not fire them for inefficiency. Something similar occurred in the private sector, where some large firms—steel companies and railroads among them—provided light work assignments for employees deemed superannuated, and even firms using scientific management methods retained older employees beyond the point of greatest usefulness. Undoubtedly, some older workers benefitted from accumulated experience and knowledge.[8]

Also of benefit to older workers were artificial job ladders, developed after about 1910 in industries in which the minimal skills required of most workers would normally have restricted upward mobility within the enterprise. Defined (until the final rung) by time on the job rather than chronological age, job ladders created a sense of mobility, providing gradually higher wages to workers as they aged, even as their skill levels and contributions to the bottom line declined or remained unchanged. Older workers received more money, and a feeling of moving up, while management reduced turnover and raised productivity. But job ladders and seniority systems also created problems for older workers. One was that the ladders worked only if filled from the bottom, by younger workers, a process that shut out older job seekers. More important, ladders and seniority systems produced an aging, and at some point inefficient, workforce. "The solution to the dilemma," write Haber and Brian Gratton, "was mandatory retirement."[9] Therefore, while ladders and seniority systems may have protected older workers, they also subjected them to two forms of age discrimination: one at hiring, the other at forced retirement.

Did age discrimination (the scrap heap) and/or the "rational" desire for younger, more efficient workers result in involuntary retirement? Both logic and statistics are in play here. The logical argument is that if industrialization, bureaucratization, or modernization in general had marginalized older workers, then, as these processes gathered speed in the late nineteenth and early twentieth centuries, an increasing percentage of older workers, especially those over fifty, would be found on the sidelines, unable to find employment, involuntarily retired. But that apparently didn't happen. Labor force participation rates (LFPRs) for older (sixty plus) men were quite stable at roughly 60 to 65 percent over the 1870 to 1930 period, an era corresponding to the emergence of virulent age discrimination. Had age discrimination (whether rational or irrational) significantly affected older workers in this period, the LFPR for the group would have fallen significantly.[10]

Even if one assumes stable LFPRs for the sixty-year period, to properly evaluate the impact of age discrimination on retirement one must explain why about one-third of the older, male population was out of the labor force. If they weren't victims of the industrial scrap heap, why weren't they working? One answer is that farmers, once thought to be lifelong workers, actually did retire, often setting up households in small towns where the census listed them as "urban."[11] In addition, some turn-of-the-century workers, especially but not solely the self-employed (including farmers), had sufficient savings to afford a voluntary "modern" retirement.[12] Both these groups were "pulled" into retirement, rather than "pushed" by discriminatory practices.

Although evidence for the idea that income and savings produced significant numbers of voluntary retirements around the turn of the century is limited, one element of the population seems clearly to have been encouraged to retire, pulled into retirement by windfall benefits not available to the general population: Civil War veterans. From modest beginnings in 1862 compensating disabled veterans of the Union army (those who were unable to perform manual labor) and dependents of those killed or injured in military service, by the turn of the century Civil War pensions had become a social service behemoth, making up about 25 percent of the national budget and, in 1910, delivering benefits to 28 percent "of all American men aged 65 or more"—and to many widows and dependents. At first designed to compensate soldiers for war-related disabilities, the program evolved into something resembling old-age welfare (though only for veterans and their dependents), the payments triggered by chronological age. In 1890, under pressure from Republican politicians who stood to gain the most from enlarging the ranks of those receiving veterans' benefits, Congress dropped the original requirement of a service-related injury or death, and, through administrative rulings, the inability to perform manual labor (even as a result of just being "old") became sufficient reason for an aged veteran to receive benefits. Because of the bureaucratic complexity of investigating each disability claim individually, the next step was to generate a precise standard by which all claims could be measured. Hence a 1906 amendment stated that "the age of sixty-two years and over shall be considered a permanent specific disability within the meaning of the pension laws." Of course, this simple solution to a complex problem had the additional political benefit of producing larger numbers of grateful, voting veterans. After 1912 revisions, benefits rose automatically with age.[13]

The program is important for several reasons. Because benefits were so widely dispersed (in the northern states, that is) and generous, veterans' pensions allowed thousands of men and their dependents to voluntarily retire, perhaps accounting for a substantial percentage of the one-third of older men not participating in the labor force in the Progressive Era. Although the age-sixty-two provision in the 1906 act no doubt induced retirements at that age, it was money—now available at a specific chronological age—that drove the phenomenon. After 1890 the veterans' pension program resembled an old-age pension plan, in that age soon became the only requirement for receiving veterans' benefits, but it was not conceived or administered as an old-age pension plan; age was only a *mechanism* for distributing benefits to a carefully circumscribed group of recipients: men who had fought, sacrificed, and died for the nation and who, it was believed, had earned compensation. Aging paupers need not apply—unless, of course, they were Civil War veterans. Besides military service, the factors correlating with eligibility were residence in the North, being native-born, and living in a Republican area and outside a big city. Political sociologist Theda Skocpol describes the program, far from being social welfare for the elderly, as a product of "gender-oriented policymaking" and "white male fraternalism," facilitated by the "U.S. patronage democracy." In short, while age seems central to the system of Civil War pensions, it was largely a matter of politics and bureaucratic convenience.[14]

Relatively little is known about how women navigated the retirement matrix in this period, in part because the work experience of many women—inside rather than outside the home, child rearing, and on farms—did not result in participation in pension plans or seniority systems or make them subject to mandatory retirement. And the Civil War veterans who triggered the massive national pension expenditures at the turn of the last century were, of course, men, though widows were also beneficiaries. Like men, women were subject to age discrimination in hiring; ads for domestic servants called for "girl" or "young woman," and in 1925 AT&T announced "attractive positions in telephone work for young women between 16 and 25 years of age." Still, we know little about how age discrimination affected older women workers, those on the cusp of retirement. Like older men, who faced accusations of being "useless in the workplace," older women were, writes Lisa Dillon, "defined as useless because their mission to bear children was over"—a state David Hackett Fischer calls "maternal 'retirement.'"[15]

It is clear, too, that older women faced greater risks of poverty than men, either because their aging, employed husbands were vulnerable to ageism and unemployment, or because many older women had no paid employment or, often, no husband. In the absence of support from kin, black elderly women took menial jobs, eking out a living. Although the risks of impoverishment were higher for the elderly, whether male or female, both men and women were more likely to maintain a functioning household if they had a spouse; one might say that marriage trumped age, yielding a more comfortable and independent retirement.[16]

Despite these indications that the retirement pattern of women differs from that of men, these differences have affected the age/retirement nexus less than class. Throughout American history, the ability to choose retirement, and especially an early retirement, has depended largely on income and resources. Less successful farmers did not retire. African Americans in the post–Civil War South lacked the property that would have allowed them to retire. As industrialization gained traction in the late nineteenth and early twentieth centuries, long hours and physical labor made retirement attractive for many in the working class, yet it remained unaffordable for most, with the notable exception of pensioned Civil War veterans and their widows. The welfare state gradually changed that, as did the post–World War II pension boom; by the 1970s, the nonsupervisory working class was retiring at a mean age of 60.5 years, well below the national average, and the reason for retirement most often cited was that it was affordable. It mattered, too, that leisure had become less expensive.[17]

The starting point for understanding the third period in the history of retirement—roughly the half century after 1930—is the steep, ongoing, long-term decline in LFPRs for older workers, beginning as early as the 1930s and well under way by 1950. When the stock market crash of October 1929 ushered in the Great Depression, about 60 percent of American men over age sixty-five were in the labor force; by 1990, only about 20 percent were working.[18]

Within this frame of LFPR secular decline, the consensus is that workers were not "pushed" but "pulled" into retirement, emboldened to surrender their jobs by *money*—that is, government money: the welfare and social insurance provisions of the 1935 Social Security Act and, in progressive states such as Massachusetts, old-age assistance. Government policy was of particular importance in the decades after 1950. Congress passed changes to Social Security, including regular benefit increases and the availability of reduced retirement benefits at sixty-two for women (in 1956) and men (in 1961). Medicare and Medicaid (available at age sixty-five under the Older Americans Act, 1965) and the indexing of Social Security benefits (1972) also made retirement more affordable and more secure. Some of the sharp decline in elderly LFPRs in the 1970s was due to changes in the laws governing disability, "an important route into early retirement," according to one scholar. Government benefits (and to a lesser extent, private pension plans) were critical because Americans were such poor savers; a study of those approaching retirement age in 1984 revealed mean liquid wealth of just sixty-six hundred dollars, and renters had "virtually no liquid assets."[19] Although benefits were not especially generous compared with those in other industrialized countries, recent studies of retirement behavior suggest that retirement is less influenced by the *level* of benefits than it is by their *availability*.[20] So it was not just money, but the *idea* of money.

Declining LFPRs, especially among better paid, white-collar and career employees, were also the result of the mandatory retirement provisions of private pension plans. Many existing plans had been dissolved by corporate management in the early years of the Great Depression, but the Revenue Act of 1942, which provided tax incentives for firms establishing pension plans and required "broad employee participation," triggered a dramatic resurgence in these instruments, ushering in a four-decade era when mandatory retirement—based on chronological age and greased with money—was both legal and widely applied. According to one estimate, in the 1950s nearly half of all firms had provisions for mandatory retirement, and of those that did, whether in the 1950s or later, the great majority required retirement at age sixty-five, an age adopted from the Social Security Act.[21] Mandatory retirement was also a feature of many collectively bargained pension plans, especially those negotiated in the recession periods of 1948–49 and 1957–58, when labor unions were more likely to recognize the benefits of retiring older workers to accommodate younger ones.[22]

This package of public and private benefits available to retired workers, including Social Security and private pension plans, was made possible by a postwar American economy at the very peak of its world dominance and productive powers. When that peak passed in the mid-1970s, the benefits—Medicare, defined-benefit pensions plans, and Social Security—would become increasingly controversial and problematic.

The push/pull schematic is too roughly hewn to account for every facet of what was a very complex, and often nonlinear, historical process. Although the pre-1930 period can best be described as an era when some (male) workers were pushed into retirement, it also had "pull" elements, including federal Civil War pensions and state old-age pension laws, passed and in effect in eight states before 1930.[23] Nor did the "push" into retirement simply disappear after 1930, the beginning of a roughly fifty-year period characterized by "pull" forces. The old-age insurance provisions of the Social Security Act, drafted in 1934 by the Committee on Economic Security (CES), were a mix of features intended to promote retirement among older workers. Although neither the original act nor the 1939 amendments strictly prohibited those who received benefits (beginning in 1940) from working, the amount of allowed earned income—fifteen dollars per month—was designed to push workers, however gently, from the labor force. "He [an older worker] would not get *retirement* benefits unless he retired," recalled CES executive director Barbara Armstrong. "We *never* called these benefits anything but *retirement* benefits." Moreover, the age of eligibility enshrined in the act, sixty-five, was deliberately selected over younger ages, thought to be too costly, and older ages (including sixty-eight and seventy, the latter common in state old-age pension programs), because of anticipated public and congressional opposition to late retirement in a period of high unemployment.[24]

Even in this midcentury period, when mechanisms employing chronological age proliferated, policies based on life stage were common. Mandatory retirement was described by legal historian Lawrence Friedman as "*the* form of age discrimination *par excellence*," and its proliferation in the postwar era attests to the existence of the "push" of age discrimination well after 1930. There is other evidence. The 1949 Steel Board Report, characterized by one scholar as "the defining document in the history of collectively bargained pension plans," was famously "push" rather than "pull"; it justified mandatory retirement and the costs of pensions in language that recalled the "scrap heap" arguments of an earlier era: "human machines, like the inanimate machines, have a definite rate of depreciation."[25] A survey conducted in 1941 and 1942—after prosperity had returned—reported that over half of those surveyed said they had retired because they had been laid off.[26] Hiring age limits remained common in the 1950s; in Columbus, Ohio, 80 percent of job notices were for men under age forty-five, and in Houston in 1952, 52 percent of job notices had age requirements. In the midst of the postwar boom, the U.S. Department of Labor was awash in letters from middle-aged men and women, frustrated and angry over their inability to find work. Even in 1965, when just a few states had laws against age discrimination, and just two years before federal law made discrimination in employment illegal for most workers between forty and sixty-five, about 60 percent of employers in states without prohibitions imposed upper age limits—usually between forty-five and fifty-five—on new hires.[27]

Even in a post-1930 era when the reach of the welfare state seems clearly to have been a major factor in stimulating retirements, ideas—about age and about retirement—have remained in play. Beginning in the 1950s, sociologists of aging abandoned "activity theory," which postulated that older people required a high level of interaction, for "disengagement" theory, which presented disengagement from social relations as a reasonable and inevitable process and retirement as "permission to disengage." Theorists of leisure confronted retirees' problems and resolved to provide American men over fifty with a new concept of leisure. "Perhaps," suggested Lynn White, Jr., president of Mills College, "we have to glamorize leisure as we have not."[28] At the same time, the retired and those approaching retirement age were being exposed to a barrage of propaganda: the "selling of retirement." Life insurance companies were at the forefront of this effort, emphasizing in advertisements that retirement was the joy of being at the ball park on a weekday afternoon. Larger companies (Esso, Lockheed Aircraft) and major labor unions (United Automobile Workers, United Steelworkers) sponsored retirement preparation programs, designed in part to convince retirees and prospective retirees of the virtues of life beyond the workplace.[29]

Informing this postwar discussion of retirement was the assumption that retirement was an unnatural state, one to be taught and learned, as if age itself—being sixty-two or sixty-five or simply "old"—was insufficient preparation for a new life of play and leisure, with work and the workplace left behind. The instructions and bromides were aimed mostly at men, and white men at that, for it was this group that dominated the postwar workplace in sheer numbers, was most able to afford retirement, and was most likely to be forced into retirement by the mandatory plans that were all the rage at midcentury. A recent book by Gregory Wood suggests that most postwar men resisted retirement and were tormented by it, clinging to what remained of their work-defined masculinity by retreating to basement workshop "dens" and barbecuing outdoors—a "man's job."[30]

No doubt some men feared retirement and had to be sold on it. But by and large, it was welcomed. A 1958 survey revealed that many workers had bought into some version of the Depression-era slogan of the Townsend Old Age Pension Movement: "Youth for work. Age for Leisure." In all, 68 percent of factory workers and 39 percent of supervisory personnel looked forward to "taking it easy" in retirement. After 1950 leisure became not only more varied and attractive, but also inexpensive.[31] An elaborate survey of 849 nonsupervisory, blue-collar, sales, and service workers who retired between 1968 and 1978 confirms that most workers wanted to retire. Of those required to retire, only about one-third would have preferred to continue working. In fact, nearly a quarter of the respondents said they had retired because the pressures of work were too great. The low median age at retirement—60.5 years—suggests that many chose to retire even before they became eligible for reduced Social Security benefits. The authors of the study concluded that most of the subjects "retired early of their own free will," "apparently glad to leave the world of work behind them." Perhaps most revealing, the abolition of mandatory retirement in 1986 did not immediately result in a rise in LFPRs for older workers.[32]

Today, poverty remains a prominent issue for older women nearing retirement, especially if they are single.[33] But the mid-twentieth century yielded important changes in the situation of older women, whether retired or considering retirement. State and federal old-age assistance programs—designed for the elderly poor—established an income floor for many nonworking, "retired" women. After 1940, old-age insurance (Social Security) provided women who had been long-term, outside-the-home workers, or whose spouses had worked, with the basis for a modest retirement income, and Medicare and Medicaid provided benefits without regard to earnings or gender. While the LFPR for older men *fell* precipitously in the decades after 1950, that of women *rose* through the mid-1980s, bringing many women into the retirement game as full players rather than dependent observers. As their financial situations improved, more older women chose to retire, and they often chose to live alone, apart from kin. But a recent study suggests that for women, as opposed to men, the decision to retire has had less to do with money and more to do with the high value women place on "nonwork years"—essentially, leisure.[34]

Between 1965 and 1980, the era when retirement was strongly linked to chronological age had begun to wane. After 1967, employers were legally prohibited from discriminating in the hiring or firing of workers between forty and sixty-five, a restriction that functioned to prohibit the mandatory retirement of most workers under sixty-five. In 1978,

mandatory retirement—again operating through chronological age—
became illegal for workers between sixty-five and seventy. And in 1986,
mandatory retirement was prohibited for nearly all public and private
employees at any age. Even so, discrimination leading to involuntary
early retirement remained of consequence for some older workers. The
definition of age discrimination is important here. Those older workers
most affected were employed in traditional industries with traditional
skills, lacking the knowledge to transition into new industries with new
technologies, a common occurrence in periods of restructuring, such
as the 1970s and 1980s.[35] While this phenomenon presented itself sta-
tistically as age discrimination—older workers were fired and not hired
in larger percentages than other groups—it also reflects rational labor
market decisions by corporations eager to keep pace with technological
innovation. Yes, they "pushed" older workers out in some industries;
no, they did not discriminate. Therefore, after about 1980 neither mandatory retirement nor other forms of genuine (that is, irrational) age
discrimination were of great importance in moving workers out of the
workforce and into (earlier) retirement.[36]

At the same time, the new global, postindustrial economy made retirement less accessible for many lower-income workers, and by the mid-
1980s had halted the long-term decline in LFPRs for older workers—a
proxy for retirement. Wages declined or stagnated; many companies
eliminated defined benefit pension plans and with them the requirement that employees retire at a specified age; Congress abolished mandatory retirement (which came with a pension that made it affordable),
legally prohibiting the use of chronological age. Millions of Americans
approaching the standard retirement age had no health insurance. Well
into the twenty-first century, poverty and lower rates of access to health
benefits and Social Security limited the retirement aspirations of many
older Hispanics, blacks, women, and the less educated, and their LFPRs
had begun to rise. Those with limited resources often turned to a pattern
of "blurred" as opposed to "crisp" retirement, moving in and out of the
workplace as their resources dictated.[37]

The story of retirement is also a story of accommodation and conflict
between generations, between men and women of different ages. At the
most basic level, retirement involves the transfer of work from older
workers to younger ones. Some of this transfer has taken place through

the business system, when firms fired older workers (whether discrimination or not) and replaced them with younger ones, or created pension plans with provisions for mandatory retirement by chronological age. Some, perhaps most, of the job transfer has been generated by government: Civil War pensions (an unintentional transfer); Social Security (an intentional transfer); Medicare (likely unintentional); and postwar private pensions, a hybrid of business, labor, and government, encouraged by the 1942 federal law but private in operation. The 1934 Railroad Retirement Act was another hybrid, the product of a negotiation among business, labor, and government; enacted in the midst of the Great Depression, it was designed to transfer work from older to younger workers. Although not strictly intended to transfer work between age groups, seniority systems, by protecting older workers, essentially *required* retirement based on age and hence invoked many of the same issues.[38]

These systems pitted older against younger workers, but in complex ways. Overall, incentives to retirement would seem to have benefited younger workers by clearing crowded labor markets. But when these incentives brought large numbers of early withdrawals from the workplace—the postwar Social Security amendments, making benefits available at age sixty-two, are a good example—a shrinking cohort of younger workers found themselves paying for the lengthy retirements of older workers through hefty increases in payroll taxes. Although negotiated, many collectively bargained pension plans created jobs for younger workers only in the long term—at the end of the chain, when the elderly retired—and in the long term, many plans failed, with most of the money going to retirees and little to younger workers, even those with a vested right to a pension. They were, writes Steven Sass, "essentially social welfare schemes benefiting a specific needy class—the elderly union members."[39] Seniority systems made older workers more secure and loaded wages into later life, leaving younger workers vulnerable and able to benefit only if they remained with the company long enough to become old. Here, and elsewhere, older workers were able to prevail because they had more organizational power, especially within unions.

Intergenerational issues arose again in the 1970s and 1980s, when Congress eliminated mandatory retirement in most public and private employment. The laws of 1978 and 1986 that constituted the prohibition stand together as the last major event in the modern history of retirement, and they deserve their own history. But it might be useful to suggest a few of the factors that went into this important change in policy. The standard view is that the end of mandatory retirement was the culmination of a liberal attack on age discrimination that began in the 1960s. There is more than a little truth to that perspective, and the sense of righteous indignation at mandatory retirement was likely reinforced by lengthening life expectancy; once a reasonable representation of old age, sixty-five had become too young for the scrap heap. In Senate hearings leading to the 1978 legislation, New York's Jacob Javits railed against the use of the arbitrary age sixty-five. "All we are dealing with," he said, "is one of the shibboleths of our time. Somebody said sixty-five. They probably should never have said it. How long do you keep your job? What kind of a person are you? How can you perform?"[40]

However, as we have seen, mandatory retirement was not, or was not simply, a nasty way to get rid of older workers; it came at the end of a long-term contract that was of benefit to the aging worker. Only one cohort stood to benefit from its elimination: the oldest workers, those who had earned a lifetime of benefits from the "contract" and were now on the verge of being forced to retire. They would have their candy and eat it, too, pocketing the long-term benefits *and* yet free to keep working. In this scenario, younger workers were the losers.

But suppose the damage to younger workers was minimal. By the mid-1990s, the average age of retirement was about sixty-four, having failed to rise significantly after the last of the antidiscrimination legislation was passed; and in the 1970s and early 1980s, the vast majority of workers were retiring, voluntarily and with satisfaction, well *before* the age at which mandatory retirement could legally occur. Indeed, in the early 1970s fewer than 10 percent of workers were subject to age-based mandatory retirement.[41] Although a large group of poorly paid and marginal workers could not afford to retire in their early sixties, neither was this group represented in the pension systems requiring mandatory retirement. In short, mandatory retirement was eliminated when it no longer made much of a difference. And that means that systems of retirement based on chronological age, so important for some fifty years, were disappearing.

By far the most important cause of the elimination of these age-based systems, including mandatory retirement, was a new American economy that was emerging in the 1970s. The mass production industries—steel, autos, rubber, and the like—that had dominated the old economy and had fashioned and benefited from the postwar mandatory retirement plans and a supportive welfare state were being challenged by globalization and replaced by new industries that relied on a highly educated, professional, and technically inclined workforce. Creating and managing that new workforce required flexible employees who could be assembled and deployed in a constantly shifting constellation of new configurations. For the new breed of employers, the goal was, in historian John Myles's words, "market flexibility in all factors of production." Myles speculates that the demise of defined-benefit pension plans and mandatory retirement represents a "de-chronologising" of the life course and its replacement by a new, "craft-based model of production" that would judge older workers not by age but by the skills they possessed.[42]

Something like this perspective dominated the Senate hearings on the 1978 legislation. To be sure, testimony by representatives of the mass production industries—GM, Ford, United Auto Workers—defended mandatory retirement. But the new economy would have its way. Speaking for a number of businesses, Michael D. Batten of the consulting firm Kirschner Associates invoked the Carter administration's call for zero-based budgeting for federal agencies. "I think we ought to 'zero base' age in the labor force," he said, "and begin to examine functional criteria, functional ability as the means to 'zero base' age."[43] That viewpoint carried the day.

There was one more significant issue raised in 1978, and its exploration will take us into the present. It had been broached in 1935 by Harry Hopkins, head of the Federal Emergency Relief Administration, who was even then, at the birth of Social Security, concerned about its future costs. "The old age thing," he told Treasury Secretary Henry Morgenthau, Jr., "is a bad curve." Relabeled the "crisis of Social Security," Hopkins's demographic "bad curve" was of concern in the debates of the 1970s, when Social Security Commissioner Robert Ball registered his hope that "greater labor force participation among older people in the next century" could produce "a significant saving for social security over what is currently estimated."[44]

When the next century arrived, it was widely understood that Medicare was the more serious problem, requiring something more like prayer than hope. But Ball's solution—getting older people to work longer—remains at center stage. Some progress toward that end appeared in the mid-1990s, as the prohibition of age discrimination and end of mandatory retirement encouraged a cadre of older, mostly white male workers to remain on the job. Between 2000 and 2004, the LFPR for both men and women over sixty-five rose by about 5 percent, and by 2012, in the wake of the "Great Recession," the employment rates of three older cohorts (sixty-five to sixty-nine, seventy to seventy-four, seventy-five and over) had risen since 2006. In the oldest of these cohorts, one in nine men was working.[45] Even so, the prominent scholarly team of Alicia Munnell and Steven Sass offered a despairing look at the prospects for the nation's older workers, who faced long retirements with inadequate resources, a situation worsened by changes in the Social Security and Medicare laws that would significantly lower the rate at which Social Security replaced working income. One solution, perhaps the only one, was for older people to work longer—a good deal longer: at least two years, perhaps even four. The temptations to early retirement, with benefits at sixty-two foremost among them, had somehow to be repealed or overcome.[46] Where older workers had once been reviled as inefficient and required to leave the labor market at a fixed age, they must now be encouraged, even in some sense coerced, to remain in it. If politics would allow it, chronological age—the raising of eligibility ages under Social Security—would be one of the mechanisms. Given the history of age and retirement, change of this sort would not be easy.

NOTES

The author wishes to thank Brian Gratton and Norman Stein for assistance at an early stage in the composition of this essay.

1   Alicia H. Munnell and Steven A. Sass, *Working Longer: The Solution to the Retirement Income Challenge* (Washington, D.C.: Brookings Institution Press, 2008), 11; Nancy Brandon Tuma and Gary D. Sandefur, "Trends in the Labor Force Activity of the Elderly in the United States, 1940–1980," in *Issues in Contemporary Retirement*, ed. Rita Ricardo-Campbell and Edward P. Lazear (Stanford, Calif.: Hoover Institution Press, 1988), 42 (early Social Security benefits); Dora L. Costa, *The Evolution of Retirement: An American Economic History, 1880–1990* (Chicago: University of Chicago Press, 1998), 14 (early Social Security benefits); Edward P. Lazear, "Why Is There Mandatory Retirement?," *Journal of Political Economy* 87 (December 1979): 1261–84 (mandatory retirement age).

2 Lazear, "Why Is There Mandatory Retirement?," 1262–64, 1267, 1275; Brian Gratton, *Urban Elders: Family, Work, and Welfare among Boston's Aged, 1890–1950* (Philadelphia: Temple University Press, 1986), 70 (labor force participation rates).

3 Carole Haber, *Beyond Sixty-Five: The Dilemma of Old Age in America's Past* (New York: Cambridge University Press, 1983), 5 ("golden age"); David Hackett Fischer, *Growing Old in America: The Bland-Lee Lectures Delivered at Clark University* (New York: Oxford University Press, 1977), 18, 52 (landed wealth), 64.

4 Fischer, *Growing Old in America*, 43–44 ("duty," "cause"), 78 (enthusiasm for youth), 109; W. Andrew Achenbaum, *Old Age in the New Land: The American Experience since 1790* (Baltimore: Johns Hopkins University Press, 1978), 19, 22.

5 Haber, *Beyond Sixty-Five*, 4 ("unproductive"), 5, 7, 109, 113–15, 119, 120.

6 Ibid., 123 ("overstaffed"); William Graebner, *A History of Retirement: The Meaning and Function of an American Institution, 1885–1978* (New Haven, Conn.: Yale University Press, 1980), 21–24 (Mergenthaler); Lisa Dillon, *The Shady Side of Fifty: Age and Old Age in Late Victorian Canada and the United States* (Montreal: McGill-Queen's University Press, 2008), 180 ("age-rounding"); William Graebner, "Help Wanted: Age Discrimination in Buffalo, New York, 1895–1935," *New York History* 65 (October 1984) (newspaper advertisements); Gregory Wood, *Retiring Men: Manhood, Labor, and Growing Old in America, 1900–1960* (New York: University Press of America, 2012), 66 (private pension plans); Sir William Osler, "The Fixed Period," in *Aequanimitas: With Other Addresses to Medical Students, Nurses and Practitioners of Medicine* (Philadelphia, 1910), 391–411.

7 The term "human scrap heap" dates to the first decade of the twentieth century, the term "industrial scrap heap" to Abraham Epstein, *Facing Old Age: A Study of Old Age Dependency in the United States and Old Age Pensions* (New York: Knopf, 1922), cited in Susan B. Carter and Richard Sutch, "Myth of the Industrial Scrap Heap: A Revisionist View of Turn-of-the-Century Retirement," NBER Working Paper Series on Historical Factors in Long Run Growth, Historical Paper 73 (Cambridge, Mass.: National Bureau of Economic Research, October 1995), note 4. The idea of the scrap heap reached children's literature with Virginia Lee Burton's *Mike Mulligan and His Steam Shovel* (Boston: Houghton Mifflin, 1939).

8 Graebner, *History of Retirement*, 58, 87 (Treasury), 123 (scientific management); Steven A. Sass, *The Promise of Private Pensions: The First Hundred Years* (Cambridge, Mass.: Harvard University Press, 1997), 15 (steel companies, railroads); Haber, *Beyond Sixty-Five*, 117 (railroads); Gratton, *Urban Elders*, 175; Carole Haber and Brian Gratton, *Old Age and the Search for Security: An American Social History* (Bloomington: Indiana University Press, 1994), 96. See also Dillon, *Shady Side*, 8, 184. In their coauthored study, Haber and Gratton argue that it was "probably rare" for older workers to be thrown on the industrial scrap heap (213n83).

9 Haber and Gratton, *Old Age*, 109 ("mandatory retirement"), 106–8; Roger L. Ransom and Richard Sutch, "The Decline of Retirement in the Years before Social

Security: U.S. Retirement Patterns, 1870–1940," in Ricardo-Campbell and Lazear, *Issues in Contemporary Retirement*, 4 (ladders).

10 Not only are the calculations difficult (the U.S. census did not provide labor force participation rates [LFPRs] in this period, so they have to be generated from other sources), but there is disagreement over the basic claim of LFPR stability. For example, economist Dora Costa claims a substantial 20 percent decline in the sixty-five-plus LFPR between 1880 and 1910, followed by two decades of stability, and even Gratton's figures for that age group show a nearly 13 percent decline between 1890 and 1920. On the constant LFPR argument, see Carter and Sutch, "Myth of the Industrial Scrap Heap," 4; Gratton, *Urban Elders*, 63, 66, 70; Robert L. Lumsdaine and David A. Wise, "Aging and Labor Force Participation: A Review of Trends and Explanations," in *Aging in the United States and Japan: Economic Trends*, ed. Yukio Noguchi and David A. Wise (Chicago: University of Chicago Press, 1994), 12; Jon R. Moen, "Rural Non-farm Households: Leaving the Farm and the Retirement of Older Men, 1860–1980," *Social Science History* 18 (Spring 1994): 56; Costa, *Evolution of Retirement*, 29.

11 Moen, "Rural Non-farm Households," 56–57, 65; Costa, *Evolution of Retirement*, 1, 93; Carter and Sutch, "Myth of the Industrial Scrap Heap," 12.

12 Carter and Sutch, "Myth of the Industrial Scrap Heap," 1–2, 4, 15; Costa, *Evolution of Retirement*, 57; Ransom and Sutch, "Decline of Retirement," 16–17; Moen, "Rural Non-farm Households," 71.

13 Theda Skocpol, *Protecting Soldiers and Mothers: The Political Origins of Social Policy in the United States* (Cambridge, Mass.: Belknap, 1992), 65 ("all American men"), 1, 111–12, 122–24, 126–28, 129 ("permanent specific disability"); Costa, *Evolution of Retirement*, 198–202.

14 Skocpol, *Protecting Soldiers and Mothers*, 151, 149, 143 (paupers), 135–36 (residence in North), 37 ("gender-oriented"), 26 ("fraternalism"), 130 ("patronage democracy").

15 Graebner, "Help Wanted," 363–64 (domestic servants, AT&T); Wood, *Retiring Men*, 50; Dillon, *Shady Side*, 50; Fischer, *Growing Old in America*, 146.

16 Gratton, *Urban Elders*, 49, 126, 157 (risk of poverty); Dillon, *Shady Side*, 155–56, 273 (black women), 275 (spouse).

17 Haber and Gratton, *Old Age*, 95 (African-American property); Moen, "Rural Non-farm Households," 71 (farm retirement); Haber, *Beyond Sixty-Five*, 120 (long hours); Dean W. Morse, Anna B. Dutka, and Susan H. Gray, *Life after Early Retirement: The Experiences of Low-Level Workers* (Totowa, N.J.: Rowman and Allanheld, 1983), xii (60.5 years), 17 (affordable); Costa, *Evolution of Retirement*, 195 (leisure cost).

18 Costa, *Evolution of Retirement*, 1; Gratton, *Urban Elders*, 5–6; Lumsdaine and Wise, "Aging and Labor Force Participation," 12; Moen, "Rural Non-farm Households," 56, 60; John Myles, *Old Age in the Welfare State: The Political Economy of Public Pensions*, 1984, rev. ed. (Lawrence: University Press of Kansas,

1989), 20–21; Ransom and Sutch, "Decline of Retirement," 3–5; Wood, *Retiring Men*, 149.

19 Gratton, *Urban Elders*, 70–71; Tuma and Sandefur, "Trends in Labor Force Activity," 41–43 (early retirement benefits, Medicare, indexing); Organisation for Economic Co-operation and Development (OECD), *Ageing and Employment Policies: United States* (Paris: OECD, 2005), 91 (disability ["route into early retirement"]); Donald O. Parsons, "Discussion," following Eileen M. Crimmins and Maria T. Pramaggiore, "Changing Health of the Older Working-Age Population and Retirement Patterns over Time," in Ricardo-Campbell and Lazear, *Issues in Contemporary Retirement*, 158 (disability); Lumsdaine and Wise, "Aging and Labor Force Participation," 14, 16 (1984 study). For an elaborate chronology of Social Security benefits, see http://www.ssa.gov/history/chrono.html.

20 OECD, *Ageing and Employment Policies*, 86 and John Macnicol, *Age Discrimination: An Historical and Contemporary Analysis* (Cambridge: Cambridge University Press, 2006), 219 (replacement rates); Munnell and Sass, *Working Longer*, 59 (availability).

21 Sass, *Promise of Private Pensions*, 110 ("broad . . . participation"), 99; Lumsdaine and Wise, "Aging and Labor Force Participation," 16; Wood, *Retiring Men*, 150 (half of all firms); Lazear, "Why Is There Mandatory Retirement?," 1274 (age sixty-five).

22 Graebner, *History of Retirement*, 226 (recession periods).

23 Costa, *Evolution of Retirement*, 166.

24 Graebner, *History of Retirement*, 186 ("*retirement* benefits"), 189; Achenbaum, *Old Age in the New Land*, 136–37, 149.

25 Macnicol, *Age Discrimination*, 3 (Friedman quotation); Sass, *Promise of Private Pensions*, 133 ("defining document," "human machines").

26 Costa, *Evolution of Retirement*, 23 (survey).

27 Wood, *Retiring Men*, 214 (Columbus, Houston); Graebner, *History of Retirement*, 236–37 (Department of Labor); OECD, *Ageing and Employment Policies*, 106 (prohibitions on new hires).

28 Graebner, *History of Retirement*, 227 (disengagement theory), 228 ("glamorize leisure").

29 Graebner, *History of Retirement*, 231 (life insurance companies).

30 Wood, *Retiring Men*, 2, 8, 110, 140, 190–93 (domestic space).

31 Ibid., 103–5 (Townsend), 191 (survey); Costa, *Evolution of Retirement*, 152.

32 Morse, Dutka, and Gray, *Life after Early Retirement*, 23, 17 (survey), xii ("own free will"); Haber and Gratton, *Old Age*, 114 (abolition of mandatory retirement).

33 Jack VanDerhei, Craigh Copeland, and Dallas Salisbury, *Retirement Security in the United States: Current Sources, Future Prospects, and Likely Outcomes of Current Trends* (n.p.: Employee Benefit Research Institute, 2006), 9; Munnell and Sass, *Working Longer*, 11.

34 Haber and Gratton, *Old Age*, 112; Gratton, *Urban Elders*, 72 (Social Security and income); Wood, *Retiring Men*, 228 (LFPRs); Costa, *Evolution of Retirement*, 115

(living alone); Silvana Pozzenbon and Olivia S. Mitchell, "Married Women's Retirement Behavior," NBER Working Paper Series, Working Paper No. 2104 (Cambridge, Mass.: National Bureau of Economic Research, 1986), 2, 20–21 ("nonwork years").

35 OECD, *Ageing and Employment Policies*, 120 (discrimination statutes); Macnicol, *Age Discrimination*, 35, 37, 41; Sass, *Promise of Private Pensions*, 248.

36 Macnicol, *Age Discrimination*, 20, 21,

37 Munnell and Sass, *Working Longer*, 42 (LFPRs); Harvey L. Stearns and Boin Chang, "Workforce Issues in Retirement," in *Aging in America*, vol. 3: *Societal Issues*, ed. John C. Cavanaugh and Christine K. Cavanaugh (Santa Barbara, Calif.: Praeger/ABC-CLIO, 2010), 96–97 ("blurred" retirement); Alan M. Garber, "Financing Health Care for Elderly Americans in the 1990s," in Noguchi and Wise, *Aging in the United States and Japan*, 175 (health insurance); Jacqueline L. Angel and Fernando Torres-Gil, "Hispanic Aging and Social Policy," in Cavanaugh and Cavanaugh, *Societal Issues*, 3, 15 (Hispanics); Brian Gratton and Myron P. Gutmann, "Emptying the Nest: Older Men in the United States, 1880–1920," *Population and Development Review* 36 (June 2010): 349; Lazear, "Why Is There Mandatory Retirement?," 1275.

38 Sass, *Promise of Private Pensions*, 92 (railroad retirement), 29–31 (seniority); Graebner, *History of Retirement*, 153–80 (railroad retirement); Haber and Gratton, *Old Age*, 109 (seniority).

39 Sass, *Promise of Private Pensions*, 140 ("social welfare schemes").

40 Costa, *Evolution of Retirement*, 81–82 (age sixty-five); Macnicol, *Age Discrimination*, 121 (health); Graebner, *History of Retirement*, 246–47 (age sixty-five), 252–53 (Javits).

41 OECD, *Ageing and Employment Policies*, 53 (LFPRs); Haber and Gratton, *Old Age*, 114; Sass, *Promise of Private Pensions*, 44 (voluntary retirement); Macnicol, *Age Discrimination*, 21.

42 Sass, *Promise of Private Pensions*, 240 (new configurations); Myles, *Old Age*, 137 ("factors of production"), 138–39 ("craft-based model").

43 Graebner, *History of Retirement*, 253 (GM, Ford), 251 (Batten).

44 Ibid., 256 (Morgenthau), 257 (Ball).

45 VanDerhei, Copeland, and Salisbury, *Retirement Security*, 82 (Medicare); OECD, *Ageing and Employment Policies*, 52–53, 122 (remain on the job), 52 (LFPRs); Floyd Norris, "The Number of Those Working Past 65 Is a Record High," *New York Times*, May 19, 2012, B3 (older cohorts).

46 Munnell and Sass, *Working Longer*, 9 (two to four years), 11 (temptations to early retirement); Eduardo Porter, "The Payoff in Delaying Retirement," *New York Times*, March 6, 2013, B1, B5.

10

"The Proper Age for Suffrage"

Vote 18 and the Politics of Age from World War II to the Age of Aquarius

REBECCA DE SCHWEINITZ

"Should 18-year olds be allowed to vote?" Were young people best characterized as unruly, impulsive rebels or as responsible, politically and socially conscious agents of democratic change? What age marked the turning point between youth and adulthood? The American public began discussing these questions during World War II, and more vigorously debated them between 1968, when a range of activists, organizations, and politicians initiated a concerted campaign to lower the voting age, and 1971, when the states ratified the Twenty-Sixth Amendment to the Constitution. But if questions about "the proper age for suffrage" sparked sometimes-heated conversations about age, citizenship, and American democracy in the past, Vote 18 has generated little interest or argument among historians.[1]

Much of the limited scholarship on the movement to lower the voting age centers on the constitutional questions and legal battles raised by the way it was achieved—partly through provisions tacked on to the popular 1970 Voting Rights Extension Act and, after the Supreme Court rejected the scope of those provisions, through constitutional amendment. Largely descriptive, this scholarship repeats a number of unexamined assumptions, namely, that adults in America simply gave the vote to young people. In the "Age of Aquarius" it became untenable to force young men to fight and die in Vietnam when many of them did not enjoy the right to vote. Moreover, leaders felt compelled to channel youthful political dissent into appropriate and manageable forms.[2] Besides missing the fact that, like other successful movements to expand citizenship rights, Vote 18 involved behind-the-scenes grassroots organizing, coalition building, and mainstream politicking on local, state, and national levels, such top-down "social control" narratives simplify contemporary understandings of age and the historical context in which young people won the right to vote. Rather than a move to contain youth, Vote 18 reflected the rising significance of eighteen as a turning point in young people's lives, the successful expansion of universal secondary education, increasingly positive perceptions of young people and their role in the modern world, and the meaningful activism of youth on the nation's most pressing issues.

Old Enough to Fight, Old Enough to Vote

Proposals to lower the voting age appeared regularly before federal and state legislatures after Congress amended the Selective Service Act in 1942 and began drafting young men for the military at age eighteen. That the government deemed eighteen-year-olds "old enough to fight" made some believe that it should also recognize them as "old enough to vote." Although young men under the age of twenty-one (and even under the age of eighteen) had been fighting in the country's wars since the Revolution, most Americans believed that minimum voting age restrictions adhered to long-standing historical precedents linking "the citizen and the soldier." Twenty-one, politicians and the public widely assumed, had always served as both the minimum voting age and the age at which American men took up arms. And those customs, commentators insisted, harkened back to a medieval Anglo practice of bestowing knighthood at twenty-one.[3]

Their understanding of the past was imperfect, but those who argued for a "strong historical" relationship between taking up arms and citizenship rights had a point. African American men's military service in the Civil War and Native American men's participation in World War I played central roles in their enfranchisement in the wake of those conflicts. Women's patriotic service in World War I similarly helped justify passage of the woman's suffrage amendment.[4] Lower-voting-age supporters insisted that traditional connections between martial (or patriotic) and political citizenship rights and duties continue. If a new age marked the starting point at which youth began acting in the country's defense, whether as soldiers, nurses, or defense industry workers, then that age should also qualify them for the "most basic right of citizenship."[5]

Early Vote 18 advocates, like Georgia Governor Ellis Arnall and Representative Jennings Randolph (D-W.Va.), told stories of "intrepid, courageous, alert, and faithful" servicemen like Private John McEachern who lost his life as a paratrooper in North Africa at nineteen, and under-twenty-one-year-old James Cranford, who had been wounded twenty-two times. America denied these heroes the right to vote. Eighteen- to twenty-one-year-old young men, they pointed out, made up 25 percent of Army personnel, 37 percent of those serving in the Navy, and roughly 57 percent of the Marine Corps, while their female counterparts filled essential defense positions "in the WACS, WAVES, Spars, and elsewhere," or as "Rosies" in the shipyards.[6]

Later political allies told similar stories as they conveyed their sense of the injustice in declaring eighteen-year-olds "old enough to fight . . . to bleed and die" to carry out American foreign policy objectives while still categorizing them "as children" when it came to voting. Promotional materials for lowering the voting age in the 1960s frequently featured images of young men dressed for combat, risking their lives in the "rice paddies of Vietnam" without having ever cast votes for those establishing the nation's course of action. Youth franchise allies, such as Representatives Kenneth Hechler (D-W.Va.) and Pete McCloskey (R-Calif.), occasionally waxed sentimental about the civic burdens and interests of "young wives, sweethearts, sisters, and classmates of our younger members of the Armed Forces" "whose lives are linked with theirs." Like their 1940s counterparts, later Vote 18 supporters buttressed their emotional appeals with sobering statistics. One Ohio brochure read, "25% of our soldiers in Vietnam are under 21." "29% of those killed never reach 21." "Over 51% of Ohio's 1,673 Viet Nam casualties were not eligible to vote."[7]

But not everyone agreed that a lower draft age necessitated a lower voting age. Emanuel Celler (D-N.Y.), Vote 18's most ardent antagonist from the 1940s through the 1970s, explained the main argument: "voting is as different from fighting as chalk is from cheese." Bearing arms and exercising the franchise required different competencies. And young people, opponents insisted, developed those competencies at different ages; the physical and psychological traits that made eighteen-year-olds fit for military service were not "the qualities which are most desired in voting citizens." "Daring and impetuosity," "regimentation and physical courage" could make younger soldiers "seem desirable to the military authorities," adversaries argued, but did not make them "man enough to vote." The same was true of the "unquestioning obedience to orders from superior officers" described as an "instinctive reflex" in eighteen-year-old "boys." Military leaders could judge eighteen-year-olds sufficiently developed to follow directions and wield a gun in battle, but they lacked the "good judgment essential" to good citizenship.[8]

No Magic Age

As opponents' criticisms make clear, age, especially the years between eighteen and twenty-one, was a complicated category. At eighteen most young people exhibited the physical features of adults. But age eighteen did not signal the attainment of emotional, behavioral, and intellectual capacities associated with maturity. In fact, the late teens and early twenties were linked with decidedly nonadult qualities such as instability, inexperience, and idealism. For the first third of the twentieth century, a range of scholars and reformers had described childhood and youth as meaningful physiological, psychological, and social categories that set them apart from adults. The Great Depression had especially encouraged attention to the distinct problems of youth, particularly those between the ages of eighteen and twenty-five. Increasing support for youth's recreational needs and educational and vocational training reflected widespread understandings of this age category as a liminal space wherein young people became full-fledged adults.[9] Partly because they recognized the need to connect age eighteen with a variety of desirable developmental characteristics, Vote 18 advocates explained that military service demonstrated the intelligence, acuity, and civic mindedness of eighteen- to twenty-year-olds, even as they insisted that the age at which young people assumed "the mandatory right to die" should be aligned with the age at first vote.[10] For politicians as well as organizations allied with the Vote 18 movement, that eighteen-year-olds risked their lives for the common good and readily "mastered the art of mechanized, complicated warfare" indicated that they would "perform with equal distinction at the ballot box." Young people's involvement in the nation's defense proved their mental and physical preparation for adult citizenship responsibilities.[11]

In lowering the age for compulsory military service, Congress high-lighted the tenuous boundary between youth and adulthood and en-sured that the chronological age of twenty-one could no longer be taken for granted as a sacrosanct marker of adult status. People on both sides of the debate admitted that the ages between eighteen and twenty-one represented an ambiguous stage in human growth. The indistinctness of age as a developmental sign meant that "ultimately the decision as to voting age must be somewhat arbitrary." "There has to be a line drawn at some age and no figure is magical," allies and opponents acknowledged. Both groups also agreed that voting required a degree of common sense and social responsibility. The trouble remained because "no one really knows when adolescence reaches the age of common sense."[12]

With no "*magic* number," Vote 18 allies argued that the new draft age provided a concrete alternative age—and one at which young people assumed other adult duties and rights. Indeed, although Vote 18 advo-cates repeatedly called on fight/vote arguments as they made the case for a lower voting age, they favored broader lines of reasoning about youth responsibility and legal status. Allies in the 1940s pointed out that laws regulating juvenile courts, compulsory public schooling, relief and welfare aid, and child labor categorized young people from the age of eighteen, "essentially" as they did "older persons." Eighteen-year-olds held the same rights to property, marriage, and contracting as did their elders. And even special "youth" programs, like the CCC, treated young people in their late teens as they did those in the first half of their twen-ties. Eighteen-year-olds, proponents insisted, had more in common with twenty-five-year-olds than with seventeen-year-olds.[13]

Lower-voting-age advocates, however, began making assertions about the expansive position of eighteen-year-olds in American society shortly after the country reached a consensus about childhood and youth as dis-tinctive categories requiring distinctive relationships to the state. Young people were supposed to be protected from adult concerns and respon-sibilities. This "caretaking" understanding of young people and their rights dominated 1940s and 1950s public discourse and policy, making it difficult for Vote 18 allies to discuss eighteen-year-olds as indepen-dent contributors to the country—their position as workers, taxpayers, and heads of families. Saluting the increased political concern for young people, early advocates reassured the public that a lower voting age would not jeopardize recent, hard-won protections for youth. Unlike later allies, they avoided suggesting that eighteen-year-olds, regardless of the similarities in their legal classifications or life experiences to adults, should be considered anything other than "youth," instead proposing that since the "social rights" afforded younger citizens did not apply after age eighteen, eighteen-year-olds should be eligible for, and were in distinct need of, the right to vote.[14]

While Vote 18 supporters cautiously moved away from the nation's caretaking model of young people's rights, 1940s opponents, such as child welfare activist and education reformer Dorothy Canfield Fisher, boldly used contemporary concerns for young Americans to their advantage, warning that a lower voting age might "remove some or all of the special historic legal protections now afforded them [eighteen- to twenty-one-year-olds]." Adversaries pointed to laws that barred under-twenty-one-year-olds from jury service, purchasing alcohol, executing wills, and running for elected office as reasons to keep the voting age at twenty-one. A median age above twenty-one for first marriage allowed antagonists to dismiss age of consent statutes granting majority standing to eighteen-year-olds. There might be some laws that gave eighteen-year-olds civic rights and responsibilities, but many others, opponents argued, appropriately classified them as "legal infants," "incompetent to handle their own affairs." An ideology, backed by government initiatives, which defined work as a primarily adult concern, also enabled foes of Vote 18 to trivialize the economic contributions and interests of youth. Drawing on the philosophy of youth protection, opponents insisted that young people required "the vital two years between eighteen and twenty" in order to develop their personalities and find "direction and purpose in life." "Everyone should have the right to grow up." Youth franchise foes, like educators Alonzo Myers and Louis Hacker, further suggested that eighteen- to twenty-one-year-olds "must be protected against the consequences of [their] own blunders" and would be better served by "true equality of opportunity" than by the franchise. The universal expansion of services for youth, not the vote, was what young Americans needed.[15]

By the late 1960s, however, ideas about youth agency increasingly challenged the custodial approach to young people's rights that had predominated in the first half of the twentieth century. Both reflecting and building on a growing sense of eighteen- to twenty-one-year-olds as active participants in American life, student leaders, politicians, unions, civil rights organizations, and other groups that supported a lower voting age, like the National Education Association (NEA)–initiated Youth Franchise Coalition, all highlighted the range of ways that government impacted the lives of youth and that young people contributed to the nation. Arguing that "those most affected by a policy should have a say in making that policy" or that youth are "good enough to contribute, good enough to vote," late 1960s and early 1970s advocates painted a collective portrait of prospective youth voters as responsible citizens who undertook multiple duties associated with adulthood. Besides serving in the military, eighteen-year-olds paid substantial taxes, worked and often supported themselves, were judged as adults in criminal courts, married, headed families and raised children, entered civil service, volunteered in government programs, owned and operated firearms, and held driver's licenses. Insurance companies classified eighteen-year-olds as adults, as did the government when determining welfare benefits. With statistics placing the average age of marriage in some states at 19.7 years for men and 18.5 for women, and other figures showing some 60 percent of youth between the ages of eighteen and twenty-one worked full-time, Vote 18 allies explicitly depicted eighteen- to twenty-year-old young Americans as "young adults." Like their older counterparts, these youthful adults "bore the consequences of democratic decision making." Required to "bear the burdens of citizenship" and otherwise "behave and resume responsibility *as adults*," eighteen-year-olds essentially functioned "as other adults do under most of our laws and customs."[16]

Smart Enough to Vote

As lower-voting-age advocates also pointed out, young Americans took on "the obligations of adulthood" at eighteen because that was the age at which they graduated from high school. Eighteen might not be a "magic age," but it "marks a definite turning point in a person's life," allies such as Representative Cornelius Gallagher (D-N.J.), Senator Jacob Javits (R-N.Y.), and the NEA's Monroe Sweetland argued. While "laws covering age limits that separate the men (and women) from the boys (and girls)" offered no clear-cut answers about the transition between youth and adulthood, eighteen was the age at which the state ended its most extensive and enduring caretaking relationship with young Americans, and the age at which the nation presumed young people ready to turn their training to use in the world.[17] If Americans believed in the mission of public schools, and if those schools did what they were expected to do to prepare youth "for responsible citizenship," then why not, allies asked, make commencement day New Voters' Day?[18]

Partly due to the ascendency of custodial philosophies of young people's rights, by the time the United States entered World War II, secondary schools played an important role in the lives of young Americans. While graduating from high school had been out of reach for earlier generations of citizens, graduation rates tripled between 1920 and 1940. When Congress began debating the voting age, finishing high school had just become the norm for American youth. This trend bolstered the case for a lower voting age. "Growth in high school enrollments," 1940s advocates argued, meant that "the newly graduated youth is better informed about current affairs than he is likely to be later, better informed than the average adult. He is better educated than his parents and grandparents."[19]

If improved educational opportunities suggested the theoretical fitness of the nation's eighteen-year-olds for the right to vote, studies confirmed that contemporary high school seniors knew "as much about government and politics as the average adult voter—and perhaps a little bit more."[20] For those who insisted on "experience," not just knowledge, as prerequisite to critical thinking and good voting, advocates explained that modern schools, which emphasized social science, "presented a wider range" and "more intricate" understanding of the world and "social problems than could the *limited experiences* of pioneer days." Youth franchise supporters allowed that a few extra years of "simple community participation" helped prepare voters in the past. But, they insisted, expanded educational opportunities and the sophistication of current pedagogies and curriculum made public schools fully equipped to "combat ignorance among the electorate." According to Vote 18 allies, contemporary secondary schooling "better" prepared prospective young voters than three years of experience had prepared their elders.[21]

Besides representing the "logical climax to the amazing growth of the American high school," enfranchising those "fresh" from secondary coursework would also bring to the polls a group "more alive to civic problems than their parents." Aligning the voting age with the age at high school graduation promised to preempt the political apathy that inevitably developed during the time between when young Americans studied history, civics, and current affairs in high school and their first vote at twenty-one. "Young people should be given the vote before they cool off," allies like reformer Richard Welling argued. A lower voting age would allow eighteen-year-olds to immediately put into practice their citizenship training and help them develop lifelong habits of civic engagement.[22]

As such points suggest, early Vote 18 allies drew on ideas about youth competency and deficiency as they made the case for a lower voting age. Advocates presented eighteen-year-olds as adequately educated for the franchise at the same time they presented the right to vote at eighteen as a measure to help young people *become* good citizens. "Youth learn by doing" and "Young people need the training that participation in Government can give," youth franchise champions, like University of Texas president and American Youth Commission director Homer Rainey, argued. Participating in the democratic process would cement high school training and was necessary for young people's "full moral development." Learning theories of the 1940s stressed the principle of education through participation. Such theories reflected a growing respect for young people as active agents in society but also the belief that young people required "careful education and guidance" to achieve "their full capacities of adulthood."[23]

Opponents expressed skepticism that a few more years of schooling adequately prepared young Americans for the weighty responsibility of voting. A high school diploma, after all, signified attendance rather than competence.[24] And knowledge about the workings of government and public affairs was different from wisdom about civic matters. Misgivings seemed especially justified if, after all those extra years of formal education, eighteen-year-olds needed the franchise in order to really learn about American democracy. Foes of a lower voting age rejected the idea of the vote as a teaching tool. Voting seemed a dangerous substitute for already established ways of developing good citizenship. Requiring a few years of community participation as a type of "internship" to voting rights fit, opponents argued, with the accepted principle of "progressive stages in citizenship." While eligibility for many state offices began at the current age of first vote, citizens did not become eligible for the federal Congress until age twenty-five, the U.S. Senate at thirty, and the presidency at thirty-five. Modern eighteen-year-olds might be well educated, but it was not unprecedented, Vote 18 opponents insisted, to require the life experience that accrues with age for different levels of political responsibility.[25] Rather than hope that voting at eighteen "would make citizenship education more effective," opponents turned to caretaking ideas about youth rights, contending it would be better to maintain the traditional voting age and work to advance the educational opportunities "still lacking for millions of youth."[26]

While 1940s opponents could point to remaining gaps in America's public education system, the continued expansion and rising standards of secondary schooling significantly strengthened the case for a lower voting age. In 1970, with nearly 80 percent of American youth graduating from high school, and almost 50 percent of eighteen- to twenty-one-year-olds enrolled in colleges, Vote 18 movement backers, like the NEA, insisted that "reason does not permit us to ignore any longer the reality that eighteen-year-old Americans are prepared by education, by experience, by exposure to public affairs to assume and exercise the privilege of voting."[27] More than any other argument, youth franchise groups and their allies in the late 1960s and early 1970s turned to the "relatively high proportion of highly educated" and "politically sophisticated" youth as they tried to justify lowering the voting age. Advocates across the political spectrum, including presidents Lyndon Johnson and Richard Nixon, favorably compared well-educated American youth with already enfranchised adults. Improved education marked a "crucial difference," they said, "between this youthful generation and previous ones"; today's eighteen-year-olds should be given the right to vote, "not because they are old enough to vote, but because they are smart enough to vote."[28]

While allies in the 1960s and 1970s pointed to unparalleled levels of formal schooling and the educational benefits of rapid "advancements in technology and mass communication" as they made the case for a lower voting age, they also insisted that, smart as they were, most young people still entered the labor force as full-time workers after high school graduation, making it the best "universally applicable gauge of maturity." That more than a million youth established families before age twenty-one further underscored high school graduation as a significant milestone. Already better trained than their elders, young people in jobs, in their own homes, and at universities deserved the right to shape the policies that governed their lives. As student members of the NEA explained, "[B]etter educated than their counterparts of yesterday[,] control" of young people's interests are "at present in the hands of others. There should be provision within the democratic system for them to express their concerns."[29]

Youth Activism and Vote 18

Vote 18 allies of the 1940s *and* 1960s rightly claimed "the current generation of young Americans [as] the best educated group of 18-to-21-year-olds in the nation's history." But for advocates in the later period, high school graduation had become the most widely shared transition point between youth and adulthood—and hence, more clearly the "proper level" for the age of suffrage. In addition, while lower-voting-age advocates in both periods believed in the notion of education through participation, and expressed concern about the "vote slackers" created by "the lag between the time a student may graduate from high school and the first time he has the opportunity to vote," 1960s Vote 18 supporters did not propose the franchise as a method of instruction. Instead, they pointed to more than a decade of youth political activism as evidence that young people were already thoroughly informed *and* engaged political actors. Rather than hypothesize about the political potential of eighteen-year-olds or suggest the vote would spur those who had studied American democracy in the classroom toward active citizenship in the world, advocates, from grassroots, civil rights, and labor organizations to Republican and Democratic Party affiliates, argued that youth participation in a range of "community conscious projects," political campaigns, and protests "demonstrated the concern, energy, and ability of young people to deal with political issues." Better educated than other age groups, potential youth voters were also "actively involved in the society itself." To some, this age cohort seemed "more politically savvy than anybody else in the country." The combination of young people's increasing education levels and obvious political engagement led youth franchise supporters to joke that maximum rather than minimum age restrictions should be imposed at age twenty-one.[30]

Vote 18 supporters in the late 1960s linked expanding educational opportunities to expanding rates of youth political participation, and used these trends as evidence that young people were book smart and "care about their country and are socially aware and responsible." In congressional hearings in the nation's capitol and in states across the country, advocates like Senator Javits and Oregon's State House Representative Joe Richards (R-Eugene) "welcomed" youth activism and credited young people with prompting the important political changes of the era, arguing, "it was the nonviolent and student-led demonstrations of the early 1960s that produced the climate in this country necessary for enactment of the landmark Civil Rights Act of 1964 and 1965." Applauding young people's "enthusiastic" participation "in voter registration drives, political campaigns," and a host of "independent organizational actions," Vote 18 supporters hailed the "talent and abilities . . . energies and enthusiasm" of eighteen- to twenty-one-year-olds.[31]

The highly visible (and behind-the-scenes) participation of young Americans in 1960s civic life created new arguments for a lower voting age. Eighteen-year-olds did not need the vote to complete their education and put them on the path to engaged citizenship; they needed it to make their political engagement more effective. National and state-level allies, like the Youth Franchise Coalition and the Connecticut Committee for the 18-Year-Old-Vote, complained that at present "young people can say all they want and be ignored because they lack a real voice." "These concerned citizens can at most be only active observers, not full participants in the political process." Of course, even without the vote, young people had hardly been voiceless "observers"—which was exactly the point. Young people were already acting as responsible citizens. Youth who played significant roles in political organizations and in programs like VISTA, the Peace Corps, and Head Start seemed fully capable of watching after their own (and others') interests; eighteen- to twenty-one-year-olds needed further empowerment, not guidance. Widespread youth activism contributed to a shift from a protectionist to liberationist understanding of young people's rights, and that shift bolstered the case for a lower voting age.[32]

Clear evidence of young people's interest in politics had been harder to come by in the 1940s. "The average youth of 18 cares little about his government," opponents charged.[33] Supporters, including Arnall (whose gubernatorial campaign significantly benefited from student involvement), presented little evidence to suggest otherwise.[34] Later Vote 18 supporters, on the other hand, juxtaposed high rates of youth participation in political campaigns, programs, and organizations with their exclusion from the polls. Eighteen- to twenty-one-year-olds were asking "very real questions" with "true earnestness." But "paternalistic" voting age requirements created unnecessary "barriers" to youth participation and kept the nation from making full "use [of] their talents." Current voting-age policies, allies argued, restricted the exercise of young people's energies and ideals for the good of the country. More than that, the present voting age "encouraged irresponsible actions." Allies insisted that young people be given "the opportunity to work within the democratic process." Otherwise, politically active youth might become alienated from "systematic political processes" and driven to "search for alternative means to express their frustration."[35] Already involved, young people just needed a "constructive" way to shape "the future course of the society in which they live." As the widely circulated *Final Report of the National Commission on the Causes and Prevention of Violence* and myriad Vote 18 advocates pointed out, the youth activism of the period demonstrated the political acuity of eighteen- to twenty-one-year-olds, and signaled the possible negative consequences of holding to current "anachronistic voting age-limits."[36]

A host of congressional allies, state and national youth franchise organizations, and leaders from groups like the National Association for the Advancement of Colored People and the U.S. National Student Association vigorously saluted eighteen- to twenty-one-year-olds as "restive, concerned, earnest and informed" while also suggesting that the vote would help channel potentially dangerous youth activism into legitimate and manageable forms. Bringing politically conscious young people directly into the political process by giving them the traditional "tools of expression," Vote 18 backers asserted, would result in "enormous constructive youth activity" and forestall "nihilistic attacks on the establishment."[37] Senator Birch Bayh (D-Ind.) depicted both the political enthusiasm of youth and its potential dangers when he cautioned that young people's "energy is going to continue to build and grow. The only question is whether we should ignore it, perhaps leaving this energy to dam up and burst and follow less-than-wholesome channels, or whether we should let this force be utilized by society through the pressure valve of the franchise."[38]

Allies' warnings about "the rampant frustration" among youth, and the need to provide them with a "direct, constructive, and democratic channel for making their views felt," captured the period's anxieties about youth activism and turned those anxieties on their head—as another reason to lower the voting age to eighteen.[39] When media commentators and political opponents charged that militant youth activism disqualified young people from the franchise, Vote 18 supporters clarified that *militant* protestors comprised only a minority of youth activists. As chairman of the Young Republican National Committee, Jack McDonald said at Vote 18 congressional hearings that more young people say "build, man, build [than] burn, baby, burn." Some also indicated that most of the firebrands stirring up trouble were over twenty-one. Youth franchise supporters rejected negative stereotypes of youth activism while using those stereotypes to press for the vote. Young Americans, as eighteen-year-old Charles Koppelman explained, wanted "to be infused into the political processes of America, to have the opportunity to effect change through legitimate channels." Eighteen- to twenty-one-year-olds, the young activist and lobbyist said, sometimes turned to protests because they lacked "the most basic means by which [youth] can be involved."[40]

Even as advocates raised concerns about youth and highlighted the need to "direct" young people's activism, they circled back to positive views of youth activity—young people were agents to be empowered rather than dependents to be protected. Allies, like Youth Franchise Coalition executive director Ian MacGowan, might bring up the specter of eighteen- to twenty-one-year-olds working outside the system, but such scenes resulted only when adults "obstructed" rather than "commended and supported [youth] in its social and political commitments." "Youth is politically aware. They will not be silenced," youth-vote supporters advised. Supporters also pointed out that "other institutions—the church, the colleges, organized labor, and even corporate management" no longer expected young people to play a passive role; such groups "found ways to involve youth in their affairs and decision-making." With young people already "the most involved" of any generational cohort "in the problems of [the] neighborhood, [the] nation and [the] world," it was time to grant them the means for "the most fundamental of all decision-making."[41]

Traditional interpretations of the movement to lower the voting age fail to take into account the contemporary importance of age eighteen as a transitional marker in the lives of young Americans and of perceptions of young people as significant political actors in American society. Such interpretations ignore how the successes of caretaking philosophies of youth (the realization of near-universal secondary education for young Americans) and the shift away from those philosophies for framing young people's rights (toward youth as social and political agents) impacted the youth franchise movement. Narratives that portray Vote 18 as a measure designed to contain rather than facilitate the influence of young people on the American political system also ignore the ways that lower-voting-age arguments reflected evolving understandings of age that challenged, even reversed, earlier assumptions about the qualities most desirable in an electorate, and where they could be found.

A New Norm for Responsible Citizenship

In the 1940s, Vote 18 advocates had described potential eighteen-year-old voters as "red-blooded, high-minded." Innovative and energetic, "the young voter will bring in a larger measure of idealism and impulse." But for many, that was a central problem with the idea of lowering the voting age. Congressman Celler and other Vote 18 opponents in this era successfully associated political idealism with a lack of real-world experience and judicious thought. Foes warned that if given the vote, young people, overly idealistic, "impressionable," and prone to "hasty action" and radical solutions, would be easily misled by "propaganda" and "political tricksters." The threat of fascism—the specter of Hitler and Mussolini and the ability of such tyrants "to capture the youth of the land"—further heightened fears about "how easily the adolescent attaches himself to causes" and what might happen if the country armed young people with ballots. "We youth," one young detractor warned, "are quick to grasp at panaceas for obvious wrongs. That is how Nazism, Fascism, and Communism were spread and held in Europe."[42]

Allies of the 1940s responded to such fears by insisting that despite their idealism, most young voters would not "seek subversive or radical ends," and that ideals might play an important role "in government and in social progress." Rather than ushering power to dangerous right- or left-wing demagogues, young voters' "exalted idealism" would bring about needed democratic reforms. For most (adult) Americans at the time, however, "exalted idealism" seemed a threatening quality in the electorate.[43]

Later Vote 18 opponents also identified young people in their late teens and early twenties as naturally idealistic, and linked youth activism to the uncompromising "black and white" thinking of young people instead of to an expanded political sophistication or sense of social responsibility. Politicians whose careers and thinking had been shaped by the rise of totalitarianism continued to warn that idealism made eighteen- to twenty-one-year-olds particularly susceptible "to the arts of mass management." Their eagerness to accept "strange philosophies" made youth "easy prey" for "the political adventurer." Critics in this period also linked youth idealism and its resultant activism to subconscious, Freudian, emotional drives to rebel against authority; young people's recent penchant for political action was merely the latest manifestation of a "perennial adolescent [generational] struggle."[44]

By the 1960s, however, youth idealism seemed more a cause for celebration than for concern. "The idealism of American youth is a great national asset," Vote 18 allies and social scientists alike asserted. Rather than writing off young activists as "simplistic and naïve" radicals, condemning "the whimsicality of youth," or dismissing youth protests as generational, Oedipal responses to adult authority, scholars such as sociologist Lewis Feuer described young people as highly attuned to America's ideals, and positively characterized their political action as the "best barometers of society."[45] As one educational foundation explained, "[O]ur youth are neither blind, ignorant, nor shy; they call 'em as they see 'em. If the emperor isn't wearing clothes, they say so." While fears about youth idealism and activism remained, the participation of young people in political and social causes increasingly signified an admirable "spirit of high idealism" and commitment to a democratic society.[46] Rather than something to fear, youth idealism was generally described as a quality to embrace. Dangers remained only because the country refused to provide young people with a democratic means for conveying their idealism. As Alaska State Senator Joe Josephson (D-Anchorage) explained, "The idealism of American youth is a great national asset. It is also a fragile asset, that too often is lost to cynical forces when that idealism lacks proper expression."[47]

Successful youth activism for civil rights and young people's ongoing "self-less, generous, compassionate, and self-sacrificing challenges to the status quo" convinced many politicians, organizations, and everyday people that the idealism considered endemic among eighteen- to twenty-one-year-olds uniquely qualified them for greater participation in politics. Enfranchising eighteen-year-olds would allow idealistic, politically and democratically minded youth to even more effectively help to close the *real* gap in America—which lay not between old and young but "between the nation's ideals and actions." As Vote 18 allies explained, "active involvement in the political process can constructively focus [youth] idealism on the most effective means of change in a free society." Once a sign of their immaturity, by 1970, the "ethical, idealistic spirit" of young people represented a "new norm for responsible citizenship." Moreover, it was a quality that many supposed would positively alter (not be contained by) American democracy.[48]

Older citizenship models, which treated idealism with suspicion, also held that voters needed the experience, wisdom, and stability that accrued with age. Such conventions worked against Vote 18 in the 1940s. Then, a range of educators, psychiatrists, reformers, politicians, and local community leaders repeatedly insisted that during "the three-year age span from 18–21" young people developed "manly ideas and experience" and "a more logical reasoning." By twenty-one, opponents charged, youth also became more rooted—economically and socially. Adults still played important roles as "preceptors" to eighteen-year-olds as they established themselves in careers and homes, and worked to master matters of citizenship. After age twenty-one, youth might not be entirely steady (so perhaps thirty was a better age for voting rights), but they could be expected to have more "settled convictions" and identifiable interests than had been true a few years earlier.[49]

In the 1940s, that eighteen- to twenty-year-olds did not manifest strong party affiliations, identify with particular professions, or support special interests contributed to a sense of them as inconstant and hence unworthy of the franchise. Although property qualifications no longer restricted voting, popular thought, as well as state laws, presumed that the right to vote required some measure of socioeconomic stability. Poll taxes, strict (often lengthy) residency requirements, and public opinion all reflected a predilection for permanence.

Vote 18 allies in the 1940s and 1950s countered such views by highlighting the superiority of modern education and the responsible economic, social, and civic roles assumed by eighteen-year-olds. But allies also allowed that "youth *is* uncommitted"—that is, young people's relative freedom from the "vested interests" of adults made them "more inclined to seek answers from the point of view of the common good." If, as opponents charged, democracy is "a system of social living in which common interests have the right-of-way over special interests," then the relative detachment of the nation's eighteen- to twenty-one-year-olds might make them especially trustworthy voters. "Not addicted to party habits, not yet afflicted with the force of pressure groups," younger voters "would bring a fresh, less biased point of view to the polls." Noting "an aging population may be a force for conservatism" and that "in static societies, people reverence the past because the future will be like it," Vote 18 proponents insisted that "in a changing world young people are often superior to the older ones in meeting new problems." An eighteen- or nineteen-year-old might even be "better qualified" for voting if "capacity for adjustment" or "the energy, the will, and the courage to travel in ways we have never trod" were criteria for voting.[50]

In the 1940s, experience and stability remained the preferred characteristics of the American voter. Although the pace of change had escalated, most people believed that the future would resemble the present, and that society's elders could effectively prepare the young for what lay ahead. Within a few decades that thinking shifted. The emergence of a "world community" and the speed of technological, economic, and social change ushered in what scholars like Margaret Mead called "a new phase of cultural evolution." Not everyone used her terms, but Mead's description of a "prefigurative" phase of human civilization, in which "nowhere in the world are there elders who know what their children know," resonated with others' reconsideration of age and relationships between age groups.[51]

A growing belief that significant change was inevitable, happening quickly, and to be desired meant that young people's "susceptibility to change" increasingly made eighteen-year-olds seem like logical rather than risky participants in the democratic process.[52] Scholars' reinterpretations of the meanings of both change and age undercut traditional arguments against the eighteen-year-old vote. Social scientists and others who wrote about youth, such as former Columbia University chaplain Henry Malcolm, asserted that the mature conduct generally associated with adulthood, and often pushed on the young, "submission to authority, hard work, social conformity, and orderliness," had "very little to do with" what society actually believed to be "the real markers of adulthood"—namely independence. Contemporary scholars and observers asked whether maturity meant "freedom, self-expression, and autonomy, or structure, conformity, and group membership." "Bound" as they were "to familiar paths," the new analysis likened adults to "repressed and angry children, deeply afraid of the world, and extremely cautious in their manner of dealing with [it.]"[53] It characterized youth, on the other hand, as "healthy, creative, and spontaneous." Unchained to "institutionalized and bureaucratized patterns," and without "the same kind of emotional, financial, or 'spiritual' investment in the existing system," young people's lack of experience and unsettled nature and place in society left them free from the constraints that restricted their elders. As a 1968 White House Report explained, "the young person can take the time to look at the system, question it and attempt to change it."[54]

Waiting for the franchise made less sense if eighteen-year-olds, who felt much more "at home in *this time*" than their parents, "could not "learn [from adults] what the next steps should be." With scholars like Mead reflecting, "we need [youth] as partner in the urgent task of catching up with the time in which we live," lower voting-age advocates, too, increasingly insisted that the nation needed "the bold thinking and exciting ideas of youth." "At the most adventurous stage of his life," an eighteen-year-old now seemed particularly well suited for the vote.[55]

Critics of Vote 18 in the late 1960s still favored "settled convictions," "worldly experience [and] historical perspective" as preconditions for the franchise. But in the context of "the jet age," and the new expert opinion on age, their arguments seemed anachronistic, based on "archaic systems of authority," out-of-date age hierarchies.[56] Young people had as much, or more, to offer society than their elders. In the modern world, "wise decisions"—which, in the absence of a "magic age" seemed an appropriate "test" for suffrage rights—were likely to come from a "refreshing viewpoint and knowledge" rather than from those "encased in outmoded patterns of life."[57]

New beliefs about age and the qualities associated with particular age categories made it increasingly difficult to fault young people for traditional age-related deficiencies. In the late 1960s and early 1970s, advocates brazenly challenged standard defenses of the current voting age, suggesting that "sometimes the judgment of these eighteen-year-olds is better. Of course, experience need not be a negative quality, but those of us who are more mature cannot prevent our prejudices and backgrounds from influencing our decisions."[58] Representative Charles Diggs (D-Mich.) reflected the new conventional thinking about age and voting when he explained that eighteen-year-olds should be given the franchise since they have "a clear view [that] has not become clouded through time and involvement."[59] And on the other side of the political aisle, Representative Dan Kubiak (R-Tex.) similarly explained that young people would bring "new blood, new ideas, and clearer vision to American government."[60] Idealistic, unreserved, unfettered—characteristics strongly associated with eighteen-year-olds were to be hailed and even encouraged rather than criticized in the Age of Aquarius.

Vote 18 allies in the late 1960s and early 1970s repeatedly argued that "under modern conditions we need the tonic leaven of young adults in our decision making."[61] To many, "infusing youth," who were described as adept "structural defect specialists," into an electoral system "encrusted" "in worn out traditions" seemed less of a dangerous experiment than a recipe for the "regeneration of the democracy."[62] As Representative Abner Mikva (D-Ill.) explained, a lower voting age would act as "a fountain of youth to some of our tired institutions."[63]

The idea that there was something fundamentally wrong with American politics—that the "vital citizen engagement" that lay at the heart of America's democratic experiment "had given way to compliance and convenience"—permeated late 1960s commentary on Vote 18. Adding the voices of "restive, concerned, earnest and informed" eighteen- to twenty-one-year-olds would "provide significant revitalization to American politics and government." For Vote 18 supporters, eighteen-year-old suffrage was "much more than a youth issue." The youth vote represented the "next great step in the march of democracy," not just because it was "just and right" to give millions of young but conscientious citizens "the most basic right of all," but because, as James Graham of the U.S. National Student Association put it, "the nation needs it."[64]

American politics needed "reviving," of course, partly because young people had contributed to a "national crisis of confidence in our institutions." It was hardly accidental that a concerted campaign to lower the voting age emerged in 1968—the same year as Tet, the assassinations of Martin Luther King, Jr. and Robert Kennedy, the release of the Kerner Commission Report, contentious Republican and Democratic national conventions, and a host of militant youth protests related to those events. Student leaders explained, "the events of 1968, both within and without the system, have provided new compelling reasons why 18 to 20 year olds deserve to vote." Others similarly described 1968 as "a watershed," wherein "myths about the free society and liberalism came crumbling down."[65]

Youth activism certainly played a role in that crumbling, but lower-voting-age advocates insisted that youth activism, and the qualities it signaled, was also the solution to the political crisis of the period. Opponents of Vote 18 in the 1940s had admitted that "it is through the votes of youth of a country that reforms always find their first and strongest expression." And in 1970, America clearly needed reform. As Senate Majority Leader Mike Mansfield (D-Mont.) explained, the country "could stand a little educating from [its] youngsters."[66]

As Mansfield and other Vote 18 allies framed the situation, society's inflexible elders, afraid of the future and lacking faith in the nation's sons and daughters, were trying to manage "existing priorities along the lines of more efficient repression and control."[67] Proponents of a lower voting age characterized eighteen- to twenty-one-year-olds as fundamentally "pragmatic," dedicated to "American institutions" and to solving the "problems of the real world." Unwilling "to sit on the sidelines while the events affecting their destiny are being played out on the field," Vote 18 supporters made clear that "the conscientious, idealistic majority of young men and women" in the country desired "direct, constructive," and "responsible" participation.[68] Adults, however, prone to "fight the tide" of change, had "forced youth to become society's heretics."[69] Vote 18 allies warned that the country had a choice: "continue our useless war against our youth [and] lose those special values so much a part of a young society," or allow eighteen- to twenty-one-year-olds voters to "add some healthy dose of heart and public honesty to our style."[70]

The Only Logical Turning Point

If the nation seemed to be at a crossroads in the late 1960s and early 1970s, and needed "the positive contribution young voters can make," it seemed increasingly clear that age eighteen was "the only logical turning point" for enfranchising young Americans.[71] Never, in itself, enough to lower the voting age, the "old enough to fight, old enough to vote" "shibboleth" did throw into question traditional age hierarchies associated with citizenship, offer one straightforward argument for a lower voting age, and, especially in the context of Vietnam, give the youth voting issue considerable emotional resonance. Just as important, it provided a concrete, alternative minimum age for extended citizenship rights.

In the 1960s and early 1970s, most state referenda on the issue asked voters to lower the voting age to nineteen. Many supporters believed that a "compromise age" would be more likely to pass. Alaska, Kentucky, and Hawaii had all enacted "compromise" legislation in the 1950s. But in the early 1970s, nineteen also seemed more arbitrary, less a meaningful, and justifiable, age marker. Indeed, despite the prevalence of Vote 19 initiatives on the state level, polls found that only 7.7 percent of Americans believed the voting age should be lowered to nineteen, 4.4 percent wanted it lowered to twenty, while over 50 percent agreed that eighteen-year-olds should be given the right to vote. Eighteen may not have been any more "magical" than twenty-one. But it did align with the age at which young men registered for the draft, the age most youth entered full-time jobs, the age many of them entered colleges, and the age numerous other legal rights, responsibilities, and opportunities accrued to young people. Most significant, eighteen corresponded with the age at which the vast majority of young Americans graduated from high school. In 1967 nineteen-year-old Betsy Glasgow argued against lowering the voting age: "Let's keep the first vote at twenty-one as a symbol of our growing up." But by that time, high school graduation was the most readily identifiable symbol of growing up. It was the age at which the state relinquished the task of training young citizens; it was *the* "turning point" in the lives of modern youth. If America needed "some new blood, some new vigor, some new ideas" to help revitalize democracy, then high school graduation was the rite of passage that confirmed eighteen as "the proper age for suffrage."[72]

Of course, young people themselves had played important roles in changing how the country thought about them. As they put into practice the lessons in democracy they learned at school, eighteen- to twenty-one-year-olds had proven their political capacities and helped create new understandings of age in the Age of Aquarius.

NOTES

1 "Project 18 Bulletin," February 25, 1969, F3, box 2709, National Education Association Papers, Estelle and Melvin Gelman Library, George Washington University, Washington, D.C. (hereafter cited as NEA Papers).

2 Like other histories that address Vote 18, Alexander Keyssar's *The Right to Vote: The Contested History of Democracy in the United States* (New York: Basic Books, 2000) devotes only a few pages to the youth franchise movement and problematically bases its discussion on Wendell W. Cultice's, *Youth's Battle for the Ballot: A History of Voting Age in America* (New York: Greenwood, 1992). Mostly descriptive, Cultice's book includes faulty information and no endnotes—only an incomplete bibliography. In "Uncovering the Twenty-Sixth Amendment" (PhD diss., University of Michigan, 2008), Jenny Diamond Cheng offers useful analysis but examines only congressional debates on the topic.

3 On youth service in the military, see Caroline Cox, "Boy Soldiers of the American Revolution: The Effects of War on Society," in *Children and Youth in a New Nation*, ed. James Marten (New York: New York University Press, 2009), 17.

4 Julia E. Johnson, ed., *Lowering the Voting Age* (New York: H. W. Wilson, 1944), 111.

5 James Graham, *Lowering the Voting Age* (U.S. National Student Association, 1968), 27.

6 "Should Eighteen-Year Olds Vote?," *American Forum of the Air*, October 19, 1943, 3, 5; House Judiciary Committee, Subcommittee No. 1, *A Joint Resolution Proposing an Amendment to the Constitution of the United States Extending the Right to Vote to Citizens Eighteen Years of Age or Older*, 78th Cong., 1st sess. (October 20, 1943), 6; Johnson, *Lowering*, 210.

7 *Voting Rights Amendments of 1969*, 91st Cong., 2nd sess., *Congressional Record* 116 (March 11, 1970), 6929; Senate Judiciary Committee, Subcommittee on Constitutional Amendments, *Hearings Before the Subcommittee of the Judiciary on the President's Requested Legislation to Lower the National Voting Age to 18 Years*,

90th Cong., 2nd sess., *Congressional Record* 114 (July 12, 1968), 21068; Senate Judiciary Committee, Subcommittee on Constitutional Amendments, *Hearings Before the Subcommittee on Constitutional Amendments of the Committee on the Judiciary on S.J. Res. 14, and S.J. Res 78 Relating to Lowering the Voting Age to 18*, 90th Cong., 2nd sess. (May 14–16, 1968), 73; House of Representatives, *Extending Voting Rights Act of 1965*, 91st Cong., 2nd sess., *Congressional Record* 116 (June 17, 1970), 20174; Ohio Vote 19, "Why You Should Vote Yes," F11, box 2709, NEA Papers.

8 *Constitutional Amendment Introduced Providing That No Citizen under 21 May Have the Right to Vote*, 83rd Cong., 2nd sess., *Congressional Record* 100 (March 10, 1954), 3050; Dorothy Canfield Fisher, "Raise Don't Lower the Voting Age," *Parent's Magazine*, December 1943, 18; Virgil M. Hancher, "Too Young to Fight or Vote," *Parent's Magazine*, December 1943, 19, 20; George Fletcher, "Voting Age—Fighting Age," *Los Angeles Times*, June 30, 1952, A4; "Should the Legal Voting Age Be Reduced to 18?," *Journal of the National Education Association* (1946): 58.

9 Rebecca de Schweinitz, *If We Could Change the World: Young People and America's Long Struggle for Racial Equality* (Chapel Hill: University of North Carolina Press, 2009), chap. 1.

10 Fletcher, "Voting Age," A4.

11 "Should the Legal Voting Age Be Reduced?," 58.

12 Cornelius E. Gallagher, Statement on Vote 18, F5, box 2707, NEA Papers; "Youth Support Promised if Voting Age Put on the Ballot," *Oregonian*, February 7, 1969, F8, box 2703, NEA Papers; David Dennis, Statement on Vote 18, April 3, 1970, F5, box 2707, NEA Papers; "The Legal Age of Maturity," *San Francisco Examiner*, March 26, 1971, 34.

13 Noel Greenwood, "Lower-Voting-Age Bill May Propose Adulthood at 18 or 19," *Los Angeles Times*, November 7, 1969, 3; Johnson, *Lowering*, 119–20.

14 "Should Eighteen-Year Olds Vote?," 7; Greenwood, "Lower-Voting-Age," 3; Johnson, *Lowering*, 119. On caretaking views of children's rights, see Michael Grossberg, "Liberation and Caretaking: Fighting over Children's Rights in Postwar America," in *Reinventing Childhood after World War II*, ed. Paula S. Fass and Michael Grossberg (Philadelphia: University of Pennsylvania Press, 2011), 19–37.

15 "Should the Legal Voting Age Be Reduced?," 58; William Carleton, "Votes for Teenagers," *Yale Review*, October 1968, 45, 54; Lenore G. Marshall to Richard Welling, October 8, 1942, in "Voting Age Lowered to 18 (Pro and Con)," box 70, National Self-Government Committee Records, New York Public Library, New York (hereafter cited as NSG Papers); Johnson, *Lowering*, 174; "Should Eighteen-Year Olds Vote?," 7.

16 "On Lowering the Voting Age to 18," typescript, F9, Box 2705, NEA Papers; Graham, *Lowering*, 10; Harvey Berk, "BBYO Project 18," F9, box 2703, NEA Papers; Volunteers for Vote 19, "Old Enough to Vote," brochure, F11, box 2709, NEA Papers.

17 Berk, "BBYO Project," NEA Papers; Jacob Javits, "Lower the Voting Age," *Playboy*, February 1968, 18; Harry Trimborn, "Debate Flares on Giving Vote to 18-Year-Olds," *Los Angeles Times*, June 17, 1968, A1.

18 National Education Association, minutes, February 4–5, 1968, F1, box 1144, NEA Papers; "Excerpts from the Testimony of Monroe Sweetland to the California Assembly Hearings on Lowering the Voting Age," April 9, 1970, F9, box 2699, NEA Papers; Javits, "Lower," 176; Joy Elmer Morgan, "Old Enough to Fight: Old Enough to Vote," *Journal of the National Education Association* (February 1943): 35.

19 "Should the Legal Voting Age Be Reduced?," 58.

20 "Voting and Youth: Should the Age Limit be Lowered," *Vital Issues* 17 (1967): 113.

21 Fisher, "Raise Don't Lower," 18; Johnson, *Lowering*, 122.

22 Johnson, *Lowering*, 163; Richard Welling to Dr. James K. Pollock, Sept. 16, 1953, in "Voting Age Lowered to 18 (Pro and Con)," box 70, NSG Papers.

23 Johnson, *Lowering*, 13, 78, 121, 165; "Should Eighteen-Year Olds Vote?," 3.

24 Edgar Z. Friedenberg, "The Image of the Adolescent Minority," in *The Dignity of Youth and Other Atavisms* (Boston: Beacon, 1965), 67.

25 *Hearings before Subcommittee No. 1 of the Committee on the Judiciary on H.J. Res. 39: A Joint Resolution Proposing an Amendment to the Constitution of the United States, Extending the Right to Vote to Citizens Eighteen Years of Age or Older*, 78th Cong., 1st sess. (October 20, 1943), 8; "Youth Forum Split over Voting at 18," *New York Times*, October 25, 1953, 51.

26 "Should the Legal Voting Age Be Reduced?," 58.

27 NEA Representative Assembly Report, July 6, 1968, F6, box 2699, NEA Papers.

28 Louis M. Seagull, "The Youth Vote and Change in America," *Annals of the American Academy of Political and Social Science* 397 (1971): 89; Dwight L. Chawin (Special Assistant to the President) to Ian MacGowan, May 5, 1969, F3, box 2703, NEA Papers; "18 Is Old Enough," unidentified editorial (September 27, 1969), F3, box 2909, NEA Papers; "Excerpts from the Testimony," NEA Papers; Berk, "BBYO Project 18," NEA Papers.

29 Chawin to MacGowan, NEA Papers; Youth Vote Brochure (1968), F14, box 2700, NEA Papers; "Report of the Status of Project 18 and the Youth Franchise Coalition," F3, box 2909, NEA Papers.

30 "Let Young Americans Share in Democracy," F16, box 151, Frontlash Collection, George Meany Memorial Labor Archives, National Labor College, Silver Spring, Md.; Connecticut Committee for the 18 Year-Old Vote, "It's Time for a Change: A Report on the 18 Year-Old Voting Issue," March 12, 1967, 4–9, box 18, Senator Jacob K. Javits Collection, Special Collections & University Archives, Stony Brook University, Stony Brook, N.Y.; Youth Franchise Coalition Pamphlet, F9, box 2705, NEA Papers; Democratic Platform (1968) in "Statement on 18-Yr. Voting," F2, box 2705, NEA Papers; Citizens for Vote 18, "Radio Spot" (WKBW Buffalo, NY), F9, box 2703, NEA Papers; "Excerpts from the Testimony," NEA Papers.

31 Citizens, "Radio Spot," NEA Papers; Javits, "Lower," 176; "Youth Support Promised"; "Case for Lowering the Voting Age," F9, box 2705, NEA Papers; Graham, *Lowering*, 29.

32 "Case for Lowering the Voting Age," NEA Papers; Ian MacGowan, press release, April 14, 1969, F9, box 2699, NEA Papers; Connecticut Committee, "It's Time," 7, NEA Papers; Javits, "Lower," 176.

33 Johnson, *Lowering*, 199.

34 James F. Cook Jr., "Politics and Education in the Talmadge Era: The Controversy over the University System of Georgia, 1941–42" (PhD diss., University of Georgia, 1972), 262–63.

35 Stephen Hess, "Now Is There a Gap between the Generations or Isn't There?," *New York Times*, June 12, 1971, 29; MacGowan, press release, April 14, 1969, NEA Papers; "Excerpts from Transcript of Nixon Talk on Youth," *New York Times*, January 15, 1971, 12; John Dellenback, "The 19-Year-Old Vote" (press release, March 19), F5, box 2707, NEA Papers; Connecticut Committee, "It's Time," 7, NEA Papers; Project 18, "Fact Sheet," F9, box 2705, NEA Papers.

36 *To Establish Justice, to Insure Domestic Tranquility: The Final Report of the National Commission on the Causes and Prevention of Violence* (New York: Bantam Books, 1970), 189, 191.

37 "Excerpts from the Testimony," NEA Papers; Senate Judiciary Committee, Subcommittee on Constitutional Amendments, *Hearings before the Subcommittee on Constitutional Amendments of the Judiciary, United States Senate*, 91st Cong., 2nd sess. (March 9, 1970), 151–52; James Brown, "Report to National Convention," 1968, F6, box 5, NAACP Western Region Papers, Bancroft Library, Special Collections and Archives, University of California, Berkeley; Gloster Current, "Excerpts of the 1966 Annual Report of the Director of Branches and Field Administration," 1966, frames 2–7, reel 6, part 29, NAACP Papers (microfilm); Senate Judiciary Committee, *Hearings* (May 14–16, 1968), 45.

38 Senate Judiciary Committee, *Hearings* (May 14–16, 1968), 2.

39 Project 18, "Fact Sheet," NEA Papers.

40 "Let Young Americans Share in Democracy"; Senate Judiciary Committee, *Hearings* (May 14–16, 1968), 43.

41 Friedenberg, *Dignity of Youth*, 16; Ian MacGowan to All Members of Congress, memo (May 12, 1970), F4, box 2705, NEA Papers; "Excerpts from the Testimony," NEA Papers.

42 Johnson, *Lowering*, 122, 173, 210, 215, 219–20; "Should Eighteen-Year Olds Vote?," 13.

43 Johnson, *Lowering*, 122, 215.

44 Ben Rubenstein and Morton Levitt, "Rebellion and Responsibility," *Yale Review* 57 (1967): 23; Kenneth Crawford, "Youth Is Served," *Newsweek*, March 30, 1970, 29; Carlton, "Votes for Teenagers," 57; "Age of Aquarius," *Newsweek*, March 23, 1970, 70; Trimborn, "Debate Flares," A1.

45 Senator Joe Josephson (Alaska) to Monroe Sweetland, May 19, 1969, F7, box 2700, NEA Papers; Douglas Holmes, Monica Bychowski Holmes, and Lisa Appignanesi,

The Language of Trust: Dialogue of the Generations (New York: New York Science House, 1971), 97; F. G. Friemann, *Youth and Society* (London: Macmillan, 1971), 35; Lewis S. Feuer, *The Conflict of Generations: The Character and Significance of Student Movements* (New York: Basic Books, 1969), 46; Carlton, "Votes for Teenagers," 50.

46 *What Do Students Really Want?* (Bloomington, Ind.: Phi Delta Kappa Educational Foundation, 1972), 43; Richard Nixon, "Remarks at a Ceremony Marking the Certification of the 26th Amendment to the Constitution," July 5, 1972, online by Gerhard Peters and John T. Wooley, American Presidency Project, http://www. presidency.ucsb.edu/ws/?pid=3068.

47 Josephson to Sweetland, NEA Papers.

48 Feuer, *Conflict*, 3; *To Establish Justice*, 191; "Statement on Lowering the Voting Age," F4, box 2705, NEA Papers; Henry Malcolm, *Generation of Narcissus* (New York: Little, Brown, 1971), 20.

49 Johnson, *Lowering*, 200–205, 189, 178; Carlton, "Votes for Teenagers," 55.

50 "Should the Legal Voting Age Be Reduced?," 58; Johnson, *Lowering*, 14, 123–24, 178.

51 Margaret Mead, *Culture and Commitment: A Study of the Generation Gap* (New York: Doubleday, 1970), 54, 51, 68, 60.

52 "The Youth Vote and Change in American Politics," *Annals of the American Academy of Political and Social Science* (1971): 89.

53 Malcolm, *Generation*, 18, 155, 239; Mead, *Culture*, 56.

54 Graham, *Lowering*, 22; Rubenstein and Levitt, "Rebellion and Responsibility," 19, 22; Malcolm, *Generation*, 240; "Confrontation or Participation? The Federal Government and the Student Community: A Report to the President of the United States" (White House Fellows Association, October 1968), 2.

55 Mead, *Culture*, 58, 61; Graham, *Lowering*, 22; Democratic Platform in "Statements on 18-Yr. Voting," NEA Papers; Joseph A. Thomas quoted in NEA minutes, November 16, 1968, F8, box 2699, NEA Papers. See also F9, box 2709, NEA Papers.

56 Carlton, "Votes for Teenagers," 55, 57; Fred Graham, "Lowering the Voting Age," *New York Times*, March 29, 1970, E12; Malcolm, *Generation*, 72; Graham, *Lowering*, 18.

57 Graham, *Lowering*, 18.

58 Harriet Griffin, quoted in NEA minutes, November 16, 1968, F8, box 2699, NEA Papers.

59 Charles Diggs, Statement on Vote 18, April 9, 1970, F5, box 2707, NEA Papers.

60 Dan Kubiak, "Youth and Their Vote: A New Day Is Coming," *Theory into Practice* 10, no. 5 (December 1971): 322.

61 Monroe Sweetland, "Suffrage for Teeners," *San Francisco Examiner*, September 22, 1969, news clipping in F18, box 2700, NEA Papers.

62 Abner J. Mikva, Statement on Vote 18, F4, box 2707, NEA Papers; Morton Levitt and Ben Rubenstein, eds., *Youth and Social Change* (Detroit: Wayne State

University Press, 1972), 16; Crawford, "Youth Is Served," 29; "Testimony by Charles Koppelman," F8, box 2703, NEA Papers. See also Nathan Glazer, "Student Power in Berkeley," in Levitt and Rubenstein, *Youth and Social Change*, 269; Feuer, *Conflict*, 407; Holmes, Holmes, and Appignanesi, *Language of Trust*, 96.

63 Mikva, Statement on Vote 18, NEA Papers.

64 "Report on the Status of Project 18 and the Youth Franchise Coalition," F3, box 2709, NEA Papers; "Excerpts from the Testimony"; Dellenback, "19-Year-Old Vote"; Graham, *Lowering*, 27–28.

65 "18 Year Old Vote," unidentified news clipping, F10, box 2705, NEA Papers; Graham, *Lowering*, 2; Malcolm, *Generation*, 178.

66 Johnson, *Lowering*, 202; "Age of Aquarius," 30.

67 Malcolm, *Generation*, 102.

68 Eleanor Crocker and Maurine LaBarre, "The Silent Vigil: A Student Nonviolent Demonstration," in Levitt and Rubenstein, *Youth and Social Change*, 221; Senate Judiciary Committee, *Hearings* (May 14–16, 1968), 43; Seymour Martin Lipset and Philip G. Altback, "Student Politics and Higher Education," in *Student Politics*, ed. Seymour Martin Lipset (New York: Basic Books, 1967), 233; "Age of Aquarius," 30; *To Establish Justice*, 191.

69 *To Establish Justice*, 204; Malcolm, *Generation*, 51.

70 "Report on the Status of Project 18 and the Youth Franchise Coalition," 6, NEA Papers.

71 Mikva, Statement on Vote 18, NEA Papers; Les Francis, "Educator Urges Voting Age of 18 as 'Only Logical Turning Point,'" *Los Angeles Times*, March 3, 1969, C8.

72 Monroe Sweetland to Ian MacGowan and Rosalyn Baker, May 1, 1970, F18, box 2700, NEA Papers; Gallagher, Statement on Vote 18, NEA Papers; Betsy Glasgow, "In My Opinion: Eighteen-Year-Olds Aren't Ready to Vote," *Seventeen*, September 1967, 266; Project 18 Bulletin, "Reports from States," F3, box 2709, NEA Papers.

11

"Old Enough to Live"

Age, Alcohol, and Adulthood in the United States, 1970–1984

TIMOTHY COLE

When Harvard University student Stefan Muller turned twenty-one in March 2011, he woke up feeling like much the same person that he had been the day before. The arrival of his birthday, in other words, had not altered his personality or otherwise changed who he was. Nonetheless, Muller felt as though his life had been transformed, and in a blog post that he wrote a few days later, he compared turning twenty-one to having "a weight lifted from my shoulders." After years of waiting, Muller had reached the minimum legal drinking age. He could now order a drink in a restaurant without worrying about being asked for identification, and he no longer felt separated "by a birthday" from friends who had already turned twenty-one. Conscious that these might sound like trivial changes to some, Muller insisted that his role in American society had been fundamentally altered. "This was about personhood," he wrote, "in a society that highly values drinking," and turning twenty-one had finally made Muller feel like he was a "real person" in the eyes of other adult citizens.[1]

Muller was not a typical twenty-one-year-old. A long-time member of the National Youth Rights Association, he was more sensitive than most young people to how age shaped his social status and legal rights.[2] He was not alone, however, in believing that it was the drinking age, more than any other age threshold, that defined young people's passage into "real" adult citizenship. Since the 1980s, Americans between the ages of eighteen and twenty-one have held a legal status unlike that of any other age group as individuals who are nearly, but not completely, adults before the law. State and federal lawmakers granted these young people most of the rights and privileges of adult citizens during the early

1970s when they lowered both the voting age and the legal age of majority from twenty-one to eighteen. These reforms proved to be both durable and popular, and it is thanks to them that eighteen-year-olds are considered legal adults for most purposes today.[3] The drinking age is the most glaring exception to this rule; while twenty-nine states lowered the drinking age along with the age of majority during the 1970s, public and political support for a lower drinking age proved to be short-lived, and lawmakers in many of these states reversed or rolled back their earlier drinking age reforms within a few years.[4] In 1984, congressional lawmakers approved the National Minimum Drinking Age Act (NMDA), using a budgetary incentive to wrest control of the drinking age from the states and effectively imposing a drinking age of twenty-one nationwide.[5] As a result of these reforms, young Americans must wait three full years *after* they reach the age of majority before they can legally drink, and it is not until they reach the drinking age that young people lose the last vestige of their legal minority.

Since the 1980s, supporters of the national minimum drinking age have justified this discrepancy between the drinking age and the age of majority by making a single, straightforward argument. Eighteen- to twenty-year-olds, in this view, are far more likely to cause drunk driving accidents than are older drivers, and denying them access to alcohol saves lives. As the primary sponsor of the 1984 drinking age act, Senator Frank R. Lautenberg (D-N.J.) relied almost exclusively on this argument in making the case for his bill. Working closely with drinking age lobby groups like the New Jersey Coalition for 21, and with anti–drunk driving organizations like Mothers Against Drunk Driving (MADD), advocates of the NMDA claimed that early 1970s drinking age reforms had led to a dramatic rise in the number of drunk driving accidents caused by eighteen- to twenty-year-old drivers. Using accident statistics and traffic safety research from states that had lowered the drinking age as evidence, they suggested that eighteen- to twenty-year-olds had proven themselves incapable of drinking responsibly during the 1970s, and that raising the drinking age to twenty-one nationwide would save more than a thousand lives a year.[6]

In the years since NMDA took effect, most policy makers, journalists, and academics have taken the rhetoric surrounding the act at face value, assuming that the act's supporters were simply trying to prevent drunk driving deaths, and that they were responding to a proven link between the drinking age and drunk driving accidents. This link, however, was never as straightforward as supporters of the NMDA had claimed, and 1970s and 1980s debates over the drinking age were about more than just traffic safety. Representatives of the United States Student Association (USSA) and other students' groups—along with several prominent alcohol policy experts—challenged Lautenberg's use of statistics throughout the debate over the act, and later scholars have faulted parties on both sides of the debates for their "use and abuse" of traffic safety statistics.[7] Most traffic safety scholars do now believe that raising the drinking age led to a reduction in youth drunk driving rates, and their findings have served as the lynchpin for political and popular support for a drinking age of twenty-one since the 1980s. These findings have also faced perennial challenges, however, from dissenting scholars and activists, and academic debate over the issue has often been highly politicized.[8] From a policy perspective, determining the effect of the drinking age on drunk driving accidents is certainly important. But this utilitarian focus on the outcomes of the NMDA has also kept scholars from exploring its broader meaning, and obscured a longer, more complex history of the drinking age in the United States.

A broader historical analysis of political debates over the drinking age suggests that drinking age laws have never served solely as a means of preventing drunk driving accidents, or of protecting vulnerable children and youth. Historically, these laws have also functioned as a means of controlling young Americans' behavior, of preserving adult privileges and authority, and of drawing clear distinctions between children and adults. The NMDA is no exception. The earliest efforts to reverse early 1970s drinking age reforms and restore a drinking age of twenty-one originated at the state rather than at the federal level, and grassroots drinking age activists like Phyllis Scheps—who formed the New Jersey Coalition for 21 in 1977—were not initially concerned with preventing drunk driving accidents. Rather, they believed that a lower drinking age had precipitated a broader crisis of adult authority, and they were primarily concerned with controlling the behavior of young people in their communities. Over time, however, these activists found that they could gain far more traction by framing their campaigns as a means of preventing drunk driving accidents and saving lives, and during the early

1980s, they made common cause with anti–drunk driving organizations like MADD. Relying on a rhetoric of protecting vulnerable children and youth—and on their own identities as parents and protectors of young people—both groups would play a key role in building support for the NMDA.

While they were certainly sincere in their desire to protect young people and save lives, the activists and lawmakers who worked to raise the drinking age during the 1970s and 1980s were also expressing a deep-seated distrust of eighteen- to twenty-year-olds' ability to make responsible decisions, and asserting that these young people needed to have their rights and privileges restricted for their own protection. Rejecting eighteen- to twenty-year-olds' claims that they had a right to drink as legal adults, they sought to reassert the ability of parents, teachers, and other adult authorities to control youth. Debates in the 1970s and 1980s over the drinking age were part of a broader, ongoing struggle over young people's legal status and the timing of their transition into adulthood. The drive for a higher drinking age was in many ways a reaction against earlier reforms, which had granted eighteen-year-olds most of the rights and responsibilities of adults. By framing a higher drinking age as a means of saving "our children's" lives, in other words, MADD, the Coalition for 21, and lawmakers like Senator Lautenberg were all effectively asserting that eighteen- to twenty-year-olds *were* children—and that only young people over the age of twenty-one were "real" adults.

For all the effort that they put into championing a drinking age of twenty-one, however, activists like Scheps and MADD founder Candy Lightner sometimes expressed a surprising lack of faith in even twenty-one-year-olds' ability to drink responsibly. Lightner, for example, often asserted that she would like to see the drinking age raised "much higher" than twenty-one, even as she admitted a need to "be realistic," and acknowledged that few Americans would support a drinking age higher than twenty-one.[9] Lawmakers and activists on both sides of this debate recognized that the drinking age was a somewhat arbitrary threshold, and that age did not in itself guarantee an individual's maturity or responsibility. Virtually no one, however, seriously proposed a drinking age lower than eighteen, and while some states did try to compromise by setting the drinking age at nineteen or twenty during the 1970s, in the long run these compromises seemed to satisfy hardly anyone. Rather than attempting to determine what the best possible drinking age was or when young people actually acquired the capacity to drink responsibly, the activists who sought to alter the drinking age during the 1970s and 1980s tended to champion one of two preexisting, rival thresholds for legal adulthood. Conflict over the drinking age was largely a struggle over whether to grant young people access to alcohol sooner or later, and policy makers essentially faced a binary choice between a drinking age of eighteen or twenty-one.

***

The concept of a minimum legal drinking age is a distinctly modern invention. Prior to Prohibition, most states barred minors—which usually meant young people under twenty-one—from purchasing alcohol, but there were few restrictions on their ability to possess or consume it. For the most part, pre-Prohibition lawmakers assumed that young people's parents should be in control of whether, and when, their children could drink. While minors were barred from buying liquor in saloons, then, young people could often still purchase alcohol with their parents' permission, and "there was never a ban on all youthful drinking."[10] Children did figure prominently in the literature and rhetoric of the temperance movement, where they were cast both as the victims of adults' drinking and as "child drunkards" who had fallen victim to alcohol themselves. But temperance activists were more interested in furthering their goal of a dry society than they were in setting a minimum age for alcohol consumption, and their attempts to protect young people often focused on temperance educations programs—which were designed to keep young people from *ever* drinking—rather than on denying them access to alcohol until they were older.[11]

The ratification of the Eighteenth Amendment and passage of the Volstead Act in 1919 rendered existing liquor laws moot, including those that restricted young people's access to alcohol. During Prohibition, however, both prohibitionists and repealers frequently framed their cause as a means of protecting children and young people. Many former temperance activists, for example, noted with alarm that speakeasies "served adults and minors with impartiality" during Prohibition, and by the early 1930s activists like Pauline Morton Sabin were warning that young people were "drinking more than ever" under Prohibition in order to make a case for repeal.[12] During the Prohibition years, Americans' attitudes toward alcohol consumption changed dramatically, as drinking lost much of the stigma that had been attached to it in earlier years. After the repeal of Prohibition in 1933, more and more adults began to think of drinking as a "normal part of life," rather than a "deviant or sinful" pursuit—but they continued to fear the effects of alcohol consumption on children.[13] As a result, the drinking age laws that lawmakers instituted after repeal served a double purpose, protecting children and youth from the dangers of alcohol use while also minimizing the possibility that Americans might begin to think of alcohol *itself* as inherently immoral or dangerous. By drawing a firm line between those who were "old enough" to drink and those who needed to be protected from liquor, these laws made it possible to think of moderate drinking by *adults* as relatively harmless.

Initially, many states' post-Prohibition drinking age laws looked much like earlier statutes, setting a minimum age for the purchase but not the consumption or possession of alcohol. In nearly every state— the major exception being New York, which restored its pre-Prohibition minimum purchase age of eighteen—lawmakers set this threshold at twenty-one, defining alcohol consumption as an "adult" activity and equating the drinking age with age of majority.[14] Over time, however, Americans became more and more concerned that minors were finding ways to access alcohol, and state lawmakers repeatedly strengthened minimum drinking age laws, barring minors from possessing as well as purchasing alcohol, closing loopholes that had allowed young people to drink under some conditions, and strengthening the enforcement of drinking age laws. Throughout the middle of the twentieth century, young Americans were busy developing increasingly distinct youth cultures and identities—embracing new and unfamiliar sexual mores, styles of dress, and forms of entertainment—and more and more Americans began to worry that young people's moral values were diverging from those of their parents' generation. To many Americans, youthful drinking seemed to be both a cause and a symptom of this divergence, and the stricter drinking age laws that legislators put in place in the years and decades after Prohibition were part of a broader effort to keep young people under adults' control and prevent "outbursts of immorality" among the nation's youth.[15]

These fears were often exaggerated. In the decades that followed repeal, public discussions of young people's drinking behavior were characterized by a divergence between "a slow but growing body of genuine research on youth"—which suggested that there was no real cause for alarm—and sensational news coverage, which portrayed youthful drinking as a widespread and serious problem.[16] In 1953, for example, sociologists Robert Straus and Selden Bacon—whose study *Drinking in College* was among the first to analyze young people's drinking habits systematically—expressed frustration with reporters' tendency to assume that young people drank "frequently and to excess," when their own research had found that most students drank only moderately, and without causing serious harm to themselves or others.[17] Americans would continue to see teenage and "underage" drinking as one of the most pressing problems facing young people, however, until the late 1960s, when Americans' attitudes toward youthful drinking suddenly shifted.

During the late 1960s and early 1970s, the explosive growth of 1960s counterculture, protests against the Vietnam War, and unprecedented unrest on college and university campuses generated widespread public anxiety over a perceived "generation gap," and in this context young people who merely drank alcohol began to seem *less* threatening to many adults. Alcohol, at least, was a drug that many parents had themselves tried as youth, and one that "underage" young people had found ways to enjoy for decades. To many adults, alcohol seemed far less threatening than less familiar drugs like marijuana and LSD, which had exploded in popularity during the 1960s.[18] At the same time, a growing number of academics, educators, and lawmakers began to interpret the generation gap as a sign that the nation's college-aged youth were ready to handle greater responsibility, and to do so at younger ages than young people had in the past.[19] Eighteen-year-olds, they asserted, were better educated and more at home in the rapidly changing, technology-driven world of the late 1960s than many of their elders, and they displayed a passion and idealism that many adults lacked. These arguments helped to convince state and federal lawmakers to place an enormous vote of confidence in American youth when they lowered the voting age in 1971.[20] Driven by this same confidence in eighteen-year-olds' maturity and responsibility, and by a firm belief that the law should treat eighteen-year-olds consistently, lawmakers in thirty states voted to lower the age of majority within two years of the ratification of the Twenty-Sixth Amendment, with all but a handful of states passing similar laws in the years that followed.[21]

Changes in the drinking age were often the most controversial component of these new age of majority laws. Having struggled to keep alcohol *out* of teenagers' hands throughout the postwar decades, conservative lawmakers in many states strongly objected to the idea that eighteen-year-olds should be granted access to alcohol. One Texas state senator, for example, warned that a lower drinking age would corrupt young people, exposing young men to "lascivious, pornographic type entertainment" in bars and allowing young women to be plied with liquor.[22] Opponents of a lower drinking age often found, however, that they could gain even greater traction by warning that a lower drinking age would cause "carnage" on the highways, as inexperienced and irresponsible young people mixed drinking and driving.[23] Responding to these arguments, lawmakers in many states refused to lower the drinking age at all. California, for example, retained a drinking age of twenty-one even after granting eighteen-year-olds all of the other legal rights and privileges of adults, and in a few states lawmakers hedged their bets; Alabama, Alaska, Arizona, Idaho, and Nebraska lowered the drinking age to nineteen instead of eighteen, and lawmakers in Delaware chose to set the drinking age at twenty.[24]

For a brief period during the early 1970s, lawmakers in many states did believe that eighteen-year-olds were capable of drinking responsibly—or at least that it was important to treat them consistently. In Texas, for example, State Senator Robert Gammage convinced his fellow lawmakers to lower the age of majority and drinking age simultaneously, by asserting that eighteen-year-olds were "either adults, or they're not adults," and asking "for consistency" in the regulation of young people's legal rights.[25] Proposed at a time when feminist, civil rights, gay, and Chicano activists were making similar appeals for consistent and equal treatment before the law, this argument had a broad appeal, and by 1975 lawmakers like Gammage had succeeded in convincing twenty-nine different state legislatures to lower the drinking age. In most of these cases, lawmakers voted to lower the drinking age as part of a broader effort to lower the age of majority, and at times these reforms seemed to be an afterthought to the Twenty-Sixth Amendment. Having heard—and made—the argument that if young people were "old enough to fight" then they were also "old enough to vote" during the debate over the voting age, lawmakers like Gammage seemed to think that it was only common sense that eighteen-year-olds should be permitted to drink as well. Young people had been heavily involved in campaigns to lower the voting age during the early 1970s, but they were much more muted in their support for a lower age of majority—and most of the impetus for age of majority legislation came from lawmakers like Gammage themselves.

While they often acknowledged that there were risks in lowering the drinking age, supporters of a lower drinking age pointed out that many adults, too, drove drunk or drank irresponsibly, and argued that it was more important to treat young people fairly than to protect them at any cost. As New Jersey assemblyman Joseph Woodcock put it, eighteen- to twenty-year-olds were not "hothouse flowers," and lawmakers could not "always keep protecting them: they do not need it, nor do they want it."[26] But despite the confidence of lawmakers like Woodcock, many Americans were worried that new, lower drinking age laws would lead to more drunk driving accidents. As the first of these laws took effect in states like Michigan, Maine, and Vermont during 1971 and 1972, police, traffic safety officials, and lawmakers in other states were watching carefully. Early results were not encouraging; accident statistics compiled by the Michigan state police were among the first to be released, and they painted a grim picture of the effect of Michigan's new drinking age, appearing to show a 119 percent increase in drunk driving accidents involving eighteen- to twenty-year-old drivers. Circulated widely by the Michigan Council on Alcohol Problems—an advocacy group that had opposed a lower drinking age in Michigan—these figures won nationwide attention.[27] While influential, however, the Michigan statistics were also deeply flawed; state police had changed how and where they kept track of drunk driving accidents the same year that the new law took effect, rendering a simple before-and-after comparison useless.[28]

Controlled, scientific studies of the effects of new drinking age laws did not begin to appear until after 1974, and while these studies did find that a lower drinking age carried "a price in increased fatal motor vehicle collisions," they reported more modest changes in youth drunk driving rates of between 10 and 25 percent, with a few states and regions showing almost no increase at all. Traffic safety experts like Robert L. Douglas and Allan F. Williams were optimistic that the effects of a lower drinking age could be reduced over time, and one group of researchers at MIT asserted that new drinking age laws had merely allowed young people to drink and drive at the same rates as adults. Raising the drinking age in response to elevated drunk driving rates, they asserted, would therefore be "unduly discriminatory against this age group."[29] These more level-headed analyses emerged too late, however, to shore up support for a lower drinking age. Media reports of skyrocketing drunk driving rates in states that lowered the drinking age had already won nationwide attention, and the wave of drinking age legislation that had swept through state legislatures after 1971 had already ground to an abrupt halt.

Alabama became the last state to approve a lower drinking age in 1975, and lawmakers in states that had already lowered the drinking age faced growing pressure to reverse their earlier reforms in the years that followed. By 1984, nineteen different states had passed legislation to raise the drinking age.[30] While growing public concern over a perceived rise in drunk driving accidents had halted any further efforts to lower the drinking age, however, many of the activists and lawmakers who worked to raise the drinking age during the late 1970s and early 1980s were responding to a much broader set of concerns. Drinking age lobby groups like the New Jersey Coalition for 21 were initially far more interested in controlling young people's behavior, and in fighting what they perceived to be a broad crisis of adult authority, than they were in preventing drunk driving accidents. Their primary goal, in other words, was to reassert adults' ability to control eighteen- to twenty-year-olds' behavior, and restore age twenty-one as the threshold for becoming an adult in this key area of law. Founded by New Jersey Parent-Teacher Association (PTA) member Phyllis Scheps in 1977, the coalition quickly grew into a force to be reckoned with, claiming to represent forty-two different member organizations and 280,000 voters, running extensive and well-organized grassroots campaigns, and leveling an enormous amount of anger and indignation at lawmakers who refused to take their concerns seriously.[31]

Coalition members often made it sound as though their schools and communities were under siege by drunk, disorderly, and above all disrespectful youth. In 1979, for example, coalition member and New Jersey PTA official Manya Unger told a committee of New Jersey lawmakers that the state's parents and educators were witnessing "a growing number of instances in which alcohol played a part in the breakdown of respect for property, programs, and people." A lower drinking age, she asserted, had emboldened young people in their confrontations with adult authorities, and caused widespread discipline problems in schools, as eighteen-year-olds who were still in high school passed liquor on to younger youth.[32] Responding to these concerns, State Senator Frank X. Graves proposed a bill to raise New Jersey's drinking age to nineteen in 1979, describing his bill not as a means of preventing drunk driving accidents, but rather as a measure designed to "set these schools straight" from being under the influence of alcohol.[33]

Coalition members supported Graves's bill as an improvement over the status quo, but they made it clear that they were as troubled by the behavior of nineteen- and twenty-year-old youth as they were by the behavior of high school students. One coalition supporter shared a litany of complaints about the behavior of the young people who congregated at "youthful drinking establishments" in his community. These complaints ranged from fights, assaults on police officers, and "obscene comments" directed at women to much more minor infractions, such as littering, "illegal parking," and loud cursing. Whatever their specific complaints, however, coalition members often seemed to be most troubled by a perception that eighteen- to twenty-year-olds were no longer respecting adults' authority and had gotten out of their parents' control. By telling the story of a young woman who had been "brought in drunk" to his police station, police officer and coalition supporter Robert Fastiggi sought to bring the severity and the scale of his concerns home to New Jersey's lawmakers; when the young lady's father arrived to pick her up, according to Fastiggi, "the first thing she said to her father [was] 'you're a F__ king Douche.'"[34] Clearly, a fear that young people were rejecting their *parents'* authority lay at the heart of coalition members' concerns. They blamed lawmakers who had voted to lower the drinking age and age of majority for causing this lack of respect, and were determined to restore parents' ability to control their children's drinking behavior—even when those children were legally adults. Lawmakers, according to Scheps, had made parents' responsibility to protect youth and to "teach them right from wrong" an "impossibility," giving young people a "loaded gun" in the form of access to alcohol.[35]

In legislative hearings on Graves's bill, a number of young activists, most of whom were involved in student government at New Jersey's universities and colleges, spoke out against the bill. But these young activists rarely spoke of eighteen-year-olds' *right* to drink; the previous year, a federal court in Michigan had ruled that the state's new drinking age law—which set the drinking age at twenty-one—was constitutional, asserting that drinking was not a "fundamental right" but a privilege, and upholding states' right to set the drinking age higher than the age of majority so long as they had a "rational basis" for doing so.[36] Recognizing that they were unlikely to convince lawmakers that eighteen-year-olds had a right to drink, young people like Princeton sophomore vice president Eric Keller referred to "philosophical" arguments only obliquely. Instead, they focused on challenging the Coalition for 21's rationale for drinking age reform.

Keller pointed out that young people had been able to obtain liquor with ease even before lawmakers had lowered the drinking age, and asserted that Graves's bill would be a "singularly inefficient method of treating only one symptom of the overall problem." The college pubs that had opened since the early 1970s, according to Keller, were "clean, attractive, and efficiently managed." Raising the drinking age, in his view, would only eliminate this type of "controlled drinking" and drive students' drinking underground, while doing nothing to help young people whose drinking posed a real threat to their own and others' well-being. There was, Keller argued, "no compelling reason why the privileges of this specific age group should be rescinded," or their status before the law altered.[37] Students from other colleges and universities made similar arguments, and they were supported by policy experts like Dr. Robert Pandina and Dr. Gail Gleason Milgram—both of the Rutgers Center for Alcohol Studies—who proclaimed Graves's legislation "a bad bill," which would "have very little impact on the drinking practices" of young people. These experts warned lawmakers to take the "emotional kinds of information" they were hearing from Coalition for 21 spokespeople with a grain of salt, and that raising the drinking age would not, in itself, be a solution to any of the problems that young people's drinking caused.[38]

Coalition members' "emotional" arguments, however, often had more political force than young people's protests or experts' advice, particularly when these arguments were backed by a groundswell of voter irritation and anger and accompanied by well-organized campaigns to put pressure on lawmakers through petitions and letter-writing campaigns. Coalition members rejected the testimony of experts like Pandina and Milgram, noting that "figures can be manipulated" and calling on lawmakers to trust the testimony and experience of adults who interacted with young people every day. Unger, for example, reminded lawmakers that the state's eighteen- to twenty-year-olds were "our own children," and asserted that coalition members were not "out to get" eighteen-year-olds, or to "deprive them of some alleged right." Laying claim to a long tradition of "child protection," coalition members instead portrayed themselves as having a duty to "protect young people from themselves," so that they could grow up "strong, healthy, and well educated."[39]

Graves's bill ultimately passed, raising the drinking age in New Jersey to nineteen. Coalition for 21 activists were determined, however, to achieve their ultimate goal of denying anyone under the age of twenty-one access to alcohol. Disappointed that Graves's bill had not gone further, coalition members worked throughout the period between 1980 and 1982 to draft and build support for a new drinking age resolution, and to reframe their arguments for a drinking age of twenty-one. Folding their concerns about young people's behavior into a broader wave of public outrage over drunk driving accidents, their new resolution placed a renewed emphasis on the role of the drinking age in causing "alcohol-related arrests, accidents, and fatalities among drivers 18 to 20 years of age."[40] Thanks in large part to anti–drunk driving organizations like MADD, which had turned drunk driving into a national cause célèbre during the early 1980s, the tactic was extremely effective, and the Coalition for 21 had little difficulty convincing lawmakers to approve a drinking age of twenty-one in 1982.[41]

Much like the Coalition for 21, anti–drunk driving activists like Doris Aiken—who founded Remove Intoxicated Drivers (RID) in 1977—and Candy Lightner—who founded MADD in 1980—had used a rhetoric of protecting children in order to draw public and political support to their cause during the early 1980s. Their campaigns had provoked a broad wave of popular outrage over drunk driving deaths, and forced state and federal lawmakers to take action on the issue. Drunk driving was hardly a new issue during the 1980s, but for decades many lawmakers, judges, prosecutors, and policemen had found it too easy to imagine themselves in the shoes of these drunk drivers and "looked the other way," even when faced with incontrovertible evidence of drunk drivers' negligence.[42] As a result, drunk drivers often escaped with little to no punishment, even when they had injured or killed someone. During the early 1980s, however, activists like Lightner and Aiken used the stories and images of young people who had been killed or injured in drunk driving accidents—including Lightner's own daughter, Cari—to convince Americans that drunk driving was a "national emergency," which had reached "epidemic proportions."[43]

Thirteen-year-old Cari Lightner had been struck by a drunk driver while walking through the streets of her hometown, Fair Oaks, California, in May 1980. She was thrown nearly forty feet by the force of the collision and died within an hour. The driver, forty-six-year-old Clarence Williams Busch, had been charged with a separate drunk driving offense two days earlier, and been arrested four times for driving drunk. Devastated by her loss, Candy Lightner vowed to see Busch and other drunk drivers brought to justice. MADD began as a gathering of some of Lightner's closest friends and family in a restaurant bar, but within four years it had become one of the "best known and best loved charities in America," and Lightner had become a household name.[44] Anti–drunk driving activists used the tragic stories of young people like Cari Lightner to build support, portraying drunk driving as a danger to children's lives, and using young victims like Laura Lamb, an "adorable" child from Maryland who had been paralyzed by a thirty-seven-year-old drunk driver when she was only five months old, to bring the costs of drunk driving home to Americans.[45]

Early on, MADD focused primarily on bringing drunk drivers to justice and displayed many of the characteristics of other "law and order" and victims' rights groups. In time, however, both MADD and RID began to lobby for legislation that would prevent drunk driving deaths, and RID, in particular, was highly successful in convincing state lawmakers to fund new drunk driving prevention programs.[46] Drunk driving, however, was an endemic problem in the United States, and there was no easy way to keep Americans from driving drunk without broaching a broader, much more divisive debate over how to control Americans' consumption of alcohol. Caught between a broad constituency of Americans who considered their own drinking habits to be none of the government's business and anti–drunk driving activists' demands that they take decisive action to reduce drunk driving deaths, congressional lawmakers seized on the idea of raising the drinking age in 1983, when the Presidential Commission on Drunk Driving—which Lightner and MADD had cajoled President Reagan into appointing in 1982—released its final report. The report made a wide variety of different recommendations, but its recommendation that Congress deny federal highway funding to states that did not promptly raise their drinking age to twenty-one attracted congressional lawmakers' attention.[47]

The idea that raising the drinking age to twenty-one could prevent drunk driving accidents offered lawmakers a way of placating both anti–drunk driving activists like Lightner and drinking age activists like Scheps and the Coalition for 21. By working to raise the drinking age, lawmakers could claim to be taking decisive action to prevent drunk driving accidents without the risk of offending larger, more powerful constituencies, while also granting a complete, nationwide victory to drinking age activists like Phyllis Scheps and her fellow Coalition for 21 members. Responding to the commission's final report, several congressional lawmakers—including Representative Michael D. Barnes (D-Md.), Representative James J. Florio (D-N.J.), and Senator Lautenberg—moved quickly to propose a national minimum drinking age, and the interests of MADD and the Coalition for 21 began to converge. In their efforts to support the bill, advocates of the NMDA shifted the focus of public discussions of drunk driving between 1982 and 1984, effectively redefining the drunk driving issue—at least at the federal level—as an issue of raising the drinking age.

MADD had played a key role in creating the Presidential Commission on Drunk Driving and making drunk driving accidents a national political issue, and it was instrumental in pressuring congressional lawmakers to support the NMDA. But the drive for a national minimum drinking age also had direct connections to the Coalition for 21's earlier, state-level campaigns. A group of policy makers from New Jersey—including Governor Thomas Keane, Representative Florio, Representative James Howard (D), and Senator Lautenberg himself—did much of the political organizing that allowed the bill to pass, and congressional hearings on the NMDA heard from a veritable who's who of Coalition for 21 activists and supporters. In one congressional hearing, New Jersey PTA spokesman Arnold F. Fege even read a statement that echoed Manya Unger's testimony before New Jersey lawmakers four years earlier almost word for word. When he stated that "we are not out to get children or to deprive them of some alleged right," and that it was necessary to "protect youth from themselves," for example, Fege appeared to be reading from Unger's notes.[48]

As they had in New Jersey, student activists did their best to counter the push for a drinking age of twenty-one in Congress. In congressional hearings on the NMDA, most of the young people who spoke out against Lautenberg's bill were associated with the USSA, but other young people during the early 1980s wrote letters, held protests, and even participated in a wave of minor "beer riots" on college and university campuses to defend their right to drink.[49] These young activists were adamant that denying them access to alcohol would make them into "second class" adults. Barring young people who were legally adults from drinking, they asserted, was contrary to "fairness and reason," and would restrict the "freedoms of an entire group of citizens."[50] According to USSA spokesman Katherine Ozer, raising the drinking age meant revoking a privilege that "over 99 percent" of eighteen- to twenty-year-olds used responsibly, penalizing them for the actions of a "tiny minority," while ignoring the fact that drunk driving and alcohol abuse were society-wide problems, and "certainly not age specific." Eighteen, Ozer reminded lawmakers, had become "the universally accepted age at which individuals are considered under the law to be responsible." The ability of adults to make their own decisions, she asserted, "should not be interfered with."[51]

These had been clinching arguments during the early 1970s, in the context of broader debates over the voting age, age of majority, and drinking age. It was much more difficult for young people to claim that they had a right to be treated equally, however, when their access to alcohol was being discussed in isolation, and when MADD and drinking age activists like Scheps had so successfully framed the drinking age as a matter of saving lives. Well aware that their protests could sound selfish and callous in this context, student activists often felt the need to categorically state that they were not endorsing drunk driving, and that they too were "concerned about the loss of lives related to alcohol and traffic fatalities."[52] But lawmakers routinely dismissed such assertions, and implied that young people who opposed a higher drinking age were simply being selfish. Missouri Senator John Danforth, for example, framed the drinking age not as a matter of fairness, equality, or rights, but as a matter of "being able to drink at age 18." Contrasting young people's desire to drink with what he described as "the statistical certainty" that a drinking age below twenty-one would cause a thousand more deaths every year, Danforth made it clear which factor he considered more important.[53]

A large majority of American adults, it seemed, had grown tired of arguments that eighteen-year-olds should be allowed to drink simply because they were treated as adults in other areas of law. Between 70 and 80 percent of Americans consistently favored a drinking age of twenty-one in polls during the early 1980s, and media observers had begun to mock young people's demands for consistent treatment. A May 1982 editorial in the *New York Times*, for example, lampooned the "old enough to fight, old enough to vote" arguments that young people had made during earlier debates over both the voting age and the drinking age. "The real point," the *Times* asserted, "is not consistency but life"; all young people were "old enough to live," and this right to life trumped any claims that eighteen-year-olds deserved to be treated equally, or had a right to make their own decisions.[54]

***

In June 1984, President Reagan—who had initially opposed the NMDA as an infringement on states' rights—signaled his support of the bill by appearing with Governor Keane at a high school in Oradell, New Jersey, all but guaranteeing that Lautenberg's bill would become law. The benefits of a higher drinking age were "so clear cut," according to Reagan, that he had decided to cast aside his objections in order to "get moving, raise the drinking age, and save precious lives."[55] The lives that Reagan spoke of saving, however, were "precious" primarily because they were *young* lives, and Reagan's rhetoric implied that the young people whose rights and privileges the NMDA limited were not adults, but vulnerable children. During the debate over the NMDA, the images of young, innocent victims of drunk driving like Laura Lamb and Cari Lightner seemed to have been conflated with those of young people like Eric Keller and Katherine Ozer, and policy makers like Reagan had uncritically adopted the rhetoric of the Coalition for 21, speaking of eighteen- to twenty-year-old youth as though they were vulnerable children and in desperate need of adults' supervision and protection—whether they wanted it or not. This rhetoric melded a desire to protect young Americans with a desire to control them, and, like the NMDA itself, it barred them from true "adult" status, denying that they had either the capacity or the right to make decisions about alcohol for themselves.

The irony, of course, was that for all their talk of protecting vulnerable youth, MADD, the Coalition for 21, and congressional lawmakers had ignored a much broader range of threats to young people's safety when they chose to focus on raising the drinking age. Cari Lightner and Laura Lamb, after all, had been the victims of *adult* drunk drivers, and legislation like the NMDA would not necessarily have kept them safe. Instead of focusing on the root causes of drunk driving, working to encourage responsible drinking, or confronting the problem of drunk driving by Americans of *all* ages head-on, lawmakers had singled out eighteen- to twenty-year-olds and—on the basis of their age—made them the symbols of a much broader and more complex social problem. While it may have saved lives in the years since it took effect, then, the NMDA was at best only a partial solution to the problem of drunk driving deaths, and in many ways it represents a lost opportunity to address the broader problems that lead both adults *and* young people to drink and drive. At once the product of genuine concern for young people's safety, political expediency, and many Americans' desire to keep young people under adults' control, the NMDA created a new class of young people who were "all-but" adults, and it guaranteed that future generations of young Americans would spend the first three years of their legal adulthood as individuals who were both "adults" and "underage."

NOTES

1 Stefan Muller, "Why I Care More about Lowering the Drinking Age," National Youth Rights Association (blog), April 10, 2011, http://www.youthrights.org/2011/04/10/why-i-care-more-about-lowering-the-drinking-age/.

2 The National Youth Rights Association bills itself as the nation's "premier youth rights organization," which is dedicated to expanding the "civil rights and liberties

of young people." The group has approximately ten thousand members. National Youth Rights Association, "About NYRA," http://www.youthrights.org/about/.

3 Elizabeth S. Scott, "The Legal Construction of Adolescence," *Hofstra Law Review* 29 (2000–2001): 547–98.

4 It can be difficult to speak about state drinking age laws in general terms, because the specific provisions of these laws have often varied widely. While every state now prohibits both the purchase and the public possession of alcohol by young people under twenty-one, for example, earlier laws often set different age limits for different types of alcohol or for young men and young women and had many loopholes and exceptions. See James F. Mosher, "The History of Youthful-Drinking Laws: Implications for Current Policy," in *Minimum Drinking Age Laws: An Evaluation*, ed. Henry Wechsler (Lexington, Mass.: Lexington Books, 1980), 11–38. For a comprehensive list of 1970s drinking age reforms, see Alexander C. Wagenaar, *Alcohol, Young Drivers, and Traffic Accidents* (Lexington, Mass.: Lexington Books, 1983), 3–4.

5 An Act to Amend the Surface Transportation Assistance Act of 1982, Pub. L. No. 98-363, Stat. 98 (1984).

6 *National Minimum Drinking Age: Hearing before the Subcommittee on Alcoholism and Drug Abuse of the Committee on Labor and Human Resources*, 98th Cong. 2, 33 (June 19, 1984) (statements by Senator Frank R. Lautenberg and Candy Lightner, president, Mothers Against Drunk Driving).

7 Joy Shana Newman Getnick, "The Drinking Age Debates" (PhD diss., State University of New York, Albany, 2011), 218; *National Minimum Drinking Age*, 71 (statement by Morris E. Chafetz, president, Health Education Foundation); *Prohibit the Sale of Alcoholic Beverages to Persons under 21 Years of Age, Hearings before the Subcommittee on Commerce, Transportation and Tourism of the Committee on Energy and Commerce, House of Representatives*, 98th Cong. 417 (October 19, 1983) (statement by Katherine Ozer, legislative director, United States Student Association).

8 For a recent review of these debates, see Anne T. McCartt, Laurie A. Hellinga, and Bevan B. Kirley, "The Effects of Minimum Legal Drinking Age 21 Laws on Alcohol-Related Driving in the United States," *Journal of Safety Research* 41, no. 2 (2010): 173–81.

9 *Prohibit the Sale of Alcoholic Beverages*, 70 (statement by Candy Lightner).

10 Some states had a lower age of majority for women than for men, and thus allowed young women to drink earlier. Mosher, "History of Youthful-Drinking Laws," 11–38, 20; Clark Byse, "Alcoholic Beverage Control before Repeal," *Law and Contemporary Problems* 7, no. 4 (Autumn 1940): 544–69.

11 Mosher, "History of Youthful-Drinking Laws," 16; Jonathan Zimmerman, *Distilling Democracy: Alcohol Education in America's Public Schools* (Lawrence: University Press of Kansas, 1999).

12 Byse, "Alcoholic Beverage Control before Repeal," 564; Pauline Sabin, quoted in David E. Kyvig, *Repealing National Prohibition*, 2nd ed. (Kent, Ohio: Kent State University Press, 2000), 120.

13 Lori Rotskoff, *Love on the Rocks: Men, Women, and Alcohol in Post–World War II America* (Chapel Hill: University of North Carolina Press, 2002), 37.

14 New York Alcoholic Beverage Control Law, law 1934, chap. 478 § 1; Mosher, "History of Youthful-Drinking Laws," 18–22.

15 Paula S. Fass, *The Damned and the Beautiful: American Youth in the 1920's* (New York: Oxford University Press, 1977), 6; Grace Palladino, *Teenagers: An American History* (New York: Basic Books, 1996), 7; Moderation League, Inc., *National Conditions under Prohibition in 1928* (New York: Moderation League, 1928), 633.

16 Getnick, "Drinking Age Debates," 48.

17 Robert Straus and Selden Bacon, *Drinking in College* (New Haven, Conn.: Yale University Press, 1953), 37.

18 "The Latest Teen Drug: Alcohol," *Newsweek*, March 5, 1973.

19 See, for example, Margaret Mead, *Culture and Commitment: A Study of the Generation Gap* (New York: Doubleday, 1970).

20 Wendell W. Cultice, *Youth's Battle for the Ballot: A History of Voting Age in America* (New York: Greenwood, 1992); Jenny Diamond Cheng, "Uncovering the 26th Amendment" (PhD diss., University of Michigan, 2008).

21 Virginia Grace Cook, *Age of Majority (Updated)* (Lexington, Ky.: Council of State Governments, 1973), 1; Alabama and Mississippi still set the age of majority at nineteen and twenty-one, respectively; Ala Code 26-1-1, Miss Code Ann. §1-3-27.

22 State Senator Tom Creighton, Senate Floor Debate (Audio Tape), 63rd Texas Legislature, March 5, 1973, tape 1 of 5, side 1 (tape 34), 36:00; "Rights Bill Delayed," *Houston Post*, March 6, 1973; Jerry Gilliam, "Bill to Let Voters Decide Drinking Age Rejected," *Los Angeles Times*, June 7, 1977.

23 Senator Don Adams, Senate Floor Debate (Audio Tape), 63rd Texas Legislature, April 24, 1973 (tape 101), 20:00.

24 Wagenaar, *Alcohol, Young Drivers, and Traffic Accidents*, 3–4.

25 Robert Gammage, Senate Floor Debate (Audio Tape), 63rd Texas Legislature, March 12, 1973, tape 5 of 5, side 1 (tape 42), 17:00–20:00.

26 Linda Lamendola, "Senate Backs Full Rights for 18-Year-Old Jerseyans," *Newark Star-Ledger*, May 16, 1973.

27 "Age of Majority Backers Mum on Teen Casualty Increase," *Capital Report* 11, no. 10 (November 22, 1972), "Micap Publications: Capitol Report, 1969–1972," box 3, Michigan Interfaith Council on Alcohol Problems records, Bentley Historical Library, University of Michigan, Ann Arbor; Robert L. Hammond, "Legal Drinking at 18 or 21—Does It Make Any Difference?" *Journal of Alcohol and Drug Education* 18 (1973): 9–13; Michael J. Boylan, "Jersey Acts to Curb Potential Hazards When Drinking Age Drops to 18," *New York Times*, December 4, 1972.

28 Traffic Safety for Michigan, "Gaps Noted in Teen Driver Data," *Traffic Safety Government Bulletin* 6, no. 30 (December 15, 1972); "Minimum Age Law Mistakenly Related to Michigan Statistics," *Alcoholic Beverage Newsletter* 319 (November 1972). Both in "SB 123, 18-Year-Old Rights," box 97-230/24, Robert A.

Gammage Papers, 1971–1995, Dolph Briscoe Center for American History, University of Texas at Austin.

29 Allan F. Williams, Robert F. Rich, Paul L. Zador, and Leon S. Robertson, "The Legal Minimum Drinking Age and Fatal Motor Vehicle Crashes," *Journal of Legal Studies* 4, no. 1 (January 1975): 238; R. L. Douglas, L. D. Filkins, and F. A. Clark, *The Effect of Lower Legal Drinking Ages on Youth Crash Involvement* (Ann Arbor: University of Michigan Highway Safety Research Institute, 1974); Stephen Cucchiaro, Joseph Ferreira, Jr., and Alan Sicherman, *The Effect of the 18-Year-Old Drinking Age on Auto Accidents* (Cambridge, Mass.: MIT Operations Research Center, 1974), 30.

30 Wagenaar, *Alcohol, Young Drivers, and Traffic Accidents*, 3–4.

31 Michael Norman, "Effort to Raise Drinking Age in Jersey Unites a Diverse Group," *New York Times*, December 29, 1982; "How to Raise the Legal Drinking Age: The New Jersey Story," April 1983, in *Prohibit the Sale of Alcoholic Beverages*, 469.

32 *Public Hearing before Assembly Judiciary, Law, Public Safety and Defense Committee (New Jersey) on S-1126*, February 5, 1979, 1 (statement of Manya Unger, Legislative Activities Chairman, New Jersey PTA) (hereafter cited as Hearing on S-1126, February 5, 1979).

33 *Public Hearing Before Assembly Judiciary, Law, Public Safety and Defense Committee (New Jersey) on S-1126*, January 23, 1979, 16 (statement of State Senator Frank X. Graves).

34 Hearing on S-1126, February 5, 1979, 81–82 (statement of Robert Fastiggi, New Jersey Police Traffic Officers' Association), redaction in the original.

35 Hearing on S-1126, February 5, 1979, 84–85 (statement of Phyllis Scheps, Coalition for 21).

36 *Felix v. Milliken*, 463 F.Supp. 1360 (E.D. Michigan, 1978).

37 *Public Hearing before Assembly Judiciary, Law, Public Safety and Defense Committee (New Jersey) on S-1126*, February 6, 1979, 26 (statement of Eric Keller, vice president, sophomore class, Princeton University) (hereafter cited as Hearing on S-1126, February 6, 1979).

38 Hearing on S-1126, February 5, 1979, 15–17 (February 5, 1979) (statement of Gail Gleason Milgram, director of education, Rutgers University Center for Alcohol Studies); Public Hearing on S-1126, February 6, 1979, 1A (statement by Dr. Robert Pandina, associate director, Center for Alcohol Studies).

39 Hearing on S-1126, February 5, 1979, 1 (statement of Manya Unger).

40 "How to Raise the Legal Drinking Age."

41 NJ Stat § 2C:33-15-17.

42 Barron H. Lerner, *One for the Road: Drunk Driving since 1900* (Baltimore: Johns Hopkins University Press, 2011), 4–5.

43 Joseph D. Whitaker, "'A National Outrage': Drunken Drivers Kill 26,000 Each Year," *Washington Post*, March 22, 1981.

44 Lerner, *One for the Road*, 65.

45 Eugene L. Meyer, "Victims Testify on Drunk Driving," *Washington Post*,
    September 24, 1980; Andrea Pawlyna, "Cindi Lamb: A Lion in the War on Drunk
    Driving," *Baltimore Sun*, January 31, 1982.
46 Lerner, *One for the Road*, 89.
47 Presidential Commission on Drunk Driving, *Presidential Commission on Drunk
    Driving: Final Report* (Washington, D.C.: Government Printing Office, 1983), 10.
48 *Prohibit the Sale of Alcoholic Beverages*, 129–30 (October 4, 1983) (statement by
    Arnold Fege, New Jersey PTA).
49 Howard Witt, "Right to Drink Becomes the Latest Cause on Campus," *Chicago
    Tribune*, November 18, 1984.
50 Erik Erichsen, letter to the editor, *Los Angeles Times*, June 21, 1984.
51 *Prohibit the Sale of Alcoholic Beverages*, 417–20, 407–8 (October 19, 1983)
    (statements by Katherine Ozer, legislative director, U.S. Student Association, and
    Greg Sullivan, president, New York Student Association).
52 *National Minimum Drinking Age*, 105 (June 19, 1984) (statement of Celeste
    Bergman, Florida Student Association).
53 *National Minimum Drinking Age*, 21 (June 19, 1984) (statement by Senator John
    Danforth).
54 "Old Enough to Live," *New York Times*, May 28, 1982; "Rep Barnes' Bill Would
    Make 21 Drinking Age," *Washington Post*, February 23, 1984.
55 Ronald Reagan, "Remarks at River Dell High School in Oradell, New Jersey," June
    20, 1984.

12

Age and Identity

Reaching Thirteen in the Lives of American Jews

STUART SCHOENFELD

Adolescence is critical in the modern Jewish life cycle, in a way that is heightened from earlier historical periods. In earlier times, when Jews lived on their own land, and later became an outsider people residing in Christian and Muslim societies, young Jews generally grew up, as did their neighbors, to live lives more or less like those of their parents. In this context of slow cultural change, reaching early adolescence was an age of majority marker in Jewish law, and to some extent seen as a stage in psychological development. Modern times changed the experience of Jewish adolescence. Dramatic changes in human culture and the virtually sacred status accorded to individual choice challenged the transference of traditional social roles from one generation to another. Early adolescence became a time for rituals affirming Jewish identity from one generation to the next. Celebrating a bar mitzvah at age thirteen gradually became a more important ritual ceremony; in the twentieth century bat mitzvah for girls grew to become normative.

The Torah, the first five books of the Bible that constitute the foundational text of Judaism, has few age markers. The most notable age markers specify the ages of eight days for the male circumcision that marks entry into the Jews' covenantal relationship with God and twenty as the age of being counted in the census, contributing the half shekel for the upkeep of the sanctuary, and eligibility for military service. Although every legal system needs to distinguish minors from adults, texts of Jewish law formally addressed thirteen as an age of majority only from the second century on. Texts adding a psychological dimension supplemented the legal writing. Bar mitzvah ceremonies and celebrations became common Jewish practice only in early modern times, and bat mitzvah became common only in the twentieth century.

The widespread adoption in modern times of bar/bat mitzvah ceremonies reflects a folk custom rather than the agenda of religious leaders.[1] They are not required by Jewish law, which does have a great deal to say about the life cycle events of birth, marriage, and death. Bar/bat mitzvah speaks to the emotional needs of parents, addressing issues of intergenerational Jewish identity, extended family, and sometimes social status. Early adolescents generally experience these ceremonies and celebrations as highly positive events at which family and teen cultures come together. The experience of bar/bat mitzvah continues to change. The social patterns of contemporary American Jews are different from those of a century ago. Family and maturational challenges are different, and bar/bat mitzvahs reflect these changes.

Following the catastrophic failure of Jewish revolts against Roman occupation in the first and second centuries and the loss of many scholars, Rabbi Yehudah HaNasi compiled the Mishnah to preserve Jewish legal traditions. Its six sections deal in detail with many aspects of Jewish ritual and also cover laws of marriage and divorce, civil law, and criminal law. The Mishnah indicates that a boy is legally obligated when he understands what is expected of him; for example, "A minor who knows how to shake the lulav is subject to the obligation of lulav" (Sukkah 3:15).[2] In many traditional societies, a child who can, does, under the authority of the parent. The practice of "a child who can, does" suits parent-child relations but is insufficient for setting community standards for the age at which individuals are legally considered to be adults. In the Mishnah minors are specifically exempted (often along with women and slaves) from certain obligations or prohibited (along with mental defectives and deaf mutes) from fulfilling certain responsibilities. The Mishnah uses signs of puberty as the standard for age of majority: "A girl that has grown two hairs . . . is subject to all the commandments enjoined in the Torah. And likewise, also, a boy that has grown two hairs is subject to all the commandments enjoined in the Torah" (Niddah 6:11). A late addition to the Mishnah uses a different standard, age by itself: "He (Judah, ben Tema) used to say, At five years the age is reached for the study of Scripture, at ten for the study of Mishnah, at thirteen for the fulfillment of the commandments, at fifteen for the study of Talmud, at eighteen for marriage, at twenty for seeking a livelihood, at thirty for entering into one's full strength" (Avot 5:24). The ambiguity among competence, physical puberty, and age continues in the Talmud, the later elaboration of Jewish law codified in the sixth century. Without contradicting the Mishnah, the Talmud uses as the age of majority thirteen for boys and twelve for girls, presuming that by those ages puberty has occurred. A major sixteenth-century rabbi, Moses Isserles, endorsed using age alone: "this is the practice; one must not deviate from it" (Orach Hayyim 37:3). The context in all of these considerations of age of majority was the continuing legal authority of a father over the children in his household. Puberty might make a child legally responsible, but not necessarily, as we say today, empowered.

Other writings on attaining the age of thirteen contain a psychological dimension. Interpretations of the Torah that were not included in the legally oriented Mishnah and Talmud were collected into volumes of midrash around the time of the Talmud and afterward. Several contain references to age thirteen as a time of psychological significance, as in *Genesis Rabbah* (63:10):

> Rabbi Phineas said: They (Jacob and Esau) were like a myrtle and a wild rose bush growing side by side: when they attained maturity one yielded its fragrance and the other its thorns. So for thirteen years both went to school and came home from school. After this age, one (Jacob) went to the house of study and the other (Esau) went to idolatrous shrines. R. Eleazer b. Simeon said: A man is responsible for his son until the age of thirteen: thereafter he must say—"Blessed is He who has freed me of the responsibility for this one."

The reference here is to the twin sons of Isaac. Genesis recounts that Jacob bears the family's covenant with God; Esau does not. The midrash adds the element of choice at age thirteen to the complex biblical story of sibling rivalry. In our time the last part of this quotation is cited as a source for the bar mitzvah ceremony as a Jewish tradition. The quotation suggests something quite different, however, from modern bar mitzvahs. The focus is on the father no longer being accountable for the son's behavior; there is no indication of a ceremony involving the son.

The *Midrash on Psalms* states, "Why is the good inclination called a child? Because it becomes part of a man when the child becomes thirteen" (9:5). The *Avot According to Rabbi Nathan* declares, "[T]he evil impulse is older than the good impulse by thirteen years. The evil impulse begins to develop in the mother's womb and is born with the person thirteen years later the good impulse is born" (16:3). These quotations reflect the rabbinic view that the human personality contains an evil inclination and a good inclination. The evil inclination is not understood as purely negative. It is the impulsive, self-absorbed, pleasure-seeking part of being human. Without it, the midrash writes, no man would build a house, marry, or have children. But society would not be possible without the good inclination, which is sensitive to the needs of others, obligations to others, and obligations to God. In the rabbis' view (anticipating Freud, Jiminy Cricket, and others), people are born self-centered. By the time they are thirteen, they have achieved enough maturity to control their selfish impulses. Legal responsibility is only part of puberty. Ethical, self-controlled conduct is the other dimension of maturity. The early adolescent is now old enough for the good inclination to grow. According to some scholars, the years between thirteen and twenty were understood in rabbinic tradition to be a period of psychological maturation.

For most of Jewish history, age thirteen meant a status passage and a stage in psychological maturation. There is no clear record of the emergence of a ceremony. In the contemporary understanding of a bar/bat mitzvah ceremony, the adolescent is included as one of the adults called to the reading of the Torah, often chants in Hebrew a section from the Torah, and chants the weekly readings from the prophets. The thirteen-year-old might also take part in leading other sections of the service. There are medieval records of thirteen-year-old boys receiving such honors, but it is not clear that they refer to the first time they have participated in leading services or being called to the Torah. In contemporary practice it is customary for the bar mitzvah to deliver a commentary on the Torah portion, followed by a celebratory meal.

According to the historian Ivan Marcus, these elements of bar mitzvah ceremony and celebration appear together only in the sixteenth-century German Empire. Marcus notes variations in ritual practice in different communities and traces through manuscripts the practices that came together into bar mitzvah. He concludes that bar mitzvah was established as a ritual event outside the German Empire and Eastern Europe only in the nineteenth or twentieth century. From the late twelfth century in Germany minors were more frequently restricted from performing ritual commandments; Marcus notes similar restrictions in contemporaneous Christian practice. He cites two thirteenth-century texts. One takes for granted that a son will be called to the Torah for the first time at age thirteen, commenting that there is no evidence of how widespread this custom was.

The other states that minors could be called to the reading of Torah in Germany, but in northern France only on the holiday of Simchat Torah. Marcus reviews manuscripts—biographies, memoirs, descriptions of Jewish practices—where one might expect to find bar mitzvah mentioned and where it is absent. He finds references outside of Germany and northern Europe beginning only in the seventeenth century. He concludes that bar mitzvah practices spread beyond Europe to Muslim lands and the Americas no earlier than the eighteenth century.[3]

***

Celebrations that supplement the synagogue ceremony can be traced back to a responsum—a rabbi's reply to a formal request to clarify a point of Jewish law—by the seventeenth-century Polish rabbi Solomon Luria. Rabbi Luria was asked whether the practice of marking the age of attaining bar mitzvah by a social gathering in the home, as was reportedly practiced by the Jews of Germany, was permitted. He noted the precedent that housewarming celebrations were permitted if they included a discussion of Torah and approved similar bar mitzvah celebrations. The responsum indicates the importance of the speech. When ritual practice was routine, synagogue skills were not exceptional and could be acquired at an early age. A speech, however, gave boys the opportunity to display the learning that Diaspora Jews highly valued.[4]

Those who have researched the emergence of bar mitzvah ceremonies and celebrations have suggested that they are linked to newly intense understandings of martyrdom, the competition for synagogue honors, the rise of individualism in Western culture, and the threat to Jewish continuity from the cultural and social disruptions of modern times.

During the Crusades, mobs slaughtered Jewish communities that had been under the protection of feudal lords. Survivors, trying to find meaning in the massacres, composed laments invoking the memory of Isaac, the son of Abraham, whom God asked Abraham to bring as a sacrifice and who heroically submitted to the will of God.[5] While this parallelism interpreted the slaughters of the Crusades as heroic martyrdom, it also highlighted the precariousness of Jewish survival from one generation to another and the importance of each boy becoming a member of the sacred community.

A more prosaic suggestion focuses on the community dynamics surrounding the ambiguity between children participating in ritual as soon as they were able in contrast to the restriction of privileges to those who reached the age of thirteen. Jewish worship is traditionally lay-led. Participating in leading services and being among those called to the reading of Torah honor those who perform these roles. The distribution of honors was very meaningful in small communities with competitive status rankings. This competition could be partially managed by restricting honorific roles in the service to males who had turned thirteen. The more restrictive distribution of honors made the first occasion when the adolescent was honored along with other adult males more important.

The priority given to individual choice had cultural and social dimensions. Marcus notes the Catholic shift to the older age of thirteen in the clerical initiation practices of monasteries in the same part of Europe where bar mitzvah ceremonies became common.[6] The Protestant emphasis on the individual's relationship to God and the philosophical writings on conscience, economic individualism, and government by consent changed the world of ideas in which Jews lived. Children, rather than growing up to assume the values and ways of life of their parents, now had greater freedom to choose their own paths. The European shift from a rural-agricultural society with a literate elite to an urban-industrial society with a widespread literacy had a powerful effect on Jewish life. As wage labor and education-based careers replaced household economies, the marketplace replaced the community, raising questions about the intergenerational continuity of social identity. An adolescent ritual affirming intergenerational Jewish commitment can be seen as a response to this challenge.

***

The importance given to bar mitzvah in America seems consistent with changing times. Early Jewish settlers who were numerous enough to establish a religious community were primarily Sephardic Jews, whose Judaism had survived forced conversions, expulsion from the Iberian Peninsula, and the Inquisition. The new world was a frontier community, but rigid social boundaries of religious groups initially maintained Jewish separateness. Age thirteen was observed with bar mitzvah but not much remarked upon. Boys were prepared for Jewish life by parents and tutors and then in small schools. In the intimate Jewish settlements of the eighteenth and early nineteenth centuries, the modern disruptions of family life were not immediately apparent.

In the nineteenth century the age for an adolescent synagogue ritual became controversial. A new wave of Jewish immigration, mainly German in origin, brought new ideas about Jewish age of majority. Nineteenth-century Western European Jews were reforming Jewish practice as part of the program of leaving the ghetto and integrating into society as citizens. Respect for rabbinic scholarship and distinctive lifestyles declined; secular knowledge and modern culture increased in prestige. Reformers advocated shorter services in the vernacular, featuring hymns and sermons instead of the lengthy Hebrew prayer service that acculturated Western Jews were no longer raising their children to understand. They promoted turning to the Bible for inspiration and setting aside distinctive ritual restrictions of rabbinic Judaism, such as dietary laws, dress, and Sabbath prohibitions. Religious reformers argued that they were stripping away the ritual accretions of centuries to return to the biblical message of ethical monotheism.

Although bar mitzvah at thirteen had become an established practice, religious reformers advocated replacing it with confirmation, first instituted in early nineteenth-century Germany. This ceremony—held in the spring, in the vernacular, with boys and girls, usually fifteen or sixteen, as a group, emphasizing ethical teachings—was in keeping with their outlook. Confirmation was also consistent with contemporary Christian practices and demonstrated the similarity of Jews to their Christian neighbors.

German Jewish immigrants settled in the large cities of the Northeast, moved into the South, and followed the frontier across the central and western states, establishing congregations in the places they settled. Their children went to public schools and received religious instruction at congregational Sunday schools. Large urban congregations brought reform-oriented religious leaders from Germany. Temple Emanu-El introduced confirmation into American Jewish practice in 1847.[7] As American Reform Judaism become clearer in its doctrine and organizational structure, prominent leaders promoted confirmation, which fit well into the structure and limits of Sunday school education, in place of bar mitzvah.

In 1890 a leading Reform rabbi criticized the "abuses" associated with confirmation: "extravagance in the dress of the girls . . . the vulgar display of presents in every home on confirmation day . . . grand and magnificent receptions, rivaling the splendor of wedding receptions."[8] This criticism reflects German Jewish prosperity in the capitalist expansion of the Gilded Age. Thorstein Veblen was still nine years away from introducing the phrase "conspicuous consumption," but the phenomenon was already in evidence. Jews were participating in an emerging culture of consumption, in which the public display of wealth was considered a legitimate expression of social status. The gender reference in the rabbi's comments is also suggestive. In the conventionally religious society of nineteenth-century America, confirmation seems to reference upper-middle-class coming-out parties and to anticipate the later secularized sweet sixteen parties. Young Jewish gentlemen had various places besides the synagogue in which their growing accomplishments could be noted. For young women in mid-adolescence, confirmation was an opportunity to be acknowledged as a young Jewish woman preparing for a domestic role.[9]

The German Jews were vastly outnumbered by the largest wave of Jewish migration, begun in the 1880s, interrupted by World War I and ended by restrictive immigration legislation in 1924. Millions of Jews left Eastern Europe, which at the time had by far the largest concentration of Jews in the world, with the largest group going to the United States. This migration brought Jews who were accustomed to bar mitzvah and for whom confirmation was an unfamiliar, alien ritual. They reinforced attaining age thirteen as a ritual marker for boys. Bat mitzvah gradually developed from the 1920s on, and both became celebrated in the expressive style of American consumer culture.

The celebration of bar mitzvah within this wave of immigrants was not necessarily an expression of deep piety. Pious Jews were among the immigrants, but there were also large numbers whose Jewish identity was shaped by modern secular movements. Yiddishists advocated for recognition of Jews as a national minority with rights to a full cultural life in their own language. Zionists emphasized the national theme of Jewish history and called for Jews to establish a nation-state in their historic homeland. Many Jews had become factory workers whose identities were deeply enmeshed with labor unions and labor movements. Reaching the age of bar mitzvah had become a varied experience in Eastern Europe. It could involve a ritual of comfort in a threatening world, a reminder (with sometimes elaborate, arcane speeches) that religious scholarship was still valued, a sentimental ceremony that kept up appearances, an undemanding Monday or Thursday ceremony with a simple celebration, or no ceremony at all.

Eastern European Jews brought these ideological currents to crowded neighborhoods in large American cities. Many who were influenced by secular Yiddishism, Zionism, and socialism wanted some connection with Judaism but kept a skeptical distance from Orthodox beliefs and demands, using synagogues and rabbis as needed, but did not join. The congregations of Eastern European migrants, often small and based on area of common origin, held lengthy Orthodox services. Orthodox prayer was normal, but a fully observant Orthodox way of life was rare.

Despite the crowded, poor neighborhoods in which immigrants struggled without a social welfare net, it was important to Jewish parents that their children, especially the boys, remain in public school to acquire the skills to attain better employment than their parents. Along with American skills and values, the boys were learning popular culture and were attracted to the excitement and opportunities of the street. Reports during and following the long wave of Eastern European immigration highlight the tension between generations. Hutchins Hapgood, twenty years into the mass migration, wrote that American born sons "gradually quit going to the synagogue, give up 'chaider' promptly when they are 13 years old, avoid the Yiddish theatres, seek the up-town places of amusement, dress in the latest American fashion, and have a keen eye for the right thing in neckties. They even refuse sometimes to be present at supper on Friday evenings. Thus, indeed, the sway of the old people is broken."[10] Among poor Jewish immigrants bar mitzvah seems to have been typically simple. Parents were gratified to see the thirteen-year-old go through a synagogue ritual and children obliged. Most parents had acquired synagogue skills in the old country; their childhood conditions were not replicated in America. Tutors taught the basic skills needed. Books of bar mitzvah speeches provided texts that boys could use instead of writing something themselves. School, dropping out and going to work, popular culture, and athletics were much more on the minds of thirteen-year-old boys. Girls were similarly oriented toward an American future.

The rituals and celebrations of bar/bat mitzvah evolved along with the American development of branches of Judaism and changes in Jewish life. In this evolution, the ritual marking of attaining the age of thirteen became a more important feature of growing up Jewish. As Jews acculturated and prospered, the simple bar mitzvahs of the children of immigrants gave way to more elaborate events. Bat mitzvah, introduced in 1922, eventually became equally important as bar mitzvah. After World War II, the central institutions of the Conservative and Reform movements instituted educational requirements for these ceremonies, resulting in several years of continuing Hebrew school attendance prior to bar/bat mitzvah becoming a normal part of preteen Jewish life. However, by the end of the twentieth century, the American Jewish community had become much more internally diverse, with the experience of Jewish children turning thirteen becoming more varied.

The rise of the Conservative movement through the first half and middle of the twentieth century changed the experience of a ritual at age thirteen. Conservative Judaism was founded to be a middle way between Orthodox and Reform. As Jews acculturated, their congregations looked increasingly to English-speaking Conservative rabbis who could blend Judaism with American values, who could be their representatives in the wider community, whom their children could respect. Most Conservative synagogues were larger than Orthodox ones. Their handsome sanctuaries, in which they held more formal, shortened services with some English, were the settings for more impressive bar mitzvah ceremonies. Some congregations instituted, in addition to bar mitzvah, group confirmation ceremonies as a way of incorporating girls in a synagogue ceremony and extending adolescent contact.[11] Others later adopted the innovation of bat mitzvah, which spread to Reform and Orthodox congregations as well, eclipsing confirmation.

While historians have found earlier precedents, the 1922 bat mitzvah of Judith Kaplan is remembered as the innovation that mattered. Rabbi Mordecai Kaplan, who introduced it for his daughter, was already embarked on his long career as a creative leader in the Conservative movement and then as the head of the Reconstructionist movement. The innovation followed the 1921 convention of Conservative Rabbis, where Rabbi Abraham Hershman urged congregations to adopt bat mitzvah.[12] Judith Kaplan Eisenstein recalled, "Invitations had been sent to family and friends for a party in our home on *Motza-ei Shabbat* (the evening following Sabbath). I had asked only one or two close friends in addition to my fellow members in the Yarmuk Club (a Hebrew-speaking club of girls who met in the Central Jewish Institute). The 'club' could be depended on for sympathetic support, regardless of their precocious propensity for questioning all religious observance."[13] At the Saturday morning service, in a synagogue where men and women sat separately, she was seated in the front row with the men,

> away from the cozy protection of mother and sisters. . . . I was signaled to step forward to a place below the bimah at a very respectable distance from the scroll of the Torah, which had already been rolled up and garbed in its mantle. I pronounced the first blessing, and from my own Humash (Five Books of Moses) read the selection which Father had chosen for me, continued with the reading of the English translation, and concluded with the closing brakhah (blessing). That was it. The scroll was returned to the ark with song and procession, and the service was resumed.[14]

Not all Conservative rabbis were enthusiastic. One, replying to a questionnaire item in the early 1930s about whether his congregation conducted bat mitzvah ceremonies, wrote, "The Bar Mitzvah ceremony is enough of a farce."[15] Nevertheless, the ceremony gradually gained wider acceptance, further instantiating the age of thirteen as a significant marker for Jewish girls as well as boys.

The gap between the synagogue ceremony and the celebrations concerned leaders of the movement. In 1930, the Women's League for Conservative Judaism published a psychologist's lectures on parenting. A long section on bar mitzvah read in part,

> The . . . celebrations do much to counteract whatever good the synagogue ritual may accomplish. I have seen children brought from the inspiring and chastening atmosphere of the synagogue to fashionable hotels where a great banquet was prepared in utter defiance of the Sabbath or the Jewish dietary laws and involving an outlay which made the occasion one of vulgar display of parental wealth rather than of parental concern for the welfare of the child. . . . [V]audeville artists are sometimes engaged and one is privileged to enjoy the puerile vulgarisms of the variety theatre capping the climax of a Bar Mitzvah ceremony.[16]

Bar mitzvah, and then later bat mitzvah, became important as extended family events. Fertility was high in the immigrant generation, producing a subsequent next generation with families full of uncles, aunts, and cousins. Extended families shared each other's lives. Bar mitzvahs, then gradually bat mitzvahs as well, were occasions, but far from the only ones, when families came together. Like Passover seders, participants responded to the ceremony and celebrations with a wide range of thoughts and feelings: respect for the traditions the grandparents had kept alive, pride in the admirable qualities that the early adolescent displayed, ambivalence about a Hebrew service that was little understood, pleasure of being with family in the sanctuary and in the subsequent party, a feeling that the family shared something emotionally satisfying and meaningful, or, on the other hand, a feeling of family obligation, and, for those estranged, some degree of emotional and intellectual hostility.

The extended family dimension of bar mitzvah is likely related to its retention in the Reform movement. Confirmations, group ceremonies with many adolescents, were not equivalent extended family events.[17] Changing demographics also bolstered bar mitzvah in the Reform movement. Children and grandchildren of Eastern European immigrants found Reform Judaism appealing. They brought more positive sentiments about traditional rituals such as bar mitzvah into the movement.

Thirteen-year-old boys typically did not experience bar mitzvah as a display of a high level of Jewish literacy or an expression of deep piety. Children in Reform congregations went only to Sunday school, as did most children in Conservative congregations as late as 1945, despite the movement's advocacy of three-day-a-week congregational schools.[18] Many boys whose bar mitzvahs were celebrated in Orthodox synagogues attended, after public school, Talmud Torahs that struggled with inadequate teaching materials, variable curricula, teachers of mixed quality, a wide gap between what was taught and what was lived, financial stress, and a very high dropout rate between the beginning of the school year and its end.

Comments from the late 1940s indicate the continuing perception that the celebrations overshadowed the religious ceremony. A scholar of Jewish life observed, "[T]he reception party or dinner and ball are usually elaborate and sumptuous." He further noted the wide circulation of a film of the bar mitzvah celebration of Edward G. Robinson's son, and commented, "The child usually measures the success of the event by the value of the gifts he receives."[19]

A 1937 editorial in Mordecai Kaplan's journal the *Reconstructionist* proposed to use the importance American Jews attached to bar mitzvah and confirmation as an opportunity to strengthen their Judaism by insisting on more Jewish education.[20] The editorial proposed that the national representatives of the branches of Judaism such as the Conservative and Reform congregational federations establish minimum educational requirements for bar mitzvah and confirmation ceremonies.

The Conservative movement held its first conference on Jewish education in 1946, as Jews were beginning to move from cities to suburbs and to build modern synagogues with sanctuaries, schools, and parking lots. The Talmud Torahs were left behind, with thirteen-year-olds now prepared for bar mitzvah, and more and more frequently for bat mitzvah, in congregational schools.[21]

The movement's 1946 statement, *Objectives and Standards for the Congregational School*, included educational requirements. For bar/bat mitzvah, the Conservative movement required no less than six hours of school a week for three years above the age of eight. For confirmation, the movement required attaining the age of fifteen and attending school for five years. The Reform movement followed suit, introducing bar/bat mitzvah educational requirements of two years of school attendance and a "definite understanding" of continuing attendance through confirmation. Affiliated congregations were expected to limit the privilege of a synagogue ceremony to children who met these requirements.

The impact of these standards on turning thirteen can be seen in enrollment in Jewish schools. Between 1948 and 1958 enrollment more than doubled, raising the percentage of children between five and fourteen receiving Jewish education to over 40 percent. By 1962, over half of Jewish children between five and seventeen were enrolled in Jewish education, the large majority in congregational schools.[22] The standards had a similar effect on synagogue affiliation. Synagogue affiliation during the period of mandatory enrollment meant that thirteen-year-olds understood bar/bat mitzvah as an extended process in their lives, involving at least three years of Hebrew school attendance and family congregational membership.

Postwar thirteen-year-olds were growing up in increasingly affluent and well-educated families, relocated from central cities to suburbs but still clustered in Jewish neighborhoods. While adults who attended Hebrew school in the 1950s and 1960s often remembered them as places of poor discipline, scarce learning, and limited piety, they did create social ties, reinforcing cultural, not necessarily religious, expectations of what it meant to grow up Jewish.

Rabbinic encouragement of girls' enrollment in Hebrew school and the wider implementation of bat mitzvah went together. By 1960, bat mitzvah was celebrated by almost all Conservative congregations, most commonly as a Friday night service at which the bat mitzvah read the haftorah.[23] In the 1970s and 1980s, as congregations and the central institutions of the movement became gender egalitarian, bat mitzvah moved to Saturday morning as a ceremony equivalent to bar mitzvah. Within the Reform movement, bar mitzvah and bat mitzvah ceremonies supplemented and then gradually overshadowed confirmation. A 1950 survey of Reform congregations reported that all held confirmation ceremonies; 90 percent also had bar mitzvah for boys and only 25 percent held bat mitzvahs.[24] However by 1960 96 percent also celebrated bat mitzvah.[25]

As bar/bat mitzvah celebrations became firmly established in post-war American Judaism, they became public symbols of conspicuous consumption. A 1952 *Life* magazine photo essay portrayed a party that seems lavish even by today's standards. The 1955 best seller, *Marjorie Morningstar*, included a negative description of an elaborate party. A case before the New York State Supreme Court contested whether parents could use their son's personal injury settlement to pay for his bar mitzvah reception.[26]

Religious authorities continued their criticisms. A Reform rabbi told *Time* magazine that bar mitzvah was an "empty ceremony" with the receptions showing "conspicuous waste."[27] As early as 1955, a Conservative movement resolution reminded congregations that the celebrations of bar mitzvahs and weddings were religiously sanctioned and should be conducted accordingly. A leading Orthodox rabbi wrote that if he had the power he would abolish bar mitzvah. The Reform movement adopted a resolution in 1964 warning that "the extravagant consumption, the conspicuous waste, and the crudity" of bar mitzvah parties "were rapidly becoming a public Jewish scandal,"[28] a sentiment reinforced in a 1979 responsum of the association of Reform rabbis,[29] and a 1992 Reform movement resolution.[30]

The criticism of exceptional extravagance obscures what was more common. Teen culture grew in the 1950s and 1960s. Luncheons at the synagogue and dance parties in suburban basement recreation rooms using the new technology of stacked forty-five singles were likely as common, or more, as expensive evening affairs, but they attracted little public notice. Catered events, including more modest ones, began to incorporate "themes" drawn from sports, movies, or other aspects of popular culture. Themes serve to differentiate one party from another and can be used (but not always are) as opportunities for one-upmanship. A folklorist who interpreted bar mitzvah themes noted that for boys the themes often address images of masculinity in contemporary culture, allowing the adolescents to play at incorporating masculinity, or, for the critics, some distorted idea of it, into their identities.[31] A similar observation may be made of feminine themes at bat mitzvah parties.

A study of bar/bat mitzvah in one congregation in the late 1980s gives some indication of why they matter to the child and parents.[32] By the 1980s the culture of adolescence was well established in the American life cycle. The shared family project takes place at the time in the family life cycle when the child is changing into an early adolescent, and the relationship between parents and children is changing too. In this study, as in the one by Judith Davis,[33] it is clear that bar/bat mitzvah is a family ritual. Bar/bat mitzvah involves a child's performance in the synagogue and changing self-understanding, but is also an event in which the parents, and the family unit as a group, perform identity.

Planning for these social events often began two or three years in advance, after the bar/bat mitzvah date was set. Bar/bat mitzvah celebrations were typically weekend reunions with an intimate family dinner Friday, the party Saturday night, and the Sunday brunch or an informal Sunday at home.

Due to the postwar geographic dispersion of Jews, almost every family had out-of-town friends and relatives attending. Because of later marriage, parents were usually older than the previous generation had been when their children reached thirteen, more in a position to host an elaborate family celebration for dispersed relatives and less certain that relatives would be around for weddings. With changing American norms about family, bar/bat mitzvah parties could act as substitutes for far distant, uncertain weddings. Thirteen-year-olds increasingly saw at bar/bat mitzvahs family members they hardly knew. Business associates of parents were typically not invited, and the main question for parents concerned the criteria for which relatives were included.

The child's invitation list, invariably a matter for negotiation, varied from a handful of close friends to forty to sixty friends from public school, the neighborhood, summer camp, sports teams, dance classes, and friends of the family. Invitations to children's friends, as for parents, followed the norm of reciprocity. The formal representatives of Jewish tradition—rabbi, cantor, teachers, and tutor—were rarely invited to the social events.

In addition to the party atmosphere, the celebrations had secular rituals focused on the adolescent. Entering the reception, guests usually found a life-sized poster of the bar/bat mitzvah with places on the margins to write their well wishes. Speeches by parents and sometimes siblings combined biography, jokes about the family, and expressions of love and pride. The celebrations were videotaped and edited to include a photomontage of the child growing up.

At most social events, with fanfare from the band and scripted comments, the bar/bat mitzvah would invite thirteen groups of people to light candles, blow them out with the last group (friends), and then cut the cake. This candle lighting ceremony mimics the synagogue ritual in calling people up for an honor and incorporates the cake from birthday celebrations. The sequence in which people are usually called up— the first candle lit by grandparents, the last by friends—expresses the child's movement from extended family to peers. In the sequence of social events through the typical weekend, the child also moves the same way—from the Friday night family settings through mixed ones, ending up in the company of peers at the party.[34]

This ethnography is congruent with other reports of bar/bat mitzvah celebrations.[35] The celebrations act as counterpoint and complement to the synagogue ceremonies. At the synagogue, the adolescent performs intergenerational identification with the ethnoreligious community, demonstrating the skills to participate in Jewish worship and acknowledging Judaism's role in the family's understanding of identity. The family uses the celebration to acknowledge the movement from child to adolescent and the value they place on extended family and friends. The two guest lists—the parents' and the child's—define the social networks and cultures—extended family and peers—that the child is growing out of and moving into. The montage of the child's development, the speeches by family members, and the photographs of the child on display are the family's way of summarizing, of noting the accomplishments, of expressing pride in the child as "the product" of the family. Guests give gifts, make complimentary remarks, and share a good time. Their approving participation ensures the family that what they are going through is proper and that they have done it correctly.

For contemporary thirteen-year-olds and their parents, bar/bat mitzvah also raises issues of emergent sexuality in a highly sexualized popular culture. The rounds of bar/bat mitzvah parties are settings for experimenting with gender roles. Early adolescent awkwardness is often noticeable. Age-inappropriate sexual elements at the celebrations are the object of public ridicule.[36] Bands and DJs who work the bar mitzvah circuit use games and contests designed to help the kids have a good time without too much overt sexuality.

Two examples suggest the importance of the gender contrast at the synagogue and party. A father comments on his daughter's poise and accomplishment at her bat mitzvah service: "The bat mitzvah comes at that awkward stage in life, when young girls are getting self-conscious about their bodies. In our culture, so much emphasis is on the exterior, the physical, the appearance; but here in the synagogue, at that moment, all the emphasis was on the interior, the intelligence and the soul."[37] A mother, introducing her remarks on a "What to Wear" event at the Jewish Theological Seminary, wrote, "The idea of my child being old enough to chant Torah, let alone go forth on her own terms, makes me weepy. Of course, the notion of her dressing like a two-dollar whore while jerking her hips to LMFAO's 'Sexy and I Know It' makes me even weepier."[38] Growing diversity in Jewish life is reflected in contemporary bar/bat mitzvah practices. Among the Orthodox minority, bar/bat mitzvah is yet another performance of a distinctive identity and community. The frequent intergenerational shift away has slowed, and numbers are growing due to large families. For boys in a community of frequent ritual, reaching the age to participate as an adult has everyday meaning. Putting on tefillin (small boxes containing quotations from the Torah, bound to the head and on the arm by leather straps) at the age of bar mitzvah is important; Orthodox men will wear them every day except Sabbath and holy days at morning prayers. Boys are fluent in synagogue skills from an early age and typically take a major role in the service marking their bar mitzvahs. Bar mitzvah is marked with school friends, family members, and the congregational community. Rabbis and teachers will be present at Orthodox celebrations, sometimes in leading roles.

Orthodox bat mitzvahs are now common. Rabbi Jerome Tov Feinstein began a bat mitzvah class in 1944. At a Friday night ceremony outside the sanctuary, the rabbi gave each bat mitzvah candlesticks, quizzed and praised them, and installed them as members of the junior sisterhood; each then made a speech.[39] By the 1960s, Orthodox schools and congregations were holding group bat mitzvah celebrations for seventh graders and twelve-year-olds. It is now also common for individual families to mark a girl's twelfth birthday outside the sanctuary with a celebration at which the bat mitzvah delivers a speech. For several decades, Modern

Orthodox groups have enlarged women's place in the synagogue service, creating opportunities for bat mitzvah ceremonies in women's prayer groups, at Friday night services, at services concluding the Sabbath on Saturday night, and after the formal conclusion of other services but in the sanctuary.

Among the majority of Jews the boundaries of Jewish identity and Jewish life have become more variable with each generation, with variable formal and informal expectations for thirteen-year-olds. On the one hand, there is a group that is highly connected to Jewish life. From the 1960s into the twenty-first century, Conservative, community, and Reform day schools (all-day private schools) grew rapidly. Jewish camps, retreat centers, and adult education programs have also grown. Colleges and universities have introduced Jewish studies courses. Members who are more Jewishly literate have invigorated congregations. Congregations aspire to be communities of caring and sharing and places of innovation and creativity that respond to the emerging needs of American Jews. They aspire to be places where bar/bat mitzvah is not an exit ritual for the thirteen-year-old but a movement from being a child in the community to being an adolescent in the community, and for the parents an event that marks the family's progress through a Jewish life cycle.

On the other hand, more Jews are less connected. Intermarriage, divorce, geographic mobility, higher education, later marriage, smaller families, and later childbirth all mean that Jewish family and friendship networks are less dense and social pressure is less intense.

The religious marketplace has changed, modifying the experience and meaning of reaching thirteen. Many less connected Jews do not find several years' membership in a congregation to which they rarely go appealing. Families no longer need synagogue affiliation or formal education in order to arrange a bar/bat mitzvah ceremony. Books and websites on bar/bat mitzvah are widely available, rivaling congregations and schools as guides. Some sources give advice on how to avoid a congregational bar/bat mitzvah and spend a limited budget on other things. Orthodox outreach groups, tutors, and independent rabbis will organize a ceremony or a destination bar/bat mitzvah. Travel agents organize bar/bat mitzvah trips to Israel, complete with a ceremony.

Jewish institutions have responded to their changing constituencies. Congregational and school bar/bat mitzvah preparation now often includes classes for parents, family education programs in which parents and children participate, and family retreats. There has been a shift from classroom preparation for performance to experiential learning for a life-style. Congregations and schools use "mitzvah" programs in which the early adolescent does thirteen good deeds. The popular *Putting God on the Guest List* helps families use bar/bat mitzvah as an opportunity for spiritual and emotional growth.[40] The Reform movement, with which more American Jews now identify than any other branch of Judaism, has launched a "b'nai mitzvah revolution" in its congregational schools in order to deemphasize training for the bar/bat mitzvah service and focus instead on creating meaningful experiences for its families and promoting engagement in the synagogue community.[41] A small study of adult children of intermarriage suggests that bar/bat mitzvah matters for them. Of those who had a bar/bat mitzvah, 90 percent reported their religion as exclusively Jewish, compared to 13 percent of those who had not.[42]

The celebration of bar/bat mitzvah by adults, especially adult bat mitzvah, now widespread, is another indication of its evolving role in American Jewish life.[43] Men and especially women who did not have a synagogue bar/bat mitzvah find this an opportunity to connect to Judaism in the company of a supportive group within the congregation, typically over a two-year period, followed by the public use of the newly acquired synagogue skills and knowledge. Bar/bat mitzvah, then, has moved from a legal age marker to a complex and varied performance of the identity of early adolescents and their families and to a ritual of identification for adults as well.

It may seem arbitrary to have bar/bat mitzvah at thirteen in contemporary Jewish life. It references a legal transition that is now of limited significance, and for girls diverges from the Talmudic use of age twelve. Moreover, the daily lives of Jewish early adolescents do not change very much upon reaching thirteen. However, for most thirteen-year-olds the ritual seems to fit developmental needs. They show competence in demonstrating synagogue skills. In preparing their speeches, they are encouraged to think for themselves about the lessons to be drawn from their tradition. By attending parties in their age cohort, they are able in a structured way to explore gender roles.

At the age of thirteen adolescents, along with their parents, present themselves at bar/bat mitzvah ceremonies and celebrations. Looking back to unevenly understood traditions and family history, looking forward into an uncertain future, they perform rituals of intergenerational identity, saying through them, "Here we are. This is how we put it together. This is how we think we can make it work." As they grow, the adolescents will separate more from their parents and community and make their own lives, but the experience of bar/bat mitzvah gives them a way back, a resource for the construction of their adult identities.

NOTES

1 See Charles Liebman, *The Ambivalent American Jew* (Philadelphia: Jewish Publication Society, 1973) on the distinction between elite and folk religion in Judaism. The theme of ambivalence in Liebman's work has also influenced this chapter. For the clearest, most detailed history of bar/bat mitzvah, see Michael Hilton, *Bar Mitzvah: A History* (Lincoln: University of Nebraska Press, 2014). In *The Wonders of America: Reinventing Jewish Culture, 1880–1950* (New York: Henry Holt, 1994), Jenna Weissman Joselit vividly discusses the popular culture of bar/bat mitzvah and confirmation through the 1950s. The best collection of materials on bar mitzvah remains Sara Silberstein Swartz, ed., *Bar Mitzvah* (New York: Doubleday, 1986).

2 Quoted in Ivan Marcus, *The Jewish Life Cycle: Rites of Passage from Biblical to Modern Times* (Seattle: University of Washington Press, 2004), 82. A lulav, which combines palm, myrtle, and willow branches, is used on the holiday of Succot.

3 Ibid., 85–105. Simchat Torah takes place on the last day of Succot, when the reading of the last part of the Torah is completed and the reading from the beginning commences.

4 Hilton, *Bar Mitzvah*, 35–36.

5 Jeremy Cohen, *Sanctifying the Name of God: Jewish Martyrs and Jewish Memories of the First Crusade* (Philadelphia: University of Pennsylvania Press, 2011).

6 Marcus, *Jewish Life Cycle*, 94.

7 Ibid., 113–14.

8 David Phillipson, "Confirmation in the Synagogue," *Yearbook of the Central Conference of American Rabbis* 1 (1890): 43–57. For more details on the criticism of confirmation celebrations and its transition to "girl's business" see Joselit, *Wonders*, 105–14.

9 See further Melissa R. Klapper, *Jewish Girls Coming of Age in America, 1860–1920* (New York: New York University Press, 2005).

10 Hutchins Hapgood, *The Spirit of the Ghetto* (1902; repr., New York: Schocken, 1976), 27.

11 Joselit, *Wonders*, 118–20.

12 Regina Stein, "The Road to Bat Mitzvah in America," in *Women and American Judaism: Historical Perspectives*, ed. Pamela Nadell and Jonathan Sarna (Hanover, N.H.: Brandeis University Press, 2001), 223–34.

13 Judith Kaplan Eisenstein, "A Recollection of the First U.S. Bat Mitzvah," http://www.ritualwell.org/ritual/recollection-first-us-bat-mitzvah, reprinted from Azriel Eisenberg, ed., *Eyewitness to Jewish History*, vol. 4 (New York: UAHC, 1978).

14 Ibid.

15 Morris Silverman, "Report of Survey on Ritual," *Proceedings of the Rabbinical Assembly* 32 (1932): 322–43.

16 Jacob Kohn, *Modern Problems of Jewish Parents* (New York: Women's League of the United Synagogue, 1932).

17 Joselit, *Wonders*, 114.

18 Pamela S. Nadell and Marc Raphael, *Conservative Judaism in America: A Biographical Dictionary and Sourcebook* (Westport, Conn.: Greenwood, 1988), 342.

19 Isaac Levitats, "Communal Regulation of Bar Mitzvah," *Jewish Social Studies* 11 (1949): 153–62.

20 The following section is developed in more detail in Stuart Schoenfeld, "Folk Religion, Elite Religion and the Role of Bar Mitzvah in the Development of the Synagogue and Jewish School in America," *Contemporary Jewry* 9 (1988): 67–85.

21 Nadell and Raphael, *Conservative Judaism*, 342–43.

22 Oscar Janowsky, "Jewish Education," in *The American Jew: A Reappraisal, ed.* Oscar Janowsky (Philadelphia: Jewish Publication Society, 1964), 123–72.

23 Stein, "Road," 232.

24 Ibid., 228.

25 Ibid., 232.

26 Examples and quotations are taken from Rachel Kranson, "More Bar Than Mitzvah: Anxieties over Bar Mitzvah Receptions in Postwar America," in *Rites of Passage: How Today's Jews Celebrate, Commemorate, and Commiserate*, ed. Leonard J. Greenspoon (West Lafayette, Ind.: Purdue University Press, 2010), 9–24.

27 Ibid.

28 Ibid.

29 Janet Marder, "When Bar/Bat Mitzvah Loses Meaning," *Reform Judaism*, Winter 1992, http://urj.org/worship/worshipwithjoy/letuslearn/s14whenbar/.

30 Union for Reform Judaism, "Bar/Bat Mitzvah Resolution" (1994), http://urj.org//about/union/governance/reso//?syspage=article&item_id=1907.

31 Simon J. Bronner, "Fathers and Sons: Rethinking the Bar Mitzvah as an American Rite of Passage," *Children's Folklore Review* 81 (2009): 7–34.

32 For a fuller account, see Stuart Schoenfeld, "Some Aspects of the Social Significance of Bar/Bat Mitzvah Celebrations," in *Essays in the Social Scientific Study of Judaism and Jewish Society*, ed. Simcha Fishbane and Jack Lightstone (Montreal: Department of Religion, Concordia University, 1990), 277–304.

33 Judith Davis, *Whose Bar/Bat Mitzvah Is This, Anyway?* (New York: St. Martin's, 1998).

34 For an earlier comment on the candle-lighting ceremony, see Abraham G. Duker, "Emerging Culture Patterns in American Jewish Life," in *The Jewish Experience in*

America, vol. 5: *At Home in America*, ed. Abraham J. Karp (New York: Ktav, 1969), 413.

35 Mark Oppenheimer, *Thirteen and a Day: The Bar and Bat Mitzvah across America* (New York: Farrar, Straus and Giroux, 2005); Davis, *Whose Bar/Bat Mitzvah?*

36 A 2013 video of a bar mitzvah boy dancing with Las Vegas–style showgirls has gone viral as this is being written.

37 Rodger Kamenetz, "The Last Bat Mitzvah," http://www.beliefnet.com/Faiths/Judaism/2000/12/The-Last-Bat-Mitzvah.aspx.

38 Marjorie Ingall, "Bat Mitzvahs Get Too Glitzy," *Tablet*, March 27, 2012, http://www.tabletmag.com/jewish-life-and-religion/95152/bat-mitzvahs-get-too-glitzy/.

39 Stein, "Road," 227–28; Joselit, *Wonders*, 128.

40 Jeffrey Salkin, *Putting God on the Guest List: How to Reclaim the Spiritual Meaning of Your Child's Bar or Bat Mitzvah*, 3rd ed. (Woodstock, Vt.: Jewish Lights, 2005).

41 See http://www.bnaimitzvahrevolution.org; Isa Aron, "Supplementary Schooling and the Law of Unanticipated Consequences: A Review Essay of Stuart Schoenfeld's 'Folk Judaism, Elite Judaism and the Role of Bar Mitzvah in the Development of the Synagogue and Jewish School in America,'" *Journal of Jewish Education* 76 (2010): 315–33; Stuart Schoenfeld, "Too Much Bar and Not Enough Mitzvah?," *Journal of Jewish Education* 76 (2010): 301–14.

42 Pearl Beck, *A Flame Still Burns: The Dimensions and Determinants of Jewish Identity among Young Adult Children of the Intermarried* (New York: Jewish Outreach Initiative, 2005), 35.

43 Stuart Schoenfeld, "Integration into the Group and Sacred Uniqueness: An Analysis of Adult Bat Mitzvah," in *Persistence and Flexibility: Anthropological Studies of American Jewish Identity and Institutions*, ed. Walter P. Zenner (Albany: State University of New York Press, 1988), 117–35; Schoenfeld, "Ritual and Role Transition: Adult Bat Mitzvah as a Successful Rite of Passage" in *The Uses of Tradition: Jewish Continuity since Emancipation*, ed. Jack Wertheimer (Cambridge, Mass.: Harvard University Press, 1992), 205–19; Schoenfeld, "Interpreting Adult Bar Mitzvah: The Limits and Potential of Feminism in a Congregational Setting," in *Jewish Sects, Movements and Parties*, ed. Menachem Mor (Omaha: Creighton University Press, 1992), 205–19; Lisa Grant, "Restorying Jewish Lives Post Adult Bat Mitzvah," *Journal of Jewish Education* 69, no. 2 (2003): 34–51; Grant, "Finding Her Right Place in the Synagogue: The Rite of Adult Bat Mitzvah," in *Women Remaking American Judaism*, ed. Riv-Ellen Prell (Detroit: Wayne State University Press, 2007), 279–302.

13

A Chicana Third Space Feminist Reading
of Chican@ Life Cycle Markers

NORMA E. CANTÚ

Latinas coming of age in the 1960s, as I did, faced numerous conflicts
of identity and of allegiance. The way that our community celebrated
a young woman's coming of age, for example, was often suspect by the
hippie thinking of most of us who were protesting the Vietnam War,
joining the farmworker movement for social justice, and questioning the
established order of things in general. Despite this cultural dissonance,
a point that Michele Salcedo makes in the introduction to her book
Quinceañera!, we still held onto the traditions; we still celebrated our
quinceañeras and helped each other come of age amid the turbulence
and chaos.[1] Our parents didn't quite know what to do with our rebellion,
having themselves been raised in the patriotic fervor of post–World War
II U.S. affluence, even though things were not quite as rosy or affluent
for Chicanas and Chicanos in south Texas. I recall one afternoon in the
mid-1990s talking to my Mom's sister, my Tía Eloisa, nicknamed Licha,
who claimed that things were much better in the 1950s. She missed the
"good old days"—this coming from a woman who had been a part of the
migrant stream working long, arduous jobs in the fields and canneries
in *el norte*, up north. I remember thinking that I would perhaps one day
look back at the 1960s and 1970s with nostalgia and think that those
were the good old days. Well, here I am in the next century, and indeed
I am thinking that those were the good old days. In particular for wom-
en's rites of passage—the erosion of some traditions and the changes
that have occurred in these rituals drive me to contemplate the aspects
of these traditions that remain. So I have been studying Latina rites of
passage from quinceañeras, the long-established celebration of a young
woman's fifteenth birthday, to *cincuentañeras*, the recently introduced

celebration of a woman's fiftieth birthday. I say Latina, but in reality, Latinos—as I explain below—also celebrate; men's birthday celebrations, both at age fifteen and fifty, are gaining in popularity. My essay is laid out in parts interspersed with ethnographic data as well as historical facts that weave a tapestry made up of the concepts highlighted by the celebrations of shifts of a woman's social standing. I focus on two key rituals that signal shifts: shifts that are linked to age—the quinceañeras and the entrance into elderhood, or cincuentañeras—and to shifts in social status due to age.

In this essay I explore how these celebratory rituals—especially the markers of a change in social status—could be read as markers of a Chicana resistance, an inhabiting of what Gloria Anzaldúa calls *nepantla*, a place of transition that ultimately leads to change and transformation.[2] This concept, along with Chela Sandoval's idea of third world feminism, establishes what I and other scholars call a Chicana Third Space Feminist (CTSF) approach.

The conceptual framework for marking age, I submit, must be intimately tied to chronological, social, psychological, and emotional ages. Structuring my essay around the two pivotal *edades*—fifteen and fifty—and grounding the content on this chronological and sequential structure demands that I also disrupt it: not always can we rely on the chronological progression of time. I know, there is nothing that would be more fitting, but I resist, as I always have, the easy categorization of time. If time is fluid as the scientists are finding out, then it follows that the aging process is also fluid. In this essay, I have chosen to integrate the analysis of the quinceañera and cincuentañera celebrations instead of taking one and then the other, for two reasons. Doing so allows for easy comparison and contrast of the attributes of each, and in some ways gives both equal weight. In my work, I often rely on *pláticas*, chats or informal ethnographic observations that I braid with *testimonio*.[3]

Because south Texas was part of the nation state of Mexico a mere 165 years ago and remains culturally bound to its roots in Mexican popular culture, this colonized space presents a ripe terrain for study of cultural change as well. South Texas and northern Mexico constitute a cultural region, as cultural geographers Daniel Arreola and James Curtis have established, where traditional Mexican ways continue to dominate social, religious, and in some cases even political life.[4] At the different stages of its history, south Texas has undergone radical change; the movement of people back and forth has given the area a sense of transitoriness, but those who remain, who have been present a long time, sustain the cultural life of the region. For this essay I limit my focus to the last seventy-five years, from about the 1930s to the present, my evidence garnered from scholarly work and participant observations. In addition, I use a testimonio methodology that seeks to explore the theory in the flesh concepts that Cherríe Moraga and Gloria Anzaldúa first introduced in their book, *This Bridge Called My Back: Writings by Radical Women of Color*, and that the Latina Feminist Group articulated in their collection, *Telling to Live: Latina Feminist Testimonios*. Using testimonio allows me to insert my own experience even as I am describing and analyzing the celebrations I have witnessed as a scholar and in which I have participated.[5]

A Chicana Third Space Feminist (CTSF) Approach

The theoretical frame based on the work of Gloria Anzaldúa that posits that certain cultural expressions exist outside the mainstream and within a liminal space and time offers an exciting vantage point for analysis, especially insofar as women's rituals are concerned.[6] This third space presents possibilities but also challenges the integration of the cultural expressions within the larger panorama of the United States. Because nepantla is a recursive process continuously establishing the subject's positionality as in a liminal state, it differs from Victor Turner's concept of liminality.[7] Like Turner, though, I turn to Arnold Van Gennep's ideas on liminality, or of transitory stages, to analyze culture. In my case, I find Van Gennep's work useful in looking at the quinceañera and the cincuentañera celebrations.[8] But, it is the concept of nepantla that best establishes this for me, for unlike the more European idea, Anzaldúa draws on indigenous thought, and the idea is not linear but inclusive and encompassing, a collapsing of opposites into a third space.

Nepantla

While Anzaldúa uses the concept in a late twentieth-century context, the word's etymology resides in Aztec thought some five hundred years before; even so the word has current significance for scholars and creative writers. Writer Pat Mora titled her collection of autobiographical essays *Nepantla: Essays from the Land in the Middle*, and Walter Mignolo chose the term as the title of a journal, *Nepantla: Views from South*, employing the term to mean different yet similar things.[9] In this brief discussion on such a key concept, I want to clarify the way I am using it vis-à-vis CTSF theory in my analysis of these life cycle rituals. Unlike the concept of hybridity that Homi Bhabha, Mignolo, and other scholars have posited, Anzaldúa sees it as a stage that is recursive and in some ways a perpetual state that infuses transformative meanings for the psyche.[10] Scholars and interlocutors of Aztec thought such as Miguel León-Portilla explain concepts such as *difrasismo* and nepantla citing the epistemology grounded in an indigenous worldview that accepts two seemingly opposing views to exist simultaneously.[11] Historical documents trace the use of the term "nepantla" to Fray Diego Duran, who cites an unnamed Indian, a Nahuatl-speaking man, who claims that worshiping both Christian and Aztec deities places him in a state of nepantla; in other words, by following both his traditional Aztec belief system and the colonizer's Christianity, he is in nepantla, in between. The way Anzaldúa then takes this concept and applies it to the Mestiza, the Chicana, leads me to the discussion of Third Space Feminism.

Third Space Feminism

Anzaldúa claims that a "transitional nepantla space" leads to *conocimiento*;[12] in my view, the shift from one status to another is similarly achieved through nepantla, a moving through a liminal existence. But, while for Anzaldúa nepantla is where a rupture, a shift, happens, I see the transitions offered by the life cycle markers as places of awareness and of shifts in perception—both how the woman is perceived and how she perceives herself in the world. Anzaldúa writes, "Nepantla is the space in-between, the locus and sign of transformation."[13] A CTSF position, then, takes a woman through nepantla and into what Emma Pérez envisions as a "decolonial imaginary" that exists between the colonized and postcolonial. These two key concepts, along with Chela Sandoval's concept of differential consciousness, allow for such shifts. Pérez states, "Third Space feminism, then, becomes a practice that implements the colonial imaginary."[14] Pérez's historical focus is the Mexican Revolution, where she finds that the decolonial imaginary exists for "the silent [to] gain their agency."[15] In her book, *Methodology of the Oppressed*, Sandoval provides a useful "apparatus . . . represented as first a theory and a method of oppositional consciousness . . . which . . . transforms into a methodology of emancipation."[16] Because this "apparatus" constitutes the basis for what she had introduced as Third Space Feminism in her essay, "U.S. Third World Feminism: The Theory and Method of Oppositional Consciousness in the Postmodern World," I bring her into conversation with Anzaldúa and Pérez; thus, we have the CTSF theoretical lens through which to view the life cycle markers.

Quinceañeras and Cincuentañeras

I have been studying the coming-of-age ritual referred to as a quinceañera or *quince* (fifteenth birthday celebration) for about twenty years, and I have recently begun considering the cincuentañera as a parallel phenomenon since both signal a shift in a woman's life, bringing a new set of responsibilities along with the new status within the social structure of the family and the community. The origins of both have been traced to the Amerindian custom of marking coming of age, usually at the onset of menses, and the passage into elderhood.

While it is clear that the onset of menses is a significant change in status for a young girl, the specific age of fifteen, however, seems to have been arrived at due to the age when a young woman could marry with her parents' permission in Mexican law. The origins of this may be the Napoleonic code of 1804 that established fifteen as the marriageable age for girls. The tradition as it exists now may have its origins in the first court presentations celebrated around the time of the French occupation of Mexico in the nineteenth century. Evidence can be found in the language for certain elements of the celebration, such as *chambelán* for the escort, *damas*, or ladies, for the accompanying party, and the use of a tiara and other "courtly" accoutrements. I posit that the celebration is one of the vestiges of the French occupation; when Emperor Maximilian was executed and the French were driven out in 1867, many of the cultural expressions remained. French influence can be seen in Mexican cuisine, architecture, music, gardening, and what we know as *pan dulce*, the French-derived pastries.[17]

While the origins of the quinceañera date back to colonial times, the cincuentañera, I have found, was revived as a more traditional celebration in the 1980s and early 1990s when Chicanas took up the celebration. Prominent Latinas such as Judge Hilda Tagle in Corpus Christi, Texas, in the early 1990s can be credited with being among the first to set the baby boomer celebration in motion; soon followed male *cincuentañero* celebrations. Although the male counterpart seems not to have taken off, the celebrations do exist; typically it is a backyard *carne asada*,[18] and not always the fancy formal or semiformal celebrations that women seem to prefer. Since then, the tradition has taken off and Chicana and Chicano baby boomers turning fifty have held cincuentañeras/os honoring the tradition in their own unique fashion. I discuss some specific celebrations later on in the essay. For now, my focus is on the origins of these two celebrations.

It is easier to cite the coming-of-age rituals in indigenous cultures that may have influenced the quinceañera since many such cultures coexist and indeed still practice coming-of-age rituals. But the fiftieth birthday celebration that has become in the last twenty years as ubiquitous in Chicana and Latina communities as the quinceañera, I am claiming, is a recovered tradition that has been revived by Chicanas who may be responding to a need to acknowledge their transition to elderhood as was done by our *antepasadas*, our ancestors. Inés Talamantez, whose work with the Apache female initiation rituals likens them to quinceañeras, also has been working on markers of coming into elder status in that indigenous cultural group. If, as I claimed earlier, the quinceañera is a parallel celebration to the onset of menses, is the cincuentañera then a celebration of menopause, the end of menstruation? Conceivably yes. But it is a bit more complicated, as fifty resonates with fifteen linguistically, and may also rely on the consumerism of "over the hill" parties that signal fifty as the turning point in the United States. A proliferation of books geared for those turning fifty, and the fact that one can join AARP even if one is not yet retired, when one turns fifty, may also have an impact on the selection of this year. There are some Chicanas, though, who choose instead to celebrate turning fifty-two, the century marker according to the Aztec calendric computation. Especially for Chicanas whose ties to traditional or indigenous culture are strong, such as members of the *conchero* dance tradition, it makes more sense to hold the celebration at fifty-two and not the more hegemonic fifty of the U.S. media and greeting card industry.

***

On the other hand, as I mentioned earlier, I for one harbored a desire to mark my fiftieth birthday as I had my fifteenth. I am not surprised that it is often Chicanas who did not have a quinceañera who will have a cincuentañera, perhaps in an effort to fulfill a desire for sharing an important shift in their status. In some ways, they may also be responding to nostalgia for the celebration of their youth.

Arguably, these celebrations could just as easily be attributed to Anglo-European customs that would signal a young woman's coming of age and thus her sexual availability; I am thinking here of cotillions, and even nineteenth-century customs of presenting young women in society. The equivalent of the cincuentañera could be the various rituals that signal the transition of elders as they retire from jobs or into the status of the patriarch or matriarch within the family. The desire to celebrate older age may also come from the increasing age regimentation that scholars have shown developed over the course of the twentieth century in the United States.

While the celebrations I have studied are situated within a Mexican and Mexican American or Chicana context, they are by no means restricted to this *Latinidad* and exist across the various Latinidades, as Julia Alvarez explains in her book, *Once upon a Quinceañera: Coming of Age in the USA.*[19] In the spring of 2013 I attended a cincuentañera in California where the honoree chose a cheetah print theme. She was dressed in red, and the VFW hall in Corona, California, where the event was held, was decorated with red and black as well as the cheetah print design. Not unlike themed quinceañera celebrations, these relatively new celebrations of a change in social status based on age assign the honoree a certain degree of autonomy and agency. Her choices led me to consider how personal such decisions can be and how the way we present ourselves to the world as we age is also a progression of how we presented ourselves to the world in our youth. In Náhuatl culture, one reached elderhood at fifty-two, at what could be the equivalent age of fifty; one of the benefits—or perks—was that the individual could then drink *pulque* and in fact was expected to become inebriated at ceremonies. While some elements of the indigenous coming-of-age rituals have remained, this one for moving into elderhood had been lost until about twenty years ago, when Chicanas reclaimed it; they have instituted a celebration with the usual elements: music, food, drink, ritual, and special dress.

For the quinceañera as well, the usual festival elements—music, food, ritual, and special dress—mark the "sacred space" of the fiesta that happens in the two traditional spaces for celebration: the church and the dance hall. Thus, it fulfills the need for spiritual or religious sanction; that is, the celebration seeks to fill a void wherein religious ritual, such as the mass, and the social performative ritual, such as the dance, respectively, constitute aspects of the person's reality, her standing within the community. While the quinceañera mass is not an official liturgy of the Catholic Church, that is, it does not hold the status of a sacrament or even of a part of the liturgical calendar, the mass of thanksgiving is an essential element of the celebration.[20] It is not unusual in Latino communities to have folk Catholic celebrations that are not necessarily church-sanctioned.[21] The religious basis of the celebration reflects a syncretism as the celebration includes indigenous and European elements; we could say that the celebration occupies a liminal space within the registers of what constitutes a religious feast day. The Catholic Church has both hampered and fostered the celebration.[22] It was often allowed within the church ritual of the mass itself, though it was not always so. Norma Zuñiga Benavides writes of her quinceañera in the 1940s that the family and friends gathered in the church to say a rosary and not a mass;[23] perhaps the mass was too akin to a wedding ceremony.

To assist the family planning a quinceañera, a number of publications have sprung up, such as Michele Salcedo's *Quinceañera! The Essential Guide to Planning the Perfect Sweet Fifteen Celebration* and the Catholic-sponsored Mexican American Cultural Center's publication.[24] The former serves as a guide to the parents and the honoree as they plan the fiesta; the latter serves as a guide for a church-sanctioned mass liturgy.[25] Some dioceses allow the priests to conduct their quinceañera celebrations as they best see fit, so some churches will have an annual celebration in May honoring all the parishioners who have turned fifteen the previous year. On any given Friday or Saturday evening from Manassas, Virginia, to Omaha, Nebraska, to Fresno, California, young Latinas are celebrating their fifteenth birthdays with a quinceañera mass surrounded by family and friends. The Church insists on focusing on the responsibility of the young woman, and some parishes require the young woman and her court, as the members of the party are called, to attend classes for a few weeks before the celebration. In her work on the tradition in Chicago, Chicana anthropologist Karen Mary Dávalos noted that the Church uses the occasion for socializing the young woman in proper behavior and instilling a cultural identity.[26] Other actions and artifacts signal the religious meaning of the celebration. For instance, one of the honoree's relatives is selected as the *madrina de medalla*, the sponsor for the religious medal. It is usually the medal of the Virgen de Guadalupe, thus reinforcing the connection with the indigenous, for Guadalupe, the indigenous dark-skinned Madonna, appeared to a Nahuatl-speaking Juan Diego in sixteenth-century Mexico. I have also witnessed quinceañeras where the combination of indigenous and Catholic ceremony elements blend. Should the family choose not to have a mass of thanksgiving, for whatever reason, it is often the case that a deacon or priest offers a blessing for the young woman, as was the case for one such celebration I attended in San Antonio, Texas.

While the cincuentañera is gaining in popularity, it is still not as common as the quinceañera. Baby boomers, however, have taken the elements of the quinceañera and created a similar age marker that signals a shift in status.[27] The cincuentañera, too, may include religious elements, albeit in a much more subdued fashion. If a mass of thanksgiving is offered, the priest offers a blessing for the honoree and her family; I have attended over twenty such cincuentañeras over the past fifteen years, only five of which included a mass. During the mass, instead of instructing for the future, the priest dwells on the honoree's past accomplishments. I celebrated my cincuentañera surrounded by family and friends whom the priest blessed; my *madrinas* wore *rebozos*, finely woven shawls that serve as a cultural symbol. Instead of just receiving the Virgen de Guadalupe medal, I gifted my forty-nine madrinas with a small gold Virgen de Guadalupe medal, the size of a charm. In some instances, the cincuentañera celebration may include traditional indigenous elements such as a *temascal*, or sweat lodge, or other ritual welcoming the honoree to elder status in ceremony.

The cincuentañera may have more whimsical elements, and the madrinas may be selected with an eye for the aging status of the honoree; for example, there may be a *madrina de AARP*. I have never observed such an approach for the quinceañera, as it is taken much more seriously and may even take on a solemn air—especially in church—as the adults, mostly the parents and family members along with the honoree, may renew their baptismal vows.

From a CTSF approach, we can deduce that the religious markers for the quinceañera are there to instill some restraint and to curtail the young woman's sexuality; in essence, the celebration signals her coming of age to mean that she is now of marriageable age.[28] Elsewhere I have explored how this liminal space for the quinceañera constitutes a passage between one clearly defined status—child—and the next—adulthood.[29] Fifteen is critical as the age at which a woman in Mexico could marry with her parents' consent. But the religious and more sacred aspect of the celebrations gives way to a more secular and social event; in fact, in many instances it is the dance and the music where things are played out and where the societal expectations are ritualized.

Dancing

Both the quinceañera and the cincuentañera have a celebratory element that includes dancing and music. The social part of the celebrations occurs in a dance or party house. The quinceañera and her mother select a theme and colors for the decorations, the dress, and the damas—the fourteen young women who accompany the quinceañera. For the cincuentañera, on the other hand, the honoree and her daughters or sisters choose the topic and the color theme. I chose a Mexican theme for my cincuentañera, so the hall was decorated with *zarapes* and *piñatas*; the madrinas wore rebozos. The choreography is an essential part of the dance. Salcedo devotes an entire chapter to the choreography and another to the music.[30] Such attention to these elements indicates that they are metacomments on the event itself. The quinceañera dance, often professionally choreographed, signals the honoree's new status as she often changes into high heels in a brief ritual where the *madrina de zapatos* presents her with her new heels. To music from a live band (or sometimes a DJ), the young woman dances with her father, then with her *chambelán*; finally the entire court—damas and chambelanes—performs the choreographed dance. In the cincuentañera, the *Baile de las Madrinas* is usually performed, but not necessarily choreographed. The quinceañera invariably dances to a waltz, and then may perform a hip-hop or pop song for the choreographed dance; the cincuentañera and her madrinas usually dance to empowering songs, such as "I Am Woman," "Wind Beneath My Wings," and the Donna Summer classic "I Will Survive."

So far we have been focusing on the elements surrounding the individual, the honoree, as she performs her role at the center of the celebration. I have been highlighting, however, that the family and friends, especially the madrinas, are an integral part of the celebration. It is up to the *padrinos y madrinas*, the sponsors, to make the celebration a communal one; the quinceañera's family and close friends either volunteer or are invited to help pay for certain elements, such as the cake or the music, or to give the honoree particular elements, such as the religious medal, the tiara, the shoes, or the last doll. In similar fashion, friends and family of the cincuentañera volunteer or are invited to join her children or siblings to pay for certain aspects of the celebration. In discussing the various items that are under sponsorship within the context of the celebrations, we can see the communal aspect that the marking of a change in status entails. For instance, the cake, usually elaborately constructed and reflecting the theme, may include a cake topper appropriate for the celebration. The quinceañera's cake often includes the dolls representing the damas wearing similar dresses, while the cincuentañera's cake may exhibit elements that signal the life-changing moments of the honoree, such as educational attainments, a wedding, significant trips, or the birth of children.

The marking of the occasion by inscribing the date and the name on various objects signifies that the occasion is indeed a life marker. So a madrina may also be in charge of gifting an engraved cake server set that has the honoree's name, the date of the celebration, and the number "15" or "50," depending on the occasion. Similarly, napkins, favors, and champagne flutes used for the toast are engraved with the honoree's name and the date of the celebration along with the number "15" or "50."

Obviously, the age of the quinceañera and her damas and chambelanes demands that sparkling cider, not the hard liquor or wine that is served for the adult guests, be served for the toast; for the cincuentañera, the *padrinos de brindis* (toast sponsors) toast as guests raise their flutes filled with champagne.

Another item that is stamped with the name, date, and "15" or "50" is the guest registry book. It is currently customary for the sponsors of the book and of the remembrance photo album to have it hand-decorated by a seamstress with an elaborate cover. For my cincuentañera, the *madrina de Libro de Recuerdos* asked guests to write a message, listing how we met or just a message of good wishes. In the case of the quinceañera, she usually invites a family member as a sponsor for the *libro y rosario*— the missal or Bible and the rosary—that she carries into church. If the cincuentañera has a mass, she may ask a close friend to sponsor these items as well. The kneeling pillow, *el cojín*, is customarily carried by a younger sibling or a cousin of the quinceañera, who places it at the altar. I have never seen a cincuentañera have a cojín.

At one point before the quinceañera dances the traditional waltz, the *madrina de zapatos*, shoe sponsor, publicly has the young woman remove the flats she has been wearing and switch to high heels. Elsewhere I have discussed the significance of the shoes as signifiers of the young woman's new status, ostensibly her more precarious status as she can no longer confidently and easily walk but must learn to balance on high heels.[31] The quinceañera shoes clearly signal the passage from childhood to adulthood, *de niña a mujer*, from child to woman. It is not surprising, then, that nothing similar exists for the cincuentañera, who will often unceremoniously discard the dress shoes, or heels, for more comfortable dancing shoes as the party progresses. We can also now discuss the previously mentioned last doll, as this too is a clear symbol of the change in status. The *madrina de última muñeca*, last doll sponsor, will present the doll either right after the dance or right before the cake is cut. The doll typically wears the same dress as the damas or a dress identical to the quinceañera's. It is my contention that the last doll signals the end of childhood and the young woman's new status as a childbearing woman. In anticipation of a real baby, the last doll signifies her shift in status: she is no longer a child but a *señorita*. Predictably, no similar event exists for the cincuentañera.

But both the quinceañera and the cincuentañera do include similar elements; for instance, both use flowers as part of the celebration, especially the flower bouquet—or nosegay—that the honorees hold or the flowers that decorate the church or dance hall, the *salón*. The young woman, the quinceañera, carries a nosegay or bouquet—traditionally prepared of waxed flowers, but now more commonly it is a plastic or silk flower arrangement; this is also sponsored by the *madrina de bouquet*, again often an unmarried female close friend of the family, and may be interpreted as a foreshadowing of the bridal bouquet. Of course, in this case the young woman does not toss it to the young women in attendance to see who will marry next, as is done at a wedding celebration. The cincuentañera often selects a *madrina de flores* who will pay for the flowers used for the celebration: the nosegay or corsage and her favorite flowers used for the salón and church decorations. In my case it was the fragrant *nardos*, or tuberoses, that greeted guests as they walked into the salón, paid for by my madrina de flores, a friend in California who was not able to attend the celebration but who was nevertheless present in the form of her gift.

To pay for the expensive live band or even for a good DJ, the *padrinos de música*, two or three different groups of sponsors may be needed: one or two will pay for the church music that is often secured separately, the dance music, which includes a band or a sound system and may require several folks pooling their money together, and finally the mariachi band that appears as if by magic at the conclusion of the dance—around midnight—singing *Las mañanitas*, the traditional birthday song, with everyone joining in the singing in honor of the quinceañera or cincuentañera. The timing may vary, but the point is that the mariachi band adds a traditional music element to the event. Video recording services may also be sponsored and may be quite costly. For quinceañeras, too, jewelry, including a ring, a pendant, earrings, and an ID bracelet, often called an *esclava*, are gifted by various madrinas and padrinos. The cincuentañera may choose to do something different for the madrinas. The cincuentañera in Corona chose to have her madrinas write what they were gifting her on a sash that they then wore during the night. Some gifted her with good wishes, patience, or other abstract traits or attributes, while others wrote "libro de recuerdos" or "gold Virgen de Guadalupe medal."

The Dress and Other Apparel

The dress remains of utmost importance to both the quinceañera and cincuentañera. In my research I have explored the differences between the dress worn by the quinceañera in Mexico or in the United States as well as in Central America and in other communities. Rachel González has found that there are distinct differences among various groups of Latinas and their dress choices.[32] While at one time the dress was a pastel color or for Chicanas white, it is now permissible to have prints and loud bright colors for the dress. Furthermore, it is often the case that the dress is constructed in such a way as to be adapted for the choreographed dance. On several occasions I have seen young women wear demure, long, formal gowns to the church and then, at the time of the choreographed dance, remove the long skirt to reveal a short one. As a headpiece, the quinceañera will wear a *diadema*, or tiara, that matches the nosegay or bouquet. Eva Castellanoz, a master artist, creates these using the traditional dipped wax flowers and prepares the young woman for the quinceañera in her community in Nyssa, Oregon. Joanne B. Mulcahy's book *Remedios: The Healing Life of Eva Castellanoz* tells of Castellanoz's deep commitment to traditional practices.[33] She too has seen a decline in the use of the traditional diadema; the headpiece in times past would also have included a *mantilla*, or traditional lace scarf, but nowadays the diadema is all that is worn on the head.

Conclusions

The traditional quinceañera celebration has enjoyed renewed popularity in recent years as social media and marketing for the celebration attest. Perhaps it is the migrant community from Mexico that has revived the tradition in the United States, but I hesitate to offer such a simple reason, especially as it remains very popular with the nonimmigrant Latino community, especially with Chican@ communities in the Southwest that have celebrated quinceañeras since at least the early twentieth century and continue to do so. The cincuentañera has gained in popularity throughout greater Mexico.[34] For example, Chicana social psychologist Aída Hurtado combined the celebration with a New Year's Eve party, and Chicana anthropologist Olga Nájera Ramírez celebrated with close friends and family in Santa Cruz, California. Mexican historian Manuel Ceballos had an elaborate dinner for his family, friends and colleagues, and Elsa Ruiz's celebration combined her cincuentañera and her doctoral graduation party. It may be that I hang around academics and so get to attend more of their parties, but I have observed the occasional appearance of photographs in the local paper, in Laredo and San Antonio, Texas, for male *quinceañeros*. The male cincuentañeros seem to be more commonly hosted by the honoree's family—wife, sisters—or coworkers, while the female cincuentañeras seem to celebrate themselves. Olguita, whose cheetah-themed party I attended in Corona will never forget the fun-filled celebration of her fifty years on earth. She planned the celebration with the help of her family and close friends. In preparation, she sent out a "save the date" and later a formal invitation.

The "over the hill" birthday parties that tend to celebrate those turning fifty—both male and female—in the mainstream culture seem not to have had an impact on the cincuentañera, where the celebrants stress the honoree's life achievements and do not necessarily dwell on the aging aspects. Except for some instances of gag gifts that include a madrina or padrino de AARP, reading glasses, or other signifiers of aging, the sponsors are much more positive and even as they may be in jest, such as a madrina de shopping, the celebration is just that: a celebration.

Insofar as the quinceañera and cincuentañera celebrations often signal changes and commemorate shifts in status for the honoree in her community, they easily gauge the sentiment of Latinas in terms of their social standing and the accoutrements that go along with these shifts. Not necessarily a major paradigm shift in terms of the ways that they will now be perceived, the celebrations do mark a change in status. Whether looking at the traditional and well-established quinceañera or the more recently "created" cincuentañera, one can see that they serve a function in the Latino community: first, they honor women transitioning from one status to another at a critical age; second, they bring the community together in the celebration; and third, they attest to the social and religious palimpsest for the entire social contract among an ever-diverse Latin@ community. From a feminist perspective, they may appear to be anything but feminist, as they often reinforce strict gender stratification and restrictions, perhaps even being sexist in their portrayal of women as sexual objects. But I submit that the very act of proclaiming that they celebrate their age is an act of resistance and affirmation. Furthermore, the celebrations exist and will continue to exist as parts of a technology of life that affirms identity and reinforces the communal bonds. The teenagers and the elders claim their space and their actions in asserting who they are and what they want. The passage through nepantla only renders them stronger and gives them a clearer location from where to embark on the next stage of life. After her quinceañera, the young woman becomes an adult member of the community integrated into the life of the social group and is expected to measure up to the responsibilities that her new status entails. Similarly, in the celebration of life that the cincuentañera publicly shares with the group, she prepares to enter what in Spanish is called *La tercera edad*, the third age, a transition into the next stage of life.[35] She is entering a nepantla stage that will continue. At fifty, the honoree is not yet at retirement age, or near the final stage, but she is usually at the top of her career ladder, with children mostly grown and gone or soon to be gone from the home, or with the dreams of previous decades now becoming reality. The mortgage is paid off, the children are married and living away; she will now be a grandmother and enter into a new role.

The quinceañera and the cincuentañera celebrations signal a change in status, but more importantly provide a vehicle for recognizing and celebrating the various bonds existing in one's community, one's family, and one's social world. From a feminist perspective, we must look at the ways that the women at both celebrations have indeed created a third space that allows for shifts, shifts that prepare them for the next stage.

I conclude with a question and my optimistic answer: Given the last ten years of increased border violence wreaked by drug cartels, will these celebrations continue? I conclude that they will, albeit with marked differences; as they have changed in the past to accommodate to the changing social, political, and cultural expectations of the people who live there, so they will change in the future. As young women are attacked and targeted by violence, it is in the celebrations that they can mitigate some of the ravages of such violence. In the United States as well, life is not always easy for Chicanas and other Latinas; the quinceañera and cincuentañera celebrations are a way to make life more bearable, a way to insist on celebrating the joys of moving from one stage to another along one's life path.

NOTES

1 Michele Salcedo, *Quinceañera! The Essential Guide to Planning the Perfect Sweet Fifteen Celebration* (New York: Henry Holt, 1997), xii.

2 Gloria Anzaldúa, *Borderlands/La Frontera: The New Mestiza* (San Francisco: Aunt Lute Books, 1987).

3 For a discussion of "testimonio," see John Beverly, *Testimonio: On the Politics of Truth* (Minneapolis: University of Minnesota Press, 2004); Latina Feminist Group, *Telling to Live: Latina Feminist Testimonios* (Durham, N.C.: Duke University Press, 2001), introduction.

4 Daniel D. Arreola, *Tejano South Texas: A Mexican American Cultural Province* (Austin: University of Texas Press, 2002); Daniel D. Arreola and J. R. Curtis, *The Mexican Border Cities: Landscape Anatomy and Place Personality* (Tucson: University of Arizona Press, 1994).

5 Gloria Anzaldúa and Cherríe Moraga, *This Bridge Called My Back: Writings by Radical Women of Color* (New York: Kitchen Table, Women of Color Press, 1981); Latina Feminist Group, *Telling to Live*.

6 Norma Cantú, "Sitio y lengua: Chicana Third Space Feminist Theory," in *Landscapes of Writing in Chicano Literature*, ed. I. Martín-Junquera (Boston: Palgrave Macmillan, 2013), 173–88.

7 Victor Turner, "Betwixt and Between: The Liminal Period in *Rites de Passage*," in *Proceedings of the American Ethnological Society for 1964*, ed. J. Helm (Seattle: American Ethnological Society, 1964), 4–20.

8 Arnold Van Gennep, *The Rites of Passage*, trans. Monika Vizedom and Gabrielle L. Caffee (Chicago: University of Chicago Press, 1960).

9 Pat Mora, *Nepantla: Essays from the Land in the Middle* (Albuquerque: University of New Mexico Press, 1993); Walter Mignolo, *Local Histories/Global Designs: Coloniality, Subaltern Knowledges, and Border Thinking* (Princeton, N.J.: Princeton University Press, 2012).

10 Homi Bhabha, *The Location of Culture* (New York: Routledge, 1994). José David Saldívar, in his book *Trans-Americanity: Subaltern Modernities, Global Coloniality and the Cultures of Greater Mexico* (Durham, N.C.: Duke University Press, 2012), cites a personal conversation with Mignolo (217). Saldivar writes of his own proclivity for the term: "My emphasis on *nepantla* throughout the chapter is meant to function as a reminder of the 'colonial difference' implicit in U.S. Latino/a, studies, a translational and transnational memory that all cultural difference has to be seen in the context of power and of the relations of subalternity and domination" (217).

11 Miguel León-Portilla, *Aztec Thought and Culture: A Study of the Ancient Náhuatl Mind*, trans. J. E. Davis (Norman: University of Oklahoma Press, 1990).

12 Gloria Anzaldúa, "Now Let Us Shift . . . The Path of Conocimiento . . . Inner Work, Public Acts," in *This Bridge We Call Home: Radical Visions for Transformation*, ed. Gloria Anzaldúa and AnaLouise Keating (New York: Routledge, 2002), 540–79.

13 Ibid., 99.

14 Emma Pérez, *The Decolonial Imaginary: Writing Chicanas into History* (Bloomington: Indiana University Press, 1999), 33.

15 Ibid.

16 Chela Sandoval, *Methodology of the Oppressed* (Minneapolis: University of Minnesota Press, 2000), 22.

17 Karen Hursh Graber, "Mexico's Irresistible Bakeries and Breads: Las Panaderias" (1998), http://www.mexconnect.com/articles/2260-las-panader%EF%BF%BDas-mexico-s-irresistible-bakeries-breads. On the mysterious origins of the quinceañera, see also Julia Alvarez, *Once upon a Quinceañera: Coming of Age in the USA* (New York: Viking Penguin, 2007).

18 Birthday parties for adults are celebrated with a barbecue or carne asada.

19 Alvarez, *Once upon a Quinceañera.*

20 I have also witnessed quinceañera services in Methodist, Baptist, and nondenominational churches.

21 Here I am thinking of the *matachines* dance ritual or the many saint devotions that include processions and special rituals for the feast day.

22 Eva Castellanoz tells of her disappointment with her parish's policies in Nyssa, Oregon. As Joanne Mulcahy tells it, Eva says, speaking of her daughter, "Had she completed the required religious preparation, she would've been seventeen by the time she could celebrate her fifteenth birthday." Joanne B. Mulcahy, *Remedios: The Healing Life of Eva Castellanoz* (San Antonio, Tex.: Trinity University Press, 2010), 44.

23 Norma Zuñiga Benavides in collaboration with Blanca Zuñiga Azíos, *Holidays and Heartstrings: Recuerdos de la Casa De Miel* (Laredo, Tex.: Border Studies, 1995).

24 Salcedo, *Quinceañera!*

25 The original publication by the Mexican American Cultural Center has been revised and published by Joyce Zimmerman, *The Bendición al cumplir quince años/Order for the Blessing on the Fifteenth Birthday* (Collegeville, Minn.: Liturgical Press, 2009).

26 Karen Mary Dávalos, "La Quinceañera: Making Gender and Ethnic Identities," *Frontiers: A Journal of Women's Studies* 16 (1996): 110–11.

27 Norma E. Cantú, "Chicana Life Cycle Rituals," in *Chicana Traditions: Continuity and Change,* ed. Norma E. Cantú and O. Nájera Ramírez (Urbana-Champaign: University of Illinois Press, 2002), 16.

28 My grandmother married at fifteen, as was the custom in the early twentieth century.

29 Norma E. Cantú, "La Quinceañera: Towards an Ethnographic Analysis of a Life-Cycle Ritual," *Southern Folklore* 56, no. 1 (1999): 73–101.

30 Salcedo, *Quinceañera!,* 105–17, 119–33.

31 Cantú, "La Quinceañera," 73–101.

32 Rachel González, "Buying the Dream: Relating 'Traditional' Dress to Consumerism within U.S. Quinceañeras," in *meXicana Fashions: Self-Adornment,*

Identity Constructions, and Political Self-Presentations, ed. Aída Hurtado and Norma E. Cantú (forthcoming).

33 Mulcahy, *Remedios*.

34 Américo Paredes first used the term "Greater Mexico" in 1958 in his landmark publication, *With His Pistol in His Hand* (Austin: University of Texas Press, 1958). He later refined the term to refer to an imagined homeland inhabited by people of Mexican descent, principally in the United States.

35 Curiously, people are now talking about a fourth age, *la cuarta edad*, that begins at eighty. One of my cousins is planning her eightieth birthday with a big celebration that her children are hosting.

14

Delineating Old Age

From Functional Status to Bureaucratic Criteria

W. ANDREW ACHENBAUM

Age-based criteria have paradoxical effects on defining later life, especially in modern times. Years matter in planning retirement decisions, determining Social Security benefits and health care resources, and qualifying for discounts in public transportation, movie tickets, and food stores. Gerontologists meanwhile claim that chronological age per se is a poor predictor of most pertinent bio-medical-psycho-social-spiritual dimensions of aging. In the wake of the Longevity Revolution, policy makers, media experts, and welfare agencies question the utility of *chronological age* in categorizing the potentials and needs that accompany advancing years. No compelling alternative has yet to replace chronological age as a delineator.[1] Baby boomers are trying to ascribe idioms and expectations they have experienced into fresh responses to the question "How old are you?"

Marking Old Age in the New World during the First 250 Years of European Settlement

In virtually every historical moment and site, old age was said to commence around age sixty-five, give or take fifteen years on either end.[2] No other stage encapsulates so large a percentage of the human life span (itself perennially fixed at 120 years). Chronological subdivisions demarcate stages within old age. Commentators at all times and in all places have distinguished a "green old" or vigorous "third" age (the onset of which typically marked between sixty-five and seventy-five) from a "fourth" age or "second childhood" (the latter stage that signifies diminishing physical and intellectual faculties with advancing years).

One additional parameter merits mention: premodern elders, rare in numbers, were deemed "strangers" in the community. Now, ironically, contemporary old persons often fade invisibly despite their growing proportions in the populations of developing and advanced industrial societies.

Ideas about old age in U.S. history range concurrently from notions of worth through contradictory and ambivalent perceptions of decline to fears of ignominy. Demography plays a part in this complex array. Since the beginning of old age customarily has been fixed within wide margins, acknowledging the fact that the old eighty is not the new fifty must be reconciled with two other patterns. First, in the "natural" sequence of events, the coming of old age presages death. Preparing to die shadows most executions of the completion of being. Second, between 1900 and 2000, thirty years were added to life expectancy at birth and in the middle decades. Gains in life expectancy later in life, for boomer males, have been modest; boomer females can expect to live eleven years more than their great-grandmothers.[3] Gender differences in later years are not simply cultural constructs.

Like chronological delineators, old age's iconic manifestations and accessories persist over time and place. Older persons in ancient times were depicted with gray or white hair and bald heads. Artists past and present incorporate canes and walkers in portraying elders, as well as trumpets for hearing and signs of missing teeth or gout. Attempting to disguise or erase the ravages of age long has been a rite of passage; some manage to please themselves or fool others, but most risk contempt. Renewal, not rejuvenation, can occur in late life.

Attaining old age was an achievement worth celebrating and emulating in early North American history. To survive to late life was a feat, particularly since reaching young adulthood required luck and pluck. Trumpeting instances of longevity, moreover, had political value: bills of mortality were thought to affirm the relative healthfulness of conditions in the New World compared to the Old. As John Bristed opined in *Resources of the United States of America* (1818): "The aggregate salubrity of the United States surpasses that of Europe; the males are, generally, active, robust, muscular, and powerful, capable of great exertion and endurance; the females define a fine symmetry of person, lively and interesting countenances, frank and engaging manners. . . . The Americans average a longer life than the people in Europe, where only *three* out of every thousand births reach the ages of eighty to ninety years; whereas, in the United States, the proportion is *five* to every thousand."[4]

Dr. Benjamin Rush concurred with Bristed. North America's first geriatrician "observed many instances of Europeans who have arrived in America in the decline of life who have acquired fresh vigour from the impression of our climate, of new objects upon their bodies and mind, and whose lives in consequence thereof, appeared to have been prolonged for many years."[5] In extolling elders as exemplars of rectitude, contemporaries took to heart a verse from Proverbs (16:31)—"Grey hair is a crown of glory, if it is won by a virtuous life." The aged's moral faculties, Dr. Rush reported, outdistanced their physical and mental capacities. Yet, as Scripture recognized, the miserly and avaricious, drunken and gluttonous, obstreperous and bitter were not guardians of virtue.[6] People wanted respected elders to offer advice, to be repositories of tradition, so that all ages together could build a *novus ordo seclorum*. "What a blessed influence the old exert in cherishing feelings of reverence, affection, and subordination in families, in warning the young against the temptations and allurements of the world," opined Reverend Cortlandt Van Rensselaer in a sermon on old age in 1841. "How much good of every kind is accomplished by the tranquilizing, wise and conservative influences of age."[7]

Older people in early American history offered these resources and more. In farming communities aged women and men managed homes and supervised plantings. Engaging in politics, commerce, and the professions typically sustained men of property and standing well into advanced age. Those who prospered in late life were rare, however. Auction prices of unskilled African Americans diminished conversely with advancing years. Owners freed slaves when they no longer could labor in fields. Many widows, regardless of race, ethnicity, region, religion, or class, depended economically and psychologically on children, neighbors, and strangers. Even once powerful men, like Increase Mather, perceived a mounting loss of esteem a decade before leaving his pulpit at eighty-two.[8]

Superannuation occurred more frequently than mandatory retirement. According to Noah Webster's *American Dictionary* (1828), "superannuation resulted from infirmity or poor health"; accidents, injuries, and illnesses superannuated youngish workers. "Retirement" connoted a "private way of life . . . withdrawing from company or from public notice or station." Like superannuation, retirement was a term that could be applied across age groups, not just to the old.[9] "Though age-related norms and prescriptions were not totally absent—most communities, for example, frowned upon the marriage of a young man and an elderly woman—cultural values associated with age were imprecise," contends Howard Chudacoff. "Age-graded stages of life, such as Shakespeare's 'seven ages of man' were often more theoretical than experienced."[10]

Being old and becoming older in antebellum America did not connote loss of functionality, however. Only in unusual circumstances did men in antebellum America leave office on account of age. Some jurisdictions adopted a 1780 Massachusetts constitutional precedent that required justices of the peace to renew licenses every seven years; the measure sought to minimize incompetence, not to discriminate against seniors. New York's legislature reacted to an actual case of a justice who grew senile on the bench. The state's 1777 constitution permitted its chancellor, Supreme Court judges, and the ranking judge on each county court to "hold their offices during good behavior" until reaching age sixty. New Hampshire (1792), Connecticut (1819), and Maryland (1851) set seventy as retirement age for their judges and justices of the peace. Upon becoming states, Alabama (1819), Missouri (1820), and Maine (1820) also imposed age-based ceilings on service.[11] These are the only instances of legislators and voters imposing on the aged chronological restrictions to public service.

Indeed, it is worth recalling that the U.S. Constitution and local jurisdictions curtailed the franchise of youth far more greatly than they discharged age. Men could not vote in presidential elections before they were twenty-one, nor could they serve in the House or the Senate before they reached thirty and thirty-five, respectively. (Women of all ages were disenfranchised on account of sex.) Failing to meet property requirements prevented young men from testifying in court, executing a will, or holding county offices until they were counted mature. In contrast, the influence of older men who controlled assets and/or held sway was praised or feared until death.

No wonder, then, New York's removal of senior judges at sixty was derided. Alexander Hamilton denounced the provision in *Federalist* 79.

Chancellor James Kent, upon vacating the bench, wrote *Commentaries on American Law* (1826–30). Hale until his eighty-fourth year, Kent became America's Blackstone. New York deleted the age restriction when it revised its constitution in 1846. Young Americans knew that they could not squander ripe, functional age.

The Increasing Prevalence of Chronologically Based Criteria for Defining Old Age

Urbanization and industrialization transformed the United States after the Civil War. These forces, modernization theorists hypothesize, diminished the marketplace status of older people.[12] Census data indicate otherwise. In Massachusetts, which was predominantly industrialized by 1885, the percentage of gainfully employed workers over sixty had declined very little.[13] "In its initial stages, industrial development had little direct effect on the elderly population," contend Carole Haber and Brian Gratton. "In skilled occupations, age—rather than being a handicap—led to greater mastery, better jobs, and higher income. Older craftsmen owned the tools and resources necessary to the trade, and they bartered knowledge and training for assistance from apprentices, who were often young kin. The craft system allowed skilled workers to avoid menial, physically demanding tasks by exchanging knowledge for labor."[14]

Meanwhile, federal agencies and private industry started discharging workers at a certain age and/or after a specified term of employment. The innovation set precedents that made mandatory retirement a condition for delineating old age. Congress in 1861 required naval officers below the rank of vice admiral to resign at sixty-two. Another provision required sailors to retire at fifty (1899); yet another intended to "promote the efficiency of the Revenue-Cutter service" (1902) by removing those who were incapacitated or over the age of sixty-four. Transportation companies inaugurated the earliest private pension programs. American Express (1875) offered workers over sixty a gratuity for good service, a gesture meant to purge obsolescence. The Baltimore and Ohio Railroad's retirement scheme (1884) gave pensions to employees over the age of sixty-five who had completed a minimum of ten years of service.[15]

The quest for efficiency reworking modes of productivity insinuated chronological age per se into personnel decisions that devalued and discriminated against older workers. "The practice of retaining on the pay-roll aged workers who can no longer render a fair equivalent for their wages is wasteful and demoralizing," opined professor F. Spencer Baldwin in 1911; he argued it hurt overall morale to protect individuals who could not keep up with the pace.[16] Obsolescence arose from circumstances out of elders' control, declared Corra Harris in a 1926 article in the *Ladies Home Journal*: "Old people are not so much prisoners of their years and infirmities as they are of their circumstances, after they are no longer able to produce their own circumstances, but are obliged to adjust themselves to conditions made for them by people who belong to a later generation in a new world."[17]

The practice of forcing retirement beyond a certain age gained acceptance in industrializing America. By the eve of the Great Depression there were 140 industrial pension plans, covering nearly a million workers. Stipulated retirement ages ranged from fifty to seventy-five. Meanwhile, the federal government enacted an old-age and disability insurance program (1920) for its half million civil servants; six states followed. Municipalities created programs based on age and service for teachers, police, and firemen.[18]

The imposition of chronological-age-based criteria crept downward in market determinations, targeting certain segments of the aging work force negatively and positively. To wit, while captains of industry were designing age-specific criteria for retiring employees, Henry Ford and the Studebaker Corporation inaugurated seniority-based bonuses in order to reduce job turnover. Union officials mainly fought for bread-and-butter issues for younger members, but they also understood that seniority bolstered job security for aging workers. Seniority meanwhile infiltrated elite circles: Congress between 1880 and 1910 instituted rules that restricted the flexibility of the Speaker of the House to make committee appointments; as a consequence, discretionary power accrued to older lawmakers the longer they stayed in office.[19]

Discriminatory age-based measures affected workers in their prime. "An age barrier" for those forty and older in heavy manufacturing consigned workers to an industrial scrapheap. Personnel managers in technology-rich industries in the 1920s were deploying psychological tests and other filters to discourage the recruitment and retention of mature and aging job candidates. "There is much evidence to support the growing belief that industry is honeycombed with strict hiring limits," reported contributors to Herbert Hoover's committee investigating *Recent Social Trends* (1933).[20]

Claims that capacities diminished with aging received their most celebrated exposition from William Osler, arguably the preeminent professor of clinical medicine on two continents at the turn of the century. Osler noted "the comparative uselessness of men above the age of forty. . . . The effective, moving, vitalizing work of the world is done between the ages of twenty-five and forty—these fifteen golden years of plenty, the anabolic or constructive period." To Osler's detached gaze men over sixty were utterly useless, so what "incalculable benefit it would be in commercial, political and in professional life, if as a matter of course, men stopped work at this age."[21] Osler remarked about "The Fixed Period," a reference to a novel by Anthony Trollope, which proposed that sexagenarian college professors be chloroformed after being granted a year to compose their last lectures.

Age-based criteria in evaluating worth and allocating benefits slowly pervaded U.S. society. No aspect of America's urban-industrial-bureaucratic milieu was exempt. Consider how chronological criteria were adopted in two unrelated welfare arenas—old-age pensions and old-age relief.

Although Thomas Paine pled for the creation of nationally funded pensions to prevent old-age dependency after the Revolution, his contemporaries were reluctant to compensate aging veterans. Congress restricted the scope and provisions for survivors of the Revolutionary War, War of 1812, and Mexican-American War until long after peace settlements. (The government during this period underwrote a U.S. Naval Home [1833] and a U.S. Soldiers Home [1851] for disabled and superannuated veterans.) Post–Civil War politics broke this dilatory, stingy pattern. Initially, Yankees (not vanquished Confederates) filed claims on grounds of disability. By 1912, having determined that old age per se was a disability that impeded veterans from gainful employment, Congress granted pensions to any Union soldier over age sixty-two who had served at least ninety days in the Civil War. The cost of military pensions soared to $174.2 million, roughly 18 percent of all federal expenditures.[22]

Arguing that U.S. military pensioners fared better than social insurance beneficiaries in Western Europe, Theda Skocpol underscores the important role that chronological age played as a criterion for work and retirement:

> European contributory old-age insurance and noncontributory pensions were explicitly meant for lower-income elderly people or for certain categories of retired employed workers. . . . By the turn of the twentieth century, Civil War pensions served for many Americans as an analogue to noncontributory old-age pensions, or to disability and old-age insurance without the contributions. . . . Civil War pensioners could automatically claim disability for manual labor due to old age by age 62, and in practice many started receiving pensions in their fifties or earlier. . . . Given that skilled and unskilled manual laborers in the nineteenth century often wore themselves out well before age 65 or 70, the American veterans had a distinct advantage—above all in relation to Britons—in being able to draw benefits earlier, especially since the benefits for those Americans who gained eligibility before age 62 were not necessarily any lower.[23]

The introduction of chronological benchmarks for defining military pensions foreshadowed two developments in the bureaucratization of modern America. First, setting age criteria obviated the necessity to define or evaluate a person's functional capacity. Old age was reconceived as a disabling condition conveniently—albeit arbitrarily—reckoned by calendar years. Second, it seemed fair to grant benefits to veterans who met standardized service and age requirements. Nonetheless, privileging the Union's aging veterans created a special category of entitlement. The group was overwhelmingly white and male; they had not contributed (as had European wage earners) in youth or middle age to a social insurance scheme from which they would draw in senescence. Older U.S. veterans, counting themselves lucky to have survived battle, now were recipients of a windfall at the very time when lawmakers ignored the claims and pleas made by women and men who were worn-out veterans of the new urban-industrial state.[24]

Public and private administrators of welfare agencies concurrently started to deploy age-based criteria in determining needy older people's eligibility for institutional support. Tradition dating back to Elizabethan Poor Laws dictated that upstanding, destitute elders be considered "worthy" poor who should be duly relieved from their vicissitudes. The quality of mercy then and now was strained, however. Most Americans in the nineteenth century preferred to invest in schooling native-born white children and caring for orphans. Those charitable funds and religious bodies that built old-age homes for widows and specific groups of urban elders wanted older beneficiaries—mainly "theirs"—to live out their last years in relative comfort. Accommodations varied: ethnic Catholics in the North erected parochial centers; ex-slaves, rarely admitted to public facilities in the South, contributed to private old-age homes. Age mattered. Supervisors set thresholds (sixty, sixty-five, or seventy were common) for admitting residents, and they kept track of lengths of residency. "Benevolent asylums, pension plans, and geriatric medicine all worked to remove the aged from industrialized society; they sought to shelter them in a world consciously devoid of the young."[25]

For the most part, elderly men and women relied on kin and/or applied for funds for outdoor relief or the poorhouse. Courts in four states (Colorado, Indiana, Kentucky, and Ohio) punished adult children who abandoned their parents; thirty-two states (of forty-eight) by 1914 enacted measures to reduce the threat of dependency among family members of all ages but seldom acknowledged the elderly's vulnerability. Whereas social reformers like I. M. Rubinow condemned poorhouses as "concentration camps for the aged,"[26] legislatures concluded that there were more pressing issues to attend. A 1910 survey of the extent of old-age poverty in Massachusetts presaged a conclusion reached by other jurisdictions: the "problem" of pauperism among elders was not acute. Fiscal conservatives feared that initiatives to assist aged indigents might destroy thriftiness, lower wages, and eviscerate family bonds. Measures to relieve old-age poverty passed in Arizona and Pennsylvania were quickly ruled unconstitutional.[27]

The Great Depression had a devastating impact on older workers and their kin. The aged's unemployment rates exceeded the national average. The economic crisis exhausted resources that corporations, unions, and private charities might have extended to elders in need. Providing food and shelter for children left little for aging parents. Hard times required fresh approaches to the challenges of late life.[28] "I am looking for a sound means which I can recommend against several of the great disturbing factors in life—especially those which relate to unemployment and old age," declared Franklin D. Roosevelt to a cabinet-level Committee on Economic Security and to experts from academia, business, government, and labor whom he charged to draft an omnibus bill. "These three objectives—the security of home, the security of livelihood, and the security of social insurance—are it seems to me, a minimum of the promise that we can offer to the American people."[29]

The Social Security Act (1935) mounted a two-pronged attack on the problem of old-age dependency. Title I, Old-Age Assistance, required applicants to meet the age, residency, and needs requirements established by the several states and then approved by a federal board. Benefits up to fifteen dollars per month, an amount set by the state and matched by Washington, varied from place to place; some southern states did not establish programs. To reduce future reliance on relief, Title II (Old-Age Insurance) established a pension program wherein employees (in designated sectors of the economy) and their employers contributed to an account from which workers eligible for Social Security could draw at the age of sixty-five.[30]

Setting age sixty-five as an eligibility criterion in both Title I and Title II was a compromise. Half the states wanted to select age seventy as a criterion for old-age assistance under Title I in the hope that aged citizens in their jurisdictions would not live long enough to benefit from the program. At the other extreme was the Townsend social movement, which proposed awarding two hundred dollars a month to people aged sixty and over who agreed to quit working and to spend their pension within a month.[31] (Despite mass appeal, the Townsend plan floundered on its dubious cost projections.) In prioritizing social insurance over social welfare, lawmakers designed a plan that "amounts to having each generation pay for the support of the people then living who are old."[32] Through intergenerational transfers, the needy aged would receive assistance under Title I. Aging workers who had contributed to Title II earned future protection that policy makers anticipated. Caring for the old would empower middle-aged couples to devote more of their time and money to raising their children.

Social Security transformed retirement thinking. It popularized life insurance plans and galvanized interest in corporate and labor pensions throughout the private sector. As coverage widened, Social Security increasingly made "retirement" an option for the middle class (instead of a perquisite of wealth, as it had been). Above all, it legitimated the practice of delineating old age chronologically in establishing and implementing retirement plans in the public and private sectors.

Multiplying Chronologically Based Measures of Old Age since Social Security

Rather than track the proliferation of age-based criteria for delineating late life, it suffices to document bureaucratic amendments grafted into Social Security's original chronological baseline. Age sixty-five remained for decades the best known benchmark in both the public and private sectors as Social Security coverage and eligibility expanded. Negotiations between General Motors and the United Auto Workers after World War II fostered a pension boom, which reinforced the significance of sixty-five as the "formal" age of retirement. In addition, Congress introduced other triggers. Under the 1956 amendments women could fully retire at age sixty-two, and workers of both sexes could take "early" retirement, with actuarially reduced Social Security benefits.[33]

Disability provisions, introduced in the 1950s, treated incapacitated workers between the ages of forty and sixty-five as if they were retiring early. Disability insurance subsumed health risks under age-based bureaucratic protocols. Sometimes existing criteria generated new chronological thresholds. Earnings tests under Social Security were complex. Basically by rewarding workers who postponed withdrawal from the marketplace, the provision enhanced "flexible retirement." The 1983 amendments raised the "normal" eligibility age for full Social Security benefits to age sixty-six for boomers and to age sixty-seven for younger workers.[34]

Policy makers enacted around the original 1935 Social Security Act a variety of other postwar federal initiatives.[35] Hence, Medicare (Title XVIII of the Social Security Act, enacted in 1965) provided hospital insurance for Title II beneficiaries and workers not yet drawing Social Security benefits. In 1972, consonant with bureaucratic liberalizations of Title II, federal health coverage was extended to 1.7 million people under age sixty-five who had been receiving disability benefits for two years as well as to 10,000 people who suffered from acute kidney disease. "As an insurance plan, Medicare does not create the environment needed for the practice of high-quality modern geriatric medicine," contends

Christine K. Cassel. "On the other hand, Medicare is much better health insurance than a large majority of Americans now enjoy."[36]

In addition to Medicare and Medicaid, Congress enacted the Older Americans Act (OAA) in 1965. OAA established a new contract with elders, promising an extraordinary commitment to ensuring "(1) an adequate income in retirement . . . , (2) the best possible physical and mental health . . . , (3) suitable housing . . . , (4) full restorative services . . . , (5) pursuit of meaningful activity . . . , (8) efficient community services, including access to low-cost transportation . . . , (9) immediate benefit from proven research knowledge . . . , (10) freedom, independence, and the free exercise of individual initiative in planning and managing their own lives"[37] A vast network of Area Agencies on Aging (AAA) initially addressed the needs only of citizens over sixty-five; over time AAA launched initiatives for frail elders and adults at risk (and, in 1992, provided for caregivers of the elderly) and coordinated planning and delivery services at the local and state levels.

Institutions whose founding predated Social Security expanded its age-based eligibility criterion. Since its establishment in 1930, when it was assigned oversight of 54 hospitals, the Veterans Administration (VA) has grown to include 152 hospitals, 100 community-based outpatient clinics, 126 nursing homes, and 35 domiciliary units. The VA health care system provides the fullest continuum of elder care and currently determines services on the basis of (old) age as well as extent of survivors' service-connected disabilities, length of active duty, and current income.[38]

One other initiative is worth noting. In 1967, Congress enacted the Age Discrimination in Employment Act, which applied only to workers between the ages of forty and sixty-five. The upper age was raised to seventy in 1978 and eliminated altogether in 1987. This measure effectively ended a century-long era of age-based mandatory retirement.

In all these instances, lawmakers and agents determined that defining coverage on the basis of age-based criteria had certain bureaucratic advantages. Doing so was administratively straightforward. It avoided the stigma of welfare associated with means testing. Nor did this approach require tests of income or capacity as had been required when age was a proxy for functional status. To the extent that people perceived older Americans as a group that was vulnerable financially and medically, age-based criteria seemed fair and nondiscriminatory.

As chronologically determined social, economic, and medical initiatives for elders proved to be more effective for bureaucrats, this approach ironically became a victim of its own success. By the late 1970s, thanks to Social Security, the incidence of old-age poverty declined sharply. Similarly, the introduction of Medicare clearly reduced the aged's medical costs. Friends and foes saw an ominous consequence to these positive developments. "Public policy based on advanced age has undergone a serious transformation over the last few decades, from 'We can't do enough' to 'Have we done too much?,'" argued political scientist Robert B. Hudson, a Social Security advocate who was one of the first gerontologists to recognize that the "graying of the Federal budget" invited backlash. "Addressing the needs of old people will inevitably be an expensive proposition; the key question will be how to allocate costs among older individuals, their families, community agencies, the proprietary sector, and government."[39]

Fears went deeper. Far from being celebrated as a felicitous consequence of the Longevity Revolution, the rising numbers of older people fanned ageism—especially among those who felt that caring for the aged should be secondary to investing in youth. While neoconservative pundits and politicians demanded limits to how much could and should be given to "Greedy Geezers," editors portrayed images of intergenerational warfare on the covers of the *New Republic* and the *National Journal* in the 1980s. And the message stuck: in a zero-sum game, economists insisted, young people with mounting debts and insufficient resources to buy homes should not be expected to subsidize the new old, who, by most accounts, no longer seemed as impecunious and frail as did their great-grandparents. This neoconservative line of reasoning was part of a larger campaign to undercut New Deal liberal principles that had been at the core of the U.S. postwar political economy. The tack regrettably ignored the plight of vulnerable elders, such as poor older women, who had not gained from Social Security entitlement formulae based on steadily covered employment or long-lasting marriages.

Cuts were first evident in federal age-based programs. Jimmy Carter angered Democrats by tightening eligibility criteria under Disability Insurance in 1977. Unexpected shortfalls in Social Security trust funds forced Ronald Reagan to appoint a bipartisan commission to shore up financing. The 1983 amendments in fact stabilized the funds in the short run and generated enough revenues to honor commitments to baby boomers. But these accomplishments were not enough to allay subsequent fears of bankruptcy. Conservatives continued to claim that boomers, by dint of their numbers, were going to deplete anticipated surpluses, and that the existing programs could not fulfill promises to younger cohorts of Americans. Seizing on anxieties, George W. Bush sought but failed to privatize Social Security in 2005. Barack Obama seems inclined to reduce the future costs of Social Security's age-based formulae in order to control the rate of growth of projected federal budgets.

The recent history of Medicare unfolds in similar ways: Reformers want to eliminate chronological age as an eligibility criterion. "We need to start from the bottom up, with a different vision of the future of aging, medicine, and health care than the one bequeathed us by the reform movement of the 1960s and 1970s," declared medical ethicist Daniel Callahan. In *Setting Limits* (1987), he proposed "a different way of understanding the problems of providing that care than is commonly considered: that of using age as a specific criterion for the allocation and limitation of health care."[40] George H. W. Bush, who greatly expanded coverage for disabled Americans, sought to fill a gap in elder care through the Medicare Catastrophic Care Act (MCCA, 1988). The president wanted to expand Medicare's scope only if the extra costs remained budget-neutral. Bush's advisors recommended an intragenerational transfer, a formula strategy that replaced age with class as a trigger. The designers of MCCA wanted affluent Social Security beneficiaries to underwrite the cost of covering less fortunate persons eligible for Medicare. The wealthy revolted because they generally had coverage for catastrophic emergencies through private insurance; MCCA was repealed in 1989.

In the 1980s, the prospect of injustice between age groups became an issue galvanizing commentators across the political spectrum. Social Security, once a sacred cow, had become a golden calf. Those who wanted to reduce the size of government denounced old-age entitlements as unnecessary. Columnists across the political spectrum urged elders to sacrifice claims to windfall entitlements for the sake of the commonweal. Scapegoating the aged proved a powerful strategy for reducing present and future burdens associated with population aging. Pitting old against

young was ageist, but it seemed persuasive to many audiences—despite
efforts by demographers, economists, and centrist policy analysts to undercut the message of growing age-based injustice sounded by Americans for Generational Equity and prominent conservatives such as Peter
Peterson.[41] Antagonisms between young and old abated, but they nonetheless linger. Individuals under forty want to contribute to Social Security today, although few expect to collect benefits when they reach their
"normal" retirement age of sixty-seven. Gerontologists increasingly follow Bernice Neugarten's lead in distinguishing between the young-old
and the old-old.[42]

Another motif demands attention. U.S. society has been loath to address the needs of persons in the fourth age—men and women whose
frailty and impaired functionality diminish their quality of life. Seizing
on any chronological age (such as seventy-five or eighty) in targeting the
old-old seems as arbitrary and wrongheaded as is maintaining sixty-five
as a benchmark for senescence. There are too many exceptions, physical
and otherwise, around age norms; gender, ethnicity, and resilience yield
diverse capacities in late life. Many are independent at eighty; others are
totally disabled at forty. For this reason Neugarten was a trailblazer in
juxtaposing future policy choices in terms of *Age versus Need* (1982); she
advocated that old-age social policies deploy income-based criteria for
meting benefits.[43]

***

"In the contemporary postmodern life course chronological age has lost
its potency in determining social roles. As life expectancies increase,
the heralded value of youth has been extended to age groups that had
once been considered old," observes Anne Basting. "Definitions of who
is considered 'old' have shifted without significant changes in the status
of those condemned to what remains a devalued category."[44] Age-based
criteria, which once shaped and drove policies for the aged, have proven
too imperfect to sustain as policy makers confront a new set of ideological and budgetary challenges.

Neoconservatism and globalization (among other trends) have trans-
mogrified cultural values and political priorities. By concentrating on
the demographic contours of the Longevity Revolution, we too often
lose sight of the variegated, often contested, meanings of work, commu-

nity, and love in late life. Radical changes in age-based expectations, not to mention compelling evidence that chronology per se has little bearing on cherished rights and contested responsibilities, pose a double-edged sword for all generations. The boomer vanguard, now the age at which their parents retired, may try to ignore (at considerable risk) the enormous social, cultural, economic, and political developments altering postmodern society. If this cohort defends its entitlements in an unreflecting manner, critics will seize on this response as an instance of boomer selfishness. The cohort born between 1946 and 1964 will be accused of letting down future generations. On the other hand, should boomers join others in redesigning the life course, especially the third and fourth ages, they can rightly claim a stake in the commonweal. This tack, too, poses difficulties, for it is not clear how to proceed without deploying age-based criteria. Age, like race and gender, carries historical baggage into the present moment.

One way to transcend the age conundrum may be for Americans to embrace expanded, transgenerational definitions of *social citizenship*. To achieve a full measure of citizenship entails reaching out to America's underclass, including the nation's frail elders. Resetting the prerogatives and boundaries of citizenship might consolidate and universalize existing work and welfare initiatives. We need policies that correct measures that accentuate disparities by income and health. Present-day age-based entitlements did not eliminate the stigmatizing modes of assistance, as bureaucrats had hoped.

Melding public responsibilities and private needs requires putting age, race, gender, and poverty into context. The postmodern Longevity Revolution has rendered obsolete traditional concepts of the three boxes of life—school, jobs, and leisure. Loosening the chronological links across a variety of federal (and/or state) programs must accommodate disparities in educational and employment opportunities. For example, a new map of (late) life should chart ways to make room for older women and men who want to "repot" in classrooms or community centers in order to extend jobs. It would offer fresh opportunities for those who have contributed to others all their lives to seek meaningful activities as volunteers.[45] Rethinking chronological delineators probably means returning to where we began: taking a functional view of old age, acknowledging its wide-ranging capacities and vicissitudes.

NOTES

1 W. Andrew Achenbaum, *How Boomers Turned Conventional Wisdom on Its Head: A Historian's View on How the Future May Judge a Transitional Generation. A White Paper* (Westport, Conn.: MetLife Mature Market Institute, April 2012).

2 W. Andrew Achenbaum, *Old Age in the New Land: The American Experience since 1790* (Baltimore: Johns Hopkins University Press, 1978), 2.

3 Elizabeth Atlas, "United States Life Tables, 2007," *National Vital Statistics Reports* 59 (September 28, 2011): Table 20.

4 John Bristed, *Resources of the United States of America* (New York: James Eastburn & Co., 1818), 20, 453.

5 Benjamin Rush, "An Account of the State of the Mind and Body in Old Age," in *Medical Inquiries and Observations*, 4 vols. (1793; repr., Philadelphia: Thomas Dobson, 1797), 2:300.

6 David Hackett Fischer, *Growing Old in America: The Bland-Lee Lectures Delivered at Clark University* (New York: Oxford University Press, 1977) noted examples of behavior by the aged devoid of virtue in his chapter on "the exaltation of age in early America."

7 Cortlandt Van Rensselaer, *Old Age: A Funeral Sermon* (Washington, D.C.: by the author, 1841), 10–11.

8 Carole Haber, *Beyond Sixty-Five: The Dilemma of Old Age in America's Past* (New York: Cambridge University Press, 1983), 18. On slaves, see Carole Haber and Brian Gratton, *Old Age and the Search for Security: An American Social History* (Bloomington: Indiana University Press, 1994), 92.

9 Achenbaum, *Old Age in the New Land*, 22.

10 Howard P. Chudacoff, *How Old Age You? Age Consciousness in American Culture* (Princeton, N.J.: Princeton University Press, 1989), 9–10. See also Haber and Gratton, *Old Age and the Search for Security*, 22, 89.

11 Achenbaum, *Old Age in the New Land*, 21.

12 Donald O. Cowgill and Lowell D. Holmes, ed., *Aging and Modernization* (New York: Appleton-Century-Crofts, 1972); W. Andrew Achenbaum and Peter N. Stearns, "Essay: Old Age and Modernization," *Gerontologist* 18 (1978): 307–12.

13 Achenbaum, *Old Age in the New Land*, 59, 72.

14 Haber and Gratton, *Old Age and the Search for Security*, 96–97.

15 Achenbaum, *Old Age in the New Land*, 48–49. See also chapter 9 and Graebner, *A History of Retirement: The Meaning and Function of an American Institution, 1885–1978* (New Haven, Conn.: Yale University Press, 1980).

16 Achenbaum, *Old Age in the New Land*.

17 Corra Harris, "The Borrowed Timers," *Ladies Home Journal* 43 (September 1926): 35.

18 Achenbaum, *Old Age in the New Land*, 121.

19 Haber and Gratton, *Old Age and the Search for Security*, 107–8.

20 President's Research Committee, *Recent Social Trends*, 2 vols. (New York: McGraw-Hill, 1933), 1:811.

21 Sir William Osler, "The Fixed Period," *Scientific American* 25 (March 1905).

22 Achenbaum, *Old Age in the New Land*, 84.

23 Theda Skocpol, *Protecting Soldiers and Mothers: The Political Origins of Social Policy in the United States* (Cambridge, Mass.: Belknap, 1992), 131–32. On the relation between age and extent of disability in veterans provisions, see also Haber, *Beyond Sixty-Five*, 111–12.

24 Skocpol, *Protecting Soldiers and Mothers*, 135.

25 Haber, *Beyond Sixty-Five*, 97, 126.

26 Isaac M. Rubinow, "The Modern Problem of the Care of the Aged," *Social Service Review*, 4 (1930): 178.

27 Achenbaum, *Old Age in the New Land*, 76, 82–83; Achenbaum, *Shades of Gray: Old Age, American Values, and Federal Policies since 1920* (Boston: Little, Brown, 1983).

28 The First New Deal concentrated on reconstituting major sectors of the U.S. economy. Only one measure dealt with retirement issues, the Railroad Retirement System Act (1934). The Supreme Court's ruling it unconstitutional affected thinking about social insurance. For our purposes, the chronological triggers interest us: employees who did not retire at sixty-five could renew their work status on an annual basis up to age seventy. See Larry DeWitt, "History and Development of the Social Security Retirement Earning Test" (Washington, D.C.: Social Security Administration, Special Study #7, August 1999).

29 Franklin D. Roosevelt, "Objectives of the Administration," June 8, 1934, in *The Public Papers and Addresses of Franklin Delano Roosevelt*, 13 vols., ed. Samuel I. Rosenman (New York, 1935–80), 3:291–92.

30 W. Andrew Achenbaum, *Social Security: Visions and Revisions. A Twentieth Century Fund Study* (New York: Cambridge University Press, 1986), chap. 1.

31 Jackson K. Putnam, *Old-Age Politics in California* (Stanford, Calif.: Stanford University Press, 1970), esp. chaps. 3–4.

32 Committee on Economic Security, *Social Security in America* (Washington, D.C.: Government Printing Office, 1937), 381.

33 Geoffrey Coleman, "Social Security: Summary of Major Changes in the Cash Benefits Program," *CRS Legislative Histories* 2 (May 18, 2000): 1–26; Patricia P. Martin and David A. Weaver, "Social Security: A Program and Policy History," *Social Security Bulletin* 66 (2005): 1–15.

34 Achenbaum, *Social Security*, esp. 39–45.

35 Martha Derthick, *Policy-Making in Social Security* (Washington, D.C.: Brookings Institution, 1979); Theodore R. Marmor, *The Politics of Medicare* (Chicago: Aldine-Atherton, 1973).

36 Christine K. Cassel, *Medicare Matters: What Geriatrics Medicine Can Teach American Health Care* (Berkeley: University of California Press, 2005), xi.

37 U.S. Public Law, 89–73, Title I; see also Matthias J. Naleppa and William J. Reid, *Gerontological Social Work: A Task-Centered Approach* (New York: Columbia University Press, 2003).

38 U.S. Department of Veterans Affairs, "History, VA History," www.va.gov/about_va/vahistory.asp.

39 Robert B. Hudson, ed., *The Future of Age-Based Public Policy* (Baltimore: Johns Hopkins University Press, 1997), 19. See also Hudson, "The 'Graying' of the Federal Budget and Its Consequences for Old-Age Policy," *Gerontologist* 18 (1978): 428–40.

40 Daniel Callahan, *Setting Limits: Medical Goals in an Aging Society* (New York: Simon & Schuster, 1987), 23, 203–4. For an update, see Callahan, "The Medicare Showdown," Over 65 blog, Hastings Center, April 16, 2013.

41 W. Andrew Achenbaum, *Older Americans, Vital Communities: A Bold Vision for Societal Aging* (Baltimore: Johns Hopkins University Press, 2005). For positions advanced by Americans for Generations Equity, see Peter Peterson and Neil Howe, *On Borrowed Time* (San Francisco: ICS Press, 1988) and Peter Peterson, *Gray Dawn: How the Age Wave Will Transform America—and the World* (New York: Times Books, 1999).

42 Bernice L. Neugarten, "Age Groups in American Society and the Rise of the Young-Old," *Annals of the American Academy of Political and Social Sciences* 320 (September 1974): 187–98.

43 Bernice L. Neugarten and Robert H. Havighurst, *Social Ethics, Social Policy and the Aging Society* (Washington, D.C.: Government Printing Office, 1977); Neugarten, *Age versus Need* (Beverly Hills, Calif.: Sage, 1982).

44 Anne Davis Basting, *The Stages of Age: Performing Age in Contemporary American Culture* (Ann Arbor: University of Michigan Press, 1988), 10.

45 John Myles, "Neither Rights nor Contracts," in Hudson, *Future of Age-Based Public Policy*, 46–55; Michael B. Katz, *The Price of Citizenship: Redefining the American Welfare State* (New York: Owl Books, 2002); Kathleen M. Woodward, ed., *Figuring Age: Women, Bodies, Generations* (Bloomington: Indiana University Press, 1999).

ABOUT THE CONTRIBUTORS

W. Andrew Achenbaum is a Professor of History and Social Work at the University of Houston. He holds three appointments in the nearby Texas Medical Center, where he is Deputy Director of the Consortium on Aging. He has written six books and edited a dozen others, most recently *Robert N. Butler, M.D.: Visionary of Healthy Aging* (2013).

Norma E. Cantú currently serves as Professor of U.S. Latin@ Studies at the University of Missouri, Kansas City. Her numerous publications include the award-winning novel *Canícula: Snapshots of a Girlhood en la Frontera*, which chronicles her coming of age in Laredo, Texas. She has coedited various anthologies, including *Chicana Traditions: Change and Continuity* and *Dancing across Borders: Danzas y Bailes Mexicanos*.

Timothy Cole is a PhD Candidate in American History at Temple University. His research focuses on the history of the legal boundary between youth and adulthood in the twentieth-century United States.

Rebecca de Schweinitz is an Associate Professor of History at Brigham Young University. She is the author of *If We Could Change the World: Young People and America's Long Struggle for Racial Equality* (2009) as well as articles and book chapters on youth and civil rights politics; youth in American religion; race, politics, and family and childhood ideals; and gender and youth socialization.

Corinne T. Field is a Lecturer in the Corcoran Department of History and Women, Gender, Sexuality Program at the University of Virginia. She is the author of *The Struggle for Equal Adulthood: Gender, Race, Age, and the Fight for Citizenship in Antebellum America* (2014).

William Graebner is Emeritus Professor of History, State University of New York, Fredonia. His most recent books include *Patty's Got a Gun: Patricia Hearst in 1970s America* (2008) and *Modern Rome: 4 Great Walks for the Curious Traveler* (2013).

Jon Grinspan is a Smithsonian Institution Postdoctoral Fellow at the National Museum of American History. His writing has appeared in the *Journal of American History, Journal of the Civil War Era, New York Times, American Heritage,* and many other magazines and websites. He is currently turning his dissertation—"The Virgin Vote: Young Americans in the Age of Popular Politics"—into a book.

Shane Landrum is an Instructor of History at Florida International University. Their historical research interests include women, gender, and sexuality; legal and policy history; and digital research methods. Their book manuscript in progress focuses on the history of birth certificates, government birth registration, and personal identity in the United States from the nineteenth century to the present.

Ann M. Little is Associate Professor of History at Colorado State University and the author of *Abraham in Arms: War and Gender in Colonial New England* (2007), as well as numerous articles about gender and sexuality in the northeastern borderlands. She is currently writing a microhistorical study of the life and times of Esther Wheelwright (1696–1780), an English captive of the Wabanaki who became an Ursuline choir nun in Quebec.

Yuki Oda is an Assistant Professor in the Faculty of Commerce, Chuo University (Tokyo, Japan). He specializes in modern U.S. history and immigration history. His work has appeared in *Pacific and American Studies* and *Italian Americana.*

James D. Schmidt is Professor of History at Northern Illinois University. He is the author of *Free to Work: Labor Law, Emancipation, and Reconstruction* (1998) and *Industrial Violence and the Legal Origins of Child Labor* (2010). He is working on a book on school authority in U.S. history.

Stuart Schoenfeld is Professor Emeritus, Sociology, Glendon College, York University. He has published widely on contemporary Jewish life and on efforts to develop environmental peace building in the eastern Mediterranean.

Sharon Braslaw Sundue is Associate Professor of History and Associate Dean of the College at Drew University in Madison, New Jersey. She is the author of *Industrious in Their Stations: Young People at Work in Urban America, 1720–1810* (2009).

Nicholas L. Syrett is Associate Professor of History at the University of Northern Colorado and the author of *The Company He Keeps: A History of White College Fraternities* (2009). He has also published essays on queer history in *American Studies, Genders, GLQ, Journal of the History of Sexuality*, and *Pacific Historical Review*. He is completing a book on the history of minors and marriage in the United States.

INDEX

AAA. *See* Area Agencies on Aging
Abbott, Lyman, 92
Abolition. *See* Slavery emancipation
Abortion, 12
Acadia. *See* New France
Activism: anti-drunk driving, 238–40, 245–46, 249–54; suffrage, 219–23, 224–25; youth, 219–23, 224–25, 252–53
Adams, John, 73–74, 78
Adolescence: in Europe, 31–32, 39–41; Jewish transition from, 259–62, 275–79; marriage in, 103–18; medically defined, 10; Native Americans in, 38–39, 41; psychology of transition from, 212, 225, 261–62; social pressure in, 88–93. *See also* Youth
Adulthood: citizenship and, 74–75, 94, 225; drinking age and, 237–38, 243–44, 254; emerging, 12; English common law for, 74, 112–14; female, 87, 91–92, 95–97, 112–16, 286–87, 293–94, 297; at fifteen years old, 282–83, 286–87, 293–94, 297; immigrant transition to, 94, 170–71; Jewish transition to, 259–62, 275–79; labor and, 151; male, 74–75, 86–95; marriage and, 112–16; menarche and, 10; middle age, 11, 307; military and, 7, 74–76, 210–12; neoteny in, 48–53; psychology of transition to, 212, 225, 261–62; *quinceañeras*, 282–83, 286–87, 293–94, 297; at sixteen years old, 74–75; suffrage and, 74–75, 86–95; symbolic items of, 293; taxes and, 74–75; at thirteen years old, 259–62, 278; at twenty-one years old, 86–88, 93–94

African Americans: free-born, 58–62; male adulthood of, 75, 88; retirement and poverty of, 194–95; suffrage for, 69–72, 78–79, 88. *See also* Slavery emancipation; Slaves
Age: grading, 5–6, 9; meaning of, 1–2. *See also* Chronological age; Functional age
Age consciousness: development of, 5–13; labor laws and, 159; numeracy and, 25–26. *See also* Birth records; Birth registration
Age discrimination, 188, 190–92, 194–98, 199–200, 306, 312
Ageism, 190
Age markers, 2–5. *See also* Laws
Age of majority, 6, 15, 47, 50, 53, 104, 105, 110, 111–18, 238, 242, 244, 245, 247, 248, 252, 259, 260, 261, 265
Age of reason, 30–37, 40
Age versus Need (Neugarten), 315
Aging. *See* Old age
Agriculture, 192
Aiken, Doris, 249–50
Alabama, 246, 304
Alcohol. *See* Drinking age
Algonquian, 24, 27, 38
Alvarez, Julia, 288
American Federation of Labor, 177
American Revolution, 73, 75–76, 150–51
Americans for Generational Equity, 315
Anthony, Susan B., 69–70
Anzaldúa, Gloria, 283, 284–85
A'ongote, 36–37, 42
Apaches, 287